Alexandria
and the Sea

Alexandria and the Sea

Maritime Origins and Underwater Exploration

Kimberly Williams

Maps and artwork by Mamut Atabay

Sharp Books | SHARP BOOKS INTERNATIONAL
www.sharpbooks.us

TAMPA, FLORIDA

Although the author and publisher have made every effort to ensure the accuracy and completeness of information contained in this book, we assume no responsibility for errors, inaccuracies, omissions, or any inconsistency herein. Any slights of people, places, or organizations are unintentional.

First printing 2004

ISBN 0-9753911-3-5
LCCN 2003098902

ATTENTION CORPORATIONS, UNIVERSITIES, COLLEGES, AND PROFESSIONAL ORGANIZATIONS: Quantity discounts are available on bulk purchases of this book for educational, gift purposes, or as premiums for increasing magazine subscriptions or renewals. Special books or book excerpts can also be created to fit specific needs. For information, please contact Sharp Books International, 345 Bayshore Blvd., #1109, Tampa, FL 33606; (727) 422-0754.

Table of Contents

List of Illustrations

Figure 1 "Conquests of Alexander the Great." Reprinted by permission of the publishers and the Trustees of the Loeb Classical Library from Arrian: Volume I, Loeb Classical Library Volume L 236, translated by P. A. Brunt, Cambridge Mass.: Harvard University Press, 1976. *pages 10-11*

Figure 2 Lake Mareotis as presented in "Carte Des Environs D'Alexandrine" by Mahmoud Bey in 1866. Courtesy of the Graeco-Roman Museum, Alexandria, Egypt. *page 13*

Figure 3 Map of Pharos Island and the Eastern Harbor. *page 14*

Figure 4 Plans for a trireme replica. Copyright: Trireme Trust. *page 21*

Figure 5 Coin depicting Ptolemy I Soter. Courtesy of the Graeco-Roman Museum, Alexandria, Egypt. *page 25*

Figure 6 Possible arrangements of the rowers of a 'four,' 'five' and 'six.' The upper three show a three-level, two-level and one-level 'four.' The lower two show a three-level 'five' and a three-level 'six.' Copyright: Lionel Casson. *page 28*

Figure 7 Mosaic representing the personification of the city of Alexandria as a woman dressed in military garb and wearing a hat shaped like a ship's prow. Signed by artist Sophilos 3rd-Century BC. Courtesy of the Graeco-Roman Museum. *page 41*

Figure 8 Coin image of Ptolemy II Philadelphus and wife Arsinoe II. Courtesy of the Graeco-Roman Museum, Alexandria, Egypt. *page 43*

Introduction

This is the story of the rise, fall, and rediscovery of Alexandria, Egypt—an influential trade center that had great impact on the Hellenistic World. Molded by some of the most famous personalities of ancient history, this city is associated with major contributions to science, medicine, astronomy, and economics—not to mention the opening of maritime trade routes between the Mediterranean Sea and the Indian Ocean. The vast wealth drawn from her extensive trade connections permitted the early Greek rulers of Alexandria to create a shining jewel of the Mediterranean filled with palaces, magnificent centers of learning, and the Pharos Lighthouse, one of the seven ancient wonders of the world. In addition, early trade provided the means for Alexandrian shipwrights to build an impressive fleet of supergalleys, including the largest vessel known to ancient history. Alexandria was a spectacular city by the sea, capturing the attention of all who have seen or visited her through the ages.

After 2,000 years, Alexandria is once again in the world spotlight with the discovery of a sunken city. Remnants of the old city's splendor rest below the surface of the Mediterranean and are being brought to light by the careful research of underwater explorers and archaeologists. The story of the city's rediscovery and the role played by archaeology present two equally interesting chronicles.

One revolves around the fact that the coastal regions of the Mediterranean constitute a long-inaccessible reservoir of archaeological remains. Over the past two millennia, a wealth of material has collected on the sea floor, awaiting recent developments in underwater exploration. The young science of underwater archaeology faces unique challenges in preserving and understanding artifacts recovered from the underwater realm. In addition, these new archaeological processes themselves have become a fascinating subject for an audience with disparate interests and specialties.

Second, these new developments in archaeology are having a profound impact on our perception of Alexandrian history and on the modern city itself. Egypt has long attracted archaeologists and treasure hunters through the centuries, all of whom have filtered or contributed to our image of the past. Their discoveries often led to the removal of artifacts and the introduction of foreign interpretations or inappropriate scientific processes. The new archaeological discoveries, and the accompanying international attention, have revitalized interest in the affairs of this Mediterranean port city. As people flock to Alexandria once again, they contribute to the reawakening of its glorious past and prosperous future. The underwater discoveries also provoke countless questions as artifacts are pulled from the sea. How do historians and archaeologist decipher secrets buried in thousands of underwater ruins? What role do ancient texts play and how do we verify their conclusions?

Interpretation of the facts and attempts to conjure the intentions of rulers play an important part in understanding Alexandria's past and present condition. However, trying to do so through the study of written sources is rather problematic. Much like our own era, the Hellenistic Age was extremely political. When writing about ancient cities, classical authors often had agendas that best served the Roman authority. Their surviving words may be riddled with hidden biases that do not always present a fair and accurate picture of past events. In other words, the textual record is vulnerable to subjectivity that is the result of influences of people in the past, an influence of ideas and values we do not completely understand.[1] Ancient and modern historians have long attempted to recreate Alexandria's early foundation and romantic upbringing under the Ptolemies. Contemporary writers such as Plutarch, Diodorus, and Strabo list important place names and other vital information, but they also incorporate personal prejudices and conflicting information.

---

1. Peter Kosso, *Knowing the Past: Philosophical Issues of History and Archaeology*, (Amherst: Humanity Books, 2001), 30.

2

Strabo studied Alexandria as a guest of an important Roman official and therefore depicts a Greek city in a manner flattering to the new administration. Likewise, significant portions of ancient history can only be reconstructed with Diodorus Siculus's *Biblioteke* as a guide. Yet his statements regarding important insights into Alexandrian history are conflicting in nature. Plutarch also offers important details pertaining to naval engagements and political relations. However, they were not based on first-hand observations but rather on secondary reports. And in all cases we are presented with exactly what the author chose to describe, not the hard direct evidence that archaeologists seek.

With so many doubts plaguing written sources, the physical evidence in ancient sites plays an even greater role in historical research. Therefore, it is important to delineate the many differences between history and archaeology. Even though both disciplines work toward the same end, archaeological evidence is less prone to the complicating influence of written texts.[2] However, a perfectly preserved set of artifacts does not necessarily answer all of history's questions. Usually, the physical evidence is far from perfect, amounting to but a few pieces left from the objects of interest, and they become useful knowledge only at the end of a careful, well-informed reconstruction.[3] Scattered archaeological remains are also subject to the ravages of time, particularly those submerged below the sea. And individual pieces are often discovered without any literal meaning. Spectacular sites, such as the one at Alexandria, can create opportunities for archaeologists to force their findings to fit theoretical constructs built on the basis of written sources without attempting to interpret their function within Alexandria's landscape.[4] Looking to history to validate material findings is a complicated business. Fortunately, new approaches to interpreting coastal sites challenge historical findings and offer added insight into our ancient past. Lastly, Alexandria's topography has undergone drastic changes owing to natural disasters and urban development. Soil redistribution has, therefore,

---

2. With the exception of honorary buildings and statues. Much of Alexandria's material remains were largely unattended remains and therefore less likely to carry such a particular intended message.

3. Ibid, 31.

4. Barbara Takackow, *Topography of Ancient Alexandria: An Archaeological Map* (Warsaw: Archeologii Srodziemnomorskiej, 1993), 21.

led to a restratification of many artifacts, mixing Byzantine, Roman, and Greek layers. As a result, Alexandria houses a rather large collection of objects without provenience and in some instances we are left with rather vague dates to work from. To compensate, historians rely on a variety of specialists who incorporate comparative artifact studies that can tell us a great deal about obscure findings.

Ideally, the textual and archaeological remains will complement one another and allow us to create a theoretical model of the past. A wide assortment of disciplines must come together in order to piece together an ancient puzzle in an accurate way. However, even with historical and material evidence cooperating, historians and archeologists know that findings are still subject to our own limited perceptions of the past and to our own arguments and prejudices. In examining this topic, the author considered the biases and perspectives of each source while acknowledging she may also be introducing other limitations and misunderstood notions. Nevertheless, I hope that you, the general reader, conclude that *Alexandria and the Sea* is a useful and detailed account of Alexandrian affairs.

Many articles and books detail the history of Alexandria and the archaeological investigations off her shores. Trouble is, these chronicles concentrate mostly on the same events. But once off these well-trodden paths, searchers for information must make their way through a plethora of scholarly publications and obscure journals, in a variety of languages— yet some topics have never been covered at all.[5] What is needed is a comprehensive work with a dedicated maritime perspective. *Alexandria and the Sea* endeavors to incorporate current archaeological reports with primary and secondary sources to create a unique understanding of Alexandria's maritime past, particularly as it relates to modern discoveries. Specifically, the first section of this book will include an assessment of ship construction, trade, Hellenistic warfare, ancient economies, and harbor development. The analysis of maritime trade and naval affairs confirm that ancient Egypt's economic interests and military pursuits were interwoven, meaning that sea power was an important foundation of Alexandria's economic prosperity.

---

5. Casson, Lionel. *The Ancient Mariners* (Princeton University Press, 1991) Preface. Casson is actually addressing ancient maritime history in general, which is certainly applicable here.

The second segment is assigned to recent developments in maritime archaeology, which have taken place in Alexandria and in related sites around the Mediterranean.[6] This portion of the text will explain archaeological processes as they were carried out in Alexandria and their impact on a modern Egyptian city. The final chapter of the book will also document some of the challenges and advancements within the science of underwater archaeology as the world attempts to create an acceptable formula of culturally appropriate methods for protecting our archaeological treasures.

Before beginning in earnest, I would like to acknowledge several persons and institutions that have greatly aided my efforts. In particular, I would like to acknowledge Professor Anthony Papalas of East Carolina University, Emad Khalil of Southampton University, and Mohamed Abd El-Maguid of Egypt's Supreme Council of Antiquities. This book has greatly benefited from their thoughtful remarks. Also, I should also like to thank members of the Graeco-Roman Museum, the Archaeological Society, the Center for Alexandrian Studies, the Franck Goddio Society, and the Institute of Nautical Archeology. But my greatest debt of gratitude goes to my parents, Ron and Dea Williams, my family and Randy Stowell. I am extraordinarily grateful for their never-ending encouragement and support.

---

6. Maritime archaeology is a sub field of underwater archaeology and is not limited to underwater research. Therefore, the studies are extended to include submerged artifacts, harbors, or maritime trade. It can also include the study of shipyards, boat burials, etc.

ONE

Alexander and Alexandria

Geography and Ethnography

Before Alexander the Great's conquest, Greeks and Macedonians envisioned a world with three continents.[7] Europe expanded northward to the Sea of Azov. Asia's borders ended with India, and the continent known as Libya extended no further than the Sudan. To the west, all the world ended at the Pillars of Hercules. Most countries and their residents were also mapped into a larger diagram and were accounted for in Aristotle's *Meterorologica.* In this work, Aristotle allocated people and places to the "ten winds," depending on their relation to the center of the world.[8] Aristotle's conclusions regarding geography and indigenous populations influenced the evolution of scientific map-making, and his teachings were critical to the future success of Alexander the Great.

As a student of Aristotle and an avid reader of Homer's *Odyssey,* Alexander developed an early appreciation for geography and ethnography. Consequently, he began his campaigns with serious scientific projects in mind and compiled a great deal of information on any region likely to be penetrated.[9] In addition, he took with him scientists

---

7. Nicholas Hammond, *The Genius of Alexander the Great* (London: Duckworth, 1997).

8. At this time Rhodes appears to be the center of the world, which is rather understandable considering Rhodes had a long-standing naval tradition and was likely to have built up a considerable mass of nautical information. O.A.W. Dilke, *Greek and Roman Maps* (London: Thames and Hudson, 1985), 59.

9. Ibid.

from various disciplines and kept detailed records of his expeditions. Well-informed about the world around him, Alexander was logistically prepared to move a large force through the Persian Empire and India. At the same time, he successfully conducted scientific surveys of many uncharted locations, opening lines of communication and trade throughout a vast empire.[10]

To assure the success of his campaigns and the survival of his army, Alexander relied on careful surveys, particularly of coastal regions and sea routes. To depend on land support in foreign, hostile territory was not only risky but also inefficient. Sea transport provided a more reliable lifeline to supplies, especially in light of the fact that the largest merchant ship of the time could carry 400 tons while a packhorse could only carry 200 pounds and would consume twenty pounds of foodstuff daily.[11] The increasingly large number of people in Alexander's following (87,000 infantry, 18,000 cavalry and roughly 52,000 noncombatants) meant a heightened dependence on deep-water harbors and protected sea lanes.[12]

Once new territory was secured, Alexander ordered garrison commanders and economic administrators to harvest local resources. As his supply base increased, his expedition was free to explore uncharted territory and establish bases in the distant lands of Arabia and India. Preliminary surveys at sea continued to play a vital role in this aspect of his campaign. Alexander's numerous scientific surveys ultimately led to the foundation of more than seventy new cities in Iran, India, Afghanistan, and Central Asia, many with the name Alexandria.[13] In addition, he established direct links between distant lands through economic and political ties. At the end of his campaign of conquest, Alexander had expanded the known frontiers of the world from Sri Lanka to Ireland. Distant residents were already looking toward a new ideological center of the world.

---

10. Diodorus 17.25

11. Donald Enlges, *Alexander the Great and the Logistics of the Macedonian Army* (Berkley: University of California Press, 1978),3.

12. Ibid, 111.

13. Peter Green, "Alexander's Alexandria." *Alexandria and Alexandrianism* (Malibu: J. Paul Getty Museum, 1995),6. Also noted in Pliny 62, 6.26,6.49, 6.107, Strabo 11.8.9, Arrian 3.28.4, 4.1, 5.19.4, 6.21.5 and Curtius 7.3.23, 9.8.8.

The young city of Alexandria fit neatly into this expanding global community and emerging world market system. Egypt was already an attractive base as an international trade center because it bridged eastern luxury items with western markets. Moreover, it bordered on the final leg of ancient caravan routes and was open to trade along the Red Sea coast. Within its own borders, the Nile Valley was a potential breadbasket for much of the Mediterranean and came complete with a highly organized system to maintain grain production. Furthermore, Alexander's seven-month long siege of Tyre had left an important port demolished and created a subsequent void in Mediterranean trade. All these conditions created a unique opportunity to establish Egypt as a central pivot in Greek commerce.

At first, Alexandria lacked a well-developed harbor. Egypt could only claim a number of small Mediterranean harbors, which served as useful outlying settlements against pirates and were active in trade. Evidence of earlier activity comes from Homer's *Odyssey*: "There is an island in the ever-surging main, offshore from Aegypt: and the men call it Pharos."[14] Later, ten harbors were accounted for in 500 BC when a Greek geographer visited Egypt and described the area west of the Nile Delta, including ten ports in the *Periplus of Scylax*.[15]

Many ports, particularly Canopus and Pelusium, were at the mercy of Nile floods. In addition, annual silt deposits collected along the northern mouths of Nile branches and required the rebuilding of these ports every few years.[16] Pharos served as the only permanent harbor and had already been in use for centuries.[17] Despite its long history, it is likely that Pharos did not maintain a trade center comparable with Canopus because Alexander ordered the Canopic market relocated to Alexandria.[18] However, the expansive area neighboring Pharos did sustain its own maritime economy.

14. Homer, *Odyssey* 4.354-55.

15. *Periplus of Scylax* as cited by Mohamed Abd El-Aziz Negm, "Recent Excavations Around Abu Mina." *Commerce et Artisanant dans l'Alexandrie hellénistique et romaine, actes du colloque d'Athénes Bulletin e Correspondance Hellénique Supplément*, (Paris: Ecole Francaise D'Athénes, 1998), 96.

16. Mustafa El-Abbadi, "The Greatest Emporium in the Inhabited World" *Underwater Archaeology and Coastal Management: Focus on Alexandria*. (Washington DC: UNESCO, 2000),17.

17. Strabo 17.1.19

18. Ancient texts also mention a custom's house located in Canopus attesting to their developed trade. There is no evidence of such an institution in Rhakotis.

FIGURE 1: Conquests of Alexander the Great. Reprinted by permission of the publishers and the Trustees of the Loeb Classical Library from Arrian: Volume I, Loeb

Classical Library Volume L 236, translated by P. A. Brunt, Cambridge Mass.: Harvard University Press, 1976.

Foundation and Development

The outpost near Pharos was officially known as Rhakotis before Alexandria itself was founded. Rhakotis literally meant "building site" and comprised sixteen fishing villages forty miles west of the Nile River mouth. It stretched along a narrow strip of land resting between the Mediterranean Sea and Lake Mareotis.[19] Researchers initially found it difficult to determine the extent of local maritime activity, since there was no physical evidence that any of these ports existed. The growth of Alexandria over the centuries and topographical changes has significantly contributed to the lowering of Lake Mareotis. As a result, more of the lake islands and traces of harbors are beginning to emerge.

Based on Scylax's observations, Alexander and his team of engineers would have known about several large harbors. Obviously, they would have recognized the port site on Alexandria's Mediterranean shore, then a second lake harbor 30 kilometers southwest of Alexandria. Preserved relics, documented in 1866 by Mahmoud el-Falaki, demonstrate that the harbor was active from the fifth century BC until the fourteenth century AD.[20] In addition, modern investigators have noted several stone piers marking other harbors between them on the northern and southern coasts of Lake Mareotis.[21]

The trade that occurred in these harbors may have simply supported a local community. Historians have speculated that Rhakotis and the regions to its west were known in antiquity for their highly developed agriculture. This area supported a number of local factories and industries that had existed since ancient times. Recent archaeological investigations have uncovered evidence of wineries, oil mills, and numerous pottery kilns.[22] The expansive territory, which would one day

---

19. Pliny, *Natural History,* V,XI, 62.3, noted that Lake Mareotis included many islands being thirty miles in length and 250 in circumference.

20. Archaeologists have also examined Taposiris Magna. The site was very extensive and may represent some of the forms of Alexandria's lake harbors. In addition, the harbor utilized an artificial jetty, which linked the port with the southern shore and forced ships to pass through the harbor. Mohamed Abd El-Aziz Negm, "Recent Excavations Around Abu Mina," *Commerce et Artisanant dans l'Alexandrie hellénistique et romaine,* 101.

21. Ibid.

22. Elzieta Rodziewicz, "From Alexandria to the West" *Commerce et Artisanant dans l'Alexandrie hellénistique et romaine,* 93. These factories were small manufacturing establishments consisting of about a dozen people. They were usually a family business based on slave labor.

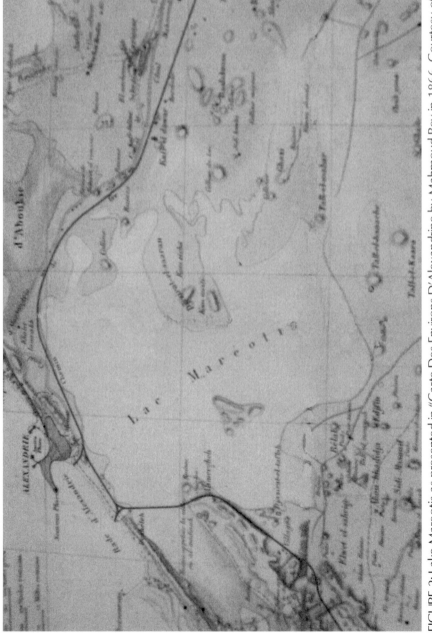

FIGURE 2: Lake Mareotis as presented in "Carte Des Environs D'Alexandrine by Mahmoud Bey in 1866. Courtesy of the Graeco-Roman Museum, Alexandria, Egypt.

include Alexandria, may not have been as well developed as other centers along the Nile or the Mediterranean, but on the future site of Alexandria a maritime base had been created with its own sector of commerce.

Brief accounts survive regarding early investigations of Egypt's north coast. Plutarch wrote that Alexander ordered surveys of the long limestone ridge between the lake and the sea, noting the deepwater harbor, the protection afforded by Pharos, and the lack of comparable facilities elsewhere along the shore.[23] Natural reefs and Cape Lochias to the east also formed a protective barrier around a deep-water harbor.[24] Additional reefs, located closer to land, later restricted harbor access to three channels. Pharos was undoubtedly a physical barrier, yet the offshore island served an additional purpose. The Greeks had developed a special affection for its strategic value when their control of the mainland was uncertain and the local population hostile.[25] The nearby island could

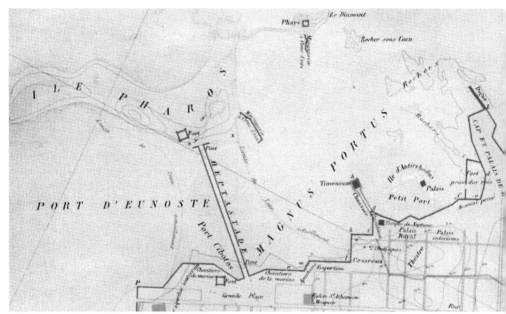

FIGURE 3: Map of Pharos Island and the Eastern Harbor.

23. Plutarch, *Alexander,* 26.

24. Submerged reefs act as a natural breakwater, reducing the wave height and changing the wave direction close to the shore. Emad Khalil, Maritime Activity in Alexandria Harbor from the Bronze Age to the Roman Period, (Southampton: Southampton University, 2002), 2.

25. Jean-Yves Empereur, *Alexandria Rediscovered* (New York: George Brazillier, 1998), 43.

have served as a protective shelter while the mainland was under construction.

Natural conditions were favorable but an international trade center would require more developed waterways and greater protection for the harbor. Therefore, Alexander ordered the construction of a causeway quite possibly to prevent the buildup of silt as was experienced in nearby seaports. The barrier was placed between Pharos and the mainland, which divided the large port into two harbors. The western harbor remained connected to the lake through a navigable channel, and an engineered "box," or *kibotos*, barred unrestricted access to the waterway.[26] In turn, the lake was connected to the Nile, bridging the gap between Egyptian grain and a growing Mediterranean market.

With Alexandria's foundation in place, Alexander was prepared to leave Egypt under the supervision of two monarchs, two garrison commanders, and two overseers. Eventually, Cleomenes of Naucratis, a prominent businessman and engineer, came to control everything when Alexander made him treasurer.[27] Cleomenes's rule marks an interesting component of Alexandria's history for he was chiefly responsible for the city's early success. He is credited with building the city walls and Alexander's palaces. Cleomenes also earned himself a distinct reputation as a corrupt ruler who profited from other's misfortune. The best-known complaint against him pertained to the public market located in Canopus. In accordance with Alexander's orders, he prepared to move the market to Alexandria. Reluctant to move, the Canopic community showered him with bribes. When the project was completed, Cleomenes attempted to extort more money. Unable to pay, the Canopic community was forcefully relocated.[28]

Both ancient and modern historians have condemned Cleomenes's corrupt administration, but Karl Polany defends him, arguing, in the alternative, that Cleomenes's bribes paralleled the local priesthood's practices.[29] Polany also argues that too little attention is paid to Cleomenes's

---

26. Strabo 17.1.7

27. Alan K. Bowman, *Egypt After the Pharaohs* (Berkeley: University of California Press, 1986), 22.

28. Xenophon, *Oeconomica*, 2.2.33.

29. Karl Polany, *Livelihood of Man* (New York: Academic Press, 1977), 242, Polany based his argument on taxes listed from the stele of Naucratis cited in *Zeitschroft fur Agypische Sprache*, Vol. 38, 133.

accomplishments: He was responsible for raising a fleet, creating a mercenary army, reorganizing the finances of Egypt, and the building of the city. He was also accountable for finances in Libya, Cyrenaica, and Marmarica.[30] Polany makes a number of strong arguments in favor of Cleomenes, adding that "individual motives and personalities are quite unimportant compared with institutional changes."[31]

The ethics of Cleomenes's actions remain questionable, but his role in the establishment of a world market system should not be understated. Greeks had already been traveling the seas in search of surplus grain; once found, they stored it in ship bottoms.[32] Athens's hold on the grain trade was loosely organized, but it did demonstrate certain market tendencies in the fourth century.[33] The famine that struck the Mediterranean between 330 BC and 326 BC led to the emergence of a new grain market because it exposed the disorganization of the then-current system.[34] Although money was available to buy grain and plenty of the crop was around, Athens was simply unable to connect supply with demand. Alexandria was soon to take up the task

The role that Alexandria and subsequently Cleomenes were to take is best known to modern historians through Demosthenes's *Private Orations*. In one section of his work, Demosthenes discusses a court hearing regarding a shipment of grain. The ship was intended for Athens, butits cargo was sold in Rhodes. The prosecutor argued that the mix-up was intentional and caused by Cleomenes's monopoly over the grain trade. The case against the defendants is explained in the following:

> "All these men ... were underlings and confederates of Cleomenes,
> the former ruler of Egypt, from the time he received the government
> did no small harm to your state, or rather the rest of the Greeks as
> well, by buying up grain for resale and fixing the price, and in this he
> had these men as his confederates. Some of the men would dispatch

---

30. Arrian, *Anabasis,* III, 5.

31. Polany, *The Livelihood of Man,* 240.

32. Xenophon, *Oeconomica,* XX, 27-28; Polany, *The Livelihood of Man,* 228.

33. Polany, *The Livelihood of Man,* 229.

34. Michael L. Rostovtzeff, *The Social and Economic History of the Hellenistic World, Vol. 1* (Oxford: Clarendon Press, 1941), 168-9.

the grain from Egypt, others would sail in charge of the shipments, while others would remain in Athens and dispose of the consignments. Then those who remained here would send letters to those abroad advising them of the prevailing prices, so that if grain were down in your market, they might bring it here, and if the price should fall, they might put it in some other port. This was the chief reason why the price of grain advanced; it was due to such letters and conspiracies ... When these men dispatched their ships from Athens, they left the price of grain there pretty high ... Afterwards, however ... when the ships from Sicily arrived, and the prices of grain were falling, and when their ships had reached Egypt, the defendants straight away sent a man to Rhodes to inform his partner, Parmeniscus, of the state of things here, well knowing that the ship would be forced to touch at Rhodes. The outcome was that Parmeniscus discharged his cargo of grain at Rhodes and sold it there."[35]

Another source, Xenophon, adds that Cleomenes attempted to freeze grain exports when Egypt suffered from the same famine plaguing the Greek world.[36] Local officials argued that the loss of profit from the freeze would be too great, and Cleomenes agreed to buy the farmer's crop directly and then resell it with a heavy embargo.[37] In doing this, Alexandria organized a much-needed system to distribute grain under a regulated government administration. The city profited greatly, since the middleman had been cut out on a local level. Then Cleomenes stretched Egypt's influence through the rest of the Mediterranean. He made agreements with Rhodes to serve as a major transporter of grain and stationed government officials in various trade centers to handle consignments and inform Rhodian agents of price movements. As a major distributor of the grain, Rhodes housed the crop and played a crucial role within international trade. The Rhodian grain price essentially set market standards, and other ports paid a comparable rate once transport charges were factored in.[38] Supplies began to move rationally

35. Demostanes, *Dareius Against Dionysodorus in the Matter of a Loan,* LVI, 7-10.

36. Xenophon, *Oeconomica,* II 1352b.

37. Ibid, 15-20.

38. Polany, *The Livelihood of Man,* 229.

in accord with actual need rather than erratically in accord with political influence or military power.[39] In such fashion, Alexandria established itself as an influential economic authority early in its history. Successful growth allowed Cleomenes to develop a large mint and he began circulating a new system of coins. Trade flourished as the young city attracted merchants and investors from the far corners of Alexander's empire.

Alexander's Navy

Alexandria's economic success was directly related to her position as a naval power, and control of the seas was directly related to Egypt's longstanding wealth. Military pursuits and economic interests were interwoven.[40] Greek politicians used military pressure to extort taxes and natural resources, which fattened treasuries and built fleets. As Alexander expanded his empire, he established a new monetary system, facilitating trade throughout the Mediterranean. He also recruited soldiers and mariners from various regions, developing a mercenary military system and changing the nature of a standing army. Hellenistic soldiers were professionals who made a career in the military, allowing farmers and merchants to work uninterrupted and without worrying about a call to arms. At the same time, mercenaries were paid frequently and traveled enough to circulate coins. Macedonian conquests encouraged piracy throughout the Mediterranean by impairing the Athenian fleet, which had previously kept pirates at bay. Though not new to the Mediterranean, piracy was affected by the growing number of mercenaries who took advantage of increased trade and the subsequent cash flow.[41] The well-trained soldiers and seamen who developed under Alexander eventually became an important fighting force in the Hellenistic Age. Alexander's successors, known as the *diodochoi,* later employed as many as 1,000 pirates at a time.[42]

Alexander's fleet changed drastically during his campaign as the utilized the flexibility of mercenaries and pirates to keep his ships manned.

---

39. Polany citing Rostovtzeff, *Livelihood of Man,* 250.

40. See W.L. Rodgers, *Greek and Roman Naval Warfare* (Annapolis: US Naval Institute, 1964), 230, for this Mahanian interpretation of Sea Power.

41. Ibid.

42. This instance specifically refers to Demetrius's blockade and later siege against Rhodes.

His navy secured supply links, explored uncharted territory, and staged attacks on coastal cities. The size of his fleet, therefore, reflected the magnitude of the naval engagements within his campaign. Ships were unquestionably a large expense and were released from service when finances were low.[43] Then, whenever the need arose, Alexander would call upon various Greek states, especially Rhodes, to supply him with galleys and sailors. The fact that Alexander was slow to establish a standing navy makes sense in light of his Macedonian background. Ironically, it was his Macedonian fighting style that played an influential role in the development of larger supergalleys.

To clarify, ancient galleys were, in many respects, "works in progress," changing along with battle techniques. The emergence of a ram called for a more powerful vessel, which led to attempts to improve speed and maneuverability, causing traditional galleys to evolve into a two-banked war ships.[44] A third level of rowers was added around 600 BC when naval architects devised an outrigger above the gunwale that projected laterally beyond it to accommodate a third line.[45] By the end of the sixth century BC, the three-banked galley, or trireme, was an important element in the Greek navy.

Triremes varied in construction, depending upon the navy that used them. Corinthian and Syracusan navies preferred to fill their decks with marines and fight alongside the enemy as opposed to ramming. Triremes were even used as horse transports in the fifth century BC. The Phoenicians also made use of the trireme, but placed the oars of their thranites, or highest level of rowers, over the gunwale. Then a second set of stanchions, planted in the railing itself, supported the raised fighting deck, which extended from gunwale to gunwale. A row of shields was placed along the deck to form a pavesade.[46] The three-banked warship varied in size and on some occasions could accommodate fifty soldiers. Other variations had special hull configurations allowing for a more streamline build. In some instances, leaner shapes restricted a vessel to

---

43. Nicholas Hammond, *The Genius of Alexander the Great* (London: Duckworth, 1997), 62.

44. Lionel Casson, *Ships and Seamanship in the Ancient World* (Baltimore: John Hopkins University Press, 1971), 80-81.

45. Ibid.

46. Ibid, 93.

no more than ten marines but such ships had greater maneuverability for ramming.[47] The trireme was not Alexander's ship of choice, even though he incorporated various styles of galleys into his fleet and then modified them as needed. In fact, the original Macedonian contingent of his navy consisted of sixty ships with a complement of 100 Greek vessels.

Alexander's navy reached the Hellespont at the beginning of his expedition, in 332 BC. When his army arrived at Sestos, Alexander placed Parmenio in charge of ferrying over troops and cavalry as well as towing a large number of round ships.[48] After reaching Sestos, Alexander continued south with sixty of the heavier ships—a distinctly Macedonian squadron that served as the fleet bodyguard.[49] Darius, on the other hand, had more than 400 Phoenician, Egyptian, and Ionian warships, most of which were triremes. Despite Alexander's smaller naval force, he successfully captured Miletos and disbanded the opposing fleet. Land forces then maintained Asia while Alexander continued to capture main ports along the coast, leaving the Persian fleet without safe harbor and virtually ineffective.

Alexander continued south, capturing 230 Phoenician and Greek ships, 224 of which were triremes. Alexander deployed the new fleet in a seven-month siege of Tyre. During this long-term assault, Alexander used a torsion catapult from the sea by mounting several of them to his second-class triremes.[50] The technique was unprecedented in naval engagements. It also dramatically influenced fighting at sea because the hull of the ship had to sustain the weight and force of the catapult. Catapults gained in popularity, which lead to a greater production of larger ships. Then, as more navies incorporated the new weapon, battle tactics changed accordingly.

Larger ships required the heavy timber indigenous to Cyprus and Phoenicia. Possession of the two territories was therefore critical to establishing and maintaining a powerful navy. Alexander recognized that by taking Tyre the rest of Phoenicia was in his hands. He also expected

---

47. J.S. Morrison and J.F. Coates, *The Athenian Trireme* (Cambridge University, 1986), 152.

48. Plutarch, *Moralia*, 327.

49. J.S. Morrison, *Greek and Roman Oared Warships* (Oxford: Oxbow, 1996), 4.

50. Casson, *Ships and Seafaring in Ancient Times*, (London: British Museum Press, 1994), 91.

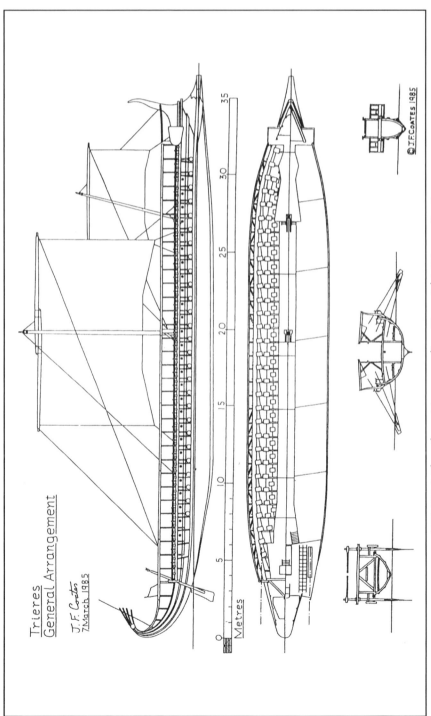

Trieres
General Arrangement

J.F.Coates
7March 1985

FIGURE 4: Plans for a trireme replica. Copyright: Trireme Trust.

that the Phoenician fleet, which was the most numerous and efficient contingent in the Persian navy, would come over to him.[51] Alexander did gain 120 ships from the Cypriot king, creating a combined fleet of 224 vessels, in addition to the Macedonian sixty. With Phoenicia and Cyprus firmly under his control, Alexander sought out Egypt to deprive Persia of any sea command.[52] Then the Macedonian army spent the summer months marching through the Levant toward Egypt, Alexander's companion, Hephaestion, followed along the coast with the fleet, mooring in Pelusium.[53] Alexander arrived, garrisoned the city, and then ordered the fleet up the Nile to the capital city of Memphis.

Eastern Campaign

With Egypt secure, Alexander began his campaign of the east in 324 BC, starting, as usual, with surveys for establishing additional cities. Then he planned to circumnavigate Arabia and finally gain entry to India. Alexander ordered ships to be built in Babylon and chose Nearchus the Cretan, an experienced ship's captain, to command his naval expedition in the east and write up an account.[54] Nearchus's squadron sailed up the Euphrates with the idea of establishing settlements along the Persian Gulf.[55] As ships came over from the Phoenician coast, they were dismantled and the pieces transported overland to Thapsacus on the Euphrates. They were reassembled and sailed the river to Babylon, where they divided into three expeditions to scout out new locations.[56] In addition, Alexander built a harbor to accommodate 1,000 ships and hired men from Phoenicia and Syria to operate them.

Alexander's expansion opened up new markets and secured caravan routes to the east. His bodyguard, historian, and future king of Egypt,

---

51. Morrison, *Greek and Roman Oared Warships,* 6; Arrian 2.17.1.

52. Ibid.

53. Ibid, 9; Arrian 3.1.1

54. Nearchus's chronicle was written before 312 BC and is cited in Strabo and Arrian. Lionel Pearson, "The Lost Histories of Alexander the Great," *The American Philological Association.* (New York: Philological Monographs, 20, 1906), p.112-49; Dilke, *Greek and Roman Maps,* 134.

55. Mustafa El-Abbadi, *The Life and Fate of the Ancient Library of Alexandria* (Paris: UNESCO, 1990), 29.

56. Ibid.

Ptolemy Son of Lagos, undoubtedly benefited from survey findings as well as trade contacts. The future king of Egypt had grown familiar with the entirety of Alexander's empire and recorded his accounts in the *Journal of Alexander.*[57] This journal included day-to-day records of Alexander's activities including detailed matters of diplomacy and official correspondence.[58] It is very likely that Ptolemy's records were filled with important information regarding the monetary wealth of distant lands along with their natural resources. Clearly, Ptolemy sought Egypt as soon as he became a contender for a share of Alexander's empire. Not only did he recognize Egypt's potential as an economic power but he also understood how it could become a key maritime base.

Alexander's campaign was nearing a close but his influence over Alexandria's future remained certain. With the death of his companion, Hephaestion, Alexander ordered Cleomenes to build temples in Hephaestion's honor on Pharos and in Alexandria. In exchange, Alexander agreed to ignore all of Cleomenes's wrongdoing.[59] Then he spent two days drinking until he fell ill with what appeared to be malaria. On his deathbed, Alexander presented Perdiccas with his ring and reportedly said, "The strongest man gets the empire."[60] In turn, Perdiccas presented the royal ring to an assembly suggesting that they should make the decision. The settlement resulted in joint rule between Alexander's infant son and the king's idiot brother with Perdiccas serving as the chiliarch, or adviser and "real power."[61] This arrangement was short-lived and trouble soon brewed between Alexander's generals. Both the infant son and the brother were assassinated, and the generals divided the empire. Perdiccas held Alexander's royal seal and therefore had first

---

57. *Life of Alexander* survived in Alexandria for some time and is paraphrased by Plutarch and Arrian 1.27.

58. Hammond, *The Genius of Alexander the Great*, 42.

59. This statement is cited frequently in historical texts. However, scholars have argued that Alexander's letter was a forgery because it was not in his style and because Alexander would not have confused the location of Hephaestion's honorary temple with the Pharos lighthouse. J. Maffy, *The Ptolemaic Dynasty* (London: Methuen and Co. 1899), 23 note 1; W. W. Tarn *Alexander the Great* (Cambridge: University Press, 1948), Vol.2, 303-4; Polany, *The Livelihood of Man*, 241.

60. Walter Ellis, *Ptolemy of Egypt* (New York: Routledge, 1994), 21.

61. At the time, the struggle of the strongest fell to Perdiccas, Antipater, who served under Phillip II, and Craterus. However, all three men perished within four years of Alexander. Ibid, 22.

choice of territories. He passed over Egypt and Libya, which went to Ptolemy. Two other of Alexander's generals went on to create lasting empires: Antigonus the One-Eyed in Asia Minor and Seleucus in Babylon.

The disputes that arose between the successors created a system of checks and balances throughout the Hellenistic Age. Practically overnight, Ptolemy turned his new capital city of Alexandria into a maritime power. He also took steps to secure his position as a rightful heir. He even went so far as to capture Alexander's remains in Syria and bring them to Egypt in 320 BC. Grandiose gestures aside, Ptolemy already had everything he needed to establish Egyptian supremacy at sea. He had gained control of the Mediterranean grain trade along with access to India, Arabia, and the rest of Alexander's empire. These contacts opened avenues of future trade, leading to increased revenues that financed naval expeditions and secured new territories. More important, Ptolemy was the benefactor of new naval battle techniques, weaponry, and the Phoenician contingent of Alexander's fleet.[62]

---

62. Diodorus 19.58.2.

TWO

The Ptolemaic Empire

FIGURE 5: Coin depicting Ptolemy I Soter. Courtesy of the Graeco-Roman Museum, Alexandria, Egypt.

When Ptolemy Son of Lagos claimed Egypt in 323 BC, he immediately demoted Cleomenes to deputy governor.[63] Ptolemy went to Alexandria, ordered Cleomenes's execution, and claimed over 8,000 talents that had been amassed in the state treasury.[64] The execution made Ptolemy popular for ridding Egypt of a corrupt ruler and financially prepared him to build his city and build his empire. His early steps became critical to the city's later financial prosperity. In particular, by connecting with Rhodes, Cyprus, and the Levant, he secured the territories required to establish a powerful fleet. In doing this, Ptolemy Soter recognized that sea power in the Hellenistic Age arose from the ability

---

63. Justin 13.4.11, Green, "Alexander's Alexandria," 6.

64. Pausiaus 1.6.3 cites Cleomenes's execution and Diodorus XVIII, 14.1 accounts for treasury holdings.

to control strategically placed naval stations from which operations could be made.[65]

Dispersed bases made sense for a variety of reasons. Oared galleys carried little room for provisions and therefore required added logistical support. Egypt was also dependent on mercenaries and safe harbors made ideal recruitment centers. In addition, a complex of widely distributed bases made it feasible for squadrons to exercise control over adjacent seaboard, protect trade routes, and stage surprise attacks.[66] New garrisons also guaranteed a substantial income for the Ptolemaic empire. The Ptolemies were free to place embargoes on various items, ensuring that outside territories purchased Alexandrian goods. External imports and exports were also subject to taxes, of which Egypt received a percentage. Controlled territories allowed the Ptolemies to establish royal mints in Cyrene, Cyprus, and Syria in order to circulate their own currency outside Egypt.[67]

Ptolemy had good reason to expand on political fronts as well. Enemies were close at hand and prepared attacks soon after Ptolemy settled into Alexandria. Perdiccas immediately staged an invasion of Egypt with his share of Alexander's fleet, an effort that failed when Ptolemy bribed the invading mercenaries. Ptolemy also fought on the front line beside his men, establishing a heroic image of a strong leader. Perdiccas, on the other hand, continued to make some rather senseless mistakes. He lost 2,000 men only to follow up with an even more disastrous second attack. His army proved incapable of crossing the eastern branch of the Nile. Many drowned, got stuck in the mud, or were attacked by crocodiles. Afterward, Ptolemy cremated all of Perdiccas's dead and sent the ashes to surviving family and friends. The remaining enemy soldiers were so impressed by Ptolemy and displeased with Perdiccas that they killed him.[68]

---

65. Vincent Gabrielson, *The Naval Aristocracy of Hellenistic Rhodes* (Aarhus: Aarhus University Press, 1997), 43.

66. Ibid.

67. Roger S. Bagnal, *The Administration of Ptolemaic Possessions Outside of Egypt* (Leiden: Brill, 1976), 229.

68. Plutarch *Eumenes* 5-7.

As the disputes between the Alexander's successors raged, the victors sought to secure resources. Not only did Hellenistic leaders need to maintain large fleets, but they also began increasing the size of ships, which required innovative shipwrights and specific types of wood, all in the effort to outdo the competition. Cyprus, Rhodes, and the Levant supplied a wealth of timber, shipwrights, and seamen. Therefore, these three areas became the focus of major confrontations between Ptolemy Soter and his adversary, Antigonus. The struggle that ensued between the two men and their successors was not only demonstrated in naval engagements but also in an arms race that drastically altered the traditional warship.

The Evolution of the Supergalley

The trireme was the mainstay of navies at the beginning of the Hellenistic Age. Later, changes in naval tactics led to the need for larger versions of the three-banked galley. Increasing the size was not terribly difficult since weight correlated closely with beam. The length remained similar for most ships and draft would not have varied much for reasons of stability.[69] 'Threes'—three-banked ships—had evolved into 'fours' under Alexander. In many accounts of the time, 'fours' are not well regarded in terms of speed and sea-keeping qualities. However, they were crucial to the development of larger galleys, which could support more marines and afford a height advantage from which to fire missiles.[70] Like the trireme, the 'four' demonstrated a good deal of variation and adaptability, depending on its use. Navies that preferred greater speed and a height advantage could simply place two rowers on the thranite oar. However, Macedonian preferences for hand-to-hand combat would have required a broader beam to accommodate additional marines, suggesting that some 'fours' had two levels instead of three.[71]

---

69. Morrison, *Greek and Roman Oared Warships,* 257.

70. Livy 20.25.2-8 distinguished a substantial difference in height between a 'four' and a 'five.' The Alba Fucentia grafitto, which dates to the first century ad, depicts the four as a long, low warship with a deck but no visible oarbox or oarports and a distinct ram. It has since determined that the height above waterline for a four was 2.2 meters. Morrison, *Greek and Roman Oared Warships,* 268.

71. Ibid, 269.

In this case, the ship would have forty-four oars per side and an oar crew of 176. The 'four' was fast and maneuverable, which at first made it more preferable than the 'five.' The 'four's' low profile offered less drag and allowed for easier rowing in adverse wind conditions.[72] The creation of various 'fours' demonstrated a certain degree of flexibility in changing naval tactics. However, Ptolemy's naval engagements proved that size mattered. In fact, height advantages and the ability to fire missiles from a greater distance contributed to the evolution of a larger ship.

'Fives' met the demands of Ptolemy and Antigonus and performed well against 'fours.' The larger galley employed double manning at two of the three levels and single manning at one.[73] A 'five' had an oarcrew of 300 with a complement of 120 deck soldiers. Naval engagements between the successors proved that the 'five' was considerably larger and slower when compared to a 'three.' Still, the 'five' marks an interesting point in the evolution of galleys. It was light enough to be easily pulled ashore and maintained a reasonably low freeboard.[74] It was also

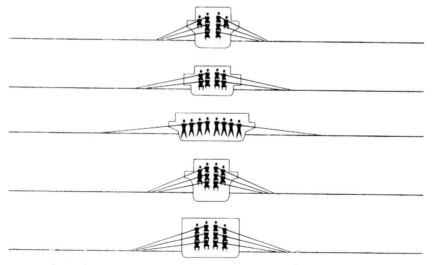

FIGURE 6: Possible arrangements of the rowers of a 'four,' 'five' and 'six.' The upper three show a three-level, two-level and one-level 'four.' The lower two show a three-level 'five' and a three-level 'six.' Copyright: Lionel Casson.

72. Ibid.

73. Ibid, 170.

74. W. W. Tarn, *Hellenistic Military and Naval Developments* (Cambridge University Press, 1930), 124.

more economical than larger ships and required considerably fewer oars-men than later supergalleys. Despite the poorer performance of larger galleys, Hellenistic navies continued to develop larger ships for their height advantage and ability to launch missiles.

The transition from a 'five' to 'six' was also a rather simple proce-dure. Double manning was extended from two to three levels.[75] However, Soter did not utilize the larger ships. His decision appears to be one of personal preference. Egypt certainly had the resources to build larger galleys and the 'six' certainly proved effective in many naval engage-ments. The introduction of a 'six' marked a considerable increase in size as indicated by the number of oarsmen. The 'six' contained approxi-mately thirty oarsmen, totaling 360 rowers and could accommodate 140 marines.[76] Antigonus's benefactor, Demetrius, is credited with the development of the 'seven' and used them effectively against Ptolemy.[77] The 'seven' was also a fairly simple transition from a 'six' as it merely required the addition of a third oarsman to one of the double-manned rows on a 'six.' The 'seven' also seems to have had better sea-keeping qualities than smaller ships.[78]

Egypt and Rhodes

Rhodes was at the top of the list as Ptolemy sought to secure ship-building resources in Rhodes, Cyprus, and the Levant early in his reign. Rhodes was already dependent on Egypt's lucrative grain trade. The fact that Cleomenes had selected Rhodes to be the center of grain op-erations suggests that the island traded with Egypt before Alexander's conquest.[79] The Rhodes-Egypt route was also navigable in winter.[80] To further secure relations, Egypt established "nonaggression" pacts and other alliances as early as 312 BC, while customs reports suggest strong economic ties between the two countries. In addition, the Graeco-Ro-

---

75. Morrison, *Greek and Roman Oared Warships,* 360.

76. Ibid, 272.

77. Tarn, *Hellenistic Military and Naval Developments, 360.*

78. Morrison, *Greek and Roman Oared Warships,* 272.

79. Demosthenes 56; Richard Berthold, *Rhodes in the Hellenistic Age* (Ithica: Cornell University Press, 1984), 48.

80. Ibid, Demosthenes 56.30.

man Museum in Alexandria now holds some 80,000 Rhodian amphorae handles recovered in Egypt.[81]

The role of the Rhodian handles in Alexandria has been subject to much speculation. Originally it was thought that these containers carried wine. However, no surviving texts indicate that Rhodian wine was very popular in Egypt, and the Ptolemies charged high tariffs on wine to protect the local market. At the same time, numerous accounts state that Egypt produced a fair amount of wine on its own. In his study of the Rhodian carrying trade, P. M. Fraser concluded that empty amphorae were shipped to Alexandria as clay storage vessels. Other scholars have accepted Fraser's theory because Alexandria did not appear capable of manufacturing enough clay jars of its own. Other evidence shows that Rhodian amphorae were frequently used to transport goods from other countries all around the Aegean.[82] Fraser's theory has been undercut, however, by recent archaeological investigations that have uncovered numerous pottery kilns along Egypt's north coast, proving that the Ptolemies would have not required imported jars.[83]

The Rhodian handles are an important indicator of how much trade occurred between Rhodes and Alexandria, and their frequency of discovery throughout the Eastern Mediterranean attests to Rhodes's role in Mediterranean trade. What is also interesting is that the rest of the area is lacking in amphorae—with one exception. The Black Sea has also been determined to be rich in amphorae; it was, coincidentally, the other breadbasket of the ancient Near East. Clearly, many questions regarding the amphorae go unanswered. Archaeologists still need to translate with numerical precision the existing handles into complete containers, and they must determine their intended use as well as their quantities within short chronological periods.[84] Each container bears a stamp, and researchers still need to prove formally why they were stamped

---

81. Fraser, *Ptolemaic Alexandria*, 165. Ch. 4, note 227. Fraser states that he could not provide a complete citation of the evidence. His information was provided by Miss V. Grace, who studied the collections in Alexandria.

82. Rhodes shipped wine, olive oil, figs, and other food stuffs in exchange for grain. Gabrielson, *The Naval Aristocracy of Hellenistic Rhodes*, 65

83. Ahmed Abd El-Fattah "Recent Discoveries in Alexandria and the Clora." *Commerce et Artisanant dans l'Alexandrie hellénistique et romaine*, 33.

84. Berthold, *Rhodes in the Hellenistic Age*, 48.

in the first place. Were the amphorae stamped for fiscal purposes, to guarantee capacity, or as form of administrative control?[85]

Cyprus and the Levant

Like Rhodes, Cyprus and the Levant were critical to maintaining the Egyptian navy, and Ptolemy sought to secure relations by political alliances as well as economic agreements. Soter's daughter even married one of Cyprus's nine kings. Then, in 319-18 BC, Ptolemy invaded Phoenicia and Ceole-Syria, establishing naval squadrons in several key port cities until 315 BC.[86] Though Ptolemy quickly amassed a strong maritime empire, his success was short-lived. Antigonus managed to gain favor with Rhodes and intended to use Rhodian vessels to invade Cyprus. The agreement was that Rhodes would build the warships from timber that Antigonus imported from his Syrian possessions.[87] Ptolemy responded in 315 BC when he sent 10,000 men and 100 ships to Cyprus under the command of his brother Menelaus and 100 more ships under Seleuko. From this force, fifty ships departed under Polyperchon into the Peloponnese.[88] The squadron of fifty was cruising the Eastern Mediterranean en route to Asia Minor when they intercepted Antigonus's commander with eighty Rhodian ships.[89] The Egyptian naval force defeated Theodotus and captured his fleet.

The following year Ptolemy lost Syria and Palestine. He returned to Egypt, but his troubles were far from over. In 313 BC, Cyrene, the first territory to fall under Ptolemy's control, revolted against Egypt, prompting him to send envoys to silence the protesters. Agis led the land army and Epaeneus followed with a fleet.[90] Ptolemy defeated the rebels and

---

85. Ibid.

86. Diodorus 18.43.1-2; Morrison, *Greek and Roman Oared Warships,* 20.

87. Richard Berthold, *Rhodes in the Hellenistic Age,* 61.

88. Ibid, 21.

89. Diodorus 19.62.7-8.

90. Ptolemy placed Ophellas as general, but Cyrene was already gaining a certain degree of independence in its foreign policy and soon formed an alliance with Syracuse. Later, Ptolemy Soter placed his own son, Magas, in charge. After Soter's death, Cyrene once again broke away from Alexandria. This settlement did not appear to have a well-developed bureaucracy and there is no evidence of regular tribute to Egypt. However, the placement of a garrison in Cyrene demonstrates that Ptolemy's power went well beyond guaranteeing the settlement that he had brought about. Diodorus 29.79.4, 29.80.2.

then ordered Epaeneus to Cyprus.[91] The fleet was ordered to confront the island kings, who had apparently refused to recognize Ptolemaic authority.[92] Next, Egyptian troops were sent east toward Syria. They managed to sack Poseidium, Potami Caron, and Malus. After plundering these cities and rebuilding confidence in the armed forces, Ptolemy sent troops to Cyprus. All along, Demetrius was waiting in Ceole-Syria, to attack the Egyptian army but missed Ptolemy, who sailed home in 312 BC. Then Ptolemy returned with Seleucus, taking Gaza and many other Phoenician cities.[93]

The same year, Nikokrean, Ptolemy's most powerful ally in Cyprus, assumed complete control over the island. Ptolemy felt the other governors had turned on him and therefore handed all cities over to Nikokrean until his death in 310 BC. Ptolemy then appointed Menelaus as king,[94] who asserted his new role by issuing his own royal coinage.[95] Cyprus was, by virtue of its metals, forests, and agricultural wealth, an important part of the Ptolemaic economy, but there is little evidence of how the island was exploited.[96] However, it is clear that Ptolemy's longstanding ties with Nikokrean and his brother allowed Egypt to maintain garrisons in Cyprus's major cities.

Ptolemy had secured his position within Cyprus, but Antigonus was determined to match Ptolemy's fleet. Antigonus attempted to establish good relations with Greece as he needed its harbors, and the islands literally served as a stepping-stone through the Aegean. Then he moved into Phoenicia and ordered Syrian kings and viceroys to construct a mighty fleet. Shipwrights and woodcutters from various regions assembled in Phoenicia to build Antigonus's navy, including 8,000 men and 1,000 pairs of pack animals. This small army cut timbers from the

91. Diodorus 29.79.4

92. Diodorus 29.80.2

93. This is probably the time when Soter encouraged Jews to move to Alexandria.

94. Nikokrean supported Alexander in Tyre and then supported Soter early in his career. Arrian 2.22.3; Plutarch, *Alexander*, 29.2. Bagnal, *Ptolemaic Possessions Outside Egypt*, (Leiden: Brill, 1976) 39.

95. Ibid. 41.

96. Ibid, 73.

mountains of Lebanon and Taurus and carried the timber to shipbuilding centers in Cilicia, Byblos, Sidon, and Tyre.[97]

Battle of Salamis

After Antigonus built his fleet, he continued to try to secure the great timber resources of Cyprus. Ptolemy was undoubtedly aware of the potential impact of such a threat, since the ancient world provided only two reliable sources of timber: Cyprus and the stretch of land between Lebanon and Lycia.[98] Antigonus's power base in Syria already restricted Ptolemy's access to timber in the Levant. Cyprus represented his last dependable supply of wood with which to build and maintain the fleet of a superpower. The two opponents finally clashed in a great naval confrontation in 307 BC near Salamis, Cyprus. Demetrius convoyed 15,000 troops and 400 cavalry to Cyprus with 110 triremes and fifty-three heavier transports.[99] He also employed 'fives,' 'sixes,' and 'sevens' in his fleet. The larger ships probably accommodated the stone-throwing catapults that he incorporated into his naval tactics during this battle. Demetrius also prepared for arrow bombardment, as naval gunners were becoming a fixed element of galley crews. Small arrows, if they reached the deck, could strike a rower, causing a break in stroke and interrupt the vessel's advance.[100] Both technical weaponry and ship construction were demonstrated in Demetrius's navy.

Egypt's forces also displayed advancements in naval warfare. Ptolemy readily accepted Antigonus's challenge and sailed to the southern port of Paphos where he incorporated Cypriot ships into his fleet.[101] Ptolemy already held a substantial navy of his own. The combined Cypriot and Ptolemaic fleet totaled 140 ships and was comprised entirely of 'fours' and 'fives.' In addition, no less than 200 roundships carried roughly

97. Diodorus 19.58; Robert Moore, *The Evolution of the Greek Warship and Its Tactics in the Fourth Century BC.*(Greenville: Unpublished MA Thesis, East Carolina University, 1992), 52. Moore addressed the important changes that developed in naval weaponry during several key naval battles.

98. Russell Meiggs, *Trees and Timber in the Ancient Mediterranean World* (Oxford: Clarendon Press, 1982), 163.

99. Xenophon HG 1.1.30; Morrison, *Greek and Roman Oared Warships, 21.*

100. Casson, *Ships and Seafaring in Ancient Times, 92.*

101. Morrison, *Greek and Roman Oared Warships, 22;* Diodorus 20.49.1.

10,000 soldiers. Then Ptolemy ordered sixty ships to be sent from Salamis under his brother's command. Despite Egypt's larger numbers, Demetrius realized that an attack on Salamis would pull Ptolemy away from his large land force in Egypt and force him to fight on Demetrius's own terms.[102] Demetrius also knew that Menelaus's fleet was essential to the success of the Egyptian campaign. These same sixty ships were currently tied up in the Salamis harbor. To guarantee that Menelaus never reached his brother in time, he blockaded the harbor overnight. While seldom attempted in the ancient world, such an undertaking nevertheless proved beneficial.[103] The following morning, Demetrius left ten quinquiremes under Antisthenes's command to block the narrow strait and placed men along the shore to capture or assist any sailors who found themselves stranded.

Demetrius learned of Ptolemy's approach and sailed out to meet him. Ptolemy had intended to arrive at Salamis early enough to break through the straits before Demetrius had properly prepared his defenses. Instead, he found Demetrius's fleet in formation, barricading the harbor. Demetrius faced Ptolemy with 108 ships, mostly 'fives' but also containing 'sevens' from Phoenicia and fifty-three ships of unspecified sizes.[104] Based on these numbers, J. Morrison has suggested that Demetrius's left wing was comprised of seven 'sevens,' thirty Athenian 'fours,' ten 'fives,' and ten 'sixes.' The right wing probably contained fifty-eight 'threes' and the center maintained fifty 'threes', roughly totaling 170.[105] Because Menelaus never reached Ptolemy in time, the Egyptian fleet totaled 140. Diodorus states that Ptolemy made preparations for the battle by placing himself and the largest ships on the west wing and therefore closer to the shore.[106] Ptolemy's fleet stretched from the shore eastward for more than three miles, while Demetrius's fleet extended nearly two miles with its stronger ships on the seaward end. Not all ships were on the first line as both sides held reserves behind them. The fleets moved within three stades of each other, or 530 meters, and then the men raised their shields to commence battle.

102. Moore, *Evolution of the Greek Warship,* 56.

103. Morrison, *Greek and Roman Oared Warships,* 24.

104. Diodorus 20.47.1.

105. Diodorus 20.50.5.

106. Diodorus 20.49.5.

The battle of Salamis was a major turning point in the evolution of naval strategy.[107] By utilizing catapults and arrows, the two sides demonstrated the importance of long-range weaponry in ship-to-ship combat.[108] Heavy fire took immediate and multiple causalities as catapults and ballistae launched rocks and darts. As the two fleets approached each other, archers and javelin throwers joined in. Finally the vessels locked and "…the picture of the battle as a whole was obliterated by the bloody details of the fighting near the land."[109] Demetrius's men had a clear advantage as they had the opportunity to rest throughout the night, despite the fact that they were anchored at sea. Ptolemy's men were unquestionably tired after rowing out to greet them. With the battle underway, Demetrius employed the standard trireme tactics of *periplous* and *diekplous*.[110] By overloading one side, Demetrius assured himself of the collapse of the opposing flank and by overloading the outmost flank, he trapped the enemy against the coast, effectively combining the *periplous* and *diekplous* maneuvers.[111] This innovative tactic pressed Ptolemy against the jagged shoreline that was monitored by Demetrius's men. Ramming occurred frequently, even bow-to-bow, as did sheering off enemy oars. Diodorus accounts for numerous vessels locking together when rams penetrated another vessel and did not break away. Therefore, clusters of ships literally transformed into floating fighting platforms. The boarding and fighting that occurred is significant because the tactic was used less frequently with triremes. Larger vessels were able to accommodate more marines to engage in hand-to-hand combat. At the same time, larger warships had the benefit of higher decks from which to fire missiles. The larger ships clearly had an advantage over the speed and agility of smaller vessels.

Weaponry played an important role in this battle as the two sides attacked each other with an assortment of missiles mounted to the bows

---

107. Moore, *The Evolution of the Greek Warship and its Tactics in the Fourth Century*, 51.

108. Diodorus 20.46-7.

109. Ibid, 33.

110. *Periplous* literally translates into "sailing around" with the intention of outflanking the enemy and attacking from the rear or side. *Diekplous* meant to sail through an opening in the enemy line to gain a better position for ramming and/or sheering off the enemy's oars. Trapping the enemy against the coast was also critical as it was difficult to pursue a fleeing ship out to sea.

111. Moore, *The Evolution of the Greek Warship and its Tactics in the Fourth Century*, 65.

of ships.[112] These catapults had been invented at the turn of the fourth century BC in Sicily and Magna Graecia and were capable of firing bolts or arrows three spans in length.[113] Alexander used them in his siege against Tyre, but they had never been deployed in a naval engagement. Catapults, however, posed certain risks when used in conjunction with ramming. Sea conditions also brought natural obstacles for free movement, and accuracy was problematic. To overcome the possibility of misfires, missiles were fired from the broadside of the ship. Therefore, as the ship rocked back and forth, it increased an arrow's elevation but generally remained on target with the approaching vessel. This tactic created an interesting game of chance with the attacker because it left the broadside of a ship exposed. Long, narrow targets allow more room for error in respect to distance than do a thin, wide vessels lying directly to one's side. The risk of exposing one's broadside while firing was minimal because direct hits were rather effective. In a minor instance, one arrow could strike a rower and throw off the count. In addition, many ships also supported ballistae, which were devices capable of throwing stones up to three talents in weight (180 pounds).[114]

By the end of the day, Demetrius had lost no ships, and the twenty that were disabled eventually returned to service. He had captured 100 of Ptolemy's transports plus 8,000 of his men, in addition to forty galleys and the crews.[115] According to Plutarch, Ptolemy fled with a squadron of eight ships, suffering the loss of seventy ships to the sea and seventy to the enemy.[116] In the meantime, Menelaus had broken free to find that Ptolemy had already departed. Menelaus returned to Salamis and surrendered Cyprus, marking two noteworthy transitions in Hellenistic history. First, the victory prompted Antigonus to proclaim himself king. Demetrius, Ptolemy, Seleucus, Lysimachus, and Cassander[117]

---

112. Ibid, 60.

113. Diodorus 20.49.

114. Diodorus 20.48.

115. Diodorus 20.49.

116. Plutarch, *Demetrius,* 16.

117. Lysimachus served as Alexander's bodyguard and after his death received a province consisting of Thrace and northwest Asia Minor. Cassander was the son of Antipater, who served under Phillip and Alexander. After his father's death, Cassander drove the regent from Macedonia and Greece.

quickly followed this trend. Second, the new timber supply in Cyprus would enable Demetrius to build even larger ships in an arms race with Ptolemy's successor, Philadelphus.

Antigonus returned many prisoners to Ptolemy, including his son, but he still had his eye on Egypt. Preparations for an invasion began as early as 306 BC. Antigonus led 80,000 troops and thousands of horses along the coast opposite Demetrius's fleet of 150 warships and 100 trans-ports. When Demetrius departed from Gaza, he used his fastest ships to tow the transports.[118] Demetrius also left his 'sixes' and 'sevens' behind, which were probably not necessary since Ptolemy now relied upon 'fours' and 'fives.'[119] The decision was unfortunate, because terrific storms forced many ships to seek the safe harbors of Gaza while others perished. Few ships from Demetrius's fleet actually reached their destination at Kasion. In the meantime, Antigonus's army suffered terribly in the desert. When enemy forces finally reached Egypt, they found themselves without safe harbor. Beaching was not an option since Egyptian shores were well protected. Storms persisted off the coast and Demetrius barely survived the ordeal.[120] The Nile was also high at this time of year, preventing an attack on the coastal city of Pelusium. Antigonus recognized that the invasion was ill planned and the army voted to withdraw.

Having failed in his invasion of Egypt, Antigonus set out to destroy trade with the neutral island of Rhodes. After several unsuccessful at-tacks on Rhodian vessels carrying Egyptian goods, Demetrius established a blockade reaching from the mainland to the island that lasted more than a year. Rhodes was hardly an insignificant seapower. The island maintained a substantial income as a carrying trade and therefore fi-nanced an effective navy.[121] As a result, Rhodes drove away small squadrons. Despite such early successes, island officials were receptive to initial agreements with Demetrius. Rhodian officials were even re-

---

118. Diodorus 20.74.1; Morrison, *Greek and Roman Oared Warships*, 30.

119. Ibid, 31. Morrison also suggests that there may have been problems with 37 'sixes' and 'sevens' in terms of seaworthiness. No records indicate if these larger ships were manned with catapults or other devices. If so equipped, that may have also hindered speed and maneuverability.

120. Ptolemy captured three of Demetrius's 'fours,' which were described as two-decked with forty-four double-manned oars per side. Diodorus 20.74.1-6; Morrison, *Greek and Roman Oared Warships*, 31.

121. In fact, Rhodes was the only force that sought to control the increasing number of pirates in the Eastern Mediterranean.

ceptive to talks of war against Ptolemy. Confident in his progress, Demetrius soon went too far and demanded that Rhodes hand over 100 hostages and grant his fleet access to its harbors. Rhodes closed its gates and prepared for war. When he laid siege to the island, Demetrius employed roughly 1,000 pirates from the eastern Mediterranean. Interestingly, Egypt was prepared to aid its largest customer, despite Rhode's willingness to war with Egypt. The Egyptian fleet and treasury had suffered a considerable blow after the loss at Salamis, but they managed to tip the scales in Rhodes's favor. The economic ties between the two locations must have remained in good standing, given that Ptolemy also ignored the fact that Rhodes's influence aided in Demetrius's victory at Cyprus. However, it is also possible that Ptolemy recognized that every day Demetrius was tied up in Rhodes was another day he could not apply his massive resources against Egypt.[122]

The island survived because Ptolemy's fleet constantly broke the blockade, forcing its way into the harbor with badly needed supplies. Ptolemy delivered 3,000 *artabai* of grain and legumes, which allowed Rhodes to hold its own until Demetrius finally gave up. For his role in the war, Ptolemy earned the name Soter or "Savior." Arguably, Alexandria had already endeared itself to Rhodes, since Egypt provided the majority of Rhodian revenue.[123]

Ptolemaic Garrisons

Disputes with Antigonus ended with his death in 302 BC. The following year Egypt won Syria and Phoenicia back and kept them until the reign of Ptolemy V Epiphanes. Numismatic studies suggest that northern boundaries of Ptolemaic control ended at the Eleutheros River.[124] Garrisons remained in the main cities of Phoenicia and Syria, comprised of the same ranks and ethnic makeup as Ptolemaic forces everywhere.[125] A surviving grave stele indicates that the military con-

---

122. Berthold, *Rhodes in the Hellenistic Age,* 77.

123. Diodorus 22.81.4.

124. H.Seyrig, *Syria* 28, 1951 p.206-220 cited in Bagnal, *The Administration of Ptolemaic Possessions Outside Egypt,* 13.

125. Herbert Liebesny, *Ein Erlass des Konigs Ptolemaios II Philadelphos uber die Deklaration von nein und Sklaven in Syrien und Phonikien* (PER inv. Nr. 24.552 gr.); Bagnal, *The Administration of Ptolemaic Possessions Outside Egypt,* 16.

sisted of men from Asia Minor, Cydia, Carra, Greece, and Crete. These garrisons were of particular value after Demetrius inherited considerable sea power. Ptolemy II Philadelphus wisely expanded his defenses, especially after Demetrius invaded Attica—only to lose much of his fleet to storms. Ptolemy was able to send 150 ships to Aegina but was forced to retreat when Demetrius was able to assemble 300 warships from the Peloponnese and Cyprus.[126] Fearful of his naval superiority, Lysimachus, Seleucus, and Ptolemy formed an alliance to keep Demetrius in check. In 287 BC, the Egyptian fleet sailed to Greece and forced Demetrius out. Two years later he surrendered. Then Philocles, Prince of Sidon, who had commanded the Phoenician contingent of Demetrius's fleet at Miletus, defected to Egypt, bringing with him Tyre and Sidon.[127]

With all these developments, Ptolemy reestablished his presence in the Aegean. Evidence found in Ios indicates an important connection between Ptolemy I Soter and the League of Islanders. The League was established in 315 BC by Antigonus Monophthalmus and included most of the islands in the Aegean. Egypt's maritime supremacy was based on an alliance with the League, and archaeological remains now account for early relations between the two regions. The description of Ios, circa 286 BC, is generally taken as the first evidence to illustrate Ptolemaic control over the League because the Ptolemaic appointee bears the name of *nesiarch,* royal agent.[128] Soter had also established a third major naval base in the Aegean, which remained under Ptolemaic control until the end of the century.

Under Soter, Egypt had become an independent Macedonian kingdom engaged in a hard struggle for independence and a leading role in world affairs.[129] Soter had a firm understanding of Egypt's strengths and weaknesses and built his empire accordingly. Having successfully taken over the grain trade and treasury from Cleomenes, he used the distinctly Greek city of Alexandria to attract foreign merchants and in-

---

126. Morrison, *Greek and Roman Oared Warships,* 35. Plutarch, *Demetrius,* 43.2 states that Demetrius's fleet had increased up to 500.

127. Ibid. 33

128. *Mitteilungen des deutchen archaologischen Instituts, Athenische Ab teilung 59,* [1934], 57 no. 16. Cited in Bagnal, *The Administration of Ptolemaic Possession Outside Egypt,* 137.

129. Rostovzeff, *The Social and Economic History of the Hellenistic World,* (London: Clarendon Press, 1941), 262.

vestors. Once complete, Soter set out to acquire areas key to maintaining Ptolemaic control. In both economic and political respects, he laid the foundation for Ptolemy II Philadelphus to become one of the more powerful of Hellenistic monarchs.

THREE

Mistress of the Sea

FIGURE 7: Mosaic representing the personification of the city of Alexandria as a woman dressed in military garb and wearing a hat shaped like a ship's prow. Signed by artist Sophilos 3rd-Century BC. Courtesy of the Graeco-Roman Museum.

Ptolemy II Philadelphus (283-246 BC) inherited an empire that extended over Libya, Rhodes, Palestine, Cyrenaica, much of the Aegean, and the Levant. Because his predecessors had encouraged foreign residents to immigrate, Alexandria was a mixed community whose

41

connections extended throughout the empire, securing trade and establishing new markets. As trade increased, so did Ptolemaic control. His intricate administration regulated the local economy of imports and exports. Taxes were attached to every aspect of Egyptian maritime commerce, and the proceeds allowed Ptolemy II to build a strong navy. He also exploited the rising number of immigrants, which included a wealthy Greek community and a vast supply of manpower to build his fleet. Alexandria became a leader in shipbuilding and established a strong presence in the Aegean and Mediterranean.

International Community

Greek immigrants—from the mainland, Macedonia, Thrace, the Aegean Islands, and Greek cities in Asia Minor—brought a great deal of the capital and the industriousness needed to develop a strong maritime economy. In return, Alexandria promised new opportunities.[130] Immigrant merchants could access a virtual treasure trove of Egyptian and foreign goods to sell in their homelands. Likewise, skilled labor could find employment in developing shipyards and warehouses.

As a relatively new Greek city, Alexandria lacked a long-standing, traditional system in which a few families dominated the social elite. As the city developed, the social and political leaders were often determined by territorial boundaries instead of familial ties. This new aristocracy played a unique role in Alexandria's maritime economy as the leaders and their extravagance created a consumer society.[131] New wealth led to increased demands for luxury items throughout the Hellenistic world. In turn, rising demand for foreign goods established important trade links between the Greeks in Alexandria and their homelands.

---

130. The *Mimes* of Herondas state that Egypt has everything that exists or is made anywhere in the world.

131. Examples of Greek extravagance are well recorded in Ptolemy Philadelphus's Grand Procession, which required an enormous circle of gold couches for the spectators placed in an arena filled with gold statues and implements. E.E. Rice, *The Grand Procession of Ptolemy Philadelphus* (London: Oxford University Press, 1983); Fraser, *Ptolemaic Alexandria*, note Ch.5, 38; see also L. Pearson, *Lost Histories*, 193.

FIGURE 8: Coin image of Ptolemy II Philadelphus and wife Arsinoe II. Courtesy of the Graeco-Roman Museum, Alexandria, Egypt.

Above the aristocracy was an almost divine presence. Indeed, the Ptolemies asserted Alexander's claim to be the son of a god in order to justify their own divine status. This was particularly apparent with Ptolemy's wife, Arsinoe II, who was often portrayed as the Egyptian goddess Isis. Her image was frequently tied to Alexandria's proclamation to be the queen of the sea. As a result, Arsinoe/Isis became the patron saint to whom sailors prayed when in peril on the sea.

The Greeks also provided much-needed mercenaries to replace the old Egyptian warrior class and control a growing Egyptian population that had now exceeded eight million.[132] Ptolemy was able to support his military by offering land grants. The soldiers were required to work the land in times of peace, for which the state received its share. Furthermore, the land was forfeited back to the state if there was no male heir to inherit it, allowing the Ptolemies to perpetuate a military class.

Alexandrian Jews also made important contributions to the Egyptian economy. Jewish immigrants first appeared after the Battle of Gaza (312 BC). Ptolemy Soter's victory is undoubtedly linked to their arrival either through economic opportunity or as prisoners of war.[133] They

---

132. Diodorus 1.31.6-8 states that Egypt had a population of seven million with a free population of 300,000 in Alexandria. Fraser points out that Diodorus also claimed that Alexandria was the largest city in the world. Rome had a population of 900,000; therefore Alexandria should have exceeded this number. Further studies by Fraser now suggest the higher figure. Fraser, *Ptolemaic Alexandria*, note Ch 3.358.

133. Ptolemy had led expeditions under Alexander and relayed first-hand knowledge of the Indus valley in his memoirs and later ensured that his possessions included Palestine and Phoenicia. Lufti A. W. Yehya, *India and Egypt: Influences and Interactions*, (Marg Publications and the Indian Council for Cultural Relations, 1993), 53.

retained their own quarter of the city, had their own magistrate, and enjoyed many liberties that were not available to other minorities within Alexandria. Their success may be connected to their position in Palestine, which was under Ptolemaic rule from 309 to 219 BC. Palestine created unique opportunities for the Jewish community because the Ptolemies relied heavily on the Palestinian population to maintain their interests and protect their frontiers. The Zenon Papyrus accounts for Jewish men rising to substantial heights within the military.[134] This feat would have been unheard of in Alexandria because the Greek ruling class strongly distrusted non-Greek foreigners. Palestinian Jews may have been required to keep Syrians at bay while maintaining key trade posts. As a result, Hellenized Jews enjoyed a considerable amount of freedom as they amassed their own possessions and consequently created their own elite community within Palestine.

Alexandrian Jews soon distinguished themselves from their neighbors to the east. In fact, the Jewish community in Alexandria outnumbered the Jewish population in Jerusalem, and more Jews spoke Greek than Hebrew.[135] They also adopted Greek customs, which aided them in normal business transactions. Cultural blending, however, remained somewhat limited and anti-Semitism was rampant by the end of Ptolemaic rule.[136] Their position in Egypt appeared to be directly related to the state of Ptolemaic affairs in Palestine, where Jews played a critical role in maintaining the final leg of the ancient caravan route. Palestinian Jews had traded with eastern merchants for centuries and undoubtedly had a thorough understanding of the luxury trade. Early

---

134. Zenon was an estate manager in the Fayum for Apollonios, Ptolemy Philadelphus's finance minister. Zenon's extensive trading activities brought him into direct contact with many foreign officials.

135. Ellis, *Ptolemy of Egypt,* 44. Fraser, *Ptolemaic Alexandria,* 284, notes 5, 777. Fraser refers to the Nash papyrus, which dates to the Hellenistic period. See E.B. Lachemann, *Jew. Quart. Rev.* 40 91949/50), p.15-39. After the Pentateuch was translated into Greek under Ptolemy Philadelphus, "...Greek became an urgent necessity for synagogal purposes." Fraser argues that it was the only place where Hebrew was likely to be preserved, and religious centers were practicing Hebrew less frequently.

136. Greek acceptance was limited. More specifically, there were cultural limitations and little intermarriage. If such cultural blending were frequent, it might have deterred the anti-Semitic movement later on. Intermarriage was a means of upward social mobility for Egyptians, but even these situations were limited. Fraser, *Ptolemaic Alexandria,* 58.

Ptolemies utilized these merchants for both business purposes and as military protection.

Ptolemaic Bureaucracy

The Ptolemaic administration allowed the state terrific control over its territories through extensive supervision and taxation. Alexandria brought in great sums by managing its natural resources and by placing strict regulations on all the members of its empire. At the same time, customs duties brought in considerable profit and protected state-run monopolies from challenge in the marketplace. The tax system developed under early Ptolemaic rule was strict and comprehensive, but it was greatly expanded under Ptolemy II Philadelphus in what are referred to as the Revenue Laws of Ptolemy II.[137] More than 200 different taxes were imposed by 258 BC, with import fees as high as 50 percent on such items as vegetable oils.

The tariffs, which allowed strict control over foreign trade, were extended into domestic transport. International taxes were placed on goods transported from Upper Egypt to Lower Egypt and then along the Nile in numerous locations. Guard posts, or *phylake,* enforced tariff regulations and were noted as early as the second century BC by Agatharchides of Cnidus.[138] The actual tax amounts have survived through the Papyrus of Zenon, as it accounts for the records of Apollonius. These documents include a declaration of goods as well as a bill of charges while in Alexandria. Apollonius carried goods from the Aegean and Asia Minor, and the papyrus reflected the tax paid on each item.[139] These goods included Chian wine and cheese as well as Rhodian honey and Pontic nuts. Wine and oil were the two most heavily taxed items, and a merchant was usually taxed more than once. For example, a tax could be imposed once a ship reached Egypt and then again when it transported goods out of Alexandria. The second tax was known as the "Custom-Gate Toll." Oil was probably taxed more than any other item because of attempts to protect the government monopoly. Olive

---

137. Bernard P. Grenfell, *The Tentunis Papyri* (London: Oxford University Press, 1902), XL III 11-12.

138. Fraser, *Ptolemaic Alexandria,* 148.

139. Ibid, 150.

oil, however, was a clear exception. Egypt could not really produce its own, and the Greek population demanded a great deal of the product. Otherwise, the tax system continued to generate a considerable fortune for the Ptolemies and became a source of contention among its individual members. Citizens living under the Ptolemaic empire paid higher taxes than anyone else in the ancient world.

Customs tolls generated income in two ways: first through direct taxation, and second when the Ptolemies developed and required the use of their own coinage system. Arriving merchants were forced to trade in their own currency for Ptolemaic coins at a nominal charge. The foreign money was then melted down and recycled into Egyptian currency. Alexandria's system for regulating funds and collecting taxes was more sophisticated than any other in the Hellenistic world. This was partially because of the size of the Ptolemaic kingdom and the far-reaching trade contacts that developed under its administration. A broad-based economy required a more rigid system of finances. Oral agreements lost their place when international investors came together and businesses began insisting on written contracts. In response to these trends, the Ptolemies developed a centralized banking system with a head office in Alexandria. Local branches acted as receiving agents, collecting taxes from Egyptian workers and making the necessary payments to maintain a local community.

Ptolemy II required detailed reports from his entire empire in order to utilize his resources in the most efficient manner.[140] He maintained accurate records of flood patterns, crop reports, and manufacturing production, which allowed him to manipulate even the private acts of Egyptian citizens. Since the Ptolemies had established their divine right to all of Egypt, the land and its people became property of the king or queen. The state then determined how the land was to be used and how much was to be harvested. Every attempt was made to improve agriculture because the Ptolemies profited most by exploiting the land. In fact, Ptolemy Soter and Philadelphus made more contributions to improving Egypt's natural resources than any other ancient ruler. They reclaimed

---

140. Serge, "Note Sull'economica dell'Egito ellenistico nell-eta Tolemaica," *Bulletin de al Societe Archaeologique d'Alexandrine.* (1934), 15ff, cited in Rostovtzeff, *Social and Economic History of the Hellenistic World,* 276.

desert land and called upon Greek engineers to introduce more scientific methods of irrigation.[141] The Ptolemies also supervised the sowing and harvesting of every crop. Their control was so strict that workers in Alexandria's spice factories were stripped and searched before they could leave their jobs. Farmers, who received a small payment for the crops they sold to the state, were not even allowed to change their places of residence.[142] In such fashion, Ptolemy Soter and Philadelphus developed the most extensive and complex bureaucracy the world had ever

141. Michael Grant, *From Alexander to Cleopatra: The Hellenistic World* (New York: Scribner, 1982), 43.

142. Rostovtzeff, *The Social and Economic History of the Hellenistic World*, 279.

FIGURE 9: Map of the Nile during the Ptolemaic period. Copyright: Bob Brier.

known.[143] Proceeds from customs duties and various taxes allowed Alexandria to maintain two harbors, a system of waterways, warehouses, and dockyards. Ptolemy II achieved great efficiency in manufacture, production, and distribution, which directly contributed to his brimming treasury.

Distribution followed uniform patterns. Once an item was manufactured, it came down the Nile to Lake Mareotis until it could be taxed and transferred to the Mediterranean port. Then, near the center of the Great Harbor, was the Emporium. This area served as a customs checkpoint at which items were inspected, taxed, and probably even traded. Strabo mentioned warehouses, called *Apostasies*, located nearby. Immediately next to the Emporium was the Cesareum. On the other side of the Cesareum were naval dockyards, which ended at the Heptastadion. This area also marked the entrance to the "Kibotos," a small artificial harbor and dockyard connected to the western harbor. Beyond Kibotos was a navigable canal, extending to Lake Mareotis.

The Ptolemies also controlled local industries. Linen was traditionally manufactured in temples.[144] As a diplomatic gesture, the state allowed priests to continue production. However, the linen could never leave the temple, because that would directly compete with the state. The priests were also required to offer certain quantities as gifts to the state every year. The remainder of Egyptian linen was produced in large weaving houses controlled by the government. The Ptolemies also had monopolies in textiles, papyrus, salt mines, and banking. Papyrus making was one of the larger enterprises, since it was used in sails, mats, ropes, baskets, and clothes, in addition to paper. The Ptolemaic administration was also engaged in the manufacture of dyes, leather, perfume, cosmetics, glass, pottery, and beer. Oils grew into one of the more profitable monopolies under the Ptolemies. Sesame and flax produced the greatest quantities as the king determined how much of each herb was to be grown in a given year. Farmers sold the oil to the state at a fixed rate. The price of the oil was marked up and put into Alexandrian markets (and, of course, it was taxed at the point of sale).

---

143. Grenfell, *The Tentunis Papyri*, 11-12.

144. K.F.W. Schmidt, *Philologische Wochenschrift.* (1934), 1313 cited in Rostovtzeff, *Social and Economical History of the Hellenistic World*, 307.

While Egypt was literally a gold mine of natural resources and industries, Alexandria made contributions of its own. Specifically, archaeologists have located bone-carving workshops three blocks from the shore behind the Cesareum.[145] What appears to have first served local interests eventually developed into an international trade. Elizbieta Rodziewicz claims that it was well known that an ivory industry and vast trade flourished in Graeco-Roman Alexandria, possibly as a royal monopoly.[146] Tracking the degree to which this industry prospered is difficult. Ivory simply has not held up as well in Alexandria's soil as other substances like bone and therefore little archaeological evidence of ivory exists. One final problem is that surviving artifacts in Alexandria were acquired not by archaeologists but by art dealers who have no record of their provenance. It is also difficult to establish centers of manufacture because of the mobility of the production and portability of the products.[147] Archaeologists have, however, now uncovered evidence of overseas export of bone carvings from Alexandria.

It is not surprising that bone carving developed in Alexandria, given the city's reputation for metalworking. Ptolemaic and Roman records indicate that Alexandria produced bronze along with other metals, and the Graeco-Roman Museum currently possesses molds for the mass production of bronze.[148] Provenance of these items is still lacking. The molds indicate that the bronze goods were commonly used for household or daily use and not art. Consequently, many bronze items were overused or recycled and simply did not survive into the present day. However, the existence of the bronze molds demonstrates that metalworking was an important industry and probably extended into other metals as well. Egypt and her subsidiaries possessed a vast supply of precious metals and other stones. Cyprus and Syria supplied Egypt with copper and

---

145. Elizbieta Rodziewicz, "Archaeological Evidence of Bone and Ivory Carvings in Alexandria." *Commerce et Artisanant dans l'Alexandrie hellénistique et romaine,* 136.

146. Ibid.

147. Ibid,135. Workshop products included women's hairpins, cosmetic pots, spoons, mirrors, handles, fans, etc. However, ivory production was not confined to women's personal effects but was used in making furniture as well.

148. Papyrus Zenon Cairo 59021 states that bronze workers were greatly concerned with the manufacture and repair of tools for agriculture and navigation. Fabiene Burkhalter, "The Production of Metal Objects in Hellenistic and Roman Egypt as Found in Papyrological Sources," *Commerce et Artisanant dans l'Alexandrie hellénistique et romaine,* 96.

silver. Egypt also produced silver and a variety of building stones, primarily granite. To the south were the gold mines of Nubia.[149] Callixeinus's account of the Procession of Ptolemy Philadelphus attests not only to great resources in precious metals, but also to a high degree of artistic skill based on a long tradition of metalworking.[150]

In addition to evidence of metalworking, Egypt's northwest coast is scattered with the remains of Greek wineries, similar to ones found in Delos.[151] Archaeologists were able to identify eight specific types of wine operations with several similar features.[152] Further investigations have determined that Egyptian wine was more popular than first imagined. Surviving records state that the most distinguished Egyptian wineries were Mareotic, Sebentic, and Taeniotic. These three were also available during the late dynastic and Graeco-Roman periods.[153]

Philadelphus's Fleet

Egyptian industries remained under tight supervision from the manufacture of products until their arrival in distant markets. The Ptolemies protected Alexandria's influence around the world by building a powerful navy to maintain its trade and colonies. Maintaining a fleet was no small expense because supergalleys of the Hellenistic Age required ever-greater resources. Still the expense was entirely productive because it allowed the Ptolemaic fleet to clear the Red Sea of pirates and encourage trade to new destinations. Economic lines of transport also became tools in political struggles, primarily between Alexander's

---

149. Rostovtzeff, *The Social and Economical History of the Hellenistic World,* 298.

150. FgrH 627 cited in Fraser, *Ptolemaic Alexandria,* 130.

151. Ahmed Abd El Fattah and Mieczyslaw Rodziewicz, "Recent Discoveries in the Royal Quarter of Alexandria," *Bulletin of the Society Archaeology D'Alexandrie,* (Alexandria: Society Archaeology D'Alexandrie, [1991]), 29.

152. Each had a platform where grapes were crushed by feet. Then the juice would overflow into a basin found just beneath the surface where it was separated. Mechanical presses were available at this time, as indicated in paintings in Pompeii and other iconographical sources. All the wineries were built of stone, irregular or dressed clay, dry bricks, mortar, and red plaster. The main structural material depended on the location of the winery.

153. The Mareotic wine came from the spring of Marea in Alexandria and was described as "...white and sweet, a good bouquet, digestible and light, did not effect the head and is diuretic." Taeniotic wine came from Tanea and is considered comparable. It was "pale yellow and something of an oily quality, which was soon dispelled by mixing with water, as in the case of Attic honey when it is diluted." It was also sweet, somewhat spicy and slightly astringent. Athenaeus, I 33de.

successors. The struggle for the control of trade not only led to advancements in ship construction, banking, coin systems, and the development of new trade routes, but they also created a balance of power that stabilized the Eastern Mediterranean throughout the Hellenistic Age. Ptolemaic political success was directly related to the intricate tax system that exploited Egypt's natural resources, financed naval expeditions, and maintained its outside territories.

Alexandria was an ideal base for developing the large-scale navy required to protect the empire. Ptolemy Philadelphus was able to build an impressive sea force for two reasons. First, because he had inherited his father's resources and ships, which included the Phoenician contingent of Demetrius's fleet and, second, because Alexandria attracted shipbuilders, foreign shippers, sailors, merchants, and money lenders.[154] Outside Egypt, Tyre and Sidon remained peaceful and allowed Ptolemy II a constant timber supply from these regions. As a result, Egypt built and acquired more than 4,000 ships throughout the empire.[155] Two thousand of the vessels were barges, pole boats, and smaller craft, 800 cabin vessels with gilt sterns and rams, and 1,500 ships measuring up to 'fives.' By the end of Philadelphus's rule, the fleet had two 'thirties,' one 'twenty,' four 'thirteens,' two 'twelves,' fourteen 'elevens,' thirty 'nines,' thirty-six 'sevens,' five 'sixes,' seventeen 'fives,' and 222 'fours' and 'threes.'[156]

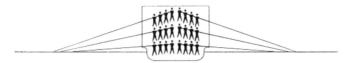

FIGURE 10: Possible arrangement of a 'twelve.' Copyright: Lionel Casson.

---

154. Diana Delia, "All Army Boots and Uniforms in Ptolemaic Egypt," *Alexandria and Alexandrianism,* (Malibu: J. Paul Getty Museum, 1995), 44.

155. Athenaeus 5.203.

156. Robert Gardiner, *The Age of the Galley: Mediterranean Oared Vessels Since Pre-Classical Times* (Annapolis: Naval Institute Press, 1995), 67. The absence of an 'eight' is not an indication that no such ship existed. A historian of Heraclea accounts for an 'eight' in the fragments of Memnon. He remarked that the ship, the Leontophoros, was named for the 100 men rowing each file so that there were 800 men from each side. Twelve hundred fought from the deck and there were two helmsmen. Judging from the length of required rowing space for 100 men, the length has been estimated at 100 meters. A probable distribution of the files was to triple-man the zigian and thalamian oars and double-man the thranite oars and a corresponding length accommodated the broad beam. FgrH III 13 p. 344 cited in Morrison, *Greek and Roman Oared Warships,* 36.

The increased size and expansion of Ptolemy II's fleet was directly related to development by the competition. Antigonus incorporated three 'nines' into his navy by 315-314 BC, later prompting Ptolemy II to add thirty 'nines' to his fleet. No surviving historical texts or iconographic evidence depict a 'nine' or a 'ten.' The lack of evidence suggests that the incredibly large ships of the Hellenistic Age were rarely used in naval engagements. This is understandable, considering that large galleys were inefficient, owing to a shortage of oarsmen. Moreover, problems with complex rowing positions eventually showed up in design flaws. For instance, vessels created to ride low in the water were susceptible to ramming from smaller vessels. Regardless, the supergalley continued to undergo changes and served as an important symbol of strength throughout the Hellenistic Age.

Not only did the large ships represent advancements in engineering, but they also demonstrated an empire's access to important resources. Demetrius's conquest of Cyprus enabled him to acquire the island's timber supply. Without specific types of trees, it would have been impossible to build anything bigger than a 'ten.' Plutarch mentions a great fleet of 500 ships, which included 'fourteens' and 'fifteens.'[157] Antigonus Gonatas most likely inherited his 'thirteens,' 'fifteens,' and 'sixteens' from him. The larger supergalleys appeared more practical because they carried greater force and required less building material than needed for two smaller ships. However, the larger ships were less manageable; ultimately these floating fortresses served as little more than showpieces.

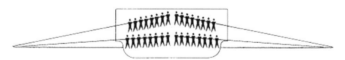

FIGURE 11: Possible arrangement of a 'sixteen.' Copyright: Lionel Casson.

Maritime historian Lionel Casson suggests that none of the ships were ever more than three banks high and, in agreement with Morrison, maintains that they evolved by adding rowers. This way a 'three' could easily be converted into a 'six.' However, operations became more complicated when a third man was added to the oar, making it too long for

157. Plutarch, *Demetius*, 20.4.

the rowers to manipulate from a seated position. Therefore Demetrius's 'seven' would have required men to stand up and sit down in a manner that was like climbing stairs.[158] Casson suggests that Demetrius used as many as eight rowers per oar in a double-banked ship in 288 BC. This method made some matters easier since only the last oarsman had to be trained. The others were considered "muscle." In addition, more rowers led to a broader beam and therefore greater deck space. This allowed for more marines, which was a considerable advantage when grappling and boarding.[159] The next galley designed after the 'sixteen' was the 'eight,' briefly described as the *Leontophoros* by Heraclea on the Black Sea. This particular ship appears to have prompted the design of an even larger ship by Antigonus Gonatas, followed by the Ptolemy's 'twenty,' two 'thirties,' and a 'forty.'

The arms race that was spurred by Ptolemy and Demetrius produced a number of impressive vessels, although nothing above a 'ten' appears to have participated in any naval engagement. W. W. Tarn argues that the standard warship of the time was the quinquireme, and large ships fell out of use in the second century BC because they were expensive and required too many men. The new masters of the Aegean, Rhodes and then Rome did not use anything larger than a quinquireme.[160] By 288 BC, Demetrius had invented the 'fifteen' and the 'sixteen.'[161] When he fell, Ptolemy acquired the 'fifteen,' but there is no record of Egypt ever owning a 'sixteen.' The largest galleys of the Hellenistic period were no longer in use by the mid-third century BC, while 'sevens' and 'tens' were used until the battle of Actium. However, once Rome officially controlled the Mediterranean, there were no challengers and therefore no need for larger ships.[162]

---

158. Casson, *Ships and Seafaring in Ancient Times*, 84.

159. Ibid. This does not indicate that ramming was uncommon. This tactic remained very popular with 'fours' and 'fives.'

160. W.W. Tarn, *Hellensitic Naval and Maritime Developments* (New York: Cambridge University Press, 1910),122.

161. Callixenes ap. Athen. V 203 d (133).

162. Casson, *Ships and Seafaring in Ancient Times*, 94.

Harbor Development

In addition to a tremendous fleet, Ptolemy II completed a number of projects, which collectively earned Alexandria the name "Mistress of the Sea." His most remarkable achievement was the erection of the great Pharos lighthouse between 285 and 280 BC. This structure was more than 330 feet tall, projecting rays up to seventy miles out to sea. The light was projected through a large wrought-glass mirror that reflected a constantly burning fire. Archimedes is credited with the creation of the light-reflecting system, which required fuel to be regularly hoisted to a parapet. The Pharos lighthouse was the largest structure of its kind in the ancient world; the greatest in an evolutionary line of similar buildings.

FIGURE 12: The Marble Watch Tower or Lighthouse Erected by Ptolemy Soter on the Island of Pharos, near the Port of Alexandria. Copyright: O'Shea Gallery, London, UK/Bridgeman Art Library.

The role of the lighthouse cannot be understated as a symbolic beacon and as much-needed protection at sea. The common belief that sailors never left sight of the shoreline and only traveled by the summer sun is not accurate.[163] Too often, sailors met circumstances well beyond their control, such as mists, winds, and delays, any one of which might cause disembarkation at an undesirable time. In addition, good weather is no protection against an unfamiliar coast with reefs and walls lying just below the surface. Any foreign sailor would naturally require assistance entering a harbor. Lighthouses also proved beneficial during daylight hours when sailors were out of sight of land, since daytime fires made ideal smoke signals.

Ptolemy II also completed the Heptastadion, effectively dividing the waters into eastern and western ports. This causeway was seven stades in length (1,200 meters) with two openings on each end that permitted direct communication.[164] The openings also served as a desilting tool by allowing the western current to pass through the harbor in a continuous fashion.[165] The Hepstadion also carried an aqueduct to supply the island with water, probably using terracotta pipes buried underground.[166] Cape Lochias served as a natural protection from the winds and current, while Pharos Island helped shield the harbor from the sea. Combined with the Heptastadion, Alexandria's port became a well-protected and bustling harbor. The western harbor was also significantly shallower than its eastern counterpart but afforded better protection when the wind changed directions.[167]

The development of the harbor continued over time, and today we have a fairly good idea of what it looked like. Investigators and engineers have put together an interesting picture of the Eastern Harbor using underwater GPS and sophisticated mapping systems. While an exact image cannot be created, many of the major ancient harbor's structures have remained intact. One engineer was able to speculate on the

---

163. Frost, Honor. *Under the Mediterranean; Marine Antiquities.* (London: Routledge, 1963), 64.

164. Most likely, the openings were connected by land bridges.

165. Khalil, Maritime Activity in Alexandria Harbor from the Bronze Age to the Roman Period, 22.

166. Ibid.

167. In 1870 the western harbor was artificially deepened to accommodate ocean liners.

arrangement of ships within the harbor based on standard requirements for establishing a port. For instance, the plan of the harbor depends on the conditions of the navigation (winds, swell), ship type (oared, sailed), size of the ships, the choppiness of the sea arising from swell, and the eventual necessity of building a defensive breakwater against storms.[168] Taking the number and size of merchant ships and warships believed to use the harbor allows an investigator to determine the length of quays and surface area of required basins.[169] In Alexandria, the wind moves from west to north in the summer and sometimes north to east in the winter. This, along with swells from the sea, would explain the need to develop a double harbor.

Alexandria's harbors unquestionably accommodated large vessels. The Ptolemies had a substantial navy with incredibly large supergalleys, and trade activity suggests large merchant ships frequented the port. Because the standing navy would require a more permanent anchorage, an examination of possible moorage was based on the size of the Ptolemaic fleet. Ptolemy II had dozens of vessels in his fleet, ranging from fifty by ten meters, to seventy by twenty meters in size. He also had eighty medium-size ships, forty-five meters by eight and 175 small ships. These varied between twenty meters by two-and-one-half to thirty-five meters by five. At the end of the Ptolemaic rule, Antony employed a fleet of 220 ships with the biggest being a 'ten.' The fleet that was burned by Caesar in the Battle of Alexandria consisted of fifty triremes and quinquiremes, twenty-two other vessels along with thirty-eight ships in arsenals.[170] Judging from the size of these fleets, de Graauw suggests that the first harbor housed the ten large supergalleys of Ptolemy II. The second harbor could have held eighty of the medium-size ships and twenty-five small ones. The third harbor would have been able to house the remaining 150 small ships.

Under Ptolemy II, while Alexandria was developing into a thriving maritime city, the empire continued to add ports of call. These far-flung garrisons not only provided logistical support for Egypt's navy

---

168. Antione de Graauw. "An Engineer's Viewpoint on the Eastern Harbor," *Alexandria: Submerged Royal Quarter* (London: Periplus 1998), 53.

169. Ibid, 58.

170. Ibid, 55.

but also bridged the empire's military and economic interests. Garrison commanders protected the financial pursuits of governed territories and even managed funds. This was a major problem with Ptolemy's administration because monies were easily diverted to finance military endeavors.[171] Though distant, these naval garrisons mirrored the homeport of Alexandria and were manned by the same international mix of Greeks found in communities throughout Asia Minor, Greece, and the Aegean.[172] The crown still enforced royal ordinances and taxed the local population. In this manner, resources and even slaves could be efficiently used to benefit the crown.[173] Ptolemy also received substantial lump payments from cities in lieu of taxation.[174] In addition, such areas as Cyrene, Cyprus, and Syria were taxed directly through the use of royal currency minted and circulated within their own territories.

Garrisons

Key garrisons were already established under Ptolemy Soter in Asia Minor and maintained under Ptolemy II. Zenon in particular retained contacts in the area and recorded the on goings in the peninsula of Halikarnassos. Pieces of this correspondence concerned royal naval funds, including an advance of 5,465 drachmas to Antipatrus, a ship commander in the Ptolemaic navy.[175] Ptolemy II also maintained courteous relations with Kos, which may be related to the claim that he was born there in 309-308 BC. Such personal and political ties suggest that Ptolemy controlled the island, but the truth is still unknown. Ptolemy also relied on Aspendos as a source of mercenaries and may have relied on Pamphylia for the same reason. Pamphylia left no indication of any garrison but was controlled by a regional governor.[176] Itanos became a long-standing site of a garrison established under Ptolemy II. Patroklus, an admiral

---

171. Bagnal, *Ptolemaic Possessions Outside Egypt,* 221

172. Ibid, 17, A diverse population is indicated by a painted stelle recovered in Sidon listing a mixed party of soldiers from Asia Minor, Lydia, Caria, Greece, and Crete. (Pros. Ptol.).

173. Zenon was concerned with the slave trade, mostly importation in Egypt (P. Cairo Zenon 59804).

174. Papyrus Cairo Zenon. 90-91, Bagnal, *Ptolemaic Possessions Outside Egypt,* 227.

175. Papyrus Cairo Zenon 59036.

176. Bagnal, *Ptolemaic Possessions Outside Egypt,* 114.

during the Chremonidean war, stopped in Itanos in 266 BC en route to Attica, and it is generally accepted that he planted a garrison there.[177] In Asia Minor, Ptolemy II briefly held Ephesus, demonstrating the importance of the site. It was confirmed as a military base comparable with Samos.[178] The Ptolemies also held Lebelos, Kolophon, Magnesia, Priene, Miletos, and possibly Teos.

Two particularly key bases were in the Cyclades, the island group containing Delos. One base was established in Samos although there is no record of any action taking place. In addition, records of Philip V taking the island in 201 BC state that the ships were not fitted out for action.[179] The second Cycladic garrison was located in Thera and protected important sea-lanes, including routes to Crete. The Ptolemies even retained Thera long after they lost influence over the rest of the Cyclades. After 250 BC, Allarian from Crete raided Thera, and the Ptolemaic garrison defeated the pirates who attacked Oia at the northeastern edge of the island. Ptolemy II held undisputed control over Cyclades from 285-260 BC, then he turned his attention to Asia and the Levant.[180] After the battle of Ephesus, generally dated to 258 BC, the Rhodian forces quickly appeared in Delos. Then Rhodes and Egypt restored peace in 255 BC and Ptolemy returned to the Cyclades. By the start of the third Syrian War (246-241 BC), the Ptolemies were holding the islands. Ptolemy finally withdrew from the Aegean in 246 BC when Gonatas defeated him at the battle of Andros. The collapse of Egyptian interest in Greece accompanied the collapse of their interest in the Aegean.[181] This happened twice. The first instance occurred in 260 BC after their defeat in the Chremonidean War, and the second departure occurred after Andros.[182]

---

177. Spyridakis, *Ptolemaic Itanos and Hellenistic Crete,* (Berkley, 1970), cited in Bagnal, *Ptolemaic Possessions Outside Egypt,* 117. This idea also fit well with the later presence of a garrison in the same location.

178. Polybios 5.35.11

179. Polybios 5.35.11, 16.2.9

180. Gary Reger, *Regionalism and the Change in the Economy of Independent Delos, 314-167 BC.* (Berkley: University of California Press, 1994),18.

181. Berthold, *Rhodes in the Hellenistic Age,* 24. Chremonides, for whom the war is named, was an Athenian statesman who sought refuge in Egypt after Athens surrendered. He later became an Egyptian admiral and was defeated off Ephesus by Agathostratus of Rhodes.

182. Ibid, 24.

Thera had garrison commanders as early as 265 BC. Apollodotus was the first to hold this position, but the subsequent commanders are not known. The next record comes during the rule of Philometor, who attests to Apollonios as a garrison commander in 163 and again in 159 BC.[183] The single Ptolemaic base on mainland Greece was Arsinoe/Methana, chosen for its strategic location near Attica and probably was established during the Chremonidean War because of its excellent port facilities.[184] A peninsula projecting out from the Peloponnessos, Methana was probably renamed Arsinoe under Patroklus. Used to regulate affairs elsewhere, the base appears to have remained until the third century AD.[185]

Battle of Ephesus

Egypt's withdrawal from the Aegean midway through the third century coincides with an important naval engagement between Rhodes and Egypt under Ptolemy II. Rhodes and Egypt had developed a strong economic relationship, and the two remained neutral on the political level. However, Egypt was growing more powerful among Alexander's successors, with Rhodes actively trying to balance that power. As vital players who depended on and catered to so many parts of the Mediterranean, Rhodian officials recognized the threat posed by the dominance of any single power. If Egypt were allowed to pull ahead of the competition, the island's autonomy would be severely threatened.[186] Therefore, Rhodes opted to preserve its interest across the board instead of risking Ptolemaic control.

Two sources depict the Rhodian victory. The first was recorded in the Lindus Temple Chronicle and served as a dedication to the surprising fact that Rhodes was at war with its most important business associate. Polyainus 5.18 also records an account of the war between the two states in 256 BC near Ephesus.[187] Chremonidas of Egypt and Agathostratus of

---

183. *Inscriptiones Graecae* 3 320, OGIS 44 and IG XII 3.327, cited in Bagnal, *Ptolemaic Possessions Outside Egypt,* 124.

184. Bagnal, *Ptolemaic Possessions Outside Egypt, 135.*

185. Ibid, 145.

186. Gabrielson, *The Naval Aristocracy of Hellenistic Rhodes,* 91.

187. Polyainus 5.18.

Rhodes led the two opposing fleets. Agathostratus led the Rhodians out in a single-file line, abruptly changing formation when the Egyptian fleet appeared. After positioning itself line abreast, the Rhodian fleet then altered its position one final time. Chremonidas interpreted the changes as a sign that Rhodes was not prepared to fight. The Egyptian fleet pulled out of formation and headed back into the harbor. At this moment Agathostratus faced off with the enemy. As the Rhodian fleet closed in, commanders thickened their line on both flanks and moved against the Egyptians as they were disembarking. The result was not entirely devastating to Ptolemy, who still maintained a strong military presence at Ephesus,[188] but the loss would have far-reaching implications in other respects. In particular, the Rhodian victory allowed the Seleucid king Antiochus II to take Ephesus. He then unsuccessfully attempted to take Syria from Ptolemy Philadelphus.

Economic changes were also underway. New efforts to expand and control Red Sea trade had already began. Ptolemy II ordered the Egyptian navy to clear Nabataean piracy in the east and began systematic explorations of the African coasts. Ports emerged along Egypt's shores, and Philadelphus attempted to reestablish a canal from the Sea to the Nile. With a diminishing presence in the Aegean and former dependents now growing their own grain, Alexandria expanded on a luxury market few others had access to. The outside possessions of Cyprus and the Levant, which supplied timber and crews, would eventually fall out of Ptolemaic hands. This loss is mirrored in Egyptian economic and political failure. Attempts to regain outside possessions would gradually subside, as would the need to build larger galleys. Egypt had reached her climax of power under Ptolemy Philadelphus and was now about to begin her decline.

---

188. Ibid, 5.35.11.

FOUR

Trade With the East

FIGURE 13: Coin image of Ptolemy III Euergetes. Courtesy of the Graeco-Roman Museum, Alexandria, Egypt.

Ptolemy III Euergetes I (246-221 BC) inherited from Philadelphus a powerful empire with numerous territories, trade contacts, and vast financial resources. Ptolemy III was also the benefactor to a large fleet and the technical understanding for advancements in ship construction. Unfortunately, many events that took place under Philadelphus's reign had negative repercussions for his successors. As a result, future Ptolemies had to accept the burden of an overworked and overtaxed community brimming on revolution. Extravagance and oppression had gone too far. Internal struggles triggered weaknesses abroad, and Egypt continued to be pushed out of the Aegean. The pressures of political disputes and market competition coincided with new developments in Red Sea trade. The Ptolemaic decline marked important transitions in world trade, as Egypt prepared to open its doors to the east and shift its influence out of the Aegean.

Philadelphus initiated Red Sea trade by reopening the ancient canal from the Nile and directing coastal explorations. He is also responsible for suppressing Nabataean piracy, making agreements with the Arabs of Yemen and establishing trading stations along the east coast of Africa.[189] He encouraged scholars to research uncharted coasts and waters. His admiral, Timosthenes of Rhodes, wrote a treatise, now lost, on harbors.[190] Euergetes also placed a special interest in exploration and received great support from the geographer Eratosthenes, who maintained that the world was round and estimated the circumference of the earth. In Alexandria, Eratosthenes served as a family tutor and a library director. He also wrote *On the Measurement of the Earth* and *Geographica,* which made vital contributions to the craft of map making.[191] Information amassed under the Ptolemies opened doorways to resources as far away as the Atlantic, southern Sudan, and India. Egypt continued to trade a large variety of luxury items. By the reign of Ptolemy III, merchants from all around the Mediterranean called upon Alexandria to acquire exotic goods.

But Alexandria had competition. Although the Ptolemies successfully exploited Lebanon's iron and copper mines, as well as its forests of fir, cypress, cedar, and juniper, the Levant eventually began competing with Egypt in two areas. Papyrus, in particular, became a tough market, with Palestine becoming the second largest producer. Meanwhile, Sidon and Tyre possessed beaches whose sand was especially adapted to fusing;[192] as a result, these two cities produced the finest glassware in the world, which now competed with Egypt's long-standing glass producers. The Ptolemies established favorable relations with Byzantium by offering considerable gifts and land grants. Surviving records mention frequent contact between the two cities. Trade with the Black Sea was probably established for Pontic nuts, Byzantine peas, and dried fish.

---

189. O.A.W., *Greek and Roman Maps,* 137.

190. Agathemerus Cn. 8. Ii.7. from Geographi Graeci Minores cited in O.A.W., *Greek and Roman Maps,* 31.

191. R.M. Bentham, *The Fragments of Erastosthenes* (PhD thesis: University of London, 1948), Ibid, 32.

192. Philip K. Hilti, *Lebanon in History: From the Earliest Times to the Present,* (London: MacMillan and Co., 1957), 176.

Alexandria established a trade connection with Carthage in the western Mediterranean. Archaeologists have recovered Ptolemaic silver in Cyrene dating from the third century, but the findings become less frequent in later years. Trade was probably upset by the Second Punic War (218-202 BC) and ceased by the third (149-146 BC). Also supporting the possibility that the Egyptians traded with Cyrene is the fact that Cyrenaica was the only exporter of Silphion, a crucial ingredient to a well-known Greek drug. Cyrene, on the other hand, appeared to have been self-sufficient and required few imports.[193]

Papyrus texts also document one-way trade relations between Sicily and Alexandria. The records state that Egypt received wine, amphora, and prized Sicilian pigs, but there is no sign of Egyptian exports to Sicily.[194] Apula pottery shards from the Adriatic have turned up in Alexandrian gravesites dating to the early part of Ptolemaic rule. Mention of this type of pottery fails to appear in Egyptian papyrus, and it can be argued that the Apula pottery was restricted to Alexandria. A Roman ambassador reportedly visited Alexandria in 269 BC, and thereafter Romano-Campanian coinage developed two new lines of mintage.[195] The first line directly borrowed from the Ptolemaic style, while the second line displayed Greek lettering.

In other areas, Alexandria was not so progressive, and despite cultural blending, many Egyptians were brutally mistreated. State-controlled monopolies tightly regulated the local population, while strict tax codes prevented any Egyptian from breaking free of a domineering system. The intricate tax system literally held many people in a state of serfdom. They were never allowed to leave and paid an exceptionally high rent. The state taxed animals and even garden produce, all while religious orders lost economic privileges to the new Greek rulers. Resentment brewed within the native population.

---

193. Close political ties remained between the two countries and a fair number of Egyptian refugees did settle there.

194. Picard, *Bulletin de Correspondance Hellénique* 35 (1911), p.177-230 cited in Fraser, *Ptolemaic Alexandria,* 154.

195. Pliny NH 33.44, R, Thomsen, *Early Roman Coinage,* (Aarhus: Aarhus University Press, 1971), 19ff.

Ptolemy IV Philopator

Meanwhile, after a number of successes, the Ptolemaic Empire began to lose its hold on outside territories. Euergetes I initiated a campaign to assert Egyptian sea power and did so by capturing Seleucia Pieria, which was an important port for Antioch. This capture was an affront to the Seleucid kingdom of Syria and demonstrated that the Levant was still vital in regard to men and shipbuilding material.[196] Euergetes's efforts continued into the reign of Ptolemy IV Philopator (221-204 BC), but was not to last. Euergetes's successor entered Hellenistic politics at roughly the same time as Philip V of Macedonia and Antiochus III. The two other leaders demonstrated great interest in Ptolemaic possessions, especially after Philopator's government became corrupt and he took little interest in running it.

Despite Ptolemy IV's obvious shortcomings, he was successful in some ventures. He managed to collect tribute from Lycia, Caria, Thrace, Lesbos, and Ephesus.[197] His general, Theodotus, was also effective in keeping Antiochus III of Syria from encroaching on Ptolemaic possessions in Ceole-Syria. Theodotus's success appears to have threatened the king's control, leading Ptolemy IV's officials to make preparations to get rid of him before he became too influential.[198] In response, Theodotus defected to Syria, helping Antiochus III to reclaim Seleucia in 219 BC, along with Tyre, Ptolemais, and forty Egyptian vessels.[199] Ptolemy IV gathered up his fleet, amassing thirty cataphracts[200] and 400 transports. Ptolemy faced a serious dilemma, since his mercenary force had lain idle with no training for several years. Therefore, Ptolemy Philopator was forced to call upon native Egyptians and to recruit Libyians, Cyrenacians, Gauls, and Thracians. The new mercenaries performed well, and Ptolemy IV reclaimed Ceole-Syria and Phoenicia.

Philopator had effectively rebuilt an army with Egyptian mercenaries. Now, disgruntled natives possessed the military know-how to stage

---

196. Morrison, *Greek and Roman Oared Warships*, 57.

197. Polybius 42.2 adds that he still protected Creole-Syria.

198. Bevan, *History of Egypt Under the Ptolemaic Dynasty*, 222.

199. Ibid. Twenty of these ships were well equipped with a rating of at least a 'four' and the other twenty were open 'threes.' Polybius 5.62.3

200. Cataphracts mean that the men are deck are protected by mesh netting as opposed to open-air aphatacts.

powerful uprisings.[201] His complacency toward his administrative duties chipped away at his empire from the inside out. Unlike his forefathers, Philopator made little effort to invest in Alexandria's economy, spending his fortune on entertainment instead. His navy suffered likewise, for he had more of an eye for the grandiose than the practical. Ptolemy's incredible treasure ship attests to his preference for the luxury. The floating palace maintained lavishly decorated saloons, bedchambers, and colonnades.

Ptolemy IV is also responsible for the creation of the 'forty.' The ship was clearly not built for functional purposes and was never used for anything more than a showpiece. Ptolemy II had already demonstrated Egypt's ability to produce the "grandest" ship when he created the 'thirty.' Athenaeus provides an account of the 'forty,' noting that it was double prowed and double-ended. The 420-foot 'forty' required 4,000 oarsmen to operate it, along with 400 crewmen, and could carry 2,850 marines. The 'forty' was approximately fifty-seven feet in beam. The height from the waterline to the tip of the prow was seventy-two feet and the distance from the waterline to the tip of the stern was seventy-nine and one-half feet. The draft when empty was under six feet, and the four steering oars were forty-five feet in length.[202]

The description states that the thranite oars were fifty-seven feet in length. The reference to the thranite probably indicates the existence of zygites and thalamites.[203] The double-prow suggests that the vessel was actually double-hulled and, therefore, may have resembled a modern-day catamaran.[204] This would divide up 4,000 rowers into four sides instead of two. By allowing at least thirty feet between the two sides, the designers would have created enough room for oarsmen on the inside to row freely. While it is still unclear exactly what configuration the rowers took, Casson has suggested that with twenty men to distribute over three oars it would be most practical to place eight on the thranite

201. The Rosetta Stone attests to conflict not only because it dates to a period of unrest but because the Greek royalty is clearly attempting to connect with the Egyptian community. Greek, Demotic, and hieroglyphic texts reassert the Ptolemies' divine status through Alexander's coronation in the ancient city of Memphis.

202. Casson, *Ships and Seafaring in the Ancient World,* 111.

203. Ibid, 189.

204. Ibid.

oar (which would work best with a fifty-seven-foot sweep), seven zygites, and five thalamites. Regardless of how the rowers were placed, by "…assuming a double-hulled vessel with rowers on both sides of the hull, we arrive at a system of oarage that is well within the bounds of credibility and squares in every respect with the evidence."[205] The 'twenty' and two 'thirties' were very likely of similar design. The 'twenty' probably had two banks with five rowers and the 'thirty' would only need fifteen men spread over three levels.

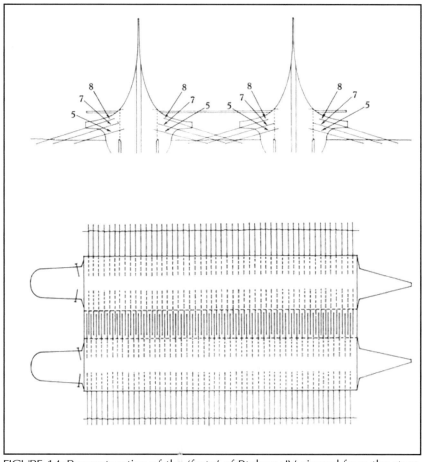

FIGURE 14: Reconstruction of the 'forty' of Ptolemy IV viewed from the stern. Copyright: Lionel Casson.

FIGURE 15: Reconstruction of the 'forty' viewed from above. Copyright: Lionel Casson.

205. Ibid, 190.

Philopator's prize ship may have impressed many, but it contributed little to the Ptolemaic navy and to solving problems abroad. In 205 BC, another war broke out, causing him to lose many Syrian possessions. Antiochus III and Philip of Macedon plotted to take over the Egyptian Empire and divide its holdings between themselves. By 201 BC Philip V took Samos and the Ptolemaic naval base stationed there. This garrison was the only known base in the Ionian area at this time and held dedications to Ptolemy III and IV, thanking Egypt for protecting the city.[206] Furthermore, after Philometor's death, Egypt appears to have abandoned Samos, but Ptolemy V Epiphanes (210-180 BC) interfered freely with international affairs on the island through his admiral, Philocles.[207] Philip then claimed the remaining Ptolemaic possessions in Thrace by 200 BC. Egypt would also lose Ionia under Ptolemy V. Yet ties were obviously established in new directions as Epiphanes married the Seleucid princess Cleopatra I. Their son became the next heir to the Egyptian throne.

The empire, however, continued to decline and the Sixth Syrian War (171-168 BC) dramatically reduced Egypt's holdings. During an invasion, Ptolemy VI Philometor (180-145 BC) was captured, and Alexandrian citizens handed over the throne to his brother Ptolemy VIII Euergetes II (145-116 BC) in his absence. Antiochus withdrew and the two brothers attempted to rule jointly. The arrangement was short-lived and resulted in a dispute that effectively divided the empire. Egypt had lost Cyrenaica and by the end of the war, her outside possessions had been reduced to Cyprus and Cyrene.

Rome and Delos

The second century BC not only marked a period of decline for Ptolemaic trade but also Italy's encroachment on Egypt's Mediterranean influence. After Rome defeated Hannibal in the Second Punic War (202 BC), it adopted an expansionistic policy,[208] first setting its sights on Rhodes. Rhodes was still an independent economic power with ter-

---

206. M. Guarducci, *Inscriptiones Creticae* (Rome: 1935) 4.4 and 4.18.

207. Bagnal, *Ptolemaic Possessions Outside Egypt,* 82.

208. El-Abbadi, "The Greatest Emporium in the Inhabited World," 18.

rific influence throughout the Hellenistic World. The aftermath of a devastating earthquake that toppled the Colossus of Rhodes and severely damaged the great harbor attests to the island's high reputation in the later part of the second century.[209] Nearly every major power responded with help. Ptolemy III donated large amounts of timber and other shipbuilding materials, 450 paid builders and masons, 1,000 talents of coined bronze, 300 talents of silver, 3,000 talents of bronze for the Colossus, and over one million artabai of grain.[210] It is likely that Alexandria's generosity was based on self-interest. Ptolemy III and the rest of the Greek world recognized that Rhodes's disaster could disrupt trade and banking.

Rhodes's influence also extended into political arenas as its leaders attempted to intervene in western affairs. Their interference was not well-received, and Rome launched economic blockades by inducing other countries to switch their routes and agencies from Rhodes to the nearby island of Delos.[211] Alexandria also switched, and Delos began to play a more influential role in Alexandrian affairs. As suggested by the Zenon Papyrus, maritime agencies that formed in Delos were similar to those in Alexandria. These groups, known as *koinas*, primarily identified themselves through their geographical affiliation. Then they were subdivided into divisions of labor such as ship owners or captains, freight contractors, warehouse owners, and others.[212] This is an interesting note in Alexandria's history, as maritime-related workers seem to be the only group organized well enough to demand higher wages while every other category of workers was subjected to constant abuse under Ptolemaic rule.

Delos became a central power in the Aegean trade and by the end of the third century BC, it was considered an important meeting place for merchants. Delos specialized in transit trade while surviving warehouses indicate a considerable storage capacity.[213] Alexandria's merchant fleet and navy made frequent use of its ports as surviving statues and tributes testify. Alexandria also relied on Aegean suppliers for pitch, metals, and

---

209. Diodorus Siculus, *Library of History I, 50,* 6-7; Strabo, *Geography,* 14.2.5; Polybius 5.88, 1090.2
210. Polybius 5.88. 1-90.2
211. El-Abbadi, "The Greatest Emporium in the Inhabited World," 18.
212. Fraser, *Ptolemaic Alexandria,* 184.
213. Ibid,171.

ship timbers, as well as for shipwrights and navigators. In turn, Egypt actively sold grain in Delos's markets.[214]

Delian independence extended into other arenas as well. Despite Egypt's rule over the Cyclades, of which Delos was a part, the Ptolemies did not attempt to pull Delos into their financial administration.[215] Delos also maintained its own administrative responsibilities and was expected to make tributes. Still, Egypt did not profit from the island as it did from other possessions. Trade between the two regions was limited to small shipments of high-value goods, like Rhencian and Kythnian cheeses, Kimolian fuller's earth, or a few amphorae of Parian wine.[216]

The Cyclades therefore housed an important Egyptian garrison maintaining Aegean trade. Delos, in many respects, was a commercial success because of its location and the important role it played in the Mediterranean's maritime economy. Egypt found the island's central location attractive as a stepping-stone to Greece,[217] and Delos was un-doubtedly affected by the Ptolemaic presence in the Cyclades. In this respect, Alexandria's relationship may have developed around the fact that Delos did not maintain a navy. The Ptolemies, on the other hand, had a very powerful fleet, which was garrisoned at the nearby Thera. It is also likely that Alexandria depended on Delos's ports for other reasons. French excavations uncovered a large ship house in Delos decorated with bullheads. The building contained a dock, which once housed dedicated ships much larger than a trireme.[218] Not only does the architecture point to Ptolemy Soter, but Egypt was also the only power at that time able to maintain a fleet with this size supergalley.[219]

Delos served as a neutral meeting place between the East and West.[220] It grew more influential toward the end of the Hellenistic Era as Rome

---

214. While many other areas of the Aegean and Asia Minor were dependent on Egypt's crop, Delos was not. In fact, it produced a fair amount of its own.

215. Reger, *Regionalism and Change in the Economy of Independent Delos*, 314-167 BC, *268;* Papyrus Cairo. Zenon 1.59110, r. 25-6 (cf.v. 35-6) 59548, 59547.

216. Ibid, 268.

217. Ibid, 269.

218. W.W. Tarn, "Greek Warship," *Journal of Hellenistic Studies* (XXV, 1905) , 139; BCH XLV 1921, 270.

219. Ibid, 142.

220. Fraser, *Ptolemaic Alexandria,* 170.

began to emerge as a world power. Italy became a great consumer of grain and luxury items and many of these items passed through Delos. Syrian, Anatolian, and perhaps Bosporan merchants also exported similar commodities here in huge quantities.[221] Delos fixed the prices, distributed goods, financed enterprises and, in a word, acted as the clearinghouse. It was quite natural for a special relationship to develop between Delos and Alexandria, which used the island as a transit point for its goods to Italy.[222] Alexandria, however, also enjoyed direct relations with Rome.

Rome contributed more money to Alexandrian markets as trade expanded into the Red Sea. Ties strengthened between Alexandria and Rome, and many Roman merchants settled in Egypt as early as 200 BC. Italy demanded a great deal of glass, papyrus, linen, and wheat, the latter of which became the most important commodity. As India opened her markets to the west, Alexandria acted as a go between. Merchants from Pompeii also sought out Indian goods by way of Alexandria and may have supplied the Ptolemies with Spanish silver. Thus, Egypt bridged the gap between eastern luxury items and western markets. Inscriptions have survived demonstrating the relationship between Delos, Rome, and Alexandria. One inscription, located in Delos, is a dedication made by Italians at Alexandria. Another dedication made by Roman ship owners expressed their gratitude to King Ptolemy Euergetes II in 127 BC.[223] In addition, inscriptions have been located in Egypt near the island of Philae dating to 116 BC.

Rome became a factor in Alexandria's markets by the mid-second century. The ensuing rise in demand for oriental goods prompted Egyptians to bypass Arabian ports and venture across the Indian Ocean directly to Indian markets.[224]

---

221. Rostovtzeff, *The Social and Economic History of the Hellenistic World*, 923.

222. Ibid.

223. Dittenberger, *O.G.I.S.* 132, Op. Cited in El-Abbadi, "The Greatest Emporium in the Inhabited World," 19.

224. El-Abbadi, "The Greatest Emporium in the Inhabited World," 20.

Indian Ocean

Strabo explained that Greeks began sailing to India after Eudoxus of Cyzicus discovered the route around 116 BC.[225] Before Eudoxus, Egypt and the Mediterranean world relied mainly on land routes over which Indian merchants delivered luxury items from the east. The Greek discovery of the route has been associated with a stranded Indian seaman. Rescued and brought to Egypt, he learned Greek and was able to explain the seasons of the monsoons and how merchantmen used the weather to their advantage. The story is that the Indian then led Eudoxus on a journey, from which he returned with a shipload of goods. Ptolemy Euergetes II promptly relieved Eudoxus of his prize. Eudoxus returned to India under Cleopatra, who relieved him of his exotic goods once more.

There is a different version, however. The anonymous *Periplus Maris Erythraei* states that Hippalus discovered the monsoons, without mentioning the exact date. Hippalus was probably a fictitious character, and Strabo makes no mention of him. Greek sailors had been sailing the monsoons nearly 100 years before Roman rule. Despite this discrepancy, the author of the *Periplus* felt the need to create a handbook for merchants and sailors demonstrating the frequency of travel under early Roman rule. The instructions explain that the best routes branched off Egypt's coast even though a large percentage of trade was directed in and out of Alexandria. From Alexandria, goods traveled through the lake harbors and up the Nile to Coptos before shipment overland by camel to Myos Hormos or Berenice.

Ideally, merchants left Egypt in September, although travel was recommended anytime between September and January. Winds that aided the sailors blew from the northwest between October and April. During this season, the weather was balmy and calm, unlike conditions between May and September. These months brought heavy winds from the southwest along with constant rain and storms. The *Periplus Maris Erythraei* recommended two main routes. One followed the coast of Africa to Rhapta or all the way across to India.[226] A second route to

---

225. Strabo, *Geography,* 2.98 57:19.5-7.

226. Lionel Casson, *The Periplus Maris Erythraei,* (Princeton University Press, 1989), 15.

India and Arabia followed the Red Sea to Muza and then along the coast as far as Kane. Afterwards, merchants could head north to Barbarikon and Barygaza or south to the ports on India's Malabar Coast.[227] In addition, the *Periplus Maris Erythraei* mentions that one could also set course from Cape Guardafui to reach the Malabar Coast.

Lionel Casson suggests that ships that left Egypt in July and sailed to the Gulf of Aden were aided by northerly winds and transversed the Gulf by taking advantage of the southwest monsoon. July departures also permitted sea captains to take advantage of northerly winds, which prevailed in the summer.[228] Afterwards the southwest monsoons would carry merchants across the Arabian Sea or Indian Ocean. A return departure after November would then take advantage of northwest winds that blow right up to the entrance of the Red Sea. According to the author, crossing these winds was hard going but absolutely favorable and shorter.[229] The troublesome southwest winds were also reflected in insurance rates. Marine insurance was typically between 1 percent and 1.75 percent from October to April rising to 20 percent by the end of May and nonexistent during the summer months.[230]

The *Periplus* also lists luxury items to be found along the Red Sea and Indian coasts. Since many desired commodities in this area were luxury goods and rather compact, it made sense to stop off in several ports to fill one's bottom. Ethiopia excelled in producing adulis, ivory, tortoise shell, aromatics, and rhinoceros horn. Northern Somalia produced frankincense, myrrh, aromatics, slaves, drugs, ivory, and tortoise shell.[231] The East Coast of Africa also produced ivory, tortoise shell, rhinoceros horn, and the nautilus shell. Arabia yielded aloe, frankincense, and myrrh. India "delivered the widest spread of goods," including spices, drugs, aromatics, gems, textiles, ivory, pearls, and tortoise shells. In addition, Alexandria received cinnamon, cattle, dogs, and women from India. And Egypt also imported gold, elephants, and iron from Nubia.

227. Lionel Casson, "Graeco-Roman Trade in the Indian Ocean," *The Greeks and the Sea* (New Rochelle: Aristide D. Caratzas, 1993), 69.

228. Ibid. 70.

229. Ibid.

230. Ibid.

231. Casson, *PeriplusMaris Erythraei*, 37-63.

The flourishing trade with India is often credited to Ptolemy Phila-delphus (283-246 BC) and Euergetes I (246-221 BC). Philadelphus made numerous efforts to explore and expand trade through Alexandria. He sent Dionysius as ambassador to the court of the Indian King, Asoka. Under the king's instruction, Dionysius wrote a book on India.[232] Ptolemy II also strengthened the roads between Coptos and Berenice and restored the ancient canal linking the Heronpolite Gulf and the Red Sea with the Nile. During the early years of the Ptolemaic reign, Egypt constructed several harbors along the Red Sea Coast. Indian and Arabian merchants primarily used these sites. Otherwise, Egyptian mer-chants used traditional coastal routes known to Ptolemy Soter. However, these routes were considered lengthy and expensive and therefore rarely used. Despite the expense, systematic explorations of the Red Sea coast began with Ptolemy Philadelphus.[233]

Satyrus was the first to sail down the African side and founded Philotera before 276 BC. Ariston was later ordered to explore the coast as far as the ocean. Ptolemy II was trying to redirect the incense route to Egypt by establishing relations with northwest Arabia.[234] He also con-structed such important ports as Arsinoe, which is currently Suez; Myos Hormos, now Qoseir El-Qadim; Philotera or Marsa Gasus; and Berenice Troglodytica, now known as Medinet el-Harras. These ports were linked by land to Edfu and Koptos. Then he supplied land passes with water cisterns and armed guards. Ptolemy II also reopened the canal between the Nile and the Red Sea. It did not receive much use, however, as Berenice was often favored for her southern location, even though it required a longer land journey to the Nile. The overland route was still more desirable than facing a few additional miles of strong current and unpredictable winds.

Ptolemy Euergetes I was the first to use a direct sea route from Egypt to the East, which helped restore Alexandria's foreign trade. After Eudoxus's expeditions, Egypt became proactive in establishing safe mari-

232. Lufti, Yahya, *Indian and Egypt: Influences and Interactions,* 53. Bevan, *A History of Egypt Under the Ptolemaic Dynasty,* 155. Pliny NH 58. Specific citations to the treatise on India have survived in Pliny.

233. W.W. Tarn, "Ptolemy II and Arabia," *Journal of Egyptian Archaeology XV* (1929), 4.

234. Ibid, 16.

time routes between Arabia and Egypt. Alexandria also secured command over oriental merchandise. Then Euergetes I improved harbors, roads connecting to the Nile, and even the Red Sea routes. He also developed new officer positions directly related to the Red Sea travel. There are surviving records accounting for travel conditions under his rule. Agatharchides of Cnidus then compiled travel logs using literary sources and official documents of explorers and merchants.[235] The information was kept in Alexandria and was intended to spark further interest among other merchants rather than serving as a guide through the Red Sea.[236]

Trade with the east via the Red Sea was clearly just beginning under the Ptolemies. The trade routes would be further exploited under Roman rule. Strabo attests to 120 ships per year traveling to India one decade after Cleopatra's death, an impressive increase from the approximately twenty vessels per year under the Ptolemies.[237] However, no one knows the source of Strabo's information and he may have been citing sources from time periods in which trade was infrequent. Bias or a desire to flatter Rome may have altered Strabo's depiction.[238] Likewise, he may not have accounted for outside influences. For instance, travel after the discovery of the monsoon patterns would still be slow to develop. Travel at the end of Ptolemaic rule may have been slower owing to political problems. However, other periods may have been rather prosperous. In the same regard, Egypt held too much control over the Indian market to have made so few sea voyages, even in the early stages of direct trade. Otherwise, Alexandria's monopoly on Indian goods could not have had such profound implications on the rest of the Mediterranean.

Trade with the east became critical to Egypt as Rome gained greater influence in the Aegean. By redirecting the focus of commerce, Egypt ensured its financial independence for a time. However, Rome consumed a considerable amount of Alexandria's luxury items. As Roman interest in these luxury items developed, so did its interest in control-

---

235. Rostovtzeff, *The Social and Economic History of the Hellenistic World*, 925.

236. Ibid, 925.

237. Strabo 17.1.13.

238. El-Abbadi, "The Greatest Emporium in the Inhabited World," 20.

ling the Indian trade and its involvement in Egyptian affairs. Much like the Ptolemies's efforts to bypass Arab middlemen when trading with the east, Italian merchants sought to bypass Alexandrians. Agatharchides noted that Rome, greedy for gain, would eventually take over the riches in Arabia.[239] Egypt's weakened administration led to Ptolemaic decline in the Aegean. It is likely that Alexandrians realized that Rome would eventually assume control of the eastern trade as well.

By the end of Ptolemy XII Auletes's (80-51 BC) reign, a new office known as the Commander of the Red and Indian Seas is noted. The new title indicates increased activity with regard to sea trade and therefore naval involvement. Not only had Rome extended its reach into the Indian Ocean through Alexandria, but it also clearly took a special interest in Egypt's political struggles. Ptolemy XII Auletes attempted to remain in Rome's good favor by bribing Caesar with 6,000 talents in the year 59 BC. In return, Caesar passed a law acknowledging his kinship.[240] The political, and now personal, ties did not prevent Rome from moving into Ptolemaic territory. Rome claimed Cyprus, prompting the island's king, Ptolemy's brother, to take his own life. Alexandria reacted with disfavor and allowed Auletes's oldest daughter to lead an insurrection. After numerous bribes to various senators, Rome took a greater interest in Alexandrian affairs. Auletes returned to Egypt in 55 BC with the Roman army to assassinate his daughter and restore his throne. Rome's interest in Alexandria would not have rested entirely with Ptolemy XII. Italian merchants in Egypt and elsewhere had grown dependent upon a thriving Indian trade. Roman assets were clearly at risk, which explains why Roman representatives remained as "protectors" of the Egyptian throne.

---

239. Robin Lane Fox, "Hellenistic Culture and Literature," *The Oxford History of Greece and the Hellenistic World* (Oxford: Oxford University Press, 1991), 399.

240. Bevan, *History of Egypt Under the Ptolemaic Dynasty,* 111.

FIVE

Fall to Rome

FIGURE 16: Coin depicting Cleopatra. Courtesy of the Graeco-Roman Museum, Alexandria, Egypt.

The final days of Greek rule in Alexandria are well-recorded by ancient and modern historians.[241] The transition from Greek to Roman control took place over many years, leading to the collapse of an empire and the immortal stories of Cleopatra, Caesar, and Antony. Historical texts and great works of literature portray the Hellenistic queen and her two lovers with colorful narratives and romantic storylines. Unfortunately, we are pressed to draw heavily from textual evidence, which is very political in nature. Legend has altered history, not only because of the intense subjectivity of ancient authors but also because of modern

---

241. See Plutarch *Caesar* and *Antony* Arrian *Annabis;* Michael Chauveau, *Egypt in the Age of Cleopatra: A History and Society Under the Ptolemies.* Translation by David Lorton. (Ithica: Cornell University Press, 2000); Edith Flamarion, *Cleopatra: From History to Legend* (London: Thames and Hudson, 1999); Lucy Hughes-Hallett, *Cleopatra: Histories, Dreams and Distortions* (New York: Harper and Row, 1990); Robert S. Bianchi, *Cleopatra's Egypt: Age of the Ptolemies* (Brooklyn: Brooklyn Museum in association with Verlag Philip von Zabern, 1988); Michael Grant, *Cleopatra* (New York: Simon and Schuster, 1973); W.W. Tarn and M.P. Charlesworth, *OctavianAntony and Cleopatra* (Cambridge University Press, 1965)

glamorization of Cleopatra. Speculation appears to plague this era of Ptolemaic historical reconstruction more than any other time frame. Despite the romanticism that may have played a part in Egypt's history, certain facts remain.

Cleopatra assumed her throne at a time when Rome had already begun to take firm control of Alexandria. Many cities throughout the Aegean and Mediterranean had already fallen to Rome, and the Ptolemaic administration had lost a great deal of political and economic influence in world affairs. The arrangements made by Cleopatra's father and Caesar ensured a direct political connection between the two states, while the growing numbers of Roman merchants in Alexandria were beginning to play an integral part in the luxury trade. The level of maritime trade in the last two decades of Ptolemaic rule was surely limited, given that Egypt was in a state of famine and Rome was engaged in numerous conflicts. Cleopatra's frequent travels, decrees limiting grain exports, and political infighting all attest to restricted commercial activity.[242] Despite these obstacles, Egypt was still considered a land of vast natural resources and a highly prized addition for an empire. In light of this, Cleopatra is credited with a great accomplishment in that she managed to keep Rome at bay. We know of the final days of Ptolemaic rule today through the limited and biased perspectives of a new Roman administration. Nevertheless, this historical record provides important clues about the state of Egypt's navy and maritime economy under Cleopatra's command.

Cleopatra's sovereignty was precarious from the beginning when she assumed her command as co-regent with her younger brother Ptolemy XIV (51-47 BC). A provision of their arrangement stated that the two should eventually marry, but the young Ptolemy drove his sister into exile. She gathered forces in Syria but to no avail. Meanwhile, Rome was entrenched in its own civil war between Pompey and Julius Caesar. Alexandria was intimately involved in the conflict, since Ptolemy Auletes and Caesar had established formal ties with one another. In 49 BC, Pompey arrived in Alexandria and collected fifty ships and 500 merce-

---

242. A royal decree made in 27 October of year 50 BC with Ptolemy XIII's seal banned shipping of grain anywhere but Alexandria. Grant, *Cleopatra,* 48-53; Peter Green, *Alexander to Actium* (Berkley: University of California Press, 1990), 644.

naries to battle Caesar.[243] The war was effectively decided by the battle of Pharsalus. Pompey then fled to Egypt, hoping that old ties, which bound the royal family[244] to him, would secure him refuge. Caesar followed close behind, arriving in Pelusium three days after him with a force of two legions, 800 cavalry, and limited supplies.[245] His intentions were clear, but ill fated. Pompey was already dead—the young Ptolemy had ordered his assassination. When presented with Pompey's head, Caesar was rather disgusted. He had missed his opportunity to finish off his enemy, but he nevertheless remained in Egypt. He intended to honor Ptolemy Auletes by resolving the dispute between the siblings. He also intended to collect on the 6,000 talents owed to him by the late Egyptian king for re-instating his command in Alexandria.

Battle of Alexandria

Caesar performed poorly as an intermediary. He was quick to take Cleopatra's favor, and Alexandrians were easily excited at the prospect of Roman domination. By November, Caesar found himself surrounded by 20,000[246] of Ptolemy XIII's soldiers, and he had little time to prepare for battle. It was late in the year and Caesar needed to cut Alexandria off from the sea. He began by burning fifty galleys anchored in the harbor. The impact must have been significant because the vessels were 'fours' and 'fives,' fully equipped and manned in all respects for sea service. He also destroyed twenty-two cataphracts, which formed part of the normal Alexandrian garrison,[247] as well as craft within the royal shipyards. Egypt was not entirely helpless, but Caesar had eliminated any chance that Ptolemy XIII would force the Romans out to sea. Caesar then landed on Pharos and garrisoned the island, which gave him full control of the harbor and prevented ships from delivering supplies.

---

243. Bevan, *The House of Ptolemy: A History of Hellenistic Egypt under the Ptolemaic Dynasty,* (Chicago: Ares, 1985), 361.

244. Bevan, *The House of Ptolemy*, 362.

245. Caesar *Bellum Alexandrianism*, 3.111.3.

246. The Alexandrian army was comprised of numerous foreigners, including many Guals and Germans who had undergone Roman discipline. It also included a considerable number of refugees and slaves from Italy and the west and pirates and bandits from Asia Minor and Syria—relics of the great pirate power disbanded by Pompey. Bevan, *The House of Ptolemy*, 364.

247. Ibid.

Despite Caesar's efforts, Alexandria could still call on upon vast resources within Egypt, while the Roman's resources were greatly limited. Aulus Hirtius, Caesar's legate, states that Caesar called for ships of all kinds from Rhodes, Syria, and Kilikia, then he summoned archers from Crete and cavalry from the King of the Nabataeans.[248] Meanwhile, he expanded his defenses and prepared for the upcoming winter. The changing climate inevitably challenged any ships attempting to reach Alexandria. Rhodes retained the most navigable sea-lane to Egypt in winter and responded to Caesar's request with ten ships.[249] His new fleet also included eight Pontic, five Cilician, and twelve Asian ships. The fleet's arrival prompted immediate response and an engagement occurred soon after. Domitius Calvanus's ships, filled with weapons and corn, were unable to make anchor.[250] Caesar received word of the distressed vessels and immediately responded. His entire fleet, minus deckhands, sailed out to receive the supplies. Caesar was concerned that his navy would be at sea for a long period, leaving his fort exposed. Therefore, he rounded up all possible soldiers to defend his stronghold.

The Egyptians learned that the Roman fleet had set sail without deck soldiers and immediately sailed out to meet them. Caesar initially refused a naval engagement, finding justification in the coming nightfall. But a single Rhodian ship had pulled away from the Roman fleet and soon found itself under attack by four cataphracts and a number of open ships.[251] Caesar's forces pulled back into the battle and managed to capture one Egyptian 'four,' swamp another, and kill a great many deck soldiers. Caesar had secured his supplies, but he had also pushed Alexandrians into taking more serious action. The residents had now lost 110 ships to Caesar, which ignited great excitement throughout the city. In response, Alexandrians decided to build up a new fleet in order to prevent any further reinforcements from reaching the Roman garrison. Egyptian officials called in guard ships from all the Nile mouths and used their timber to replace old ships inside the hidden dockyards

---

248. Aulus Hirtius, *Bellum Alexandrinum,* 3.4. Accounts by Caesar and Hirtius were written to explain their actions to the senate. Hirtius completed the Alexandrian accounts after Caesar's death.

249. Only nine made it. One deserted en route.

250. HBA, 9.3.

251. HBA 10.6.

of the royal palace.[252] They removed the roof timbers of public buildings and converted rafters into oars. Within a couple of days, the
Egyptians had completed twenty-two 'fours' and five 'fives.' Hirtius adds
that Caesar then had nine Rhodian ships, eight Pontic, five Lycian, and
twelve from Asia Minor. Ten of these ships were 'fives' and 'fours.' The
rest of the fleet consisted of smaller aphracts and some cataphracts.

Ready for battle, Caesar pulled his ships single file out of the Eastern Harbor around Pharos and into the western harbor to meet the
Egyptians. The Roman fleet faced the enemy in two line-abreast formations. The front right wing consisted of the Rhodian ships and the front
left wing, the Pontic ships. They were followed by seventeen of Caesar's
smaller vessels. The Egyptians drew twenty-two of their 'fours' and 'fives'
into line and placed the remainder of their fleet behind them. Other
Egyptians rowed out in small craft with fire-bearing missiles,[253] as both
sides waited to see who would first cross into the shallow waters of the
western harbor. Finally, the Rhodians pulled ahead and bravely fought
the Alexandrians.[254] The remaining Roman fleet followed and managed
to capture one enemy 'five,' a 'two' and its crew, and then swamp a
'three.' The Egyptians retreated to Pharos seeking solace with others
who appeared to have reclaimed the island.

Caesar retaliated by attacking one part of the island to distract the
enemy's attention, while sending 6,000 men to another part for a separate, surprise attack.[255] The assault was slow moving at first, but the
Romans soon gained ground, causing the Alexandrians to flee from
Pharos into the main city. The Egyptians had not given up hope, however, and still attempted to prevent Caesar from securing supplies in the
future. This resulted in one final sea battle in which the Rhodian commander Euphranor pulled aggressively ahead. Egyptian vessels
surrounded him with no aid from the Roman fleet. He perished and
the Alexandrians claimed his 'four.' This engagement did not determine the outcome of the Alexandrian war, but reinforcements from
abroad did. Mirthridates of Pergamon led an overland army from Syria

---

252. Hirtius, *Alexandrian War,* 12.

253. HBA 14.5.

254. HBA 15.1.

255. HBA 17.

to take Pelusium, reaching[256] Alexandria soon after. The dual efforts of the Roman force decided a victory in Caesar's favor, and Cleopatra was proclaimed queen of Egypt.

The Roman victory is significant to ancient history, but it also sheds light on Alexandria's political and economic landscape. Politically, the Ptolemaic administration had fallen into an unprecedented lull, owing to years of abusive administrators, revolts, and warring heirs. Though he had arrived in Alexandria with a small force, Caesar was able to challenge a country with substantial resources. Egypt's population exceeded eight million, with many Egyptians located right along the Nile borders. The frequency of river travel would have made it feasible to move a large number of men to Alexandria with relative ease. Yet, the historical record is clear that the Egyptian majority played little part in this engagement. The Greek city had always considered itself separate from Egypt.[257] The young Ptolemy XIII sent officers and recruiting sergeants to levy troops from all the regions belonging to Egypt[258] and amassed a fighting force, which even included slaves. Why, then, was Ptolemy unable to overpower the smaller Roman squadron? The answer most likely lies in the fact that Macedonian royalty had been overworking the local population for several centuries, leading to irreparable feelings of resentment. The country had developed a reputation for having angry mobs, and the Ptolemies were cautious before they called upon Egyptian assistance. In addition, Ptolemaic rulers had in many ways neglected Egypt over the preceding decades, and it was very likely that Alexandria was too unorganized to amass its idle forces. The Battle of Alexandria underscores how much the city had declined. Such an invasion under Ptolemy II would have been unthinkable.

Alexandria's mercantile fortunes mirrored its political state. Hirtius mentioned that the Alexandrians were anxious to return to the sea and

---

256. Ptolemy attempted to intercept them before reaching his capital city but failed. In his own attempts to escape, Cleopatra's brother vanished. The generally accepted theory is that he was killed trying to cross the Nile later records indicate that the river was dredged in search of a body. His body was never located. Butler, Alfred J. *The Arab Conquest of Egypt and the Last Thirty Years of Roman Domination.* (Oxford: Clarendon Press, 1978), 293.

257. Hirtius also made comments on Alexandrians and Egyptians, distinguishing the two groups. HBA 17.

258. HBA 17.

commented on their proficiency in the water. Hirtius added that many were trained from childhood and were experts in small boats.[259] However, their presence in the Mediterranean Sea had clearly dwindled. Demand for Red Sea trade had shifted their attention elsewhere but this activity was still in early development. Alexandria now mostly acted as a receiving agent for goods and a distributor of luxury items brought up the Nile from Red Sea ports, removing itself more from sea trade and the protection of trade routes. Historically, Egypt relied heavily on grain exports as a key component of its financial success. By Cleopatra's reign, however, many of Alexandria's former customers were growing their own crops. Water shortages, famine, and debt also contributed to Egypt's failing economy. In spite of adversity, Cleopatra still had great financial resources. Indeed, there were many possible sources for her fortune, but it is very likely that her greatest profits came from increased trade with the east. Alexandrian trade with India was certainly favorable under the later Ptolemaic rule. Rome's increasing interest in eastern luxury items corresponded with Greek exploration and the establishment of Red Sea trade. Strabo stated that Rome far surpassed the Ptolemies in developing trade with India.[260] This is probably an overstatement intended to compliment the new Roman administration, not to mention the fact that the prefect of Egypt was Strabo's personal friend and host for five years.[261]

For Cleopatra, Egypt's weakened condition presented a window of opportunity. And through her, Alexandria regained a position of power in world affairs. This time, however, Egypt was under Rome's influence, a situation in which Cleopatra played an active part. With her country securely under her command, she left for Rome. She remained as Caesar's mistress and gave birth to their son, Caesarian, later known as Ptolemy XV. After Caesar's death in 44 BC, Cleopatra returned to Alexandria, where she is believed to have killed her brother/husband Ptolemy XIV. She made her son co-regent.

---

259. HBA 17.

260. Strabo 17.1.13.

261. Strabo stayed with Aelius Gallus from 25-2 BC. El-Abbadi, "The Greatest Emporium in the Inhabited World," 21.

Rome was experiencing its own turmoil. Dolabella, Caesar's former fleet commander and consul, had been actively pursuing Brutus and Cassius, who were seeking to claim Syria and Macedonia.[262] A naval engagement finally occurred between Dolabella and Cassius in which both sides suffered losses. To replenish ships, Cassius made requests to Cleopatra and her commander in Cyprus, Serapion. Tyre, Arados, and Serapion reportedly sent all their ships without Cleopatra's consent.[263] At the same time, Cleopatra sent four legions left by Caesar in Alexandria to Dolabella in show of her true support. Cassius defeated Dolabella in another sea battle, prompting Dolabella to take his own life. Cassius then got word that Cleopatra planned to supply a fleet of heavy ships to Octavian and Antony.[264] Angered, he planned an assault on Egypt but his attention was redirected when Cassius learned that Octavian and Antony were crossing the Adriatic in pursuit of him and Brutus. The pursuants defeated Brutus and Cassius. Antony then settled into Tarsus and summoned the Queen of Egypt.

Soon after their notorious love affair began, Antony left for Rome and married Octavian's sister, Octavia. Cleopatra remained in Egypt and gave birth to twins. Marc Antony returned to Alexandria, where he married Cleopatra, and they had their third child. At this time, Antony began petitioning Rome. He called for land grants to be awarded to Cleopatra and her children and for the acknowledgment of Caesarian as Caesar's child. As a result, the queen acquired Cyprus, Phoenicia, and Ceole-Syria along with parts of Judea, Arabia, and the Cilician coast.[265] The marriage triangle was the talk of Alexandria and Rome until 32 BC, when Antony officially divorced Octavia, prompting Octavian to declare war.

Battle of Actium

Antony recognized that a settlement of differences was unlikely, and he began war preparations in 33 BC. The successful Armenian campaign

---

262. Appian Civil War 4.57.

263. Ibid, 4.60.

264. Ibid, 4.63.

265. Plutarch, *Antony* 36; Strabo 14.5.3.

emboldened his men and fattened his purse.[266] Antony assembled 500 warships, including many 'eights' and 'tens' in addition to 100,000 infantry and 12,000 cavalry.[267] Cleopatra added 200 ships, 20,000 talents, and supplies for the fleet. Mismanagement, however, forced Antony's men to wait out the winter. Many deserted or fell prey to illness. One-third of his oarsmen died of starvation. By spring, many ships were only partially manned by poorly trained rowers and, as a result, the vessels maneuvered badly in the water.[268]

During this time, Octavian's commander, Agrippa, moved over to the southwest coast of the Peloponnese where he cut off Antony from his supplies by sea. Octavian led his army and 230 ships to Actium in the hope that Antony's men would abandon his camp for more favorable conditions. Octavian established his headquarters at a point where he could see over the open sea as far as the Praxos Islands and inside the Ambracian Gulf.[269] Minor conflicts ensued in which Octavian won two naval actions and performed equally well on land. Disease and starvation continued to plague Antony's men, and morale suffered greatly. Ultimately, a modern understanding of either side's intentions is difficult to determine. The historical record is inconsistent on the character of important figures, making behavior difficult to assess. Contemporary accounts portray a camp in continual decay, even though later writings idealized the bickering between Cleopatra and Antony. Desertion was highly likely, as was the loss of men and ships due to poor morale and a poor climate. All signs indicate that Antony had ample incentive to flee from battle.

Diodorus adds that Cleopatra had been pleading with Antony to engage in a naval attack while his advisers repeatedly suggested a land invasion. His decision to attack by sea caused him to lose one of his top consuls, Ahenobarbus. Antony decided to move a small army in from the north and made arrangements for a sea battle in the south. After the sea engagement, Antony's army would be ideally placed to intercept Octavian's fleeing forces. Ancient sources suggest that if the plan were a

266. Orosius 6.19.4, cited in Morrison, *Greek and Roman Oared Warships*, 157.

267. Plutarch, *Antony*, 56.1;61.1.

268. Diodorus 50.11.2, Orosius 6.19; Plutarch, *Antony*, 62.

269. Diodorus 50.12.3-4.

FIGURE 17: 17th-Century painting of the Battle of Actium by Castro Lorenzo.

Copyright: National Maritime Museum.

failure, Cleopatra would still have time to flee in her ship while Antony retired to the Gulf and destroyed any remaining vessels. Once Cleopatra was secure, he could continue ashore, with the idea that Octavian would follow him into battle. He also ordered that his men to carry large sails, which could permit the navy to move quickly to Italy once they had won the battle. This order is certainly peculiar, as it presupposes that Antony's men would fight, conquer, and then sail to Italy without rest. Once preparations had been made for battle, Cleopatra readied her ships with all of her personal effects. Antony burned smaller vessels in case they were captured by the Romans and used against him later.[270] Antony's men must have also suspected that he was planning to abandon them upon destroying his own vessels.[271] Consequently, Antony found it difficult to fill the ships with enough rowers and to withdraw his troops south. This position would ensure a second chance, should his fleet lose, because he could drive the battle ashore and continue fighting there. The remaining troops on the other side would simply have to surrender to Octavian if he gained control of the sea. Antony also placed the cavalry to the north, but fighting was at a standstill owing to heavy winds. Poor morale and repeated delays apparently made the cavalry nervous. Not only did this lead to further desertions, but higher ranking officials also reportedly took Antony's plans over to the enemy.

Diodorus remarked that Antony employed a great number of archers, slingers, and heavily armed troops, which he placed in his ship towers.[272] The advantage of height seemed to belong to his fleet whose towers rested on 'fives' to 'tens.' Florus stated that Octavian had at least 400 ships to the enemy's 200, but Antony compensated for number with size. His ships ranged from 'sixes' to 'nines' with great towers, having the appearance of floating cities.[273] Florus added that size itself was, in fact, their undoing. Orosius's report states that Octavian had 230 ships with rams and thirty without.[274] Morrison has suggested that

270. Plutarch, *Antony,* 64.1.

271. William M. Murray, "Reconstructing the Battle of Actium," *New Interpretations in Naval Warfare: Selected Papers from the Eleventh National History Symposium* (Annapolis: Naval Institute Press, 2001), 30.

272. Diodorus 50.23.1-2.

273. Florus 2.21.6.

274. Orosius 6.19.8-9.

Octavian's fleet consisted of 230 warships with rams, thirty transports, and 140 smaller warships including 'threes.'[275]

Diodorus insists that Octavian acknowledged the tremendous size of Antony's ships, some of which stood sixteen feet above the waterline, including towers.[276] But he recognized the value of the smaller, more maneuverable ships. Then he filled his warships with as many marines as possible. He also incorporated auxiliary vessels to sail in and out of the larger ships, providing encouragement and information.[277] Octavian had drawn his fleet into three squadrons and placed them one mile from the Gulf. Octavian's position out at sea would have allowed him to surround Antony's fleet of large ships with his smaller, more maneuverable ones. Antony began his formation in two lines and then condensed his fleet into three rows where the ships were more tightly packed together. Octavian had anticipated Antony would "seek the deep water" and attempt to break through the line. No such action occurred. Antony sounded the trumpets but came out no farther. Octavian hesitated, since "he did not know what to do."[278] Ultimately, he pulled forward and the Roman fleet attacked, taking full advantage of its size and being careful to stay clear of the enemy. With every swift approach, a Roman ship rammed or fired, and then quickly pulled away before Antony's archers could retaliate. Antony's fleet hurled stones, arrows, and grappling hooks at the enemy and in some cases even damaged their own ships. Ramming was a fairly ineffective tactic because the ships were too large to gain the proper momentum. Plutarch refers to the battle as more of a siege, with several of Octavian's ships moving in on one of Antony's large ships.[279] Finally, Antony's left wing pulled forward and Octavian's right wing backed away. The implication was that Agrippa wished for the left wing to move farther out to sea and thereby encircle Antony with his larger numbers.

Ancient texts contend that the battle was still undecided when Cleopatra and sixty of her ships suddenly took flight. Antony followed.

---

275. Morrison, *Greek and Roman Oared Warships,* 163.

276. Diodorus 50.24-30.

277. Morrison, *Greek and Roman Oared Warships,* 164.

278. Diodorus 50.31.4.

279. Plutarch, *Antony,* 66.1.

Octavian did not make chase, as his own ships were not equipped with sails. The remainder of Antony's fleet grew discouraged and reacted accordingly. Those who continued to resist Octavian finally submitted when he incorporated fire into his battle tactics. In total, 300 ships were captured. Then Octavian sent ships to chase after Antony, who had fled in a 'five,' and then boarded Cleopatra's flagship. Eurycles, of Octavian's fleet, managed to ram one of Cleopatra's ships but did no harm to Cleopatra or Antony, who made their escape to Tainaron. The other escapees from the battle eventually joined Antony in Tainaron after the battle, which also suggests that a plan to flee was in place. How else would they have known to go there?

Cleopatra re-entered the harbor with sixty galleys garlanded as if for a great victory in order to deceive her people and allow her troops to take command of the city.[280] It was another ten months before Octavian would reach Egypt. Antony retreated in solitude to the Timonium, while Cleopatra actively planned her escape. She had her ships transferred overland to the Red Sea in an attempt to flee to India. Hearing of her plan, the Roman governor of Syria induced the Nabataeans of Petra to fall upon her ships and burn them.[281] Antony eventually met his death in 31 BC, and Cleopatra was soon to follow. With the end of the infamous love affair came the end of Greek rule in Egypt.

A.T. Mahan writes that several factors determine the sea power of a nation: geographical location, natural resources, climate, population, the extent of one's territory, and the character of one's government and its people.[282] In the Hellenistic Age, seapower was particularly reliant on a nation's ability to control strategically placed naval stations from which operations could be undertaken.[283] Warring successors were un-

---

280. Bevan, *The History of Egypt Under the Ptolemaic Dynasty*, 380.

281. Ibid. Bevan adds that the fact that these ships were transported overland indicates that the canals were too shallow to accommodate large vessels. Her consideration of such a move suggests direct and frequent lines of communication between the two countries

282. A.T. Mahan, *The Influence of Sea Power Upon History, 1660-1805* (Englewood, NJ: Prentice Hall, 1980), 28.

283. Gabrielson, *The Naval Aristocracy of Hellenistic Rhodes,* 43.

successful at securing and then maintaining these garrisons. Cleopatra possessed the unique opportunity to expand upon trade with the east by developing garrisons in new directions. However, it is evident that she wanted to restore the glory of her ancestors, and this meant re-taking the Mediterranean. The eastern market developed during the later years of Ptolemaic rule but did not play a major part in Cleopatra's grand vision. In fact, it is possible that she pulled all of her ships out of the Red Sea when amassing a fleet for the battle of Actium. The evidence for this argument stems from the fact that Cleopatra returned to Egypt in 31 BC with sixty ships. When she planned her escape to India, she had sixty ships carried overland. They were ultimately destroyed. No further attempts to escape were made and there were no ships to call upon for protection. This incident suggests that Cleopatra may have completely exhausted her naval resources, even in the Red Sea. The problems plaguing her administration and the citizens of Alexandria would quickly disappear. The Mediterranean Sea was securely under the control of Rome. One man would now rule the empire.

SIX

Site Formation:
Alexandria's Changing Face

FIGURE 18: Fort Qaitbay. Building stones of the famous lighthouse of Alexandria were later recycled into the medieval fort. Photo: Kimberly Williams.

Alexandria fell in prominence from a maritime capital to just one more (although essential) port within the vast Roman Empire. The city would fluctuate between prosperity and turmoil under the influence and rule of foreign nations for another 2,000 years as religious clashes, revolutions, and economic activity tore down her temples and erected modern business parks. The long, slow process of these man-made and natural alterations will be recounted here as Alexandria's site formation. More specifically, this chapter will cover the history and known geological changes that led to the creation of a "city beneath the sea." Our understanding of how Alexandria changed over the millennia comes from current physical remains, ancient historians, and writings of Arab travelers.[284]

Roman Rule

The Roman era is marked by political unrest. Alexandrians disliked the new administrators and their policies, which eliminated local political power. Augustus abolished the Alexandrian Senate and granted extended freedoms to the Jewish community. Revolutions continued to erupt, only to quickly dissipate. Alexandria's social elite persecuted the Jews while making a public mockery of the city's Roman leaders. The disputes between the two communities remained of primary importance during the early years of Roman rule, and Alexandria saw repeated unrest coupled with long periods of famine and destruction. Its inhabitants were also subject to slaughter at the hand of angry Roman emperors.

Revolutions, large-scale massacres, and the adoption of Christianity resulted in the destruction of many temples and monuments in addition to the ancient library. Alexandria lost its prominence as a cultural icon when it developed a new affinity with the Coptic Church, which also contributed to the restructuring of the original landscape. Constantine endorsed the Christian church during the fourth century AD. Christianity gained acceptance throughout the empire, and pagan cults were banned. After two centuries in which Christians had been persecuted, in a complete reversal, Christianity was now brutally imposed on the population, and the pagans were put to flight.[285] With this

---

284. New items have been incorporated into the original locations, and, therefore, also become part of the archaeological, or physical, record; as does anything that is included between deposition and recovery.

285. Jean-Yves Empereur, Alexandria: Jewel of Egypt, (New York: Abrams, Inc., 2002), 59.

movement, several key features of the ancient city were destroyed including palaces and the great ancient library.

Alexandria and its great harbor, meanwhile, enjoyed increased economic activity under its Roman rulers. Rome had effectively brought peace to the Mediterranean, permitting Alexandria to become the largest commercial market in the world. The Romans freed the Mediterranean of pirates and loosened up the world economy in many ways. Private owners soon claimed state-owned agricultural lands, made possible by the fact that "Alexandrians were greatly enriched particularly by foreign trade." Emperor Hadrian (128-117 AD) adds that Alexandria was:

> ". . . a rich city, having both wealth and prosperity. This city does not ail from unemployment, some work in the glass industry, others in the papyrus industry; others work in textiles or any other industry. Even the handicapped or the eunuchs or the blind each has a job to do. Those who have lost their hands do not remain idle. All worship one god, Money. Christians, Jews and others pay homage to money."[286]

The favorable circumstances that prevailed across the empire during the first two centuries of the modern era resulted from the unification of the world, the end of wars, and the flourishing of trade unlike any other previous time. The Alexandrians were able to navigate their fleets on the both the Red Sea and Mediterranean very successfully.[287] In the Mediterranean, they possessed the primary commercial fleet, with Alexandria serving as the point of contact with all ports to the east. Alexandrian merchants also monopolized trade by fixing the prices of goods and by providing for their transportation. Therefore, the harbor structures at Alexandria should have remained intact for much of this time period.[288] However, the harbors were certainly used for different purposes, given the reduction in the size and number of war ships stationed there.[289]

---

286. Ibid, 49.
287. Ashour, Mohamed Hamdi. *The History and Civilization of Alexandria Across the Ages.* (Kalyoub, Egypt: AL-AHRAM Commercial Presses, 2000) 50.
288. Khalil, Emad. Maritime Activity in Alexandria Harbor From the Bronze Age to the Roman Period. 37-8
289. Ibid.

The harbor was also vulnerable to natural disasters and foreign invasions. The Mediterranean suffered a series of earthquakes, tidal waves, and changes in sea level. A particularly devastating earthquake shook northern Egypt on July 21, AD 365, along the fault line between two continental plates. The African shelf was forced downward beneath the European plate, causing the whole coastal region to subside.[290] Current evidence suggests that the old city has sunk as much as twenty feet over the past 2,000 years. Sea levels have risen over the same period, effectively dropping the city another four or five feet. Alexandria also had the added disadvantage of being positioned west of the Canopic branch of the Nile, which carried out silt into the Mediterranean and into Alexandria's harbor.

Drastic changes in the physical landscape were compounded in AD 395 when the Roman Empire divided and Alexandria fell under Byzantine control. In the next two centuries, political unrest and invasions continually claimed monuments and buildings.

Arab and Ottoman Periods

Arab armies began their conquest of Egypt during the seventh century AD and captured Alexandria with minimal resistance. In the same way Egypt submitted to Alexander the Great in 332 BC to rid itself of the Persian yoke, now it hoped its conquerors would deliver it from Graeco-Roman rule.[291] The new Arab rulers were dazzled by what they saw. They encountered beautiful architecture, splendid planning, and expansive buildings. And under the new administration, Alexandria achieved a substantial level of autonomy despite her deteriorating legacy as a cultural and political leader of the ancient world. Physical changes had inevitably begun to occur, and it is probable that both sides of the Heptastadion dike had started to silt up.[292]

Alexandria was replaced by Fostat as the country's capital because its location was considered too far removed from the rest of Arab world, particularly during the Nile floods.[293] Also, the port was susceptible to

---

290. Foreman, *Cleopatra's Palace,* (New York: Discovery Books, 1999) 161.

291. Empereur, Alexandria: Jewel of Egypt, 66.

292. Harry E. Tzalas, "The Two Ports of Alexandria: Plans and maps from the fourteenth century to the time of Mohamed Ali," *Coastal Management Sourcebooks II,* (Washington: UNESCO), 23.

293. Fostat was situated northwest of Cairo.

raids from the Byzantium fleet, and the large Roman community in Alexandria was threatening to the new rulers. The seaport declined even more when wealthy foreign merchants deserted the city, prompting a depression in trade. The remaining citizens then suffered increased taxes and continued raids. Afterward, the southern and southeastern walls were destroyed and Alexandria began to lose its foreign characteristics. Attempts to reconstruct the aging lighthouse and the city walls after the earthquake of AD 797 were minimal, and even those that went forward would begin to favor Arabic expression and design.

On the waterfront, Alexandria maintained a part-time garrison during the summer months. Repeated attacks by sea no doubt contributed to the local interest in shipbuilding and secured the existence of a semipermanent naval base. Alexandria became a center for shipbuilding and a place of political refuge, which was of particular importance when citizens of nearby countries later defected from caliphate rule. Arabs were great navigators and established remarkable naval supremacy. In the Ayyubib period, naval salaries improved and the city was refortified. However, many members of the city administration moved west, abandoning the royal palaces and creating significant changes in the Eastern Harbor. Men pulled chains across the harbor to prevent ships from entering. Apparently for the same purpose, they also poured fragmented monuments and masonry stones into the harbor where they remain today. In addition, Christian merchants were prohibited from entering the old western harbor. That left the ancient port a place where access was tricky and involved narrowly skirting the Pharos to avoid the shallows of the old royal berths.[294]

After the Arab conquest, Alexandria retained some of its Greek architecture, with the conquerors settling in houses abandoned by the Byzantiums.[295] Sections of Alexandria's walls, towers, and fortresses were demolished, leading the general population to move into the inner parts of the city. The years following the Arab conquests also coincide with the drying of the Nile riverbed at the Gulf of Alexandria. Increased sand deposits, mud residue, and the city inhabitants's dependence on

---

294. Empereur, Alexandria: Jewel of Egypt, 70.

295. El Sayed Adbel Aziz Salem "The Planning and Development of Alexandria in the Islamic Age," *The History and Civilization of Alexandria Across the Ages*,111.

wells and cisterns—all contributed to the general depletion of river water. Mamluk rulers decided to re-dig a canal to bring additional water from the once dry Canopic Branch into the city. The city administrators enslaved approximately 40,000 men to carry out the task.[296]

Alexandria continued to attract a diverse population of foreigners. Members of tribes from Yemen, Lakhm, Gozam, Kenda, Azod, Khozaa, Mazaghna, and Hadareya acted as coast guards,[297] with each culture contributing in some way to the contemporary landscape. During the two centuries of the crusades, Alexandria suffered frequent attacks. Even though the town developed as a fortress in the middle of those holy wars, trade still flourished. The historical record adds that the port city remained garrisoned into the thirteenth and fourteenth centuries. Walls were rebuilt in AD 1265, and Alexandria continued to serve as an important base for the Arab fleet.

The Pharos Lighthouse received considerable attention from travelers. Their letters and journals provide insight into the eventual destruction of the extraordinary monument. Historian El Masoudi provided a particularly beneficial description in AD 944. He confirmed that the stone structure was made up of three levels. The lowest level was square, the middle an octagon built of pebbles and gravel, and the upper level was circular. He then noted that each section was less in diameter than its lower counterpart, creating a three-tiered lighthouse. History has recorded similar accounts with varying additions and omissions. In one particular account, a traveler noted a mosque at the top of the lighthouse, which also appears to have served the coast guard. Testaments to the size and shape of the lighthouse can also be tracked in other countries as the Pharos design influenced church towers throughout Egypt, Syria, Lebanon, and parts of Europe. In AD 1183, Andalusian nomad Mohamed Ibn Gobier Al Kenany recorded his description of the lighthouse and mentioned that it projected light up to seventy miles out to sea. He, too, prayed at its mosque. The fourteenth century marks the final destruction of Pharos lighthouse. An earthquake in AD 1303 appears to be the culprit. The actual earthquake first occurred in Crete but the ensuing tidal wave is credited with severely damaging the light-

296. Ibid, 151.
297. Ibid, 112.

house. Ibn Battuta, from Tangier, tells us that in AD 1329 he could get up to the door of the first floor, but that it was impossible when he returned to Alexandria in AD 1346.[298]

In AD 1365, warriors from Cyprus laid siege to the city, plundering it and setting numerous fires. This same year, the Mamluk Sultan Qalaun increased security in both harbors and ordered the construction of a "little Pharos" in the east. Alexandria thus began another long period of decay and restoration. The persistence of harbor facilities eventually led to a resurgence of trade from the sixteenth to the beginning of the nineteenth centuries when Alexandria was an active port in the Mediterranean Sea. However, the renewed trade did not resemble earlier achievements and much of the new activity was now being directed toward the harbors in nearby Rosetta. In addition, the Portuguese discovery of the Cape of Good Hope in 1498 ultimately led to considerable transformations in the Mediterranean. Alexandria was progressively abandoned. The number of residents dwindled and the remaining population now congregated on the peninsula that connected the city to the ancient lighthouse. The Ottomans continued this shift to the extent that, three centuries later, the ancient city was little more than a vast field of ruins while a new town was growing up on the spit of land leading to the ancient Pharos. Alexandria enjoyed a modest prosperity through its maritime ventures until the conclusion of Ottoman rule. Goods from China to Morocco continued to cross through its harbors in spite of increased global trade and numerous developing ports in Egypt. Alexandria truly showed its former prominence when her harbors welcomed Napoleon Bonaparte's military and scientific expedition.

European Influences

Napoleon Bonaparte arrived in Alexandria in 1798 with the purpose of disabling British trade with Egypt. The French Navy was accompanied by a scientific commission to study and record the country's current condition in addition to its long, illustrious history. The brief French occupation also left behind its own contributions to the modern archaeological site. Napoleon's navy remained in Alexandria while

---

298. Ibid.

the military and scientific expedition continued through Egypt. While stationed in the ancient city, European engineers created a dockyard, which served as a training center for a new fleet that transformed Alexandria into a stronghold once more. In addition, Alexandrians witnessed an important naval engagement near modern-day Abu Kir between French and British forces. The battle claimed a number of French ships, which added to the immense field of ruins already beneath the sea.

Napoleon's scientific expedition not only provided vivid details of Alexandria just before modern development, but has enabled researchers to gage natural shifts as well. Geological factors make all harbor archaeology both multidisciplinary and long-term. (The comparable site of Caesarea in Israel has undergone three decades of investigations.) Napoleonic documents of a well-known landmark, known as Diamond Rock, indicate that water levels have drastically changed over the last 200 years. Diamond Rock is located at the northeast limit of fallen Pharos and is now a formless shallow covered by some ten feet of water. When Napoleon's cartographers recorded it around 1798 for *Description l'Egypte,* the rock was well above the surface, towering above the human figures beneath it.

After Napoleon, Alexandria experienced a period of anarchy, followed by the reign of Mohamed Ali from 1807-1848.[299] Ali revitalized the former cultural center and strengthened commercial relations with Europe. Under his rule, Alexandria flourished and the population increased from 7,000 to 143,000. He attracted foreigners in Alexandria, and they built low-lying structures atop shallow foundations, which actually protected the ancient site underneath. The Roman quarters were also redeveloped, often with ancient building stones, to create a community with both European and Egyptian influences. Mohamed Ali cleared the ancient channel to meet the Rosetta branch of the Nile and opened the channel to the western harbor. He also commissioned French engineers to construct a large dock in the western port and reopened the harbor to Christian traders after more than 1,000 years.[300]

---

299. The English occupied Egypt after Napoleon left in 1801 but Mohamed Ali defeated the British in the Battle of Rosetta in 1807. In 1811 Ali invited 400 Mamluk leaders to a feast at his palace in Cairo and massacred them all. Empereur, Alexandria: Jewel of Egypt. 88.

300. Empereur, Alexandria: Jewel of Egypt, 90.

Not only was the physical terrain reconstructed, but the population also surged with increased trade. Foreign faces flocked to the growing opportunities in Alexandria. This had immediate cultural impacts on the growing city, one of which was the escalation of trade in antiquities. What followed was a tremendous amount of destruction in the old parts of town, which led to the loss of many significant artifacts to museums around the globe. Mohamed Ali continued to contribute to the accelerated changes by choosing the western end of Pharos as the site of his planned palace. Meanwhile, in Cairo, he argued in favor of destroying the ancient pyramids and replacing them with a modern dam.

The Modern Site

Modern Alexandria occupies ten times the space of the ancient city. Four million permanent residents are now joined by millions of tourists in the summer months. The population size has a significant impact on archaeological sites since development, human waste, and trade in artifacts damage the physical record. The sites are also impacted by aquatic environments, which encircle the city. Alexandria's northern border is the Mediterranean Sea. To the south, city limits end at Lake Mareotis, and Abu Kir Bay forms its eastern edge. The natural and manmade water systems of Alexandria drain domestic and industrial wastes directly to the sea. The cumulative volume of wastewater disposed into the sea from all point sources along this stretch of coast is roughly 9 million cubic meters per day.[301] A daily volume of more than one million cubic meters of mixed sewage water is drained from the city.[302] Such materials present serious health concerns for archaeologists working in this environment and adversely impact the artifacts themselves. Contaminated water comes in contact with artifacts lying on the seabed, having the potential to accelerate corrosion through chemical processes and depletion of oxygen.

Alexandria has once again gained prominence as a social and economic contender in Mediterranean affairs. The renewed interest in financial gain and cultural heritage has educed coastal engineering ef-

---

301. Ibid. 138
302. Ibid.

forts. In many instances, reconstruction of the coastline profoundly impacts underwater sites. In the case of the great Eastern Harbor, efforts to protect the fifteenth century Qaitbay Fortress from constant wave action has prompted officials to dump large blocks over the archaeological site near the fort. Dredging navigational channels and breakwaters prevent the free exchange of inshore waters with the open sea, leading to contaminated water. The impact of commercial expansion on the underwater site is impossible to calculate, and the threat of future construction projects still looms. A project has recently been submitted to the Governorate for the building of a marina in the inner Eastern Harbor precisely on the site of the recently discovered Ptolemaic harbors.[303] At the time of this writing, the project has been placed on hold. However, the fact that the commercial efforts are a contender for harbor space over a highly publicized site of great significance points to an unmistakable trend. Alexandria today faces the same problems as many growing metropolises with economic expansion offering more immediate benefit than cultural conservation.

City administrators also have to contend with an expanding metropolis, whose citizens face housing and development problems of their own. Therefore, the current archeological site is continuously subject to degradation and destruction by human pressure, accelerated urbanization and land-based pollution, which all contribute to the deterioration of submerged artifacts and structures.[304] In Jean-Yves Empereur's book, *Alexandria Rediscovered,* he adds that "the move to remodel the city center, which is making Alexandria one of the major urban conglomerations of the Mediterranean, involves irreversible sacrifices—and the pace is quickening. The defeat of archaeology in Alexandria is by no means due to natural conditions: Its causes are human."[305]

---

303. Ibid. 139

304. Ossama M.T. Aboul Dahab, "Environmental Concerns in Alexandrian Underwater Archaeology," *Coastal Management Sourcebook II* (Washington DC: UNESCO), 140.

305. Empereur, *Alexandria Rediscovered,* 33

SEVEN

Archaeologists and Explorers

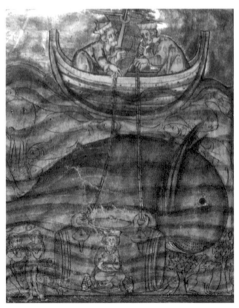

FIGURE 19: A 16th-Century French illustration shows Alexander the Great being lowered to the sea floor in a glass cage where the fish crowd around him and pay homage from "L'histoire du noble et valliant roy Alixandre. Copyright: le Biblioteque Royale de Belgique, Brussels, Belgium/ Bridgeman Art Library.

Interestingly, the history of underwater exploration can be said to begin with a mythological tale about Alexandria's founder, Alexander the Great. An Ethiopian legend says that the great king prayed for the ability to venture below the sea. Then he ordered the construction of a wooden box with glass windows to carry him to the ocean floor in what is pictorially represented as a diving bell. According to the legend, two draughtsmen accompanied him, and they saw demons with human bodies destroying harbor works with saws, hammers, and crowbars.[306] Amazed with his findings, Alexander ordered life-size reproductions

---

306. Honor Frost, *Under the Mediterranean.* 87.

103

of the monsters to be placed around the construction site. Later, the demons discovered the frightful images and fled the harbor forever.

Seventeen hundred years later, European travelers began mapping the ancient harbors.[307] As mentioned above, Napoleon Bonaparte was instrumental in recording Egypt's historical monuments. He brought with him to Egypt a scientific team of more than 120 artists and scientists to create the widely used *Description de l'Egypte* between 1798 and 1801. The description included maps by Alexandre-Saint Genis and Gratien Le Pere, which represent Alexandria at the turn of the nineteenth century. Then, in 1865, Napoleon III developed a keen interest in Julius Caesar's campaigns and requested a detailed map of Alexandria in preparation for his book. Mohmoud Bey (later known as Mahmoud el-Falaki) was a prominent engineer and astronomer trained in cartography.[308] He accepted the assignment and documented the existing remains of the Ptolemaic city in addition to later periods. El-Falaki even conducted hundreds of exploratory digs in areas now inaccessible to archaeologists and completed the first known survey of the Eastern Harbor. In 1866, he also noted the location of the submerged island, which is still visible on a good day, and remnants of the royal harbor. Napoleon never completed his biography on Caesar, which was to have include maps of Alexandria's ancient city. El-Falaki ultimately published his findings, which he presented in 1872. Today, modern scholars frequently draw upon his thoughtful examination.

While el-Falaki's map afforded Alexandria some recognition, many early archaeologists were disheartened by the lack of monumental finds. Notable researchers who met with great success around the Mediterranean failed in their attempts to locate Alexander the Great's tomb. Alexandria did not attract earlier scholars, as its few remaining monuments did not compete with the colossal well-preserved monuments of Upper Egypt. In addition, historical data was lacking, because papyrus did not survive well in Alexandria's climate versus that of the arid desert regions. Local interest still abounded but resources failed to match their

---

307. These detailed recordings also include a description of rocks no longer seen today and thus indicating additional geological disturbances.

308. The term 'Bey' denotes a special ranking within Egyptian society and el-Falaki literally translates into "the astronomer."

enthusiasm. In response, Alexandria developed its own Archaeological Society in 1893, following the opening of the Graeco-Roman Museum in 1892.

Together, these two organizations began conducting terrestrial excavations in the wake of modern development. The museum also helped bring recognition to Alexandria's archaeological efforts. Concurrently, other scholars began to take interest in Alexandria's rediscovery. D. G. Hogarth, from the British School at Athens, began a short-lived survey in 1894. He performed exploratory digs, uncovering late Roman remains, yet he did not come across exciting finds as quickly as he had expected. He widely publicized his troubled search, effectively discouraging other scholars from excavations on Egypt's Mediterranean port cities. Enter Heinrich Schliemann. Famous for his discoveries at Troy and Mycenae, he came to Egypt in search of Alexander the Great's tomb. However, he quickly came to the same conclusion as Hogarth, and he too also lost hope in Alexandria.

A major breakthrough occurred in the early 1900's. 1908 marked an important discovery in the easternmost point of the western harbor, including some monumental finds. Two years later French engineer, Gaston Jondet, began an additional examination of the western harbor. Assigned with the task of enlarging Alexandria's western port, he happened to notice what might well have been ancient harbor structures. These structures included a massive stone breakwater north of the modern coast in the open sea. His report notes a fragmented, yet expansive breakwater north of the present-day coast. The width on the surface was approximately forty-five feet, which could easily withstand the most violent storms known to the Mediterranean. When Jondet published his careful survey, he broadened it to include the site near Pharos, prompting excitement and speculation among European scholars, including the suggestion that the fragmented water features were constructed long before the Greeks arrived. Incidentally, no further examination has been made of the western harbor to this time.

Alexandria's submerged remains lay untouched for another twenty years until a British pilot reported seeing ancient remnants just below the surface. The site included numerous artifacts resting in the shape of a horseshoe in the bay of Abu Kir near the modern-day city of Alexandria. The discovery prompted Prince Omar Tousson to inquire further, and he soon learned what local fishermen had already discovered. Alexandria's waters were filled with ruins all along the Mediterranean coast. The prince was encouraged and initiated a series of excavations from 1933-42. The excavations were fruitful and his research determined the location of the ancient cities of Menouthis and Herakleion.

Alexandria was clearly an extraordinary archaeological site with infinite potential. However, Egypt was engaged in a steady stream of conflicts right after World War II, and underwater sites were unavailable for exploration. A new era of research was opened by Kamal Abou Abu el-Saadat in the 1960's.[309] Abou Abu el-Saadat was an Egyptian diver and spear fisherman with a strong enthusiasm for history. In his exploratory dives, he came across several key sites in Alexandria's waters. He made a number of other discoveries, as well, including the remnants of colossal statues, which presumably stood at the base of the Pharos lighthouse. He also located large, fragmented granite blocks scattered throughout the harbor. Abou Abu el-Saadat presented his findings to the Graeco-Roman Museum, whose members now began to solicit aid from the Egyptian navy. The naval support team kindly responded and soon recovered a life-size male statue of Aswan granite and the statue of Isis Pharia from the waters near Cape Lochias.[310] Despite Abu el-Saadat's early success, his pioneering efforts to fully excavate Alexandria's harbors met with considerable resistance. A brief sign of hope occurred in 1968 when the United Nations Educational, Scientific, and Cultural Organization (UNESCO) sent British archaeologist Honor Frost to perform a preliminary survey with Abu el-Saadat as a guide. Frost reacted with great enthusiasm and seemed confident that an excavation would be easily funded. Unfortunately, Frost's and Abu el-Saadat's discoveries coincided with war between Egypt and Israel and officials closed off Alexandria's harbors once again.[311] However, Frost's

---

309. Emad Khalil and Mohamed Mustafa, "Underwater Archaeology in Egypt" *International Handbook of Underwater Archaeology.* (New York: Kluwer Academic/Plenum Publishers).

310. Both statues date to the Ptolemaic Period.

311. El-Saadat, however, maintained enough good favor with the navy that he was permitted to dive. He set out once more on his explorations and subsequently charted the remains of Pharos lighthouse, the eastern harbor and other ruins. He was supported by members of the University of Alexandria and later presented his findings to the Graeco-Roman Museum.

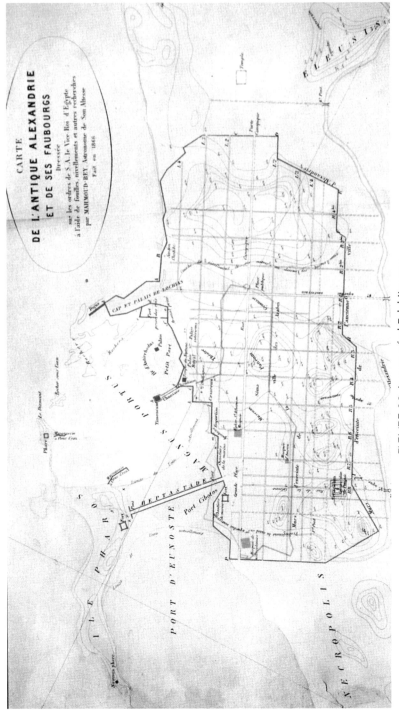

FIGURE 20: Image of el-Falaki's map.

preliminary examination and study continued to interest scholars abroad and her findings would later benefit archaeologists completing a full-scale excavation.

Interest in the harbor continued in spite of its inaccessibility. During the 1980s, the president of the Egyptian Antiquities Organization, Dr. Ahmed Kadry, grew increasingly concerned with Egypt's underwater national heritage. Through his efforts, the Ministry of Culture was placed in charge of the underwater relics recovered in Abu Kir in 1983. Then in 1996 the Egyptian Supreme Council of Antiquities (SCA) officially claimed jurisdiction over the underwater excavations and the SCA has supervised and carried out all archaeological work in Egypt since this time.[312] In light of recent history it made perfect sense for the government to be involved. Over the years, foreign expeditions in Egypt had carried off countless artifacts, contributing to the archaeological record more often in the form of filters than contributors. Now, all foreign-based campaigns are required to obtain work permits from the council. In addition, all excavations are conducted under government supervision, and site studies are based on collaborative efforts of Egyptian and foreign experts.

One of the first and most influential collaborative expeditions was under the direction of Dr. Jean-Yves Empereur, the director of research at the National Center for Scientific Research (CNRS) and director of the Center for Alexandrian Studies (Centre d'Estudes Alexandrine or CEA). Empereur has dedicated many years of study to Alexandria and the Hellenistic Period. Former secretary-general of the French School at Athens, he studied Classics at the University of Paris and has directed underwater excavations in Greece and Cyprus. The CEA's primary aim is to study the long and rich history of Alexandria. These studies involve terrestrial and underwater archaeological excavations, surface prospections, and the examination of historical archives, journals, and ancient maps. In the early nineties, the CEA began a series of emergency excavations in various sites around Alexandria to recover sites threatened by economic development. Empereur has developed a vast understanding of Alexandria's past through a broad range of study and through fragmentary excavations performed around the city.

---

312. Khalil E. & Mustafa M., "Underwater Archaeology in Egypt."

The 1990s were a particularly fruitful time for archaeologists in Alexandria, advancing considerably our general knowledge of the area.[313] In 1993, shortly after the government began placing concrete blocks at the base of Qaitbay on top of important archaeological finds, a local filmmaker captured the goings-on as part of a documentary on the Graeco-Roman museum. She used the footage to encourage authorities to discontinue their operations. The Egyptian Supreme Council of Antiquities responded quickly to the request for a submarine excavation and called upon the services of the CEA. Within months, a team of French and Egyptian archaeologists began the first series of excavations at the foot of Qaitbay Fort.

During the 1990s, Alexandria also attracted the interest of underwater explorer Franck Goddio who, like Empereur, brought a great deal of attention to the new discoveries under the sea. Goddio began his career in finance and developed an interest in archaeology while studying wreck sites in Asia. In 1987 he founded the Institut Européean d'Archéologie Sous Marine (IEASM) in Paris. In general, his expedition concentrated on the eastern part of the great harbor, also known in antiquity as the "Royal Quarter." He has also mapped wrecks of Napoleon's fleet and sites of ancient cities near Alexandria to include Pelusium and Canopus. Like Empereur, Goddio's project attracted international acclaim, yet he has come under critical scrutiny from the archaeological community for his lack of a traditional academic training and for his highly commercialized approaches to archaeology. In spite of criticism from academia, Goddio maintains that the local government has always approved his projects and that artifacts are protected for public use.

Goddio and Empereur prepared their large-scale excavations with the invaluable aid of the Supreme Council of Antiquities (SCA), which has been involved in numerous terrestrial and underwater projects. However, Egypt had no dedicated Department of Underwater Archaeology (DUA) until 1996. The mid-nineties necessitated a dedicated department as underwater excavations had become highly involved campaigns and opened new opportunities to explore sites outside the harbors. Not only does the DUA assist the French delegations under Empereur

---

313. Empereur, *Alexandria Rediscovered*, 33.

and Goddio, but they collaborate with other international organizations as well. Most notably, the DUA collaborates with the Hellenic Institute for the Preservation of Nautical Tradition of Athens. Together, the Greek and Egyptian archaeologists have conducted an underwater survey of the seabed off Alexandria, which led to the discovery of ancient harbor structures and a large building. The survey also revealed an important number of man-made cuttings in the natural limestone, amphorae shards, and stone weights in the reef.

Last, the SCA/DUA has worked side by side with American and Egyptian archaeologists from the Institute of Nautical Archaeology (INA). Together they have developed the Laboratory for the Conservation of Submerged Antiquities on the site of the Alexandrian Maritime Museum. The relatively new facility has been used to conserve artifacts from Red Sea and Mediterranean campaigns. In addition, INA has organized training programs to educate Egyptian conservators in wet-artifact conservation. INA has initiated surveys and excavations around the country and aims to investigate Red Sea wreck sites from the Roman era. As with all archaeological campaigns in the Mediterranean and Red Seas, each new discovery enhances our general understanding of ancient Alexandria. However, for the purposes of this book, we will limit our study to the excavations of the Eastern Harbor as they directly relate to Alexandria's maritime origins.

EIGHT

The Pharos Excavation

Jean-Yves Empereur's archaeological contributions in Alexandria have been shaped by the city's growth over the last few decades. The old city is scattered with many delicate buildings assembled upon shallow foundations. As these structures are pulled down to make room for modern office parks, Empereur is periodically allowed to carry out a hurried excavation. Shallow foundations often mean that remnants buried beneath it are fairly well preserved. In many areas, Empereur has uncovered more than 2,000 years of history buried in thirty feet of earth. (Underwater sites have also been protected by the nature of their environment and have benefited from being off limits to a majority of the modern population. In essence, they are more readily available for archaeological research.)

Working in the shadow of bulldozers is not easy, however. Developers in Alexandria often attempt to evade conservation efforts, and Empereur has been forced to work within their commercial-minded restraints. Excavations of this nature are often limited to a few short months, and archaeologists rarely have the luxury of choosing where to explore. The underwater location near Pharos Island was no exception, when the government began placing breakwaters on the site in 1993. Assigned the task of surveying Pharos, Empereur set out to define the archaeological zone and determine its nature.[314] However, he often had to rely on operators of very same barges who were destroying his site to complete his excavation—and at a rate and pay of their choosing. Nev-

---

314. Jean-Yves Empereur, "Underwater Archaeological investigations of the Ancient Pharos" *Coastal Management Sourcebooks 2,* (UNESCO).

ertheless, Empereur's projects have proven beneficial in two important aspects. First, the members of CEA who have worked on digs throughout Alexandria have witnessed the ancient city being fitted together like a jigsaw puzzle.[315] Secondly, rescue digs have formed a discipline of their own and a beneficial model for similar sites under similar constraints.

Diving on a Sunken City

When Empereur first dove on the site of ancient Alexandria, he encountered a jumbled field of ruins spanning more than five acres.

"At first glance, the chaos was incomprehensible. There were elements of Pharaonic history and others [that] had been part of Greek monuments. We quickly elaborated several hypotheses. One took into the account the collapse of the Pharos. The huge blocks were disposed as though they had fallen in a line, and yet they are so imposing that they could have belonged only to a monumental edifice, and certain pieces resemble parts of corners or parapets, such as the Pharos would have incorporated."[316]

The initial campaign established a base map charting some thirty pieces of archaeological interest. The seemingly random and, in some areas, dense scattering of remains complicated methods for identifying an artifact's provenance. In order to determine where the objects came from and how they were deposited in the sea, he required a better-equipped and longer campaign to chart and illustrate all the architectural elements discovered. Complexities within an archaeological investigation also emerge from working with a close-knit team for extended periods of time.[317]

---

315. Empereur, *Alexandria Rediscovered,* 30.

316. William La Riche, *Alexandria: The Sunken City,* (London: Weidenfield and Nicholson Ltd. 1996), 52.

317. La Riche *Alexandria,* 71. Empereur is joined by Nicholas Grimal of the Institut Fracais d'Archaeologie Orientale, representatives of the Louvre, of the Foundation Elf, of the foundation Electricité de France, Stephane Compoint and the photographers of SYGMA, the filmmaker Andrew Snell, Thierry Ragobert and Stephane Milliere of Gèdèon, divers of the Egyptian Navy, representative of the Supreme Council of Antiquities, the Graeco-Roman Museum, and numerous others.

Empereur employed a team of French archaeologists when he be-gan his excavations in 1995 with Egyptologists Jean-Pierre Corteggiani, Georges Soukissian, Sameh Ramses, Mohamed El-Siad and Mohamed Abd El-Maguid. The initial crew also included volunteers from the lo-cal community and members of the SCA. In some instances, these numbers would rise to forty or fifty people with a variety of specialties. Not surprisingly, a large team creates added dimensions to any project in the field. As Empereur explains:

> ". . . It is therefore necessary to know how to live together on a daily basis. . . if not, the group stops, it can be paralyzed by a little grain of sand. There's a psychological phenomenon to be managed in this, and its extremely interesting because it brings a completely human dimension to the excavation. . ."[318]

On a more permanent basis, Empereur retains surveyors, conserva-tors, photographers and artists who aid with reconstruction and mechanics in charge of equipment.[319]

Modern developments and human factors compound the usual challenges of underwater archaeology. It is an occupation involving highly precise operations, which are extremely dependent on the environment. Diving in Alexandria is generally restricted to the fall and spring months because vigorous waves near Qaitbay require careful timing. Other con-straints have included the fact that the city's harbor also once suffered from severe pollution and short-term weather forecasts are difficult to obtain.[320] Safety is another important concern since mapping the har-bor may require moving large blocks weighing thousands of pounds.

Once underwater, Alexandria's archaeological zone presents a most astounding encounter, with more than 4,000 blocks covering five-and-

---

318. William La Riche *Alexandria: The Sunken City*, P. 28.

319. A more comprehensive site study requires reliance on a number of disciplines. For example, biologists can provide great insight into the role of marine life as it may affect a site. A basic understanding of chemistry and physics offer explanation for corrosion development and alter-ation. Geology and oceanography provide laws for understanding the impact of the natural environment, tectonics, and wave action on a site. Engineers aid in reconstructing ancient har-bors and, in some instances, the researcher can obtain services from professionals with backgrounds in more than one of these fields.

320. The city did have a number of sewer pipes, which extended into the ancient port. Now, however, this water has been redirected to the nearby lake.

a-half acres. Within the mix, twenty-eight sphinxes have been found from different Pharaonic periods[321] and the number of columns and column fragments runs in the hundreds. In addition, numerous artifacts have been disfigured in attempts to transform them into the masonry of newer projects. A majority of the recovered artifacts date to Pharaonic times rather than the Greek period. Notable exceptions include a colossal statue of a man preserved from the base of the neck to mid-thigh. It is similar to the earlier female colossus preserved from the top of her head to the mid-leg and measuring twenty-three feet.[322] Empereur speculates that she would have been more than forty feet tall when complete.[323] He also speculates that the pair originally stood at the base of the lighthouse and were probably joined by others, given that he has located six bases altogether. The removal of the modern concrete blocks from the site in January 2001 exposed parts of legs that belonged to what was an ensemble of huge statues, but these fragmentary pieces have yet to be pieced together.

Equally exciting is the discovery of gigantic granite blocks linked with the Pharos Lighthouse. The collection of stones evenly formed a line across the site, indicating that they may have fallen from a single building. The uniform arrangement of these roughly seventy-five stones does not correspond with barricades placed by Arab defenders in the medieval period, since their position and form would not necessarily create an effective blockade into the harbor entrance. There are some thirty pieces of extraordinary size, some up to thirty-three feet long and weighing more than seventy-five tons. In examining the particularly large pieces, Empereur noted individual stones that were broken into two or three pieces. Given the stones's immense size, numerous breaks indicate that they collapsed from a certain height. The added implication is that they fell during a very strong earthquake or tidal wave.

---

321. There is a difference of 1,300 years between them. There are no patterns between them indicating that they formed a row of sphinxes similar to those found in Luxor or Karnak.

322. William La Riche *Alexandria: The Sunken City,* 76.

323. Ibid.

Shipwrecks

The search for a new site for a breakwater to protect the Qaitbay Fort led to northward exploration in the vicinity of the Eastern Harbor, which in turn led to the discovery of Greek and Roman wreck sites dating between the fourth century BC and seventh century AD. These locations provide new insight into our understanding of maritime trade between Alexandria and the rest of the Mediterranean. Cargo ships were typically filled with wine amphorae, oil lamps, bronze vases, and even anchors. Since 1996, more than fifty anchors of all eras have been mapped and studied. Empereur has also completed one excavation of a first century wreck site resting near the Pharos remains. The vessel originated from the southeast coast of Italy before traveling to Crete, Rhodes, and then Alexandria. Based on its intended path, Empereur has determined that the ship sank some 300 feet away after hitting a submerged rock still visible today. A number of wrecks still need to be explored and studied. During the 1996 excavation, Empereur's team discovered Greek and Roman shipwrecks not far from where the lighthouse was found in November.[324]

Their discoveries are not surprising. The historical record makes clear that Alexandrian harbors were dangerous and required port facilities to aid in navigation. Strabo in particular noted the jagged rocks, which hid just beneath the surface. Most of the shipwrecks occurred about 1,000 feet from the harbor entrance. The special danger of the Egyptian coast arises from its lack of relief, so that mariners only saw catastrophic accidents coming at the last possible moment. The same rock formations that once menaced ancient seamen provide important clues to underwater archaeologists today. Their position now lies at a depth of approximately thirty-six feet. Current studies put the maximum swell at fifteen feet, which indicates that the rock wall, which claimed many ships, must have subsided by roughly twenty feet since ancient times. Empereur is incorporating the wreck sites into the overall plan of his excavation and is including a computerized survey of this new archaeological zone. These shipwrecks are full of wine amphoras imported from Greece, northern Turkey, Italy, Spain, and North Africa.

---

324. The ships and their well-preserved cargos lay only a few hundred meters from the entrance of the Eastern Harbor. Empereur, *Alexandria Rediscovered*,32.

Plain pottery and fine pottery lamps have also been found, all of which attest to the trade connections established by Alexandria's ancient residents.

Amphoras have been found in large numbers throughout Alexandria's terrestrial and underwater sites. Within one wreck site nearly 500 were discovered, many still bearing their stoppers. These particular amphoras came from Apulia in southeast Italy and date to the first half of the first century BC. The inside walls of the amphoras are covered with pitch, meaning that they probably held wine.[325] Another wreck site details the history of a ship coming from Rhodes in the third century BC. It also carried wine amphoras, but in some of them pine nut cones have been found. This is direct evidence of the importation of this "fruit" used in cooking and baking described in historic texts. Farther out to sea a fourth shipwreck—from the sixth century AD—is now being excavated, and all four sites are being mapped into a larger diagram as a Greek team from Patras University establishes a map of the seabed using sidescan sonar.

Mapping the Pharos Site

Alexandria is one of the largest underwater archaeological sites in the world, with enormous objects piled one upon another. Deciphering the chaotic location near Pharos is a considerable challenge, yet a detailed site map is necessary for interpretation. In order to understand each artifact's origin and how it came to rest in the harbor, Empereur had to map the objects into the modern terrestrial terrain. To accomplish this, he established a transit station on shore to record the location of underwater objects. A reflector, which is attached to a buoy, floats on the surface of the sea. This is in turn connected to an adjustable cord affixed to a small, weighted pointer. Under the water a diver aligns the pointer upon the object to be plotted. For example, to precisely measure a large stone, the diver may place the pointer on each corner. Once in place, the diver will adjust the cord so that the buoy is perfectly vertical above the point. The topographer on shore takes the measurement with electronic survey equipment; thus the team obtains an accurate

---

325. Italian archaeologists are at present excavating the wineries where these amphoras were produced.

FIGURE 21: Diver taking measurements of a sphinx. Copyright: Stephane Compoint/www.stephanecompoint.com

measurement, which can be mapped into an entire city plan. The dry team and the diver communicate through simple hand gestures, requiring sharp eyesight and excellent concentration. Simple hand gestures lose their efficiency beyond 1,800 feet, and this system is further limited by the effects of the swell, which causes the buoy to move on the surface. Undersea currents may also prevent the cord from being vertical. Thus this method is only practical in calm seas close to shore. Another important method utilized in the field is triangulation. Divers may simply align the artifact with one of several permanently fixed reference markers. Then a measurement is taken between the two points. The process is repeated with additional points and mapped out on shore.

Finally, archaeologists have employed the Global Positioning System (GPS) to map the underwater site in Alexandria. The system was originally developed by the United States Department of Defense, but is now a standard work tool of topographers all over the world. To implement this system, Empereur placed a fixed station receiver as a known reference point within Fort Qaitbay. Then a mobile receiver is taken

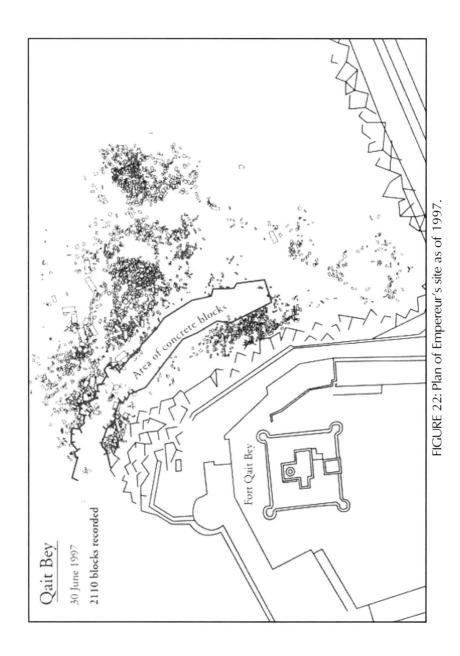

FIGURE 22: Plan of Empereur's site as of 1997.

onboard a Zodiac dinghy, and the system instantly obtains the co-ordinates of any point within his local work system. The principal advantage of GPS is that it allows someone to plot points farther from shore. At the same time, however, it cannot bypass problems posed by the sea swell or current, yet it has proven particularly beneficial in mapping outlying wreck sites.

Below the surface, divers complete artifact drawings using polyester tracing paper or synthetic calque paper and a mechanical pencil. Once they map the top layer of blocks, they uncover what lies below, which requires complicated and highly dangerous underwater maneuvers. Each block must be carefully elevated with airbags. After securing the device to the block, the divers slowly force compressed air into the bag. As the divers peel back the top layer of blocks, they make careful records of each discovery. Each block is cleaned, carefully measured, and drawn in detail. Drawings and measurements are then analyzed and classified in a computer database. Survey findings are also inserted into the database each day and allow CEA cartographers to continuously plot a revised site plan. The following day, divers can collect partial plans to re-orientate themselves underwater and to allow the divers to plot and sketch complementary features of the blocks. This 24-hour turnaround has contributed enormously to the progress of the excavation, providing updates in multiple forms. This includes written notes made in the field pertaining to the individual artifact, environmental conditions, drawings, and film footage. All of the artifact details are recorded and synthesized into on-screen or hard-copy identification sheets.

During the course of the entire campaign, relevant artifacts were removed from the sea floor to much excitement by the press and the world. The torso of King Ptolemy was lifted out of the water in October 1995. That year, thirty-three other architectural pieces, colossi and sphinxes, were also excavated and removed. A large white balloon marks each piece that is removed from the sea. Divers are then responsible for connecting cables to the underwater artifact. The cable from the winch on a barge is lowered toward the diver who will connect cables from below to the surface line. The most spectacular recoveries include the colossal statue of Ptolemy. The team also recovered the only sphinx with a head still intact.

Block Identification Sheet

Location: Qaitbay   No. 1027

Date: 10/2/95	Illustrator: John Smith	Lifted: NO
		Moved: YES

Beside Block No.	Orientation:	Max Depth	Min Depth
1634	north-south	15 feet	15 feet

✔ Complete Element or   Markings
___Fragment   ✔ Fastening Marks   No. 1
                               ___Cut Marks   No. __

Material: Granite   ___Lifting Marks   No.__
Type of Block: Slab   ___Assembly Marks   No.__
Color: Red
Inscription: None   Estimated Weight: 2.5 tons
Dimensions: 18 ft. 3 in., 9 ft. 6 in. and 3 ft. 2 in.

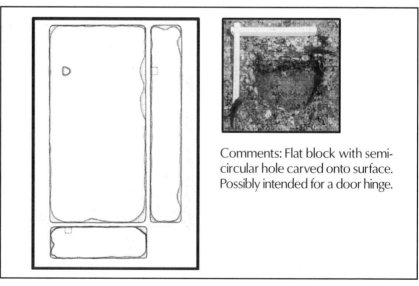

Comments: Flat block with semi-circular hole carved onto surface. Possibly intended for a door hinge.

FIGURE 23: Identification sheet based on CEA's ID forms as presented by NOVA.

Technology in the Field

Advancements in remote sensing are in a constant state of improvement and greatly facilitate archeologist's ability to map underwater sites with precision. By coupling a digital camera with electronic survey equipment, CEA investigators can collect photo images and measurements directly on portable computers. This method is considerably swifter than conventional site drawings on calque paper, which must be cleaned and digitized. Such technological efficiency and accuracy is much appreciated during urgent salvage excavations.

Whenever possible, Empereur has incorporated new advancements into his mapping processes, which have aided his divers in recording more than 4,000 blocks near the Qaitbay fort.

Topographers are an essential element in the CEA team, as they survey the excavations and create accurate site plans. Their technology goes far beyond the immediate archaeological zone. The increasing reliance on GPS led Empereur to install a reference point on the roof of the building of his downtown headquarters in Alexandria. The CEA topographers completed two twenty-four-hour observation sessions and then calculated the permanent coordinates within a global reference system. After completion, this point has linked all of Empereur's archaeological digs into one reference system. By the year 2000, Empereur decided to transform this reference point into a permanent GPS station. Since December 1, 2001, the resultant data has been available for free downloading from the Internet, which represents a first for Egypt. This same year, CEA divers also benefited from a new tool for underwater measurements known as the D100 aquameter. This acoustic system registers relative co-ordinates between a fixed receiver base and a hand-held pointer-emitter. The topography team plots the position of the base receiver and its reference points within Alexandria's local co-ordinate system.

Technology plays a greater role in archaeology than ever before. Survey equipment facilitates discovery, global positioning systems capture locations within an archaeological site, and geographic information systems (GIS)[326] allow archaeologists to form inter-relationships for

---

326. The GIS is a complicated ensemble of information held within a database that can be represented graphically. It is conceived to respond to all questions with a geographical implication. It is, at the same time, a technical tool for use in cartography and the management of data whose purpose is to rationalize the management of space, natural resources, the environment, and human interaction.

analysis and display. Everything noted in the field may be incorporated into one database, including hand drawings made underwater, which can be copied into software systems through computer-assisted design (CAD). Empereur places all of his site facts and features into one system, allowing him to examine his plan in its entirety or one section at a time. This includes photographs and videos, which can be paused and rewound, making the site much easier to study. Furthermore, GIS permits archaeologists to simply click on any individual element within the computerized site plan to view the relevant block identification sheet. The system can also respond to specific demands and plot only those blocks corresponding to certain criteria such as size, position, and material. For example, at the push of a button, the computer will bring on screen a map of only those blocks identified as columns, statuary, or those over a certain weight. Empereur can also pull up artifacts weighing at least thirty tons within close proximity to Pharos. The software returns an image of specified blocks on a screen without the thousands of other artifacts jumbled on top. In this manner, he can ascertain that these large blocks fell into a line, which may suggest that they all fell from the great Pharos lighthouse.

The CEA's database maintains computerized maps of 50,000 urban parcels throughout Alexandria, but it also has the ability to manage and manipulate historic plans as well. Given the limited technology possessed by previous mapmakers, it is rather understandable that differences appear between the sources. Now topographers can superimpose these maps with modern plans, providing archaeologists with the opportunity to compare and extract added information relative to Alexandria's shifting landscape. The CEA team carefully examines landmarks within each plan in order to align the most significant sites. The rest of the map is shifted around them. Once these maps have been geometrically corrected they can be integrated into the CEA database. The final systematic product serves as a valuable tool for consultation and comparison. Topographer Xavier Ablain and archaeologist Christophe Requi have done an analytical reconstruction of the engineer Mahmoud el-Falaki's plan,[327] determining that the former plan is flawed. Through GPS, CEA topographers compiled and analyzed sonar readings taken from ships

---

327. William La Riche *Alexandria: The Sunken City*,39

pinpointed with GPS coordinates. This information is compared with existing maps and refined methods of triangulation to chart the Pharos site.[328] When the hand-made drawings of Frost and Abu el-Saadat were overlain with the computer-generated drawing of the 1995 expedition, the lines of the two maps converged.[329]

Study and Conclusions

As with technology, our understanding of ancient Alexandria is in a rapid state of change. Despite close examination of the historical record, archeologists still have an incomplete picture of the early city, particularly the Pharos lighthouse. Reports about the seventh wonder of the ancient world often lack detail. Contemporary writers generally assumed that the reader would already have some familiarity with the subject. In a modern comparison, a visitor might write home about the magnificence of the Eiffel Tower or the Great Pyramids without including the exact height and measurements. Even if the reader has never visited these monuments, he or she would have a general idea about its structure and history. Quite naturally, such details were omitted from the records of Greeks, Egyptians, Romans, Arabs, and the many foreigners who passed through Alexandria's harbors.

What does remain, however, are numerous coins and small souvenirs that provide clues regarding the shape and size of historic monuments. The examination of such physical remains is an interesting and important study in itself, given the way images transform drastically throughout the ages. Equally important, archaeologists must contend with the irregularities and corrosion of surviving physical remains while sorting through chaotic relic alterations on land and in the sea. Empereur's team has excavated more than 4,000 architectural pieces. Only a handful are likely to have belonged to Pharos lighthouse and Empereur's maps have helped determine where many of the artifacts came from. Topographers are now able to draw lines on this map and examine concentrations of artifacts. As a result, Empereur has pinpointed several large blocks, which indeed formed a line beneath the sea (a phenomenon that would be difficult to visualize in the water). In addition,

---

328. Ibid. 46
329. Ibid. 67.

some of the larger blocks were broken into pieces, suggesting a fall from a substantial height. Based on current findings, Jean-Yves Empereur is convinced that he has found the first components of the lighthouse at Alexandria. Not only do the large blocks lie unilaterally east of Pharos Island but their composition attests to their origin as well. The impressive size of these Aswan granite blocks reaches more than thirty feet in height and seventy tons in weight. These components combined with their underwater position indicate that they are, indeed, part of the Pharos of Alexandria.

As for the rest of the site, archaeologists have proven that many of the artifacts are composed of materials that have been recycled or pillaged. The shifting of ancient monuments—a time-honored tradition in Egyptian history—has resulted in a harbor filled with remains of pre-existing structures from the Nile Delta and Heliopolis. Despite the fact that the finds are overwhelmingly Egyptian, there are clear signs of Graeco-Macedonian technological influences imparted upon Egyptian architectural materials.[330] The fact that Alexandria's monuments reflect Greek and Egyptian influences has gained growing acceptance among historians. It is not likely that the Pharos, nor the city, was built in a purely Greek fashion because the Greeks had no experience in building with granite and would have required local labor.[331] However, the Pharos could not have been purely Egyptian, either, because the Greek kings commissioned it and employed foreign architects to design it. Finally, archaeologists have uncovered a significant quantity of statuary as well as evidence of other complete structures underwater. The new discoveries have prompted new theories, which postulate that Pharos may have been part of a greater structural complex, inviting new questions about the island's civic and religious functions.

Each new discovery potentially creates more questions than answers, especially since the Alexandrian artifacts present scarce clues. Exact dates become elusive when decorative markings such as moldings and inscriptions are lost through years of reworking and decay. Recycled materials also create confusion when someone is trying to date an artifact's original and later functions. Evidence from construction techniques,

---

330. Colin Clement, "Diving on a Sunken City" NOVA.
331. Ibid

such as mason's markings, now provide a wide range of dates from the original structure to the building of the Pharos itself. Historians and archaeologists therefore wait patiently while divers and surveyors accumulate a massive database of images, video footage, and measurements. Once hand-drawn and computer-generated diagrams of architectural elements have reached completion, scientific researchers can explore new evidence for dating and create general hypotheses as to the spatial arrangement of the site.

The excavations continue on land and under the sea. The Supreme Council's success in stopping the construction of a protective breakwater has also led to the removal of the modern concrete blocks that covered part of the ancient site. Once lifted, Empereur's team discovered hundred of new architectural elements. Mapping of the underwater zone is nearly complete and Empereur has begun to focus on conservation and architectural analysis. Efforts in these specific fields have enabled him to create an image of what the ancient lighthouse might have looked like based on physical findings rather than iconographic evidence. Site studies pertaining to spatial relationships and an architectural analysis of the 4,000 blocks will still require several more years of research in a variety of fields.

Of particular importance are the conditions that cause sunken cities in the first place. Empereur's land excavations suggest that Alexandria was the victim of subsidence. To be exact, the Earth's crust under Alexandria has sunk more than fifteen feet in the last 2,000 years. To study this phenomenon, a team of geographers and marine geologists have begun to examine micro-fauna both underwater and in the silt deposits on either side of the Heptastadion. In addition to the geological surveys and underwater explorations, Fort Qaitbay is being closely examined with the hope that terrestrial excavations will uncover traces of the Pharos foundation. Empereur and the members of CEA have completed a great deal of topographic work, allowing the formation of new hypotheses regarding the provenance of each artifact. Now, as artists reconstruct images of ancient structures and historians search for missing pieces, conservators are beginning the painstaking and delicate task of preserving and restoring crumbled monuments from the sea.

Conservation

The study of artifacts from Empereur's excavations now falls to specialists already familiar with Alexandria's rich historical and physical remains. Conservation, like archaeology, is not just a set of techniques, procedures, and treatments; it is a state of mind that holds deep concern for the integrity of the artifacts, which represent remains of history.[332] With submerged artifacts, conservation becomes a strategy designed to combat loss, injury, decay, and waste. In this way, conservation can be seen as a combination of preservation and restoration.[333] Conservators are in a unique position because they are able to supply archaeologists with valuable data that would be impossible to determine in the field. Conservators not only perform basic operations to protect archaeological records, but they also take care to prevent adverse reactions once an artifact leaves the conservatory for public display. This phase in artifact preservation also ensures that precise details of the artifact are recorded with careful study, which is difficult in the field.

Artifacts immersed in seawater for long periods are prone to chemical, physical, and biological breakdowns. However, Alexandria's unique historical and modern landscape present added challenges to the artifacts resting off her shores. The degree of alteration is dependent on the nature of the artifact's composition, the time the object has been under water and prevailing conditions such as pollution and sediment type.[334] Untreated human waste, which has been deposited into the harbor, may potentially harm artifacts and accelerate corrosion. Lastly, mechanical damage occurred when concrete blocks were dumped on top of archaeological zones and when engineering works were ill planned. On a smaller scale, anchors from smaller vessels, as well as erosion and sedimentation, all contribute to mechanical deterioration as well.[335] To combat corrosive elements and to record every clue that an artifact may offer,

---

332. D.L. Hamilton. "Conservation". *Encyclopedia of Underwater and Maritime Archaeology*. (New Haven: Yale University, 1997) 106.

333. Bradley Rodgers, ECU Conservator's Cookbook. (Greenville, NC: East Carolina University, 1992) 5.

334. Ossama M.T. Aboul Dahab "Environmental Concerns in Alexandrian Underwater Archaeology" UNESCO, 141.

335. Ibid.

the center has invested in a dedicated conservatory, which serves as a storehouse for the excavations as well as a space for restoration and study. Different areas are designated for the study of specific types of artifacts, including stonework, painted plaster, mosaics, and metals.

The centralization of artifacts and analysis within one building facilitates organization and permits immediate access to the information kept there. Empereur's objective is to preserve the totality of the material and the site data that accompanies each artifact. The CEA team also welcomes experts and students from a variety of specialties to study the diverse collection and encourages outside investigators to publish their artifact and site findings. Researchers into very specific categories of material have looked at, and in some cases confirmed, evidence of the importation of such materials to Alexandria, aiding in our general understanding of its maritime history.

Specialists also shed new light on Empereur's efforts in regard to specific finds like metals. Metals are rather common in underwater archaeological sites and require special consideration and study in the field and the laboratory. One reason metals are problematic is that they can be visually difficult to detect under water. Typically, iron objects that have been submerged for extended periods will be completely encrusted and may easily blend into their surroundings. These encrustations may also distort the shape of the artifact, which may only be detectable when placed against a magnet. In other instances, the concretion may maintain the shape of a completely eroded artifact, with the inner shell providing the only evidence of the artifact. When it comes to conservation, metals such as iron will continue to corrode at a very rapid rate after they have been excavated and, as a result, require immediate treatment to retain all the original details on surface layers. Mechanical cleaning is very important, and it is critical that a conservator have a thorough grasp of the corrosion process. Finally, metals present many challenges for interpretation. The archaeological vestiges connected to the production and working of metal is difficult to understand because metal has often been re-used and reworked. As a consequence, artifact studies for metals demand a basic understanding of metalworking, for the craftsmanship associated with metal leaves very few traces. Historians and archaeologists are therefore reliant on the residues found in workshops. These specialized studies all aim to bring the thousands of tiny fragments of material history into one neat picture.

The Alexandrian finds have similarly created the need for specialized studies relative to a unique and expansive amphora collection. These storage vases held wine, oil, and fish brine and are found by thousands throughout the ancient city. The Graeco-Roman Museum houses no fewer than 140,000 amphora handles with the manufacturer's stamps, the largest collection in the world. Amphoras are of particular interest because they allow us to retrace trade routes, and not only those in the exchange of ceramic vases, but also of agricultural produce. At the same time, the marks stamped in the pre-fired clay permit dating with great precision since certain stamps bear an indication of the year and sometimes even the month of production. Archeologists are studying the amphoras both from the Museum and excavations. At the same time, a computerized database gathers together all the information on all the amphoras discovered during these excavations.

Lastly, the stone blocks receive a fairly simple treatment once they are recovered from the sea floor. Because of salt inside the epidermis of these large pieces, researchers have to remove it the same day that the blocks are taken from the bottom of the sea. First, the blocks are put in water tanks containing the same percentage of sodium found in the seawater. Then the conservator smoothly reduces this percentage of sodium. Once the blocks cease to release any salt into freshwater, the process is finished. Salt removal can take as long as six months, with conservators adding fresh water every ten days to two weeks. Currently, this process has been reduced to just a simple fresh water treatment, which appears to work quite well. The blocks can then be exposed to the open air without any problem.

In each case, the process of restoration and preservation are vital components of the excavation process. Empereur's dedication to the literal "life" of his findings ensures that future historians and archaeologists have the opportunity to re-examine these objects through a variety of cultural perspectives and scientific viewpoints. In the next chapter we will look at the legacy of historical maps made possible through underwater surveys.

NINE

Underwater Surveys of the Eastern Harbor

Franck Goddio received authorization to survey the Eastern Harbor in the early 1990's and began a full-scale excavation in 1996. Goddio's archaeological practices have received mixed reviews from academia but terrific support from general audiences and the media. Goddio's approach differs from Emperuer's in many respects, particularly in the manner in which he publishes his fieldwork and in the way he engages in spectacular publicity campaigns around the world. By contrast, Empereur has dedicated a lifetime to slowly piecing together Alexandria's entire history. This is not to say that Goddio does not carry out detailed finds and does not make accurate recordings of sites and relics, but his excavations do tend to rely heavily upon attention-getting discoveries. Goddio's descriptive approach leads to the finding of sensational sites like "Cleopatra's Sunken Palace" but does not follow all the practices of stringent archaeological guidelines. Goddio centers on artifact collection and documentation, which is tremendously beneficial in attracting attention to his ventures, yet limited in historical interpretation. The greatest credit to his projects is the immense detail to which he captures the site and his collaboration with well-known scientists from notable institutions around the globe. The Eastern Harbor project is no exception. Goddio's undertaking of the surveying and excavation of Alexandria's submerged resources has served to reopen the harbor in terms of global interest from both commercial and academic venues.

His work provides remarkable detail in his methodology for mapping the Eastern Harbor and is worth discussion and evaluation.

Surveys

Goddio began with the primary objective of mapping 800 acres of the Eastern Harbor, using a series of remote-sensing surveys. Remote sensing has become an integral component of underwater investigations since a number of archaeological procedures draw from geophysical practices. The employment of non-intrusive surveys allows scientists to document environmental conditions and delimit intrasite features without the harm of a full-scale excavation. Once incorporated into a database, magnetic or photographic images may be enlarged, digitally corrected, or overlapped to provide three-dimensional views. In this way, remote-sensing surveys can tell us about the seabed, ancient shoreline, and exposed landforms while confirming the state of archaeological remains before a researcher ever steps into the water. This initial pre-disturbance inspection allows the team to assess the degree of overburden and bottom composition, the general nature of the site, and confirm the existence or state of archaeological remains.

Goddio's general survey of the harbor was conducted in several phases. He began with the aim of producing a magnetic profile of the seabed. Magnetic-resonance magnetometers, often simply referred to as magnetometers, were used in this instance to detect buried or submerged ferrous material. To search an area, Goddio carried a towfish behind his vessel, using a careful search pattern aided by GPS and a video plotter. Afterward, he could measure field magnetic intensity at various cycle rates through a continuous read-out instrument. The towfish pinpoints buried or submerged ferrous materials that distort the earth's magnetic field, which therefore identify themselves as anomalies on a computer printout. Anomalies are then recorded by GPS so divers may investigate the targeted area. Following downloading and processing of information, printouts are obtained with details of the survey depicted in dot-density, grayscale, or trace line forms. The technique is often used to get a general overview of a wide area and to indicate whether anything of archaeological interest lies within the site.

Goddio then completed a second survey utilizing sidescan sonar, which broadcasts micro-pulses of sound through the water in fan-shaped beams. Similar to the magnetometer, a sonar system will consist of a "fish" towed behind a search ship, connected by a cable to the terminal on board. A calm sea and a straight course are necessary for a legible result. Bouncing off any obstruction in its path, the pulse returns echoes that are used to create a sonograph of the seabed. As the "fish" advances, an image is displayed on a monitor or a paper plotter. Usually, the result is just an image of the sea bottom without much detail. However, the sidescan sonar is useful in areas of low visibility since it is unaffected by limited light. Last, Goddio employed a subbottom profiler to create a three-dimensional image of his site. The subbottom profiler resembles the sidescan sonar in that both systems rely on sound or echoes. The profiler directs its pulses downward versus sideways and therefore is useful in determining the degree of overburden.

Goddio's immediate findings confirmed suspicions that earthquakes greatly altered the site of Alexandria. His survey pinpointed crevices in the seabed underneath collections of ruins. In particular, Goddio noted that a collection of columns all had collapsed in one direction, suggesting the intense force of a devastating earthquake. Goddio also argues that smashed artifacts indicate a natural disaster of such magnitude and speed that the ancient inhabitants were unable to collect their valuables and flee. Other disasters that may have affected the area include a sudden rise in sea level owing to floods, subsidence, sea-floor liquefaction, and the probable shift of the Canopic branch of the Nile.

Excavations

In 1996 the Egyptian Supreme Council of Antiquities granted Goddio permission to organize a team of twenty divers to begin an extensive excavation of the Eastern Harbor. The investigation's primary aim was to complete an extended survey based on initial composites of the sea floor. The divers were charged with fleshing out site contours and investigating unusual objects uncovered by electronic renderings.[336] Goddio instructed his team members to pay special attention to a large

---

336. LaRiche, *The Sunken City*, 60.

submerged island located in the middle of the harbor. When finds were made, they took careful measurements and captured their location with GPS coordinates. As with Empereur, unique conditions within the harbor necessitated creative methods for accurately tracking points within the site. To improve accuracy, Goddio commissioned an underwater GPS device, which divers held above an object in the water. Other divers then positioned an antenna over the first diver to obtain a fixed position. The receiving memory holds up to 500 pieces of positioning data that can be connected directly to a computer database. Not only did this create a precise map of the harbor but also it helped to determine spatial relationships within the overall plan.

During the 1996 season, one diver pinpointed a sunken jetty and identified signs of pacing stones. Because the land mass was not connected to the mainland, Goddio concluded that he had found the location of the ancient island of Antirhodos. Further investigation revealed granite columns, a World War II plane, and several branches extending from the island in what may have been an enclosure for a small harbor. The divers also found wood items, including planking and stakes.[337] Goddio's team made more than 3,500 dives and recovered a "tremendous amount of architectural and artifact evidence."[338] Divers used compasses, slates, dredges, and iron trowels to remove crustations and sketch images of the sea floor and artifacts. Once details of particular locations within the site had been recorded, Goddio compiled his findings into a master plan and stored artifact and structural coordinates on his ship's computer. As a clear image of the site evolved, Goddio developed a detailed map placed on a scale of 1:500 and generated a general map summarizing all the data on a scale of 1:2500.[339]

Even though a general map was in place, many artifacts still remained hidden beneath the sea floor awaiting discovery. In order to complete his image of the site and collect artifacts for display, Goddio brought in dredges and lift bags to uncover and retrieve some of his

---

337. Goddio adds that samples of the organic material predate the founding of Alexandria but the results are questionable, especially in light of the fact that pollution common to that area could alter the results carbon dating.

338. Foreman, Cleopatra's Palace, p. 172.

339. LaRiche, *The Sunken City*, 61.

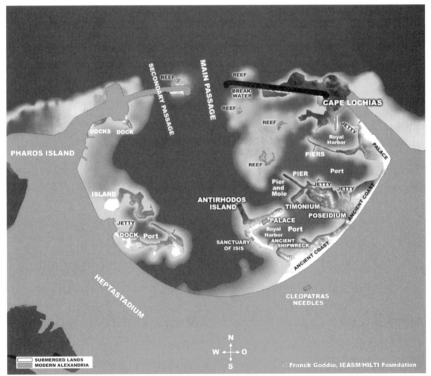

FIGURE 24: The ancient sunken quarters of Alexandria, integrated into the schematic surrounding of modern Alexandria, produced by Franck Goddio in 2000. After completion of Franck Goddio's research work, the submerged city can be charted very accurately. Since the modern city of Alexandria covers the rest of the ancient city, the layout can only be estimated, based on ancient texts and archaeological evidence on land. Copyright: Hilti Foundation/Franck Goddio

finds.[340] Larger artifacts discovered on the bottom were raised to the surface by lift bags. Not all artifacts, however, are removed from the sea. Many are simply recorded for posterity through photographs, diagrams, and reproductions. Goddio's decision to create replicas concurs with resolutions of the Supreme Council of Antiquities. With the idea of creating an underwater park, many government officials decided to wait

---

340. In its most basic form, a dredge is a large tube with a surface-supplied air hose and diver-operated valve attached near the working end. As air is introduced into an airlift, a mixture of air and water is produced that is less dense than the surrounding water. Air bubbles form and expand as they rise through the tube, which causes considerable suction at the lower end. The strong suction draws up bottom sediments, which are ejected at the exhaust end. A grate on the water intake stops larger objects that could jam inside the tube from being drawn into the dredge.

before removing many artifacts from the Eastern Harbor.[341] A few items, however, have made there way out of the sea and into museum exhibitions. Goddio lacked the permanent conservation facilities that Empereur developed and relies on outside conservatories like the lab on premises of the SCA facility to treat his findings.

Having decided to leave many artifacts in place, Goddio called on outside scholars to interpret inscriptions on the many statues, blocks, and columns. In order to facilitate further study, he made impressions of artifacts while underwater. In some instances, he temporarily retrieved objects from the sea floor to make complete three-dimensional reproductions. Divers were given a synthetic material called Tergal, cut to match the size of the block on which an inscription appeared and coated with a special silicone-rubber molding formula.[342] The synthetic material was held in place by grips formed into fasteners that were connected to lead weights. Divers first cleaned the surface and then placed the Tergal on top of the artifact utilizing the weights to keep everything in place and ensure enough pressure to accurately capture an impression. Each mold was left overnight and recovered the next day. The final result was a supple and highly resistant molding that offered an impression of the inscription details.[343] Artifacts that required a molding on board were also cleaned before the replication process. Workers covered each piece with a petroleum-based jelly to protect the outer casing before coating with modeling clay. Last, the artifact was sealed with a protective silicone and left to harden. Casts were replicated for study throughout the world.

Findings

Goddio's excavation yielded priceless finds—structures, statues, columns, and even an ancient shipwreck. However, his most valuable contribution would have to be his map of the ancient shoreline, showing the reefs, the island of Antirhodus, the promontories projecting from the ancient shore into the sea, and the collection of artificial dikes. In creating this ancient snapshot, he incorporated Strabo's contempo-

341. Foreman, Cleopatra's Palace, p. 178.

342. Ibid, p. 188.

343. Ibid.

rary harbor descriptions into the site plan. For example, when Goddio's team located two submerged reefs to the east and west of the harbor entrance, they compared the finding to Strabo's account. The ancient reefs are now partially covered by modern piers, and there is no sign of structural remains or artifacts on them.[344] Toward the center of the port is a low islet surrounded by reefs on which were discovered only a few archaeological vestiges—the foundations of a small wall coarse with uneven stones and mortar, other foundations of a small wall of the same quality in the south-eastern part, and a small pier that reinforces the eastern part of the islet.[345]

At the close of 1997 campaign, Goddio's team successfully mapped the reefs in the vicinity of the port entrance, Cape Lochias, where the kings's palaces and royal port lay, the peninsula where the temple of Poseidon stood, the island of Antirhodos, the ancient coast, and numerous ports once located inside the great Eastern Harbor.[346] Other key finds have included wood remains from an ancient pier and from a platform built during Ptolemaic times.[347] Wood remains from the platform, in particular, have been excavated on the site of a Royal House, suggesting that part of the royal district on the island had been leveled, along with the mortar platforms, before being paved.[348] In certain locations, the pavement and construction blocks have slid into the harbor and crushed ceramics such as amphorae, vases, and an oil lamp that were found underneath. Many of the artifacts date to the first and early second century AD, which may suggest the occurrence of a landslide under Roman rule.

In addition to structural finds, Goddio's team uncovered a number of artifacts, which he continues to use to fill books, museum displays, and segments of documentaries. Among his remarkable finds on the island of Antirhodos were a statue of the Great Priest of Isis holding a canopic jar and two Sphinxes, which were lying on limestone slabs. Both sphinxes have since been connected to the Ptolemaic kings, with

---

344. LaRiche, *The Sunken City*, 62.

345. Ibid.

346. Mission statements located at www.frankgoddio.org

347. Goddio has concluded that these wood remains also predate Alexandria's foundation but these findings are still under much debate.

348. Ibid.

one possibly representing Ptolemy XII, Cleopatra's father. Goddio's team also uncovered a large white marble statue depicting a Greek king in the form of the god Hermes and a fragmented head believed to be of Caesarian. In total, Goddio located and sketched more than 1,000 different artifacts, including columns, basins, sphinxes, statues, parts of obelisks with hieroglyphs, and ceramics. Goddio uncovered numerous remains bearing hieroglyphic inscriptions and uses the information to speculate about artifact use, origin and even ancient religious practices.[349] While large statuary finds typically were recycled, ceramics pulled out from under thick sedimentation clearly date from the third century BC to the first century AD.

Another landmark find was a Roman shipwreck located at the bottom of the harbor near Antirhodus Island. Most surprising, the vessel was found largely intact. Goddio's studies have since determined that the ship was empty when it went down since he found few artifacts on or near the wreck site. However, it is certainly feasible that the cargo was recovered after the vessel sank or the remains simply did not survive 2,000 years submerged in water. Artifacts that were discovered near the site include two gold rings found between two frames. Ceramics, glass, and coins were also uncovered along with rigging, ceramics and food remains. Goddio employed a naval architect to map the wreck site and documented the ship as ninety feet in length. Carbon dating places the vessel from 90 BC to AD 130.[350] The bottom of the hull lies close to the submerged antique pier, while the rest of the wreckage was found in the private harbor of Antirhodos island. Goddio believes that the ship may have been rammed by another boat, but he was unable to determine whether it was a warship or a cargo vessel.

Abu Kir

Outside of Alexandria's ancient harbors, Goddio directed other projects, including one at the Bay of Abu Kir. Located east of the old Greek capital, Abu Kir is a veritable gold mine of archaeological ruins,

349. Physical evidence relative to religious worship includes the god Agathodaimon (the 'Guiding Spirit') found in the shape of a snake is protector god of Alexandria.

350. Radiocarbon dating is based on the fact that all living things contain carbon, of which there are stable and radioactive types. Carbon-14 is the radioactive form and, once an organism dies, the level of Carbon-14 decays, shedding atomic particles at a constant rate. This rate can be

including the lost port city of Heracleion. Heracleion maintained a customs house and appears to have been an attractive entrance to Upper Egypt via the Nile. Goddio's team has dedicated several seasons to recording bottom contours and artifact locations. Through this process, his surveys also uncovered evidence of building sites, harbor structures, and several shipwrecks. Within the harbor installations, Goddio recovered a stele comparable to the Stele of Naukratis, which predates Alexandria's foundation. This particular artifact is also interesting as it specifically addresses taxes imposed on Greek items and is suggestive of the type of activity Egypt's north coast witnessed in terms of Greek trade. Other important finds include fragmented statues of a Pharaoh and a Queen. Both pieces were made of pink granite and date to the Ptolemaic period. The discovery of such important statues prompts Goddio to suggest that the site of their recovery may be the Great temple of Heracleion, which is affiliated with the Supreme God Amun.[351]

Heracleion is truly an exciting discovery for it provides added evidence of the geological changes that so greatly impacted Alexandria. The Heracleion site also opened doors for additional research in such places as the suburbs of Canopus, the more modern site of Napoleon's fleet, and other sites that have yet to be named. As sites begin to disclose artifacts from a variety of periods, historians and archaeologists develop a more complete understanding of Egyptian history and come to a better understanding of how particular sites were formed. Critical to this process is that the discoveries are made available to a wide spectrum of scholars to ensure the greatest opportunity for interpretation and understanding.

Presenting the Past

All successful historical investigations leave behind a detailed record of survey operations and findings. Without a complete site report, the world can never truly benefit from historical discoveries. Alexandria, however, is somewhat unique in that the research into the ancient city

---

measured using scientific equipment, and from it a date for the object can be obtained. Radiocarbon dating is best known for the dating of single objects and is mainly used for samples from excavations. A range of samples, rather than a single object, are taken from a site and it is important that the objects are not contaminated by modern materials. It can be used on anything that was once alive.

351. Mission reports from 1999/2000. Also included is an analysis from Prof. Jean Yoyette from the College de France in Paris.

has been recorded in extraordinary depth. Over the years countless books and articles have told the stories of ancient nobles and scholars who lived and died in Egypt's Greek city. Yet other media have had an outstanding impact on the popular audience. The principal avenue for these efforts came through television documentaries created with the cooperation of Goddio and Empereur. Goddio has established an exclusive partnership with the Discovery Channel toproduce a series of films on underwater archaeological discoveries. In return, the Discovery Channel is providing financial support to Goddio, in addition to the funds he receives from the Hilti Foundation. The initial run of Discovery's "Cleopatra's Palace: In Search of a Legend" reached 4.4 million viewers, with the expected worldwide viewership to approach 30 million. Likewise Empereur was featured in Nova's "Treasures of a Sunken City" in November 1997.

The combined excavations also produced artifacts presented in the traveling exhibit "Cleopatra of Egypt: From History to Myth." The exhibit toured Europe and the United States, attracting millions of patrons. The findings and international publicity have aided in a renaissance for the contemporary metropolis. In turn, the renewed interest sparked continued economic growth, which now presents a conspicuous danger to the submerged archaeological zone. What role does archeology play in this unique turn of events and what can we expect to discover in Alexandria now that these primary excavations have been completed?

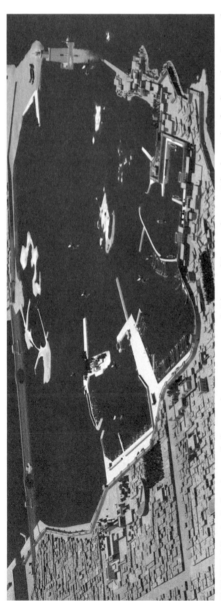

FIGURE 25: Artist's view of the sunken quarters of Alexandria as they might have looked at the time of Cleopatra. Created in 2001 and presented for the first time at the British Museum in London on April 10, 2001 by Franck Goddio. This view combines the data of the underwater surveys of Franck Goddio with information from ancient texts and archaeological evidence on land about parts of the ancient city, which are covered today by modern Alexandria. The blue structures are artistic renderings of ancient texts. The white parts of the map correspond to the actual results of Franck Goddio's surveys. Copyright: Hilti Foundation/Franck Goddio

TEN

The Future

FIGURE 26: Modern Library constructed on the site of the ancient Library in Alexandria. Photo: Kimberly Williams

More than 2,000 years after the death of Cleopatra, the ancient city of Alexander is at the center of the world's attention. The construction of the new library, coupled with modernization, means that our appreciation of the Greek city is being extended and transformed. With renewed attention, architects build tributes to the past while financiers develop a major economic center in the Mediterranean.

The role of archaeology in Alexandria's long history is a profound one. Discovery has drawn great political leaders and members of the academic community to examine the monumental finds from below the sea. The growing exchange of international co-operative movements have led to the development of even more archaeological and conservation projects, better standards in archaeological practices, and a meaningful dialogue of ideas and information concerning our ancient

141

past. This dialogue is also visible within Alexandria's academic network, as Egyptians build a community of scholars devoted to underwater archaeology and maritime history. Local archaeologists are developing their skills in European universities and returning to teach at the University of Alexandria.

While Goddio continues to investigate areas near Alexandria, the Supreme Council of Antiquities and the CEA, continue with their own projects within the city's boundaries. Members from each organization continue to share new developments and findings, while working with experts from around the globe. New government policies have been prompted by the discoveries and authorities continue to consider opening an underwater park to aid in protecting the site and to encourage tourism. In the field, INA members have completed extensive conservation workshops throughout Egypt to encourage better preservation of underwater artifacts.

In other arenas, geophysicists from France have begun a project to trace the causeway that connected the island of Pharos to the mainland. Working from the surface of the modern street network, specialists employed magnetic and electromagnetic survey equipment to uncover the line of the Heptastadion. Empereur is extending his research to include all periods of Alexandria history, working in partnerships with universities and government agencies. In particular, he is examining Alexandria's topography from the sixteenth to the beginning of the nineteenth century. Once completed, members will construct a cartographic database to display maps and the spatial organization of artifacts. All of this will profoundly contribute to our picture of early Egypt, the Ottoman Empire, and the Mediterranean Sea. The study is designed to provide a general framework of development in the area, to come to a better understanding of maritime ventures and to close gaps in our understanding of trade among these ancient ports.

International Contributions

Excavations continue in Egypt and around the world, leading to new developments within a variety of sciences and providing useful information and tools for knowledge. Just as members of the Egyptian community now refine their studies in European universities, scholars from around the globe continue their research in Alexandria. A dialogue has developed in which international thoughts and methods contribute to a greater understanding of our past. Each project opens the door to a better understanding of the ancient world as well as Alexandria. The discovery and examination of sites in the Red Sea will lend a hand to our understanding of ancient trade routes. The study of cargo remains above and below the sea have played a vital role in recreating the movement of goods.[352] Shipwreck archaeology will also shed light onto the development of Alexandria's supergalleys. By understanding harbor construction, we can gain insight into shipbuilding techniques and engineering advancements. At the same time, the collection of a database of ancient artifacts can assist with dating sites.[353] In addition, the exchange of ideas has led to the development of better archaeological practices. During the excavations in Alexandria, new standards have come together, which Alexandria's investigators have played a part in creating. Under the guidelines now extended by UNESCO, all archaeological excavations must meet specific guidelines.

The new standards stem in part from the response of the University of Alexandria, the SCA, and UNESCO to dilemmas raised by the excavations. Scientists and policymakers organized workshops in 1997 to discuss the protection of both the medieval fort and the ancient lighthouse. Archaeologists illustrated current challenges and methodological approaches encountered in underwater research. Geologists and oceanographers explained ocean current patterns, erosion processes, and their impacts on coastal archaeological sites. Coastal engineers offered alternative measures for mitigating coastal erosion. The conference resulted in a publication on a variety of specialized topics, which have proven beneficial to the academic community. Experts also recognized the importance of sound policymaking and the need for a comprehensive urban-planning process. Without an integrated management strategy

---

352. Surveys of a wreck site in Quseir have revealed Campanian amphoras from Italy dated to between the first century BC and first century AD. It is currently believed that the ship was outbound for India and was probably part of a fleet sent by Augustus to capture a controlling interest in the Indian Ocean trade.

353. For example, particular types of wood may indicate where a ship was constructed. And the occurrence of a dated object can also set a probable limit on when the site was formed, such as the occurrence of iron, which was not widely used before 1000 BC.

with expert advisers, Alexandria still faces serious problems in the areas of pollution and overpopulation.

Beyond Alexandria's borders, the joint UNESCO member states have accepted responsibility for protection of underwater sites in international waters. Because we are still in the early stages of inventing appropriate underwater preservation techniques, advancements in the diving world put underwater sites at risk. Treasure hunters have easier access to deep-water wrecks and previously unchecked pollution steps up corrosion of submerged artifacts. Therefore, UNESCO greatly needed to strengthen dialogue among decision-makers, stakeholders, and experts. Naturally, an international committee will be confronted with diverse viewpoints and understandings, but it would offer the best promise of a common, integrated solution that will allow modern cities like Alexandria to live in accord with their illustrious pasts.

The following list details the general criteria for archaeology and heritage management underwater as outlined in the charter of the International Committee on the Underwater Cultural Heritage in 1996.[354] These basic codes serve as a guideline of both archaeological record and underwater exploration as it has occurred in Alexandria, Egypt. The ICOMOS International Charter on the Protection and Management of Underwater Cultural Heritiage is intended to protect and manage underwater cultural heritage everywhere. UNESCO defines archaeological heritage as that part of the material heritage in respect of which archaeological methods provide primary information, comprising all vestiges of human existence and consisting of places relating to all manifestations of human activity, abandoned structures, and remains of all kinds, together with the portable cultural material associated with them.[355]

---

354. Preface to ICOMOS Charter by Th. J. Maarleveld. The UNESCO Recommendation on International Principles Applicable to Archaeological Excavations (New Delhi, 5 December 1956), The ICOMOS Charter for the Protection and Management of the Archaeological Heritage (Lausanne, 1990) and the new ICOMOS Charter on the Protection and Management of Underwater Cultural Heritage offer a consistent and rather comprehensive set of codes to which professionals and heritage organizations can commit themselves or on which they can base their own, more stringent codes of practice. Underwater Cultural Heritage includes any archaeological heritage taken from an underwater environment.

355. Ibid.

- *Principles* have been redefined with an emphasis on making sites more accessible to the public. Likewise, professional archaeologists are also obliged to protect sites through the employment of non-intrusive surveys and minimally damaging excavation procedures.

- *Project Plan:* Project plans must allow for conservation procedures of removed artifacts and continued historical research. Likewise, project plans must ensure that there will be adequate funding and provide contingency plans in the event that a project is left incomplete.

- *Funding:* Adequate funds must be assured in advance of investigation to complete all stages of the project design including conservation, research, report preparation and housing. Most importantly, project funding cannot include the sale of artifacts. In the event that artifacts should disappear, the entire project will be deemed unscientific.

- *Time Table:* A timetable must be clearly defined to ensure that the project plan will fall within reasonable limits and meet budget restraints.

- *Research Objectives* ensure that the investigation will maintain a conservation ethic as opposed to an exploitive base for investigation. Research objectives define the goals of the project in a manner, which will reduce contact with the site. Archaeological investigations should therefore be minimal intrusive.

- *Qualified Personnel:* As treasure hunters and "commercial" archaeologists gain access to underwater sites, the integrity of field research suffers. To counter exploitive ventures, which tend to omit conservation and limit historical research, archaeological teams need to impose tight restrictions on staff members. Ideally, the project should fall under the direction of a PhD with various specialists under his/her charge.

- *Preliminary Investigation* is critical to project planning and excavation. The initial surveys determine where divers will look for artifacts and confirm bottom conditions, which impose limitation on divers.

- *Conservation* is essential with artifact recovery as water soaked objects require special treatments if they are to survive. Artifact removal also necessitates that an object will have a home for eternity, as conserved artifacts are still prone to deterioration. Project plans should state which facility will treat the artifacts and budget concessions should provide for long-term care.

- *Documentation* should include field notes by team members, photographs, if visibility permits, detailed maps and publication in appropriate sources.

- *Management and Maintenance:* The program should include public information, monitoring and protection against interference. Site management should also include a persistent re-evaluation of procedures to assist in the development of future projects.

- *Health and Safety* is paramount. Alexandria in particular has placed divers at risk through water pollution, and the removal of colossal artifacts from the sea. Archaeological risks are then compounded by the usual hazards of diving, which can include decompression illness, strong currents and fatigue.

- *Regular Reports* are particularly important to check the project progress. Reports from the field may also open lines of communications from outside experts and permit investigators with opportunities to document processes beneficial to other underwater archaeologists.

- *Curation:* Simply because an artifact has been conserved does not ensure that it will have a long life. Conserved artifacts are still prone to deterioration and will require periodic inspection and evaluation. Therefore it is very important that artifacts remain in optimal conditions. Artifacts removed during investigation and a copy of all supporting documentation must be consigned to an institution that can provide for public access and permanent care. The host institution must be determined prior to investigation and all arrangements must be made within professional scientific standards; meaning items may not be traded for commercial value and if items are deposited in a number of institutions, this fact must not preclude reassembly to allow further research.

- *Dissemination:* Public awareness of recovered artifacts and the results of the investigations should be promoted through popular presentation in a range of media. Likewise, archaeologists should make every effort to involve local communities and interest groups in their investigations to the extent that such involvement does not threaten management or protection of the site. In addition, field projects should promote educational opportunities for the general public to develop archaeological skills. Collaboration with museums and other institutions is to be encouraged as future archaeological research will include restudy of recovered material for comparative analysis and to substantiate past research.

• *International Cooperation and Exchange of Professionals:* Underwater archaeology as a science is still in its infancy. Experts in the field are also relatively few. Therefore, it is imperative that such members endeavor to create an expanded community for which to share ideas and discoveries. Alexandria, in many ways, provides a model for this type of exchange through a broad spectrum of international communities that seek out ancient history from her shores.

Archaeologists in Alexandria have made profound and lasting contributions to the fields of history and archaeology. In addition to capturing our imaginations, the underwater sites have provided something all too real: a detailed portrait of Alexandria's great harbors. Currently, the underwater sites in Egypt continue to face decay as a modern city develops. Some nations place strict rules on underwater exploration, including the United States. Egypt, however, has taken a different approach, applying more general rules on excavations and the protection of sites.[356] Current Egyptian laws—such as the Antiquities Act No. 117 of 1983, the Law on Environment No. 4 and the Law on Natural Protectorates—could possibly create a special status for the sites by declaring them natural protectorates.[357] The World Heritage Committee may also offer protection if they accept Alexandria's Pharos site into the World Heritage List. This would represent a first for underwater sites, since the World Heritage List is now comprised entirely of terrestrial locations. Entry onto the list has proved challenging because

---

356. Legal Principles for Protecting Underwater Cultural Heritage by Lyndel V. Prott for the Sourcebook UNESCO, 131.

357. Ibid.

the Pharos site lacks a buffer zone and a detailed management plan. In general, underwater research and site management are under strong developmental pressure, which leads to critical problems in site preservation.

Alexandria's moment in the sun may be fading, but her potential as a goldmine of archaeological discovery cannot be understated. Alexandria distinguished herself in the ancient world by developing an extensive maritime network and a powerful navy. Like Athens, Rome, and countless other maritime powers, this city made vast contributions to the world through an exchange of people, goods, and ideas. Yet during the course of these events naval clashes, natural disasters, and shifts in sea levels led to the submersion of ships, cargo, and even parts of the city. An enormous wealth of archaeological record has accumulated below the surface and silently waits for underwater researchers to shed new light on the ancient remains.

Time Line

Before the Christian Era

334   Alexander departs from Athens with 160 ships.

       Siege and capture of Miletus.

332   Crosses the Hellespont.

       Siege of Tyre.

331   Foundation of Alexandria.

       Alexander returns to Tyre and reaches Thapsacus on the Euphrates.

327   Alexander begins Indian campaign.

325   Nearchus and the fleet reach Harmozia and regroup with Alexander at Salmous.

324   Nearchus's fleet sails to Susa.

       Death of Hephaestion.

323   Death of Alexander.

       Ptolemy Soter claims Egypt.

322/1   Ptolemy diverts Alexander's funerary carriage to Egypt.

321/0   Perdiccas loses two battles in the Nile and is killed by his officers.

319/18	Ptolemy annexes Phoenicia and Ceole-Syria.
315	Egypt sends 10,000 men and 100 ships to Cyprus.
314	Ptolemy loses Syria and Palestine.
313	Cyrene revolt.
312	Ptolemy takes Gaza and many other Phoenician cities.
310	Ptolemy's brother, Menelaus, becomes king of Cyprus.
307	Demetrius defeats Ptolemy in the Battle of Salamis, Cyprus.
306	Demetrius and Antigonus attempt to invade Egypt.
301	Egypt reclaims Syria and Phoenicia.
287	Egyptian navy sails to Greece to force Demetrius out.
286	Ptolemy now controls the League of Islanders.
285	Egypt claims Tyre and Sidon.
	Demetrius surrenders.
283	Reign of Ptolemy Philadelphus.
280	Pharos lighthouse completed.
276	Satyrus sails down African coast and settles Philotera.
275	Berenice becomes a trading port.
256	Rhodian victory over Egypt at the Battle of Ephesus.
246	Reign of Ptolemy III Euergetes.
	Egypt withdraws from the Aegean.
221	Reign of Ptolemy IV Philopator.
	First Roman intervention in the Greek world.
219	Antiocus III reclaims Seleukeia, Tyre, and Ptolemais.
204	Reign of Ptolemy V Epiphanes.

202	Roman victory over Carthage after the Second Punic War.
	Rome adopts expansionistic plan and begins moving into the eastern Mediterranean.
201	Philip V takes Samos and the Ptolemaic naval base stationed there.
200	Roman merchants begin settling in Alexandria.
180	Reign of Ptolemy VI Philometor.
170	Joint rule of Ptolemy VIII Euregetes II and Ptolemy VI Philometor.
167	Second Macedonian War: defeat of Macedon by Rome.
164	Ptolemy VIII Euergetes II becomes sole ruler of Egypt for one year.
146	Roman conquest of Greece.
145	Ptolemy VIII Euergetes II returns to Egypt.
	Ptolemy VII Neos Philopator assumes joint rule with Ptolemy VIII.
144	Death of Ptolemy VII Neos Philopator.
132	Cleopatra II leads successful revolt against Ptolemy VIII Euergetes II.
127	Ptolemy VIII reconquers Egypt and ruled with Cleopatra II and III.
116	Eudoxus of Cyzicus is credited with discovering the monsoons. Ptolemy IX Soter II elected joint ruler with Cleopatra III.
110	Joint rule of Ptolemy IX Soter II and Ptolemy X Alexander I.
108/7	Revolt forces Ptolemy IX Soter II to flee to Cyprus.
89/8	Ptolemy IX reconquers Egypt.
88	Thebiad revolt against Ptolemy IX Soter II.

80   Reign of Ptolemy XII Auletes.

66   Pompey the Great is given command of the Roman East.

        Final settlement of Selucid territories.

59   Caesar declares lawful kinship with Ptolemy XII Auletes.

51   Cleopatra and her young brother, Ptolemy XIII Philopator, take the throne.

48   Caesar arrives in Alexandria.

        Battle of Alexandria.

47   Cleopatra reinstated to throne with brother and co-regent Ptolemy XIV Philopator.

44   Death of Caesar.

43   Ptolemy XV Caesarian assumes joint rule with Cleopatra.

32   Octavian declares war on Antony and Cleopatra.

31   Battle of Actium.

        Death of Antony.

        Death of Cleopatra.

        Beginning of Roman rule.

Anno Domini

617   Persians capture Alexandria.

627   Persians evacuate Alexandria.

641   Romans attack Alexandria.

642   Romans evacuate the city.

645   Alexandrian revolt under Manuel.

646   Arabs recapture Alexandria.

658	Rule of Ommeyads of Damascus.
750	Rule of Abbasides.
875	Ahmed Ibn Touloum reduces Alexandria's wall perimeter.
944	El-Masoudi travels to Egypt and records the state of Pharos lighthouse.
956	Major earthquake hits Alexandria.
	Sections of the Pharos lighthouse begins to fall away.
1153-5	Normans attack Alexandria.
1265	City walls reconstructed.
1303-23	Subsequent earthquakes damage the lighthouse, reducing it to rubble.
1347	Ibn Battula reports that he cannot enter the lighthouse, nor reach its doorway.
1365	Cyprus invades Alexandria and sets fire to the city.
1480	Qaitbay constructs a fort on the site of Pharos, using fallen stones.
1892	Foundation of the Graeco-Roman Museum.
1911	Gaston Jondet discovers massive maritime structures below the sea while working on the Western Harbor.
1933	Prince Omar Tousson organizes a team to recover artifacts from Abu Kir, east of Alexandria.
1961	Kamal Abu el-Saadat discovers Ptolemaic statues submerged in the Eastern Harbor.
1962	Navy divers raise colossal statue of Isis from the Eastern Harbor.
1968	Honor Frost conducts a survey of Alexandria with el-Saadat. First plans of the Pharos site.

1993   Film maker Asma el-Bakri discovers ruins beneath construction of a breakwater.

1996   Jean-Yves Empereur begins underwater excavations of Pharos lighthouse site.

Franck Goddio begins underwater excavations of Ancient Royal Quarter in the Eastern Harbor.

Founding of the Department of Underwater Archaeology (DUA) of the Supreme Council for Antiquities.

References

Primary Sources

Appain. *The Civil Wars.* Translated by John Carter. New York: Penguin Books, 1996.

Apollonius. *Argonautika.* Translated by Peter Green. Berkeley: University of California Press, 1997.

Arrian. *Annabis.* Translated by P. A. Brunt. Cambridge: Harvard University Press, 1976.

Athenaeus. *Deipnosophists. Translated by Charles B. Gulick.* Cambridge: Harvard University Press, 1969.

Caesar. *De bello Alexandria.* Translated by Jane F. Mitchell. Baltimore: Penguin Press, 1967.

Demosthenes. *Private Orations. Translated by A.T. Murray.* Cambridge: Harvard University Press, 1954.

Diodorus Siculus. *Biblioteke.* Translated by C.H. Oldfather. Cambridge: Harvard University Press, 1935.

Dio Cassius. *Roman History.* Translated by Earnest Cary. Cambridge: Harvard University Press, 1954.

Florus. *Epitome of Roman History.* Translated by E.S. Forster. London: Heinemann, Ltd., 1929

Homer. *Odyssey.* Translated by Samuel Butler and ed. Louise Ropes Loomis. New York: Walter J. Black, 1944.

Livy. *The History of Rome.* Translated by Canon Roberts. New York: E.P. Dutton, 1924.

Orosius. *The Seven Books of Pagan History.* Translated by Roy J. Deferrari. Washington: Catholic University of America Press, 1964.

Pausanias. *Description of Greece.* Translated by W.H.S. Jones. Cambridge: Harvard University Press, 1935.

Pliny the Elder, *Natural History.* Translated by John F. Healy. London: Penguin Books, 1991.

Plutarch. *Lives.* Translated by Tim Duff. Oxford: Clarendon Press, 1999.

Polybius. *Universal History.* Translated by W.R. Paton. Cambridge: Harvard University Press, 1960.

Pseudo-Callistenes. *The Romance of Alexander the Great.* Translated by Albert Mugrdich Wolohojian. New York: Columbia University Press, 1969.

Strabo. *Geography.* Translated by Horace Leonard Jones. London: Heinemann; Cambridge, Harvard University Press, 1954.

Theocritus. *Idylls.* Translated by A.S.F. Gow. New York: Cambridge University Press, 1950.

Vitruvius. *De architectura.* Translated by Ingrid D. Rawland. New York: Cambridge University Press, 1999.

Xenophon. *Oeconomicus.* Translated by Sarah B. Pomeroy. Oxford: Clarendon Press, 1994.

Secondary Sources

Adams, William Y. *Nubia: Corridor to Africa.* Princeton University Press, 1977.

Abd El Fattah, Ahmed and Mieczyslaw Rodziewicz. "Recent Discoveries in the Royal Quarter of Alexandria." *Bulletin of the Society Archaeology D'Alexandrie,* Alexandria: Alexandrian Archaeological Society. 49 [1991].

Abd El Ghani, Mohamed. "Coptos and its Role in the Eastern Trade of the RomanEmpire." *L'egitto In Italia: Dall'antichita al Medioevo.* Roma:Consiglio Nazionale Delle Ricerche, 1995.

Aston, Mick and Tim Taylor, *The Atlas of Archaeology.* New York: DK Publishing Inc., 1998.

Bagnal, Roger S. *The Administration of the Ptolemaic Possessions Outside Egypt.* Leiden: Brill, 1976.

Ashour, Mohamed Hamdi. *The History and Civilization of Alexandria Across the Ages.* Kalyoub, Egypt: AL-AHRAM Commercial Presses.

Babits, Lawrence E. and Hans Van Tilburg. *Maritime Archaeology: A Reader of Substantive and Theoretical Contributions.* New York: Plenum Press, 1998.

Barstad, Jane and Carol Ruppe. "Underwater Archaeology in Egypt" *International Handbook of Underwater Archaeology.* Kluwer Academic/Plenum Publishers, 2002.

Bentham, R.M. *The Fragments of Erastosthenes.* Unpublished PhD thesis, London: University of London, 1948.

Berthold, Richard. *Rhodes in the Hellenistic Age.* Ithica: Cornell University Press, 1984.

Bevan, Edwyn. *History of Egypt Under the Ptolemaic Dynasty.* London: Methuen and Co. Ltd., 1927.

Billows, Richard. *Antigonus the One Eyed and the Creation of the Hellenistic State.* Berkeley: University of California Press, 1990.

Bowman, Alan K. *Egypt after the Pharaohs: 332 BCE-AD 642 From Alexander to the Arabs.* Berkeley: The University of California Press, 1986.

Brecia, E. *Alexandrea and Aegyptum: A Guide to the Ancient and Modern Town and It's Graeco-Roman Museum.* Bergamo:Instituto Italiano D'Arti Grafiche, 1922.

Blackman, D. "Ancient Harbors in the Mediterranean." *International Journal of Nautical Archaeology.* 11.2. (1982): p.79-104.

Blackman, D. *Marine Archaeology.* Hamden, Co.: Archon Books, 1973.

Brodie, Neil and Kathryn Walker Tubb, ed. *Illicit Antiquities: The Theft of Culture and the Extinction of Archaeology.* New York: Routledge, 2002.

Brown, Blanch R. "Deinokrates and Alexandria." *Bulletin, American Society of Papyrologists* 15 (1978): p. 39-42.

Burcaw, G. Ellis. *Introduction to Museum Work.* Walnut Creek; Alta Mira Press, 1997.

Butler, Alfred J. *The Arab Conquest of Egypt and the Last Thirty Years of Roman Domination.* Oxford: Clarendon Press, 1978.

Byrd, Daryl. *Piracy in the Mediterranean.* Unpublished MA thesis, Greenville, NC: East Carolina University, 1998.

Carlton, Walker. "Ancient Warships 700-31 BCE." *Journal of the Society of Ancient Numismatics* 4 (1972): p.12-17.

Carol, Michael. "Ancient Wonder Found." *Popular Science,* 248, 4 1996, p.24.

Cary, M. *A History of the Greek World from 323 to 146 BCE.* London: Metheun and Co., 1932.

Cary, M. and E. H. Warmington. *The Ancient Explorers.* London: Methuen and Co., 1990.

Casson, Lionel. *Ships and Seafaring in Ancient Times.* London: British Museum Press, 1994.

Casson, Lionel. "Graeco-Roman Trade in the Indian Ocean," *The Greeks and the Sea.* New Rochelle: Aristide D. Caratzas, 1993.

Casson, Lionel. *Ancient Trade and Society.* Detroit: Wayne State University Press, 1984.

Casson, Lionel. *The PeriplusMaris Erythraei* Princeton: Princeton University Press, 1989.

Casson, Lionel. *Ships and Seamanship in the Ancient World.* Baltimore: Johns Hopkins University Press, 1971.

Casson, Lionel. "The Supergalleys of the Hellenistic Age." *Mariner's Mirror* 55 (1969): p. 185-193.

Colt, George Howe. "Raising Alexandria." *Life* 19, 5 1996, p.70-75.

De Souza, Philip. *Piracy in the Graeco-Roman World.* Cambridge: Cambridge University Press, 1999.

Delgado, James P. *The Encyclopedia of Underwater Archaeology.* New Haven: Yale University, 1997.

Delia, Diana. "All Army Boots and Uniforms, Ethnicity in Ptolemaic Egypt." *Alexandria and Alexandrianism.* Malibu: J. Paul Getty Museum, 1995.

Dilke, O.A.W. *Greek and Roman Maps.* London: Thames and Hudson, 1985.

Dwyer, Eugene J."Temporal Allegory of the Tazza Farnese." *International Journal of Nautical Archaeology* 96, 2 (1992): p. 255-282.

El-Abbadi, Mustafa."*The Life and Fate of the Ancient Library of Alexandria.*" Paris: UNESCO, 1990.

Ellis, Walter M. *Ptolemy of Egypt.* New York: Routledge, 1994.

Empereur, Jean-Yves. *Alexandria Jewel of Egypt.* New York: Harry N. Abrams, Inc., 2001.

Empereur, Jean-Yves. "Diving on a Sunken City." *Archaeology* 52, 2 (1999), 38-46.

Empereur, Jean-Yves. *Alexandria Rediscovered.* New York: George Braziller, 1998.

Empereur, Jean-Yves (ed.) *Commerce et Artisanant dans l'Alexandrie hellénistique et romaine, actes du colloque d"Athénes (Bulletin de Correspondance Hellénique Supplément),* Paris: Ecole Francaise D'Athénes, 1998.

Engels, Donald. *Alexander the Great and the Logistics of the Macedonian Army.* Berkeley: University of California Press, 1978.

Ezzat, Dina."The Secrets of Cleopatra." *Middle East* 264 (1997): p. 38-9.

Folly, Vernard and Werner Soedel. "Ancient Oared Warships." *Scientific American.* (July 1998): p. 148-163.

Foreman, Laura and Ellen Blue Phillips. *Napolean's Lost Fleet.* New York: Discovery Books, 1999.

Foreman, Laura. *Cleopatra's Palace.* New York: Discovery Books, 1999.

Foster, John W. and Sheli O. Smith *Proceeding of the Seventeenth Annual Conference of Underwater Archaeology, 1986.* Salinas, CA: Cayote Press, 1988.

Fox, Robin Lane. "Hellenistic Culture and Literature." *The Oxford History of Greece and the Hellenistic World.* Oxford: Oxford University Press, 1991.

Fraser, P.M. *Cities of Alexander the Great.* Oxford: Clarendon Press, 1996.

Fraser, P.M. *Ptolemaic Alexandria.* Oxford: Clarendon Press, 1972.

Frost, Honor. "The Pharos Site, Alexandria Egypt." *International Journal of Nautical Archaeology* 4.1 (1975): p.126-130.

Frost, Honor. *Under the Mediterranean; Marine Antiquities.* London, Routledge and K. Paul, 1963.

Gabrielson, Vincent. *The Naval Aristocracy of Hellenistic Rhodes.* Aarhus: Aarhus University, 1997.

Grant, Michael. *Cleopatra.* New York: Simon and Schuster, 1973.

Green, Peter. "Alexander's Alexandria." *Alexandria and Alexandrianism*. Malibu: J. Paul Getty Museum, 1995.

Green, Peter. *Alexander to Actium: The Hellenistic Age*. London: Thames and Hudson, 1993.

Gardiner, Robert ed. *The Age of the Galley: Mediterranean Oared Vessels Since Pre-Classical Times*. Annapolis: Naval Institute Press, 1995.

Green, Jeremy N. *Maritime Archaeology: A Technical Handbook*. San Diego, CA: Academic Press, 1990.

Greenhill, Basil ed. *Conway's History of the Ship: The Age of the Galley*. London: Conway Maritime Press, 1995.

Goodio, Frank. *Alexandria, The Submerged Royal Quarter*. London: Periplus 1998.

Guillerm, Alain. *La Marine de Guerre Antique*. Paris: Knosos, 1993.

Haas, Christopher. *Antiquity: Topography and Social Conflict* Baltimore:Johns Hopkins University Press, 1997.

Hacket, Sir John. "Warfare in the Ancient World." *Facts on File*. New York: 1989.

Hamilton, Donny L. *Basic Methods of Conserving Underwater Archaeological Material Culture*. Washington, D.C. : U.S. Dept. of Defense, Legacy Resource Management Program, 1996.

Hammond, Nicholas. *The Genius of Alexander the Great*. London: Duckworth, 1997.

Hauben, Hans. *Callicates of Samos: A Contribution to the Study of the Ptolemaic Admiralty*. Leuven:Leuvense Universitaire Uitigaven, 1970.   Hauben, Hans. "Antigonus's Invasion Plan for his Attack on Egypt in 306 BCE." *Orientia Lovanien Sia Periodica* 6/7 (1990): p. 267-271.

Hauben, Hans. "The Expansion of Macedonian Sea Power Under Alexander the Great." *Ancient Society* 7 (1991): p.79-105.

Hauben, Hans."Fleet Strength at the Battle of Salamis." *Chiron* 6 (1976): p.1-5.

Hitti, Philip K. *Lebanon in History: From the Earliest Times to the Present*. London: Macmillan and Co., 1990.

Hyde, Walter Woodburn. *Ancient Greek Mariners*. New York: Oxford University Press, 1947.

Kemp, Peter. *The History of Ships*. London: Orbis Publishing, 1978.

Kennedy, Hugh. *The Historiography of Islamic Egypt*. Boston: Brill, 2001.

Khalil, Emad. *Maritime Activity in Alexandria Harbour from the Bronze Age to the Roman Period*. Unpublished MA thesis, Southampton: Southampton University, 2002.

Kosso, Peter. *Knowing the Past: Philosophical Issues of History and Archaeology*. Amherst: Humanity Books, 2001.

Lawrence, Bonnie S. *The Wonder's of the World*. Washington D.C.: National Geographic Society, 1998.

Mahaffy, J.P. *A History of Egypt under the Ptolemaic Dynasty.* London: Methuen and Co., 1914.

Mahaffy, J.P. *The Ptolemaic Dynasty.* London: Methuen and Co., 1899.

Mahan, A.T. *The Influence of Sea Power Upon History, 1660-1805.* Englewood Cliffs, NJ.: Prentice-Hall, 1980.

Mark, Samuel. *From Egypt to Mesopotamia : A Study of Predynastic Trade Routes.* College Station, Tex. : Texas A and M University Press, 1998.

McFee, William. *The Law of the Sea.* New York: J.B. Lippincott Company, 1950.

Meiggs, Russel. *Trees and Timber in the Ancient World.* Clarendon Press, Oxford. 1990.Moore, Robert. *The Evolution of the Greek Warship and Its Tactics in the Fourth Century.* Unpublished MA thesis, Greenville, NC.: East Carolina University, 1992.

Morrison, J.S. *Greek and Roman Oared Warships.* Oxford: Oxbow, 1996.

Morrison, J.S. and J.F. Coates. *The Athenian Trireme.* Cambridge University Press, 1986.

Mostafa, M., N. Grimal and D. Nakashima. *Underwater Archaeology and Coastal Management: Focus on Alexandria.* Washington DC: UNESCO. 2000.

Muckelroy, Keith. *Maritime Archaeology.* New York : Cambridge University Press, 1978.

Murray, William M. "Reconstructing the Battle of Actium," *New Interpretations in Naval Warfare: Selected Papers from the Eleventh National History Symposium* Annapolis: Naval Institute Press, 2001.

Naphtali, Lewis. *Greeks in Ptolemaic Egypt.* New York: Oxford University Press, 1986.

Nibbi, Alessandr. "Five Stone Anchors from Alexandria." *International Journal of Nautical Archaeology* 20, 3 (1991): p.185-194.

Parker, A.J. "Shipwrecks and Ancient Trade in the Mediterranean." *Archaeological Review from Cambridge* 3,2 (1994): p.99-113.

Page, D.L. *Greek Literary Papyri.* I. P444-447, no. 104.

Parker, A.J. "Cargoes, Containers and Stowage: the Ancient Mediterranean." *International Journal of Nautical Archaeology.* 21,2 (1992), p.89-100.

Parker, A.J. "Classical Antiquity: The Maritime Dimension." *Antiquity,* 64:335-46.

Parker, A.J. "The Mediterranean, an Underwater Museum." *Courier,* (UNESCO): 8-9.

Peacock, D. P. S. and D. F. Williams. *Amphorae and the Roman Economy.* London: Longman Group Limited, 1986.

Peacock, D. P. S. *Pottery in the Roman World.* London: Longman Group Limited, 1982.

Peacock, D. P. S. *Pottery and Early Commerce: Characterization and Trade in Roman and Later Ceramics.* New York: Academic Press, 1977.

Pearson, Lionel. "The Lost Histories of Alexander the Great." *American Philological Association.* New York: Philological Monographs, 20 (1960).

Polony, Karl. *The Livelihood of Man.* New York: Academic Press, *1977.*

Reger, Gary. *Regionalism and the Change in the Economy of Independent Delos, 314-167 BCE.* Berkley: University of California Press, 1994.

Rice, E.E. The *Grand Procession of Ptolemy's Philadelphus.* London: Oxford University Press, 1983.

Rodgers, Bradley A. *The ECU's Conservator's Cookbook.* Greenville: East Carolina University, 1992.

Rodgers, William Ledyard. *Greek and Roman Naval Warfare.* Annapolis: Naval Institute Press, 1937.

Rostovtzeff, M. *The Social and Economic History of the Hellenistic World.* London: Claredeon Press, 1941.

Rouge, Jean. *Ships and Fleets of the Ancient Mediterranean.* Translated by Susan Fraser. Middletown, Conn.: Wesleyan University Press, 1981.

Schuster, Angela. "Mapping Alexander's Royal Quarters." *Archaeology* 52,2 (1999): p. 44-46.

Sedge, Michael. "Cleopatra's Sunken Palace." *Discovering Archaeology* 1, 2 (1999): p.38-44.

Sedler, Jean W. *India and the Greek World.* Totowa, N.J.: Rowman and Littlefield, 1980.

Sekunda, Nick. *Seleucid and Ptolemaic Reformed Armies 168-145 BCE, vol. 2.* Yorkshire, UK.: Yorkshire Montvert Publications, 1994.

Sinnigen, William and Arthur Boak. *The History of Rome to AD 565.* New York: McMillan Publishing Co., 1977.

Slayman, Andrew. "Pharos Sculpture Recovered." *Archaeology* 49,1 (1996): p.22-23.

Sly, Dorothy I. *Philo's Alexandria.* New York: Routledge, 1996.

Smith, Clifford E. *Conservation of Cultural and Biological Remains : an Integral Part of the Archaeological Process Required to Preserve and Protect the Cultural Resources from the Emanuel Point Shipwreck.* Thesis (M.A.) University of South Florida, 1995.

Steffy, Richard J. *Wooden Ship Building and the Interpretation of Shipwrecks.* College Station: Texas A and M University Press, 1994.

Tarn, W.W. "Alexander's Plans." *Journal of Hellenistic Studies* 59 (1939): p. 124-35.

Tarn, W.W. "Greek Warship." *Journal of Hellenistic Studies* 25 (1905): p.137-214.

Tarn, W.W. "The Dedicated Ship of Antigonus Gonatas." *Journal of Hellenistic Studies*Vol. 30 (1910): p.209.

Tarn, W.W. "Ptolemy II and Arabia." *Journal of Egyptian Archaeology* Vol. 15 (1929).

Tarn, W.W. *Hellenistic Military and Naval Developments.* Cambridge: Cambridge University Press, 1910.

Tarn, W.W. *Antigonus Gonatas.* Oxford: Clarendon Press, 1911.

Tkaczow, Barbara. *Topography of Ancient Alexandria: An Archaeological Map.* Warszawa: Zaklad Archeologii Srodziemnomorskiej, 1993.

Throckmorton, Peter. *The Sea Remembers.* New York: Weidenfied and Nicholson, 1987.

Thomsen, R. *Early Roman Coinage.* Aarhus: Aarhus University Press, 1971.

Tilley, A.F. Warship of the Ancient Mediterranean. *The American Neptune* 50 (1990): p.192-200.

Weigall, Arthur. *The Life and Times of Marc Antony.* London: Thorton Butterworth Limited, 1931.

Williams, Kimberly. *The Development of Alexandria's Maritime History and Ptolemaic Naval Policy.* Unpublished MA thesis, Greenville, NC: East Carolina University, 2000.

Yehya, Lutfi A. W. *India and Egypt: Influences and Interactions.* Bombay: Marg Publications and the Council for Cultural Relations, 1993.

Definitions of Place Names, People, and Terms

Absolute Dating: Dates expressed as specific units of scientific measurement such as days or years; absolute determinations attempt to pinpoint a discrete, known interval in time.

Actium: The location of the naval battle between Octavian and Mark Antony. Octavian's victory left him the undisputed master of the Roman world and marks the close of the Hellenistic Age.

Airlift: An archaeological device that is used to remove sterile overburden and take sediments to the surface

Alexander the Great: King of Macedonia who overthrew the Persian Empire and laid the foundations of the Hellenistic World.

Alexandria: The capital of Egypt after its founding in 332 BC and in antiquity was a center of Hellenistic scholarship and science.

Antigonus I: Antigonus the "One-Eyed" was a Macedonian general under Alexander the Great who founded the Macedonian dynasty of the Antigonids in 306 BC.

Antigonus II: Antigonus Gonataswas the king of Macedonia from 276 BC and was responsible for rebuilding the kingdom's power and establishing authority over Greece.

Antiochus I Soter: Ruled Syria and much of Asia Minor after the assassination of his father Seleucus Nicator.

Antiochus II Theos: Reigned from 261-247 BC and made peace with Egypt after marrying the daughter of Ptolemy Philadelphus.

Antiochus III the Great: Engaged in wars with Egypt and conquered Palestine and Coele-Syria.

Antiochus IV Epiphanes: Laid siege to Alexandria between 171 BC and 168 BC until Romans forced him to relinquish his ambitions.

Antony, Marc: Roman general under Julius Caesar who was defeated by Octavian in the last of the Civil Wars, which destroyed the Roman Republic.

Aphract: Open air ship without mesh netting to protect marines from arrows and debris.

Applied archaeology: The use of archaeological techniques to conserve sites.

Archaeological record: The surviving physical remains of past human activity.

Archaeological site: Any concentration of artifacts, features, or ecofacts manufactured or modified by humans.

Archaeology: The study of human past through reconstructing past lifeways with the ultimate goal of discovering the processes that underlie and condition human behavior.

Aristotle: Ancient Greek philosopher and scientist whose writings have long influenced Western and Muslim thought.

Arsinoe II: Daughter of Berenice and Ptolemy I Soter. She eventually married her brother Ptolemy II Philadelphus.

Artaba: Egyptian unit of measurement of volume of grains.

Artifact: An object used or shaped by human workmanship.

Asp: Name used in classical antiquity to mean a venomous snake. Its bite was used in criminal executions during Graeco-Roman times.

Bas-relief: a sculpture in which the figures project slightly from the background

Berenice: Wife of Ptolemy I Soter and mother of Ptolemy II Philadelphus.

Brutus: Roman senator famed as a leader of conspirators who assassinated Julius Caesar on the Ides of March 44 BC.

Caesar, Julius: Roman general and statesman whose dictatorship was pivotal in Rome's transition from republic to empire.

Cataphract: A ship with mesh netting to protect marines from arrows and debris.

Cartouche: Oval shield or oblong scroll, used as a graphic ornament to bear the names of royal or divine personages.

Cassander: Son of Antipater and King of Macedon who gained control of Athens in 317 BC.

Casting: The process of casting natural molds left by corroded artifacts.

Cataloging: Assigning an artifact to one or more categories of an organized classification system.

Cleomenes: A prominent businessman and engineer who came to control Egypt, prior to Ptolemy Soter's rule, when Alexander the Great made him treasurer.

Cleopatra III: was the niece of Physcon (Ptolemy VIII Euergetes II) and was married to him while her mother was still his official wife. She bore Physcon two sons—Ptolemy IX Philometor Soter II (Lathyros) and Ptolemy X Alexander I as well as three daughters, Cleopatra IV, Cleopatra Tryphaena, and Cleopatra Selene. In Physcon's will he left his throne to Cleopatra and to whichever son she preferred.

Cleopatra IV: Was co-regent with her brother Ptolemy IX until her mother annulled the arrangement. Then she went to Cyprus where she tried to raise an army and to marry Ptolemy Alexander. She failed to marry him and moved on to Syria where she used her army as a dowry and married Antiochus IX Cyzicenus who was son of Antiochus Sidetes and Cleopatra Thea (her sister).

Cleopatra VII Philopator: Queen of Egypt and last ruler of the Ptolemaic Dynasty.

Culture: The nonbiological mechanism of human adaptation.

Data: Relevant observations made on objects that then serve as the basis for study and discussion.

Datum point: The zero point, a fixed reference used to keep vertical control on a dig. When combined with a grid system, archaeologists can plot any find on a three-dimensional system.

Demetrius: Antigonus's benefactor who entered an arms race with the Ptolemies, leading to the development of larger supergalleys, which he used to defeat Ptolemy near Cyprus.

Demosthenes: The greatest orator of ancient Athens who strongly opposed Macedonian expansion in Greece.

Diekplous: An important maneuver in ancient sea battles where a ship sails through an opening in the enemy line to gain a better position for ramming and/or sheering off the enemy's oars.

Diodorus: Greek historian and author of *Bibliotheca historica,* a universal history recounted in forty books.

Dionysus: The god of fruitfulness and vegetation, especially the vine, hence he is also remembered as the god of wine.

Direct Survey Method: A technique for mapping the x,y,z coordinates of a point on a site.

Egyptology: The study of dynastic Egypt and its relics.

Epigraphy: The study of inscriptions.

Eudoxus: Ancient historians argued that Eudoxus of Cyzicus discovered the sea route to India around 116 BC and opened up Greek trade in the Red Sea.

Excavation: The process of uncovering a site by removing spoil or intrusive material, observing and identifying the archaeological material, and then recording and recovering it.

Exhibition: An assemblage of artifacts through which visitors move from unit to unit in a sequence designed to be instructionally meaningful. Accompanying labels and/or graphics are planned to interpret, explain, and direct the viewer's attention.

Feature: The nonportable evidence of technology.

Field Notes: The written record containing first hand, on-the-spot observations; field notes are considered primary data in the field.

Geographical Information Systems (GIS): Computer hardware and software that allows input, editing storage, retrieval, viewing, manipulation, comparison, interpretation, analysis, and display of spatiality referenced data.

Global Positioning Systems (GPS): Twenty-four Department of Defense satellites orbiting the earth that transmit signals used for ranging to develop an accurate position on the earth's surface. **Hellenism:** The term designating the civilization produced by the ancient Greeks, of Hellenes.

Hieroglyphs: A picture or symbol representing an object, idea or sound, as in the writing system of the ancient Egyptians.

In situ: A term referring to the position in which an item was initially encountered during an excavation or survey.

Isis: In the Hellenistic period, Ptolemaic queens identified themselves with the Egyptian goddess. In earlier times she was associated with the deification of the royal throne. Later she was worshiped as a mystical mother goddess.

Karnak: Collection of temples one-and-a-half miles north of Luxor on the Upper Egyptian Nile, marking the religious capital of the ancient Egyptian Empire.

Levant: A term widely once widely used to refer to the region bordering the eastern shore of the Mediterranean Sea, compromising the present countries of Greece, Turkey, Syria, Lebanon, Egypt, and islands located near these countries.

Macedonia: A geographic area in the southern part of the Balkan Peninsula.

Magnetometer: An instrument that measures the magnetic field of the earth. It is an important tool in archaeological surveys because it can detect ferrous material buried in the sea floor.

Maritime Archaeology: The study of underwater material evidence with a focus on social and historical characteristics of the maritime environment.

Nearchus: An experienced ship's captain who served under Alexander the Great and was given command of the naval expedition in the east.

Nile: The longest river in the world extending from east-central Africa to the Mediterranean Sea.

Obelisk: A tall, four-sided shaft of stone that rises to a point.

Octavia: Sister of Octavian and wife of Marc Antony.

Octavian: Succeeded Julius Caesar as Emperor of Rome and defeated Antony in the Battle of Actium.

Papyrus: A plant cultivated for centuries before the discovery of paper in Syria and Egypt and introduced to other countries as the most important writing material of ancient times.

Periplous: Another important battle technique, which literally translates into "sailing around" with the intention of outflanking the enemy and attacking from the rear or side.

Phase: An archaeological construct possessing traits sufficiently characteristic to distinguish it form other units similarly conceived, spatially limited to roughly a locality or region and chronologically limited to a relative brief interval in time.

Plutarch: Greek biographer famed for his *Parallel Lives.*

Prefect: Governor of Egypt.

Provenance: The location from which an artifact came from. In the context of a specific site, it refers to the horizontal and vertical position of an object in relation to the establish coordinate system.

Ptolemy Apion: (116–96 BC) Ruler of Cyrenaica who separated it from Egypt and in his will bequeathed the country to Rome. Son of Ptolemy VIII Euergetes II, king of Egypt, by a concubine.

Ptolemy I Soter: (Greek: Savior) born 367/366 BC or 364 BC, died 283/ 282 BC. Macedonian general of Alexander the Great, who became ruler of Egypt (323–285 BC) and founder of the Ptolemaic dynasty.

Ptolemy II Philadelphus: (Greek: Brother-loving) born 308 BC, Cos died 246 BC. King of Egypt (285–246 BC), second king of the Ptolemaic dynasty, who extended his power by skillful diplomacy, developed agriculture and commerce, and made Alexandria a leading center of the arts and sciences.

Ptolemy III Euergetes: (Greek: Benefactor) Flourished 246–221 BC. Macedonian king of Egypt, son of Ptolemy II; he reunited Egypt and Cyrenaica and successfully waged the Third Syrian War against the Seleucid kingdom.

Ptolemy IV Philopator: (Greek: Loving His Father) born c. 238 BC, –d. 205 BC. Macedonian king of Egypt (reigned 221–205 BC), under whose feeble rule, heavily influenced by favorites, much of Ptolemaic Syria was lost and native uprisings began to disturb the internal stability of Egypt.

Ptolemy V Epiphanes: (210-180 BC) King of Egypt after 205 BC. Under his rule, the Ptolemaic empire lost Coele Syria and most of Egypt's other foreign possessions.

Ptolemy VI Philometor: (Greek: Loving His Mother) flourished c. 180 –145 BC. Macedonian king of Egypt under whom an attempted invasion of Coele Syria resulted in the occupation of Egypt by the Seleucids. After Roman intervention and several ventures of joint rule with his brother, however, Ptolemy was able to reunite his realm. The son of Ptolemy V Epiphanes and Cleopatra I, Ptolemy VI ruled as co-regent with his mother.

Ptolemy VII Neos Philopator (145 BC) was the seventh ruler of the Ptolemaic Dynasty. He was the son of Ptolemy VI Philometor and Cleopatra II. Upon Philometor's death, Cleopatra's son, who was about sixteen years old and had been appointed co-ruler by his father earlier that year, became king under his mother's regency. Philopator's uncle Physcon (Ptolemy VIII Euergetes II) wanted to rule and married Cleopatra to gain the throne. Philopator was killed during the wedding feast.

Ptolemy VIII Euergetes II (145-116 BC): Son of Ptolemy V and the brother of Ptolemy VI. Often portrayed as a cruel despot but he is credited with administrative reform and liberal endowment of religious institutions. The empire became permanently disunited after his death.

Ptolemy IX Soter II (115-107 and 88-80 BC) was initially a co-regent with Cleopatra III. She hated Ptolemy IX but Alexandrians wanted him as co-regent. He was then governor of Cyprus and brought back to Alexandria to co-rule and eventually married Cleopatra IV, his sister, but his mother repudiated the marriage and replaced her with Cleopatra Selene, who was also his sister. Cleopatra III finally succeeded in driving out Ptolemy IX in 107 BC when she accused him of trying to murder her. His brother, Alexander, returned from Cyprus and assumed the throne. After the death of Alexander in a naval battle, Lathyros was brought back to Alexandria to try to put back together the Ptolemaic empire. He died at the age of sixty-two and left no legitimate heir to the throne, both of his sons by Cleopatra Selene appear to have died at a young age. His daughter Cleopatra Berenice ruled alone for a while after his death.

Ptolemy X Alexander I (107-88 BC) Replaced Ptolemy IX as junior ruler under Cleopatra III in September 107, incorporated in the dynastic cult with Cleopatra III at that time as the Mother-loving Saviour Gods, became senior ruler associated with Berenice III. Later drowned in a sea battle while attempting to invade Cyprus.

Ptolemy XI Alexander II (80 BC) was the son of Ptolemy X Alexander. After the death of his uncle Ptolemy IX Soter II (Lathyros), his stepmother (or possibly mother) Cleopatra Berenice ruled for about one year alone. Ptolemy XI was required to marry his stepmother, who was much older than he. The marriage took place and nineteen days later; Ptolemy XI killed his new bride. He was then lynched by the Alexandrian mob, with whom his wife had been very popular

Ptolemy XII Auletes: (Greek: Flute Player), born *c.* 112 BC, died 51 BC. Macedonian king of Egypt, whose quasi-legitimate royal status compelled him to depend heavily upon Rome for support of his throne. During his reign Egypt virtually became a client kingdom of the Roman republic.

Ptolemy XII Philopator: (51-47 BC) Ruled jointly with Cleopatra after the death of Ptolemy XII Auletes. He eventually drove his sister into exile and battled Caesar in the Battle of Alexandria.

Ptolemy XIV Philopator: (Born in 60 or 59 died 47) The second brother/husband of Cleopatra who reportedly died under her orders.

Ptolemy XV Caesar: (44–30 BC), Son of Julius Caesar and Cleopatra VII. Ptolemy was his mother's co-ruler, killed by Octavian, later the emperor Augustus, after Cleopatra's death in 30 BC.

Radiocarbon dating: A physicochemical method of estimating the length of time since the death of an organism.Carbon-14 is the radioactive form and once an organism dies, the level of Carbon-14 decays, shedding atomic particles at a constant rate. This rate can be measured using scientific equipment, and from it a date for the object can be obtained.

Registration: Assigning a permanent number for identification purposes to an assession and recording this number to a system.

Relative Dating: Dates expressed through relativistic relationships, for example, earlier, later, more recent, after Cleopatra's death, etc.

Remote sensing: The battery of nondestructive techniques used in geophysical prospection to generate archaeological data without the need to for excavation.

Research design: Programmatic statement outlining four key elements as a blueprint of archaeological research: statement of prospective, synthesis of existing database, research domains, and relevant research strategy.

Rhakotis: A village on the Mediterranean Coast founded as Alexandria by Alexander the Great.

Rosetta stone: A black asphalt stone found in 1799 that bears an inscription in hieroglyphs, demotic characters, and Greek. By working from the known to the unknown, scholars were able to decipher the ancient Egyptian hieroglyphs.

Seleucus: General under Alexander and founder of the Selecuid dynasty, which extended throughout much of the Near East, from Asia Minor to northern India.

Side-Scan Sonar: A tool for mapping the topography of the surface of the seabed and for detecting shipwrecks, artifacts and other material of archaeological interest.

Sphinx: The stone figure of a lion with the upper part of the body being human. In Egypt, sphinxes usually appear to have been set up along avenues forming approaches to temples. The lion's body represents strength and the man's head symbolizes knowledge. In ancient times, the sphinx was also considered a protector of the dead.

Strabo: Geographer who recorded important details of Alexandrian harbors during the early years of Roman rule.

Sub-Bottom Profiler: An acoustic tool for mapping the sediments below the surface of the seabed and for detecting shipwrecks, artifacts, and other material of archaeological interest.

Thalamite: Rowing unit associated with ancient triremes, consisting of twenty-seven rowers on each side of the vessel. They were the lowest level of rowers and worked their oars through ports just above the water line.

Thranite: Rowing unit associated with ancient triremes, consisting of thirty-one rowers on each side of the vessel rowing on the highest level of a trireme. Consequently, their oars reached the water at the sharpest angle and were the more difficult position.

Timonium: Refuge for Marc Antony in Alexandria after his defeat at Actium. The foundations eventually were recovered underwater 2,000 years later.

Treasure Hunting: The search for intrinsically valuable objects for commercial gain versus the greater understanding of past history for greater good.

Trireme: Three-banked warship of the ancient Mediterranean.

Underwater Cultural Heritage: Any archaeological heritage taken from an underwater environment.

Zygite: Rowing unit associated with ancient triremes, consisting of twenty-seven rowers on each side of the vessel. They were positioned slightly above and outboard of the thalamites.

Index

Give the Gift of

Alexandria
and the Sea

to Your Friends and Colleagues

CHECK YOUR LEADING BOOKSTORE OR ORDER HERE

❑ **YES**, I want _____ copies of *Alexandria and the Sea* at $21.95 each, plus $4.95 shipping per book (Florida residents please add $1.54 sales tax per book). Canadian orders must be accompanied by a postal money order in U.S. funds. Allow 15 days for delivery.

My check or money order for $_____ is enclosed.

Please charge my: ❑ Visa   ❑ MasterCard
                    ❑ Discover   ❑ American Express

Name _____

Organization _____

Address _____

City/State/Zip _____

Phone_____ E-mail _____

Credit Card # _____

Exp date_____ Signature _____

Please make your check payable and return to:

SHARP BOOKS INTERNATIONAL
345 Bayshore Blvd., #1109
Tampa, FL 33606

Call your credit card order to: (727) 422-0754
Fax: (727) 456-1310

JOHN EVERSON

THE HOUSE BY THE CEMETERY

This is a **FLAME TREE PRESS** book

Text copyright © 2018 John Everson

FLAME TREE PRESS
6 Melbray Mews, London, SW6 3NS, UK
flametreepress.com

Distribution and warehouse:
Baker & Taylor Publisher Services (BTPS)
30 Amberwood Parkway, Ashland, OH 44805
btpubservices.com

Thanks to the Flame Tree Press team, including:
Taylor Bentley, Frances Bodiam, Federica Ciaravella, Don D'Auria,
Chris Herbert, Matteo Middlemiss, Josie Mitchell, Mike Spender,
Cat Taylor, Maria Tissot, Nick Wells, Gillian Whitaker.

The cover is created by Flame Tree Studio with
thanks to Nik Keevil and Shutterstock.com.
The font families used are Avenir and Bembo.

Flame Tree Press is an imprint of Flame Tree Publishing Ltd
flametreepublishing.com

A copy of the CIP data for this book is available from the British Library
and the Library of Congress.

HB ISBN: 978-1-78758-002-2
PB ISBN: 978-1-78758-000-8
ebook ISBN: 978-1-78758-003-9
Also available in FLAME TREE AUDIO

Printed in the US at Bookmasters, Ashland, Ohio

JOHN EVERSON

THE HOUSE BY THE CEMETERY

FLAME TREE PRESS
London & New York

PROLOGUE
One Night in October

The floorboards creaked as Candace crossed the room.

Ominous.

She caught and held her breath, then kept walking slowly, one careful foot at a time. Tentatively. Just like the rest of the house, this room was mostly dark. She worried with every step that something would run across her bare toes. Why had she worn sandals? A muffled red light warmed the far wall near the baseboard. Maybe *warmed* was the wrong word. The light from the hidden lamp didn't warm, it *bled* up the wall from the floor. Nearby, just barely illuminated by the lamp, a woman lay prone, unmoving on a crimson velvet duvet. She wore a frilly white nightgown, which was spotted in dark splats. The reason was obvious.

Someone had slit the woman's throat. The murder weapon lay nearby on the floor, the knife's silver blade coated in dark red. A spray of blood bled down the wall beside her in visual opposition to the light that bled up the wall. It was a study in opposites…the only constant was the color.

Red.

She could see it everywhere. Pools on the floor. Spots on the walls. The room was dripping in red.

Candace shivered. What had happened here?

The house was disturbing as hell. They'd gotten that part right.

Something tapped her shoulder. Candace jumped.

"Boo!"

Sara and Briana stood behind her grinning.

"What the hell!" Candace said. "Don't *do* that."

"Isn't this place awesome?" Sara asked.

"There's so much blood," Candace whispered.

"That's what makes it awesome," Briana said. "And they got the color right too; it doesn't just look like red paint."

Candace shivered. "It's horrible," she said.

Sara laughed. "Scaredy cat. Don't you want to reach out and touch someone? Like the witch?" She pointed at the bloody body lying by the door.

"No," Candace said. "It looks too real."

"Maybe it *is* real," Briana said. Her hands gestured dramatically. "You've heard the stories. Maybe this really *is* a slaughterhouse, and the whole haunted house thing is just a cover. Can you guess what's *really* going on down those creepy stairs in the basement?"

"You guys are mean," Candace said.

"You think so?" Briana said. A wicked smile stole across her face. "How about if we let you finish the house on your own? That way you'll get the full effect!"

"No," Candace said. Her voice took on a note of panic. "You wouldn't do that to me."

Sara grabbed Briana's hand and pulled her past the dead body and through the door into whatever horrors the next room held. "Sure, we would," her voice echoed.

Candace raced after, but they were already gone from the next room when she passed through the threshold…and she didn't know which way they'd gone. This room offered two choices of exit. A sign rested crookedly on the wall with an arrow pointing at the stairs leading down and out of sight. 'Don't Go In The Basement,' it read. The words looked as if they'd been painted freehand, in blood, with a very wet brush. A figure dressed in a black cape and holding a long scythe detached itself from the wall near the basement stairs and began moving toward her.

A second staircase was on the other side of the room, but this set of steps led up. It too was flanked by a sign with drippy red letters, this one reading simply 'Exit'.

Candace debated between the two. But only for a moment, as the reaper was between her and the stairs leading down. She began climbing the stairs leading up. 'Exit' was exactly what she wanted at this point.

The room at the top was strangely bare. The first thing she saw was the raw plank ceiling, with the beam crossing the room to form the center of the peak's A frame. The next thing she saw was the rope tied to that beam. It ended in a hangman's noose just a few feet from the floor. The loop at the end was swaying slightly.

Candace shivered. At least there wasn't a body hanging from it. But why was it moving?

Something creaked to her left. The hair stood up on the back of her neck. Candace turned to look, but saw nothing. There was an old bureau there, with an oval mirror attached above it. The mirror was cracked. And it blocked her view of whatever was in the narrow end of the room beyond. Probably someone in costume waiting to jump out at her. In a rare moment of bravery, Candace decided to beat the haunted house people at their own game. She stepped around the dresser, prepared to confront someone in a gory ghoul mask.

There was nobody there.

The hair on the back of her neck began to tingle. The small space behind the dresser was a dead zone. A shuttered window marked the wall, but otherwise…the space was empty.

Candace walked to the window, and lifted the wooden shutter slats by an inch. The window looked out on the cemetery. Even in the dark, she could see the tombstones of Bachelor's Grove in silent rows below.

Something creaked again.

She dropped the shutter and started to turn.

But someone grabbed her shoulders and gripped them tight. She struggled, but couldn't turn.

"Wha—?" she began to cry.

And then a hand covered her mouth and yanked her whole body backward.

Candace slapped and punched at her captor, but her hands couldn't make contact. The arms only tightened around her and dragged her off her feet.

Her upper body suddenly lowered. Her feet thumped down a few inches, and then her head was below the level of her toes.

She stopped struggling then and finally understood what was going on. There was a hole in the floor.

Or rather…a trapdoor.

That had been the creaking sound she'd heard. Someone coming up and through the door.

She had figured out one piece of this puzzle, but it was too late to matter.

Candace tried to scream as her head dropped down another stair below the level of the floor. A moment later, her feet dragged afterward, cracking painfully down the steps to follow her.

Her heels bounced off wood at least eight or ten times, and then the thumping stopped, and she was dragged across a floor.

She should not have walked around the bureau. Because now she had literally disappeared behind it. Maybe forever. This couldn't be part of the haunted house attraction gimmick.

Something cold touched her wrist, and then clicked. The hands abandoned her for a moment, and Candace twisted her body until she could see the chain that now locked her to an old steel bedframe. A few feet away, she heard the creaking sound again.

The trapdoor had lowered once again.

Nobody above would have any idea where she'd gone. If Briana and Sara came back to look for her, they wouldn't find a clue.

Candace opened her mouth to scream, but almost as soon as she made a sound, a hand closed solidly over her lips. The hand was cool and firm.

Her captor whispered softly.

"Shhhhhhhh."

PART ONE
THE HOUSE

CHAPTER ONE

June 23rd

"But the place is already haunted," Mike Kostner said. He shook his head and gave Perry the eye. "You want to haunt a *haunted* house?"

"That's the beauty of it," Perry said. "Half the work has already been done. We just need you to go in and put down some planks. Shore up some walls. Make sure nobody's going to fall through the floor."

Mike lifted a pint and downed a couple gulps. Stalling. Then he looked at Perry. "You don't really believe that, do you? That place hasn't had anyone living in it for fifty years. Probably more. You'd be better off knocking it down and building a new place from scratch. Actually, you'd be better off renting the space of the old Dominick's grocery store on Cicero and just setting up your haunted house there."

Perry shook his head. "We don't want to be like the Jaycees! A dead Dominick's ain't no Bachelor's Grove. You know that. C'mon. We've got access to an old cemetery in the woods, with an old spooky house behind it. And stories…lots of stories. Everyone in Cook County knows the place is supposedly haunted. Hell, everyone in Illinois who has ever heard of the place knows it. That's the beauty of this – most of the marketing is already done. People have heard ghost stories about Bachelor's Grove since they were kids. When word gets out that we're letting people into that old locked-up shack hidden back in those woods? That the police have kept under guard with chains? People will flock to this on Halloween! The place has been under lock-and-key for decades."

Mike nodded. "There's a reason for that."

"Rumors," Perry said.

Mike shook his head. "People died there. People are buried there. It's next to a cemetery!"

Perry shrugged. "People are buried everywhere. They don't come back. I don't care what the ghost stories say. They've had chains on that place because of a bunch of drug-smoking Satan worshippers who vandalized the place. That's all."

"It just seems wrong, man," Mike said. He picked up his beer, and moved the level down another inch. When he set it down, he looked at Perry. The other man had been his friend for more than ten years, since they'd met at Mike's ex-wife's sister's wedding. But Perry wore a suit, while, at his best, Mike wore jeans and a t-shirt. Even now, sitting at a sticky black round table at The Edge, a shithole shot-and-a-beer bar frequented by Zeppelin and Journey cover bands on the weekends, Perry was wearing a white shirt and tie. And Perry talked to Mia, Mike's ex, a lot more than Mike did.

"It's not wrong," Perry said. "It's business." The other man ran a hand across his balding dome, reminding Mike that when they'd first met, Perry had had a full head of blond hair. Now...he had a dome and a paunch. Things change. Kind of like Mike's marriage. Mike had kept building houses, and while he did, Mia had kept checking out other houses. In particular, the beds in those houses. That had been the sticking point for Mike.

"Look," Mike said, "I don't know what you did to bankroll this, but it just seems like a bad idea. I mean...Bachelor's Grove...they've talked about that place since I was a kid. People see ghosts out on the boulevard. I just don't think—"

Perry held up his hand. "Mike, seriously. When was the last time you had a gig? Three weeks? Four?"

Mike shook his head. "I had a roofing job last week."

"For a day?"

Mike shrugged. "Two."

Perry leveled two iron-gray eyebrows. "And what do you have lined up for this week?"

"It's Thursday."

"Okay, next week?"

Mike deflated. He said nothing. What could he say? He was a carpenter in prime season, and he'd only worked a handful of days in the past three weeks. His bank account was currently looking a lot smaller than the rent on his apartment.

Perry nodded. "That's what I'm talking about." He put his hand over the opening at the top of Mike's pint just as Mike was about to lift it.

"Look," Perry said. "You've had some bad luck. I get it. But not everybody does. You do this, and things could turn around. This is a good gig. We sold the county on a sweet deal here. They spend thousands every year trying to keep people out of that cemetery in October. Now instead of bleeding money, they can make a profit on the place. We'll fix it up, open it as a haunted house, and they get a percentage of the ticket price. If you're a part of this…there are a lot of jobs that the county could reference you on. This could put you back on the five days a week circuit instead of five days a month. I'm telling you."

Mike pulled his glass out from under Perry's hand. "I don't know," he said.

"All we need you to do is reinforce the floors and the staircases," Perry explained. "Some of it needs to be torn out, but we've already had it inspected and I think we can save a lot of the surface stuff that looks old and creepy. You'll be building a lot of new support underneath. Redo the entry, and probably build a couple room dividers once the decorators have a traffic plan."

"It's going to be a black hole," Mike said. "That place is probably ready to sink into the earth just like the coffins around it."

"What else do you have lined up this month?" Perry countered.

A tall lanky guy got up on stage at that moment and plugged in his guitar. A moment later his fingers were walking across the strings and the half-empty bar filled with steel arpeggios. The guy wasn't bad. But he was clearly a wannabe Eddie Van Halen.

Mike could sympathize. He felt like a wannabe carpenter lately.

Perry was looking at him expectantly. Mike shrugged. Noncommittal.

"This is your ticket back," Perry said. He grabbed Mike's shoulder and squeezed. "You do this, and the county makes money this fall…and you will be working again. All the time. I promise you."

Mike rolled his eyes.

"Again, what else do you have lined up this month?"

"When would I start?" Mike asked.

"Monday," Perry said. "We need the structural work done by the end of August so there's time for the artists to come in and decorate the place."

"Decorate how?"

The guitar player behind them held one note – and the guitar – high in the air. Mike put one hand over his left ear.

"Like a haunted house?" Perry said. He reached across the table and cuffed Mike. "What do you think?"

"Why don't they just leave it exactly the way it is?" Mike said. "Like you say, it's creepy and haunted now. You don't need me to do anything."

"One word: lawsuits." Perry shook his head. "You go in there and make sure people don't fall through the rotten floors. I'll make sure this thing becomes the best haunted house attraction in the state this fall. It will all be good."

"Two words back atcha," Mike said. "*Haunted* house. As in…already!"

Perry shrugged. "Two more words: Ticket sales." He paused, and looked hard at Mike. "And you pay your rent."

Mike bowed his head and stared at the half-empty glass.

"What time on Monday?"

CHAPTER TWO

Monday morning came fast. And when it did…Mike wasn't ready. He wanted to be. He'd *tried* to be. He'd loaded the truck over the weekend, putting anything onboard he could think that he might need. But the reality was, until he got into the place and really scoped it out…who could say?

Plus, Sunday had run wrong…lonely. And consequently, he'd had one too many beers again. The truth was, his head hurt, his lower back ached, and he really didn't want to be here.

The sun was still low in the sky and there was a fuzzy haze along the top of the grass when he followed the gravel path that led from Midlothian Turnpike down and into the cemetery grounds. His shoulders shivered slightly with the chill in the morning fog as he walked past the stand of silent gravestones. There honestly weren't many at this point…the place had only been a small community cemetery from the last century, after all, and some of the stones had fallen over, while others had been vandalized or removed. There was a reason the police had put chains up across the forest preserve fencing to protect what remained of this place.

It was somewhat hidden. And largely abandoned. A sad place.

And thus…ripe for abuse. Mike had heard that Satan worshippers had been run out of here on more than one occasion. There were all sorts of stories about black masses and witchcraft.

Whatever had happened before, on this particular July morning, it was just an empty and kind of forlorn clearing that he saw on an otherwise quiet morning. Behind him the echo of cars whizzed by on the asphalt. But step by step as he approached the old house…that sound receded. Ahead, there were wisps of fog rolling off the ground. And as he rounded a bend in the path, the roof of the old, abandoned cemetery farmhouse edged into view.

His summer project.

Mike walked until the full face of the old place was visible. And then he sighed. The arch of the roof lifted halfway into the tree line, and the black of the shingles was almost completely obscured in green moss. The place was sided in what was probably cedar, but whatever rustic allure it had once had, today it just looked gray, rotted and warped. There were obvious dark holes in the wood, and one of the window frames hung down in a twisted L in front of the dirty glass.

He didn't want to look inside.

But not only was he going to look inside…over the next few weeks he was going to gut the place.

His head hurt at the thought.

The porch sank, its wood spongy, as he walked up its two steps, and he mentally made a note of it. *Replace porch.* Probably the easiest repair he'd be doing here over the next couple months. He turned the key in the padlock that held the warped door closed, and took a deep breath as it creaked open ahead of him.

The sun didn't want to enter there.

He didn't want to either.

"I never wanted it to come to this," Mike said, as he stood in the door of the old house.

Thankfully, nobody answered. For a heartbeat, he'd worried someone might. But then he took a breath and stepped inside.

The front foyer was half-covered in yellowed linoleum. But there was a hole in the middle of it, where some animal had gnawed its way through the floor. Whether it had been digging into the basement below or digging its way out, he couldn't tell.

Either way, it was just one of many repairs he'd have to add to his list. First thing, was to make the list.

Perry had said that structurally the place was solid, and just needed a month or so of touch-up work, but Mike wasn't going to be responsible for people falling through the floor. Or a floor collapsing. He had his list from Perry of things their structural engineer had noted, but Mike was going to do his own assessment. And the first way to begin was 'the stomp test'.

Mike walked past the hole in the linoleum and stamped his foot down on the dusty, colorless wood that he assumed was probably maple or oak. It was impossible to tell with the grime, but that would have made sense in this area. That's what grew in the forest; that's what people had worked with a hundred years ago when the first settlement had populated this area and started to bury their dead around the small pond now known as Bachelor's Grove.

He stepped around the hole in the foyer and walked slowly into the front room. It was quiet here…eerily quiet, with the occasional hum of the road and the buzz of insects suddenly blotted out. The morning sun fought through dirty windows layered by years and years of spiderwebs and bug carcasses. He was in a different space here.

A sacred space, his mind suggested.

"A dusty place," he whispered aloud. As he walked, the dirt moved from the floor to the air in lazy currents of filth.

Mike walked around the corner. Once there had probably been a formal table and chairs in the shadowed space beyond. He could still see the dark shadows and holes where sconces had been mounted to the walls. But now…all that remained were holes…. And yellowed, faded wallpaper that had curled back from the seams at some points.

The dark plank floors might once have been varnished and shiny. Now…they were simply dark. And stained. Any beauty they once held lost in dust and neglect.

Mike retraced his steps to the hallway. The wood had creaked beneath his weight, but had not sagged. Surprising, but good.

Then he stepped through the door across the hall and into the kitchen.

"Oh shit," he said.

The wood floor suddenly turned to tile, and the tile, stained and yellowed…eventually gave way to a ragged hole in the middle of the room. There was a dark trail from the cabinets near the sink to a low spot in the center of the room that had apparently rotted through. He guessed that the water lines had been left on long after the last occupants had moved away. Or been buried out back.

"Well," Mike said. "There's one week."

He knelt down at the edge of the rotten wood and looked through the floor into the basement below.

"And there's another," he said.

The basement was a mud pit, with furrows and troughs in the bare earth where puddles of stagnant water gathered. The thick smell of rot and mildew rose up through the hole.

"Remember, you don't need to make it livable," Perry had said. "Just give us some floors, shore up the staircases and reinforce the beams in the basement. We want to make that into a crypt."

Mike stood up and shook his head. The crypt part was going to be easy.

"Well…first things first," he said. "We need to air this place out. It reeks."

He walked over to the window above the sink and after mopping away six inches of gray web with the back of his work glove, tried to lift it. A dozen spiders scurried out of the heavily webbed upper corners as the old wood creaked. But the window didn't budge upward.

"That figures," he murmured. He tried the front room window, which looked out on the porch. It shifted up a few centimeters at his push, and then stuck fast.

"No, sorry, that's not acceptable," Mike said, and reached into his portable tool bag for a small crowbar. "I'm not working in this stink all day."

The wood at the base splintered…but a minute later the window slid up the warped track and the morning air rushed over the sill.

"Better," he pronounced.

He walked around the rest of the main floor, and jimmied a handful of other windows open. The stale, mildewed stench of the house began to give way to the scent of the summer breeze.

Then he put his foot on the first step of the stairwell leading upstairs. Perry had mentioned that there was an attic suite that they had plans to use. Mike was apprehensive that the flooring would be dry-rotted…if not wet-rotted from holes in the roof. But he'd seen no signs on the first floor of black spots on the ceilings, so maybe the roof had somehow maintained integrity.

He put his weight down on the first dark-stained step, and when it didn't give, he gave it a good stomp. When nothing bad happened, he did the same to the next. And the next. There were 13 in all. When he stomped past the last one, he let out a sigh of relief. Then he looked around.

The attic room was long – it was a single open space that extended across the whole length of the house. The sun shone in through one dirty window at the far end, and dust motes swam in the murky light that filtered through. The ceiling wasn't finished; instead, when you looked up you saw the support beams and the actual upside-down V arch of the roof itself.

The room still held the remnants of its last occupant; a yellowed mattress rotted atop a bedspring to his right. Gray chunks of the bed's stuffing lay in clumps all around the bed frame, hanging from holes in the side of the mattress fabric; obviously humans hadn't been the last creatures to sleep in this bed. A night table with an old wooden lamp on top flanked the bed. On the other side, a stack of old brown boxes leaned away from the wall; the topmost box had long ago given way and toppled to the floor; its contents – a mix of books and papers – lay spread across the wood plank floor.

A tall bureau stood to Mike's left, blocking part of the light from one of the attic's two windows. But the light from that window was still enough to expose how long it had been since anyone had lived in this room. The dust on top of the dresser was so thick that if he hadn't been able to see the side, he couldn't have told the color of the wood.

Mike looked up at the wood arch of the ceiling and followed the beams to the edges. There were some dark areas in spots near the edges, especially in the northeast corner, but otherwise, the roof appeared sound. Hard to believe, but that would explain why the rest of the place hadn't rotted into the dirt. He walked back and forth across the planks, testing the give. While there were some creaks, nothing felt soft. He shrugged. Maybe Perry and his engineer were right after all. If he just had to shore up the main floor, add support to the basement beams and drop some planks across the mud down there...that would be all right with him.

Speaking of which...while he'd seen the basement through the hole in the kitchen floor, he realized he hadn't actually seen the stairs to get down there. Mike walked back down the stairs and circled the walkway on the main floor. He poked his head into two empty bedrooms there, and a bath between them with a yellowed tub and black and white granny-tile floor that looked like a power wash with bleach was in order. He opened two hallway doors and found a couple musty closets, but did not find the stairway down.

What the hell?

Mike walked outside. Maybe the only entry to the basement was exterior? Odd, but this *was* a really old house.

The sun had risen higher since he'd first stepped inside the place, and the fog had already burned away from the clearing. It was going to be hot today; the air smelled fresh, but pregnant with summer humidity. Great. He had a headache, he was going to be working in a stinking wreck of a rot-heap, and it was going to be 90 degrees. And he couldn't find the damn basement.

This week was starting out great.

He took a walk around the perimeter of the place. Once you passed the old rotten wood of the porch and turned the corner, the lower five feet of the house was obscured by scrub bushes and grass. He waded through the tall grass, sticking as close to the stone base of the old house as possible. When he hit the back, the grass began to thin as the tree cover took over. The entire rear section of the house was shaded by the tree line of the forest. He saw the entry he was looking for almost immediately. Stone steps that led down below the ground.

Mike stepped down the old stairway half hidden by a thick cover of leaves.

"The door is not going to open," he said aloud. But he reached a hand out to the old rusty knob anyway.

And damned if the thing didn't turn.

"How about that?" Mike said, and pushed the thing open. It gave a stubborn creak as it dragged along the sandy earth floor.

Inside, the place smelled dank and dead. The ceiling was barely above the top of his head, and Mike ducked beneath beams that dropped lower to support pipes from above. Everything in front of him was black as night, no windows. He pulled a flashlight from his pocket and shone it around.

The earth dipped in places where water obviously sat sometimes after a storm. And as he moved inside, he could see the one spot of light on the mud, streaming in where the floor had given way above in the kitchen.

"All right…so there's a bearing," he said, orienting himself.

Mike scoped the whole basement out. Perry said he wanted to put down a plank floor and lead people through here…but if they were going to do that, Mike needed to drop a stairway down; it had to be part of the walk through the house – you couldn't send people outside to find the basement!

But then, in the far corner, he finally saw it.

A set of plank stairs leading up. He walked over and stepped on the first stair.

And with a spongy snap, the stair broke in half.

The second one sagged when he put weight on it, and he stepped back down before it gave way. There was a wooden doorway perched at the top of the graying, rotting steps.

"Okay," he said to himself. "These go up somewhere…but where?"

He used the pipes beneath the kitchen and bathroom as a guide, and tried to figure out where the stairs had to open, based on his brief survey of the house above.

He shook his head. It seemed like the door should come out right where the den had been.

Mike made his way back out of the dark pit that was the basement, and breathed an unconscious sigh of relief when he made it back up the steps outside.

He stood at the top of the stairwell, studying the century-old stone and wood facade that stretched up and away into the tree–hidden sky.

Something tapped him on the shoulder.

"So, what do you think?" a voice asked from behind him.

Mike nearly jumped out of his skin.

"Perry?" he said, turning to face his friend. "Don't ever fuckin' do that to me again!"

Perry stood there in the grass, incongruous in his standard gray suit and blue–striped tie, grinning from ear to ear.

"Scared of an old haunted house?" Perry asked. "We ain't even decorated it yet!"

"Bastard," Mike said, and shook his head.

"Listen, I can't stay," Perry said, still grinning. "But I wanted to stop by and see what you thought of the place."

"It's a pit," Mike said.

"But you can fix it?"

He shrugged. "Yeah, enough for what you want, sure. I don't think anyone's going to want to live here again, though."

Perry nodded. "That's what I wanted to hear. Let me know if you need anything. Besides wood." Perry laughed.

Mike rolled his eyes. "I'll need plenty of that."

"I thought you had plenty of that," his friend said. "That's what you always tell me when you're drunk."

"Go to work, Perry," Mike said.

"Not before we talk through the job," Perry said. He pointed at the front of the old house. "Take a walk with me?"

Mike nodded, and a minute later, they were inside, stepping through the debris as Perry pointed out the repairs he wanted to make sure Mike made. His head swam as Perry pointed out walls to be re-drywalled, and floors to be re-surfaced. At the end of the day, his friend/boss really wanted him to re-face the whole place. The Halloween decorators would be making it look creepy, not the naturally decrepit vibe of the old, aging materials that were here. Mike would really be building a 'pathway' through the decay. A frame amid the ruin to hold their pretend decay.

After Perry had finished going on about how amazing this place was going to be and returned to his car, Mike walked back inside the old place.

He'd almost forgotten his foray into the basement until he stepped into the den at the back of the house. And then…he walked the perimeter of the empty room. Where the hell was that stairway door? It had to be here somewhere. Perry had talked so fast and furious, he'd never even brought up the question of the 'crypt'.

Mike returned to the hallway and tried the closet doors there, following it back to the family room.

He shook his head. Nope. The stairway just did not exist. Never mind that he'd seen it, along with a door…but still, it didn't exist.

"All an illusion," he murmured.

But he'd seen the evidence. And it all pointed…

Mike walked back into the den and looked harder. The room was empty, sure, but that was empty of furniture. It was not, however, simply four blank walls and a floor. There was a closet and chair rail trim and a fireplace built into one wall. He walked across the long room and opened the creaking closet door…that led to nowhere. And then turned and looked at the old wooden bookcases built into the walls next to the fireplace.

With his fist he knocked on the back wall of one of the bookcases. The echo that came back was empty, and Mike nodded.

The case might look solid, but it wasn't a permanent part of the wall.

With his hands, he began to take down the old shelves to search for the creases he knew had to be there. He was going to have to find a way to pull at least one of these cases away from the wall they guarded.

The basement was hidden from the main part of the house…and the entry had to be hidden here. He was convinced.

He traced the outline of the bookcase carefully, finding both loose shelves and solid, immovable ones. When the second shelf on the far right segment shifted at his touch, Mike didn't hesitate to lift it.

That's when things got interesting.

The back wood of the case suddenly moved away from his hand with a creak. The shelf was actually a latch, and the back of the bookcase was really a hidden door, which now hung open.

"Seriously?" he whispered. "The fucking haunted house has a hidden door?"

He punched the thing open and lifted the lower shelf so he could step through into the small hidden room beyond. He still had his flashlight from walking the basement, and he flicked it on. The space was windowless and small, and the décor didn't help make it feel any more expansive. The walls were all painted jet black, and the harsh white of what looked like bones littered the dark floor.

He reached down and picked one up. There were three teeth sticking out of it. A jawbone! He dropped it back to the floor.

"Holy shit," he whispered.

In the center of the floor was a symbol he recognized from horror movies. A circle painted in white on the dark wood...a five-point star traced in the middle. More white bones were stacked in the dead center of the circle. Dark smears of something old and previously wet marred the floor.

Blood.

And bones. In the middle of....

A witch's sign.

What kind of demonic rituals had gone on here?

"Damnit," Mike whispered. "I asked him, why haunt a place that's already haunted? Seriously."

He walked across the circle, and found the thing he'd been looking for on the other side.

A wooden frame.

A door. He turned the handle, and confirmed his suspicion almost instantly. It opened onto the rotted stairs that led down to the basement.

But why was this room hidden from the interior by a bookcase?

And who had been performing rituals there in the witch's circle?

CHAPTER THREE

Bong-Soon Mon walked up the broken sidewalk in front of Jeanie's house lost in thought. The day had not gone quite as planned; he'd been working overtime all week to try to finish a coding project and he'd hoped to have it completed by the weekend. But now he was going to be spending the next two days wondering why the Quality Assurance test failed. On any other night, he would have stayed until he'd figured a way to address the critiques, whether it took 'til eight p.m. or two a.m. But tonight, he and Jeanie had a date.

He rang the yellowed doorbell next to her beat-up old screen door and waited. She had told him in the past to just walk right in if the door was open, but he still felt funny about barging into someone else's place. So, he waited. And then rang the bell again. He knew that she was in there or the inner wooden door wouldn't be open.

Something crashed inside. It sounded like glass breaking.

"Jeanie?" he called through the screen.

He was answered a second later by a blood-curdling scream.

Bong no longer worried about being invited to enter. He threw the screen door open and charged inside. "Jeanie?" he called once more as he crossed the rug in the foyer.

The scream came again, and this time he knew for sure that the anguished sound came from his girlfriend. But before he could do anything, a second later she appeared, running around the corner from the hallway to the back bedrooms. Her face was covered in blood – she looked badly cut – as if someone had slashed her with a knife. A slab of her cheek dangled away from her head near her chin. The whole right side of her face was glistening and wet, and he could see the white of her teeth through the hole where there had been perfectly smooth flesh when he'd seen her last night.

"Bong!" she shrieked, and ran to his arms.

"Oh my God," he cried as she grabbed him. "What happened? Who did this to you? Is there someone else here?" He had a vision of a knife-wielding maniac turning the corner and coming at them any second now.

She sobbed in his arms and he hugged her tighter. Her back hitched up and down frantically and he wasn't sure if he should get her out of the house or call 911 first. Was somebody here? He needed to know what had happened.

"Jeanie," he said. "Please. Try to tell me what happened."

He could feel her sobs changing. Her back was vibrating faster, in fast panicked hitches and he gently pushed her away from his chest to see…

…that she wasn't sobbing at all.

"Gotcha," Jeanie cried. She threw her head back and let out a spurt of laughter that stopped her from speaking for a minute. When she finally regained control, she said, "Who did this to me? I did!" She fingered the flesh hanging from her face and with both hands pulled on it. It stretched like taffy.

"What do you think?" she said. "Pretty sick, huh?"

Bong pushed her away. "*You* are pretty sick," he said. "I can't believe you did that to me." His voice rose louder than he ever spoke. His words trembled with emotion. "I thought you were really hurt. You had me scared to death for a second."

"Then it worked," Jeanie said. "That's the best thing anyone has ever said to me!"

"That was mean," Bong said, shaking his head. He could feel his legs still trembling. "Really uncool."

Jeanie took his hand and pulled him closer to her again. "Oh, c'mon, don't be mad. I needed to see if I could pull this off before I apply."

Bong's brow wrinkled. "Apply for what?"

Jeanie grinned. "They're opening a haunted house this fall near Midlothian and they're auditioning for makeup people. I want to do it. You know I've always wanted to do horror makeup." She hung her head and made puppy-dog eyes at him.

They were disconcerting when she had a slab of flesh still hanging off her face. The juxtaposition of cuteness and gore almost made him laugh, and Bong couldn't help but grin. "You could totally get the makeup gig," he said. "But don't ever do that to me again."

"Cross my heart and hope to die," Jeanie said. She reached up and yanked on the fake slab of flesh. It separated from her cheek with a rubber-band effect, slapping against the back of her hand.

"I won't ever do that again," she promised. "But…could you do one thing for me?"

Bong raised an eyebrow. "Maybe. It depends."

"C'mon," she said. "I said I'd be good."

"Yeah, but you didn't say what you wanted me to do."

"I need someone to practice on. It's hard to do good zombie effects on yourself. This took forever."

"I don't know," he said. "What do I get in return?"

Jeanie pressed her hips hard to his and licked the tip of his lips. "I can think of a few things."

"Hmmm…." he said. His voice betrayed his interest. Jeanie didn't waste the moment.

"I signed up for an audition on Thursday," she said. "So, I really do need to practice. Could we stay in tonight?"

Bong thought of the potential payoff at the end of the night, and decided that a couple hours in the makeup chair would probably be worth it. Jeanie could be on fire when she was in the mood.

"Okay," he sighed. "Whatever you want."

She smiled. Kind of a weird smile, since she had painted teeth on her cheek. It was like he could see her whole jaw through half her face.

"But you have to wipe that makeup off first," he said. "It's too creepy to look at you that way."

"I can do that," she agreed. "By the way, what are you doing on Thursday?"

"Why?" he asked.

"I need to show off my work so I get the job, silly. That means you get to come with me to the audition."

Jeanie grabbed his hand and dragged him down the hallway toward the bathroom.

Bong kept up a smile, anticipating the 'payoff' to come later. But inside…he was groaning.

CHAPTER FOUR

There were now piles of 2x4s, fresh pine flooring planks and some crossbeams next to the abandoned house near the cemetery, which wasn't looking quite so abandoned anymore. Mike's friend Aaron had helped him lug the wood down here after filling up the back of a pickup truck at Home Depot, and now Mike would be spending the next few weeks installing it all. With what Perry was paying, he couldn't afford to pay for help to put it in, but he couldn't have gotten it all down here from the turnpike on his own.

For a little while, during the load-in, this gig had felt great. He was working again. Something was happening. He'd make rent again this month.

But now, as he stood in the overgrown clearing, in front of a dilapidated old house, half-obscured by trees…he felt lost. Lonely. Isolated.

Mike was completely on his own, both here and at home. It wasn't a feeling he enjoyed. Though it was one that he'd been forced to get used to since Mia had walked out last Christmas.

He started to whistle, some new pop song he'd heard on the radio just now on the drive over. But that whistle died out, quickly. It sounded false here. He felt as if he was intruding. This place had stood as it was for decades without anyone living here. And now he was changing it.

Part of him felt as if the trees themselves were watching him. And disapproving.

Mike shook it away and took his hammer to the rotted boards that comprised the porch of the old house. He'd be going in and out of this place all summer, so he might as well make sure he was not going to break a leg while doing it. So rebuilding the entryway came first.

It was also somehow comforting to be working for a while outside the house, rather than in, where every sound echoed. Where the air smelled of age. And forgotten history. Unseen death. Hidden witchcraft.

When he'd called Perry to tell him about the hidden room, his friend had assured him that whatever witchcraft or devil worship had gone on in the house had happened and stopped long ago. "No worries," Perry had said. "That shit's from like, the '60s and '70s when the teenagers and weirdos got in there. That's when all those gravestones were knocked over, and that's why the police have protected the place all these years. Keep that riff raff out."

And then Perry had laughed. "Now we're going to invite the riff raff in! Hey, make sure you open that back wall to the hidden room in the hallway, so that we can have easy access to the stairs to the basement. I don't know that we'll want people going through the bookcase in the den to get there...though you never know."

Mike wedged a crowbar between a sagging gray plank and the post that supported it, and with one long creak, the board separated and popped. Perry's story of devil worshippers hanging out in the cemetery and the house kept coming back to him. He imagined women with black capes and long silver blades walking in and out across these boards, with God knows what victims waiting in fear in the secret room inside....

He shook the thoughts away, and pulled the board free. It was just the first of many boards quickly lifted and thrown aside. In just over an hour, he'd stripped all of the surface wood, and piled it up in the long grass nearby. Most of the surface planks had come off easily; some crumbled to pieces instantly at the first prod of the crowbar. The side posts, amazingly, still seemed solid enough. He decided to simply reinforce them with new inner boards and use them, rather than replace, which would save a couple days. He pushed against a couple and they didn't move much.

Mike shrugged. A couple crossbeams on those, and the new deck would easily support throngs of people stomping up his new stairs and walking into the house of horrors that was about to be constructed. He couldn't rationalize spending any more time out here. He began to measure and mark and cut. Board by board, the new entryway to the house was born. When Mike was 'on', he was good. By four o'clock, he was done with the new deck to the old house. He could have improved its footprint and built a longer deck, but that wasn't the mission. People only needed to line up and get in the front door. And now it was time to get past that. Because the easy work was done. Mike had to go inside the house. Where the bugs lived.

Where the rot awaited.

Where, according to the stories, a witch once lived.

Mike stepped across the new porch and nodded. It felt good. Solid.

Then he opened the door and stepped into the foyer. The sunlight slipped away and the temperature dropped about ten degrees. Part of him whispered that this wasn't simply because the house was holding the cool air still from overnight. He remembered the things in the room behind the bookcase. Bad shit had happened here. Of that, he had no doubt.

He walked down the hall and looked again at the hole in the kitchen floor. He frowned. He should probably start on this room next. Cure the obvious structural problems and stop any critters from climbing up from the basement.

Something creaked upstairs. Almost like a door opening.

The hairs on the back of his neck stood up. He swore he heard footsteps above his head.

Mike cocked his head to listen closer. They couldn't be footsteps. But…it could be an animal. Maybe a raccoon had come through the roof. "Shit," he whispered. Something creaked up there again, and his vision of a raccoon sniffing around evaporated. That didn't sound like an animal.

He took a deep breath and then quietly stepped out on the new deck to grab his crowbar. He wasn't going upstairs without something to swing. No matter what it was. Mike took the stairs slowly, one at a time. He tried not to make them creak and give away his presence. Of course, the steady pounding outside for the last few hours should have done that handily anyway.

Still.

Mike reached the seventh and then eighth step. He realized he was holding his breath. His head poked above the floor of the attic, and he raised the crowbar, ready to strike, not sure what to expect. He stepped quickly through the threshold.

The room was empty.

He looked across from the dusty bureau to the boxes stacked on the other side, and watched the dust motes lazily cascade through the air in the beam of sunlight that streamed in through the small attic window.

He let go of his breath, slowly. Then he stepped onto the old plank floor. The wood creaked, and he looked back and forth across the expanse of the attic. He couldn't see anything but old boxes and chests. He walked down the center of the space, holding the crowbar at the ready, in case something jumped out from behind a box. Something fast. With teeth.

Nothing did.

He walked back and forth twice, to convince himself that there was nothing here.

He returned to the stairwell, and then passed it to walk just beyond the old bureau. There was just a small space behind it, but he looked.

Nothing.

Mike shrugged. Maybe there was an animal in the eaves somewhere. He could push Perry to have someone deal with that. All he needed to worry about was carpentry on the inside of the old house. Not pest removal.

He returned to the stairs, and was just about to step down them when a glimmer on the floor caught his eye. He must have stepped right over it on the way up.

He bent down and picked up a silver chain with a small locket in the shape of a heart attached.

Weird that he hadn't seen it before.

He opened the clasp on the locket and saw a black and white photo of a young woman's face, faded almost beyond recognition. Mike shrugged and thumbed it closed before slipping it into his jeans pocket. Then he descended the stairs, looking frequently over his shoulder.

Something just didn't feel right.

When he turned away from the last step at the bottom of the stairs, someone spoke.

"Hi there," a cool, girlish voice said.

Mike nearly jumped out of his skin. She stood just to the left of the old stairway. A slim young woman with dark black hair, deep brown eyes and an obvious spark of energy that could melt the shield of a blizzard. Her smile made his lips shift.

"Um…hey," he answered.

There was another woman, he belatedly realized, standing behind her. This one could have been a case study in opposites; she was heavyset, with long, tangled brown hair. Her face looked lifeless. No energy. Even her eyes were dull. She was the epitome of a wallflower; she seemed to literally blend into the background.

"What are you doing here?" Mike asked the first girl, stumbling over his tongue. She might be cute…but she didn't belong here. This was a construction site. He wanted to be firm, but his voice didn't carry the stick.

She didn't seem to notice his discomfort. "I just wanted to see what it was like," she said. "I heard you were going to turn this into a haunted house for Halloween."

Mike nodded. "That's the plan."

"So…where will you put the dead bodies?" she asked. She put a hand up to her face to stifle the snort.

"They won't really be dead," Mike said.

"Ahh," she answered. "They won't?"

"No one ever really dies," he said.

"Well," she said. "I don't know about *that*."

She pulled a long silver blade from the back of her shorts. "When something like this goes in…it doesn't usually come out the same way."

Mike grinned…but it was a nervous grin. His grip on the crowbar tightened.

She laughed and tossed the blade at his feet. "Don't wet yourself," she said. "It's fake."

He picked it up and realized that yes, it was just a plastic toy.

"Isn't that the kind of thing you'll be using in here when the haunted house opens?" she asked. "Toy knives? I just picked it up on the side of the turnpike."

He dropped the knife back on the floor and looked at her with his sternest expression. "You shouldn't be here."

She laughed.

"No, *you* shouldn't be here," she said. "But we can work around that. I won't tell anyone."

Mike shrugged. "Um, I was hired to be here, so yes, I absolutely *should* be here," he said. "You, on the other hand, are definitely trespassing. But I guess it doesn't matter anyway – nobody cares much about this place outside of Halloween."

"Well, then it all works out," she said.

"I suppose it does," he said. "Who's your friend?"

"This is Emery," the girl said. "And I'm Katie."

He held out his hand. "I'm Mike," he said. "Glad to know you."

Katie nodded and squeezed his palm tight. Her touch gave him a shiver.

"You will be," she said. She sounded confident. It made him nervous.

He held out his hand to Emery, but she did not reciprocate. After a moment, he dropped his arm back to his side.

"You really shouldn't be in here," Mike said again. "It's dangerous."

She shrugged. "I wanted to see what the place was all about," she said. "I heard it's haunted."

Mike nodded. "It has a bad reputation," he said. "And I guess, this Halloween, we're only going to make it worse."

Katie grinned. "I like the sound of that."

Her friend didn't say anything.

Mike pointed toward the front door. "Sorry, but you guys really have got to go now."

Katie pouted and crossed her arms. She didn't budge.

"Seriously," Mike said. "I've got work to do here. I'm afraid you're going to have to wait until Halloween if you want to see this place."

"Do I have to wait until Halloween to have a beer with you?" Katie asked.

"Are you asking me out?" he said. His voice couldn't hide his incredulity.

Katie shrugged. "I don't know about *out*," she said. "But we could sit on that nice new porch you built."

"We could," he admitted. "But there are no tables or chairs. Or bartenders."

"All we need is beer," she said. "What've you got in there?" she pointed at the red cooler sitting at the entrance to the kitchen. Mike had honestly gotten so wrapped up in the porch, he'd forgotten he'd even brought it.

He nodded, walked over to it, and popped the lid. The thought of having a beer with this intriguing (and damned cute) woman made him suddenly reconsider doing any further work today. "Don't know how lowbrow your taste buds are," he said. He held up a can of Pabst Blue Ribbon.

Five minutes later the three of them were sitting on the new planks of the deck, staring at the dark gray wood of the ancient house. Mike emptied half of his first can in about three gulps. Emery followed his example, but Katie only seemed to toy with hers.

"What do you normally like to drink?" he asked.

She grinned, looking at him with those wide brown eyes. They melted him, instantly. "Whatever's handy," she said. As if to prove a point, she took a slug of PBR.

"Do you live around here?" he asked.

Katie shrugged. "Not far. You?"

He nodded. "I've got a place in Oak Forest."

"Girlfriend?" she asked.

He shook his head.

"Hey, we have something in common," Katie said. "Blissfully single!" She tapped her can to his. "Cheers!"

He drank. And quickly popped another. He didn't even look at the can. He couldn't take his eyes off the girl.

Katie said she was twenty-three and liked baseball. Emery answered a few questions, eventually admitting to being twenty-six and also single, but really didn't say much of anything, though he tried to politely draw her out now and then. When he mentioned movies or music or other potential interests, she just smiled and answered in monosyllabic shy yeses and nos. He eventually gave up trying to pull her into the conversation and just focused on Katie, who at some point popped him yet another beer, and sat with her hand on his thigh as the sun began to set. Eventually, when the words grew slurry and the belly painfully full, he excused himself to take a leak at the side of the house.

"What are you doing?" he chided himself, once he was alone again. "These girls can't be interested in you, but you're acting like a college kid."

He shook his head and zipped up, then took a deep breath before stepping back around the corner. He needed to wrap this up and head home. It was weird to realize, but he had to work again in the morning.

The girls were gone. The deck was empty, except for a bunch of empty beer cans that lay strewn about.

"Well, there ya go," he whispered, and then picked up the empties. He grabbed one that still felt full, from the spot where Katie had been sitting. He drained a few gulps into his mouth, and then upended the rest, throwing that and the other empty cans into his now-empty cooler.

The air felt like his head…warm and buzzy, with the hum of summer locusts.

It was getting dark, and time to get out of the cemetery. His eyes were swimming, and he already knew that there was a headache in store for the morning.

"Damnit," he mumbled, and looked once more inside the old house, before closing the place up, and walking back to his truck.

"I bet she wasn't twenty-three," he mumbled to himself, as he walked down the dark trail toward the turnpike. "Lucky if she was over eighteen. Probably just wanted free beer."

He shook his head and tossed the cooler in the back of the truck bed. "Gullible," he accused himself. "With a capital G."

He started the truck and signaled to pull out onto Midlothian Turnpike. There was almost no traffic, and a moment later, the truck lurched onto the road. But even as it did, he couldn't shake the feeling that someone was watching him.

Someone from the old house.

Maybe through that attic window.

He shivered and refused to look in the rearview mirror, focusing on the yellow lines in the center of the road.

CHAPTER FIVE

"Seems like a strange place to hunt for ghosts," Ted said, slipping into the chair across from Jillie Melton.

"That's because I'm not hunting," Jillie said. She raised a paper cup with a large M on it and took a sip. "I do have a life when I'm not out with you at midnight, you know."

"Uh-huh," he said. "And that's why you're having breakfast in a McDonald's across from a cemetery."

"The cemetery has nothing to do with it," she said. "It's all about the hash browns." Jillie wrinkled one pale blond eyebrow and shook her head. "I am only here for fat."

"I hope you mean in the food," Ted said. "Because I don't think you're ever going to actually put on any. You're too twitchy to gain weight."

She laughed. "And you're too fond of burritos to lose any."

"Ouch," Ted said. "I'd be offended except…."

He reached into his bag and pulled out two breakfast burritos. And a hash brown.

"I'll take that if you're not eating it," she offered.

The idea that he wasn't eating it was somewhat ludicrous. Ted weighed in at over 220 pounds, while she might have just been able to nudge the scale over 130…if she rocked up and down on it.

"Listen," he said. "Are you doing anything right now?"

She shrugged. "Other than eating?"

"I have something I want to show you."

"You didn't just stumble on me here, did you?" she said.

He shook his head. "I saw your Facebook."

Jillie frowned. If he was stalking her to run her down….

"Okay," she said. "Care to tell me what?"

"It's at Bachelor's Grove," he said. Ted's eyebrows raised precipitously.

"Yeah…what about it?" she said. "We've recorded there a half dozen times."

He nodded so fast, the flesh of his jowls seemed to flap like wings. "I know," he said. "But I think…. Listen, I just think you need to see this."

"What?" she asked again, but he only shook his head.

"I'll take you there."

Jillie shoved a hash brown in her mouth and chewed, considering the expression on Ted's face. They'd worked together for a long time, both out of respect and love for what they did. They *believed*. Which was a lot more than could be said for most of the people who filed into buildings with crosses on top of them on Sundays.

Ted believed, just as she did. And he looked about ready to burst with whatever it was he had to say. But she knew he wasn't just going to give it up. She respected that he had a reason, and stuffed the rest of the hash brown into her mouth all at once. Before she finished chewing, she stood and mumbled, "Let's go then!"

Ted looked surprised, still working on his burrito, but he didn't hesitate. Two minutes later, they were driving in his car north on Harlem Avenue.

"You're kind of creeping me out now," Jillie said, as they sat at the stoplight of 143rd Street, waiting to turn left onto Midlothian Turnpike. The Bachelor's Grove Cemetery was just a few blocks away. She'd been there dozens of times over the years. It was one of the most celebrated 'haunted places' in Illinois, and so she'd taken her cameras and equipment there in daytime, at dusk, and at night. Ted had been there for most of those outings.

The light changed, and they finally moved down the turnpike, following an old rusted red Ford pickup. Jillie found herself leaning forward, mentally pushing the old vehicle down the road. And then finally Ted pulled over at the familiar bridge that presaged the entry to the old cemetery.

"I didn't want to just tell you this," he said, pulling the keys from the ignition. "You had to see it for yourself."

Jillie opened her door and stepped out onto the gravel. She heard the sounds of a saw echoing through the forest. And then the repetitive pound of a hammer.

"What's going on?" she said as Ted stepped around the bumper.

"Take a look," he said, and led the way down the gravel path past the cemetery. When they passed the stones and reached the clearing, she began to shake her head.

"No, no, no!" she said. "What are they doing?"

Ted made a face. "They're building a haunted house."

Jillie's eyes nearly popped out of her head. "They're doing *what?*"

"They are rehabbing the old Bremen House, and turning it into a haunted house for Halloween."

"But…they can't do that," she breathed. "This is county property. It's protected."

"Apparently the county felt otherwise," Ted said. "They've decided to sell tickets to the cemetery…and the house. I read about it in the *Daily Southtown* this morning. They're turning Bachelor's Grove into an attraction."

Jillie's face turned grim. "They can't," she said. "They mustn't. The souls that rest here…don't rest easy. You know…you've seen them."

He nodded.

"There is already too much anger here," she whispered. "You know what happened to those kids that broke into the house and woke the spirit of the witch. If they do this…."

"Something bad is going to happen, isn't it?" Ted asked.

She nodded. And then took a breath and steeled her jaw.

She began to march toward the house. "We have to stop it," she said, "before someone else dies."

CHAPTER SIX

Mike stopped swinging the hammer for a minute and just listened. The calls of forest birds filled the resulting silence. He waited a moment, then shrugged, and swung the tool again.

And again he heard the sound that had stopped him before.

A scuttling. He pressed his ear to the wall and listened.

And this time he heard it. Feet moving. It had to be feet, right? Something inside the wall was shuffling across the boards.

Mike shook his head. Just what he needed. He had visions of punching through a wall to find a raccoon family enraged and ready to pounce.

"I'm a carpenter, not an exterminator, Jim," he murmured.

Something in the wall thumped, right near his face.

Mike jumped back, shaking his head. "Not what I signed up for," he complained.

He moved a few feet to the right. Maybe if he put the braces up elsewhere, whatever was in the walls would move away. Maybe he'd trapped it in the space he had been working in.

He raised the hammer to start a new anchor 2x4. Before he could hit the wood, something slammed against it from the other side. Right where he was about to hammer. As if it knew.

He jumped backward, holding the hammer out above his head. Ready to brain anything that came through the wall.

And what, exactly, was really going to come through a wall?

He didn't want to find out. Mike decided that this would be a good time for a scene change. He needed to shore up a couple pilings in the basement. Maybe whatever it was in the wall would find an exit while he went below.

Mike picked up his thermos and walked through the house to the now unhidden room that led to the basement. He'd already fixed the rotten stairway down, and installed guardrails so that a parade of people could safely walk down them come fall. Now he needed to make sure the ceiling wouldn't cave in on them if they did.

The atmosphere changed as soon as he stepped down the first two steps. It went from musty, moldy to cool, wet, and rank.

Mike wrinkled his mouth and shook his head. They would have to do something to air this place out before people came in. Creepy was one thing, stinky was another.

He picked up a board from the stack he'd brought down earlier, turned on the string of bare-bulb lights he'd strung across the center span of the basement and went to work on one of the wooden joists. Some of the wood was solid, but he'd felt spongy patches in parts. Best to double any of the support wood and just make sure nothing was going to start sagging once a parade of people started putting weight on the floors upstairs. If this was going to be a house people lived in for the next thirty years, he would have taken a different course. But for a short-term haunted house? Reinforcement, not reconstruction.

He started nailing in one board, and wrinkled his nose. The mix of mold and…decay…was palpable. It smelled like something had died in here. He tried to block it out and focused on setting the board. He should be using his electric gun for this but sometimes he just felt like being old school. His shoulders would thank him later. Not.

He followed the beam down into the dark reaches of the basement. With every foot, the smell grew more rank. Then he stepped on something that squished.

"What the…."

The mud beneath his foot was a darker shade of black. Because a coil of something reddish black twisted out from beneath his shoe. He pulled the flashlight from his belt and shone it at the ground.

His first thought was that he'd stepped on a large dead snake.

But then he realized that there were no scales. And the flesh had ridges. It wasn't a snake.

It lay in a loose circle, and at the center was a fist-sized lump of blackened flesh. It glistened on one side in the light of the flash.

"Holy Jesus," Mike said.

It looked like a heart, surrounded by a halo of intestines.

The flies that suddenly swarmed at his face when he spoke forced him to back away.

He choked and moved quickly toward the exit, trying not to vomit.

Once outside, he pulled out his phone and dialed his friend's number through bleary eyes.

Perry laughed at him.

"It's a raccoon or something that brought a tasty little dinner down there last night," he said. "Roadkill takeout. Get a shovel. You can even expense it. Look, I gotta go. We have actual problems here."

The line went dead.

Mike considered his options. He could shovel entrails out of the basement, or fight with a raccoon or opossum or whatever the hell creature was in the upstairs wall.

After a minute, he went to his truck to find a shovel and a plastic garbage bag.

Guts didn't bite.

★   ★   ★

But no sooner did he step outside than he was faced with another problem.

A witchy-looking woman was marching across the grass toward the house. She was all pointy – bony elbows and legs, and a long beak of a nose. Blond hair sprayed away from her face like a shower of kinks and curls. She looked birdlike and fierce. And driven.

A man who couldn't have been more her opposite strode along behind her, clearly struggling to match her pace. He carried a camera in his hands, the strap hung loose around his neck. Mike stepped back on the porch.

"You have to leave this place," she announced when she put a foot on the stair to his new porch.

Mike frowned, then shook his head.

"No, I don't think so," he said. "I work here."

"Is it true then, that you're turning this place into a haunted house attraction? Something that will bring gawkers instead of reverence?"

He shrugged. "If you mean that I'm rehabbing it so they can use it as a haunted house this fall, then yeah."

"You have to stop it," she said. "Don't you understand that this whole place is a graveyard? People who come here need to do so with the proper respect that the dead deserve. This isn't the place for a carnival. There are spirits here that are better left undisturbed and unprovoked. You can't turn this place into a parade of people."

"Look," Mike said. "I'm just the carpenter. If you have a problem with the business aspect of the house, you should call the county. I can't help you."

"Well, *I* can help *you*," she said. "I can help you understand that what you're doing is akin to grave robbing."

Mike laughed. "I'm not digging up graves," he said.

"No," she said. "But you're disturbing the dead. They are everywhere here. I know you've seen the stones over there," she pointed. "But this whole clearing is an old graveyard. It should be left in peace. This is not the place for a party. The spirits get angry."

"Good thing the spirits can't throw stones then," Mike said. "Because there are going to be plenty of people here this October."

"They can do much worse than throwing stones," she said. Then she stopped talking for a moment, as if she was reassessing the situation and realizing that she was not going to get anywhere with him. Which was the truth. "Please, you have to listen to me. Stop what you're doing here. It will only lead to something…horrible."

She started to step up onto the porch and Mike put his hand up.

"Look, lady, I don't know what you're talking about, and I really don't care. I've got a job to do here, and you're trespassing. If you don't leave now, I'm calling the police."

The fat guy behind her put his hand on her shoulder, clearly trying to convince her to hold back.

"I want to see the inside of this house first," she said. "I want to see what sacrilege you've already committed."

She pulled away from the man's hand and stepped toward Mike on the porch.

He only shook his head and pulled out his phone.

"Two more steps, and I call the police, lady."

"Just a look inside?" she begged.

He shook his head. "I don't care about you, or your spirits or ghosts or whatever. I've got a job to do, and you're stopping it. If you want to complain, call the people who can answer you. They're at the Cook County Forest Preserve offices. And they're going to get on my ass if I don't get back to work."

She stopped, and the big guy put a hand on her shoulder again. Mike could see him squeezing his fingers, giving her a silent message.

She considered, and then nodded.

"All right," she said. "But I'll be back. And I know it sounds all dramatic and everything, but seriously, if you value your soul, you won't keep doing this. The dead aren't going to call the county. They're going to come to you."

She looked at him with a raised eyebrow. "Do you understand what I'm saying to you?"

"Sure," Mike said.

She turned and began to walk away, when he couldn't restrain himself. "But ghosts don't pay my paycheck and my rent."

She looked back over her shoulder and her gaze was deadly serious.

"They don't now," she said. "But if you continue this…you might find that things turn out differently."

The big guy turned and shot a photo of the house, and then quickly put a hand back on her shoulder to push her away. This time, she left without protesting.

★   ★   ★

The afternoon went better.

After disposing of the entrails of…whatever it was…behind the cemetery pond, Mike used up a good stack of 2x4s and completed his reinforcement project. At the end, he stood with hands on hips and reviewed the work. The dark gray wood ceiling of the basement was now striped with blond fresh wood. It was a jarring juxtaposition, but they were probably going to spray a coat of industrial black or dark gray paint over the whole thing anyway. Nobody would see the difference between new and old wood.

He walked over to the spot where he'd found the intestines, and was greeted with a buzz of flies. Mike swatted them away from his face and shook his head. This was not going to do. He needed to get rid of the remnants of the blood that had soaked into the earth, or he was going to be plagued with flies. And probably, in a couple days, maggots. He grimaced and his whole body shivered.

He hated maggots.

"Nope, nope, nope," he said, and walked out of the basement to retrieve the shovel. He would just have to turn over some of the earth and nip this one in the bud.

When he returned, he used the shovel to dig a shallow hole near the place where the ground was still streaked with glistening…blood? Pus? Gut slime? Whatever it was, the flies were loving it. He piled a small mound of earth to one side and then used the shovel to skim off the top of the ground where the intestines had lain. He dropped it into the hole, shovelful by shovelful, until it appeared that the area was clear of anything but dry sandy earth. Satisfied, he slammed the shovel into the ground in the center of the area, right about where the heart had been.

Instead of the shovel lodging in the earth and standing upright on its own, there was an odd cracking sound beneath the spade, and the shovel suddenly dropped a couple feet down below the surface.

"What the hell?" Mike said. The shovel lolled loosely to one side, the spade lost beneath the earth. He pushed the handle one way and then the other. It moved easily. There was apparently an empty space below his feet.

Mike pulled the shovel back up, at first gently, then with a bit more force and began to stomp his foot down on the ground around it. How far did the hollow spot extend? he wondered.

Without warning, his foot fell through the ground.

Mike yelled, and quickly jerked his leg back up. He was more careful then, and began to pile the earth from where his shovel and leg had broken through in a pile to the side of the area.

He didn't have to dig very long before his shovel kept hitting something hard. Something that scraped. It sounded like hollow wood.

Five minutes later, he was brushing the dirt off the top of an old weathered piece of wood. He cleared off more than two feet of earth before he found the edges on either side. The wood angled and grew narrower near the top. It continued beneath the earth and Mike kept digging more and more out until he was sure. The shape seemed hexagonal, flat on top, with sides sloping wider before slimming back again after a point. There was no doubt in Mike's mind as to what he had stepped in to.

"Fuckin' A," he breathed, and looked at his foot, as if to make sure that there were no bones still clinging to it.

He'd punched his shovel, and foot, into the rotted face of a coffin.

It occurred to him that there was likely a worm-eaten skeleton lying just inches below where his hand was clearing away earth. Hell, maybe the intestines and heart that hand lain on the dirt just above the coffin had been from the body buried inside it?

He jerked his hand back.

"Okay, no," he said. "No, no, no. I did not sign on for this."

Mike stepped back from the hole and shook his head. "Fuck this," he said, and turned away. He marched to the exit with the shovel, intending to go to the truck, pack up, and never come back. Let Perry find some other sucker to work on this heap.

He marched across the newly cut 'lawn' in front of the porch to where the pickup was parked in a narrow lane that entered the forest. It was a little farther to walk from the worksite, but it kept the truck cooler than parking it in the direct sun in the clearing. He stopped just before launching the shovel into the back of his pickup.

Katie was sitting on the bumper of the back of his truck.

"Going somewhere?" she said. Her eyes met his, unblinking.

"Yeah," he said. "I'm going anywhere but here."

She pursed her lips in a spoiled pout. "You can't just abandon me here. I thought you were going to build me a haunted house?"

"I don't need to build it," he said. "It already exists." He pointed at the old house behind them. "There are skeletons in the basement and monsters in the walls. My work is done here. I'm going home."

Katie stood up from the bumper and put a hand on his shoulder.

"Please don't say that," she said. "My friends and I are looking forward to coming to the haunted house when it's finished this fall. And...." She looked shy suddenly and her eyes moved to the ground, as she murmured, "I was hoping you'd show me how to build things."

"What are you talking about?" he asked, looking back at the old house.

"My dad used to be pretty handy," she said. "I loved watching him build stuff. I always wanted to learn how. I was hoping to watch you this summer."

"So ask your dad to teach you," Mike suggested.

"I can't," she answered, hanging her head. "He's dead."

"Oh." Mike felt like a shit then. He always seemed to be able to say just the wrong thing at just the wrong time. "Sorry."

He laid the shovel in the bed next to her and then walked to the driver's side of the truck. He'd left his cooler inside and needed water. And then discovered he'd automatically locked the door when he'd gotten out this morning. Mike reached into his pocket to grab his keys, and a shiny strand of metal pulled out with them and fell to the ground. He bent over to pick it up;

it was the locket he'd found in the house and shoved in his jeans the other day.

"You should put that on so you don't lose it," Katie said behind him.

He turned and she was holding out a chain around her own neck. "I have one just like it."

Mike hesitated a minute and then followed her advice, slipping the chain around his neck. The locket slipped beneath his damp t-shirt and quickly warmed to his flesh.

"Since you're going to be building stuff here all summer, I thought maybe I could kind of come by and help out," Katie said. "Plus, I could keep you company. It gets lonely out here."

Mike found himself nodding. It would make it a lot easier to work in that dump if there was a friendly voice nearby. Then he reminded himself of why he was outside. He shook his head.

"There's a coffin in there."

"Where?" she asked.

"The basement. I put my foot right through it."

She shrugged. "We are standing next to a cemetery. Maybe whoever lived here just buried one of their own close. Or…maybe they built the house over part of the cemetery. Maybe that was here first and there are a bunch of people buried down there."

She stopped and gave him an evil smile. "Think of all the ghosts there might be in your haunted house!"

Mike shook his head. "That's exactly what I'm afraid of."

She tilted her head and made a sad face. In a slightly mocking voice she asked, "Ahh, are you afraid of the scary ghosts?"

"Yes," he said. "I mean no, I'm not afraid of ghosts, but I don't want to be working around a bunch of dead bodies."

She shrugged. "I don't think they come out much during the day when you're here."

He couldn't help but laugh at that.

"So what do you say?" she asked.

"About what?"

She fingered her necklace and asked, "Will you show me the ropes?"

He hesitated, and then thought of his rent bill. Maybe he could handle this place if someone was with him. And he had to admit, he welcomed the opportunity to have the chance to spend time with her.

"I guess so," he said. "But that depends what they decide to do, now that I found this coffin. That may stop the whole project."

"Why?" she asked.

"If they decide to excavate the whole basement to look for other coffins...."

She shook her head. "Why would they do that? The bodies are buried, if there are any. And you're probably going to put in a floor down there anyway, right?"

He shrugged. "Part of it."

"There you go," she said. "Better to build right over the coffins than disturb them, right?"

"I'll have to check," he said. "That's not my decision to make."

"Can I see it?" she asked.

"The coffin?"

She nodded.

"Yeah, I guess so." He led the way back to the house. Katie followed a step behind.

"I didn't think girls were into coffins," he said.

She didn't answer.

When they reached the short staircase down, he turned and said, "It's down here."

But she wasn't behind him.

"Katie?" he called. The clearing between him and the truck was empty.

"Right here," she said. He jumped. She had slipped ahead of him and was standing on the first stair down. "What are you waiting for?"

Her head disappeared down the cellar entrance. Mike shook his head and followed her down.

The damp stink of the place got to him instantly and he grimaced. "This place reeks," he complained.

"You just need some candles," she said. "Or incense. That'd fix it right up. Where's the body?"

"Over here," he said, and led her across the sandy floor.

When they reached the spot, she bent over and looked down at the hole in the ground. "You can't really see anything," she complained. "I thought you'd dug the whole thing out."

He shook his head. "Were you hoping to see a skeleton?"

"Kinda." She grinned. "Do you have a flashlight?"

"Are you serious?" He laughed.

She met his eyes but didn't say anything. She *wasn't* kidding.

"Hang on," he said.

Mike walked to the end of the basement and lifted the work light from the nail he'd pounded into the ceiling joist. He lifted the next lamp as well and dragged the extension cord and lamps over to the hole his foot had broken through. The jagged splinters of wood suddenly shone in sharp relief to the dark space beneath. Katie got down on her knees and peered into the hole.

"All I see is dirt," she said.

"What did you expect?"

"Well, it's a coffin," she said. "There ought to be…bones."

"Maybe it was a small body?" he suggested.

Mike crouched next to her and looked into the space as well. He could see the bottom of the coffin, and a scattering of dirt where the cave-in had occurred. But she was right. He couldn't see anything else in the space, even if he angled the light right or left.

"Hang on," he said, "I'll be right back."

Mike returned from the truck a minute later with the shovel he'd just put away. Then he began to clear more of the dirt from the top of the coffin. It only took a few moments to fully clear the upper third of the coffin. Most of it appeared to be buried less than a foot or so below the surface of the earth. Mike's foot had plunged through the old wood right about where the ribcage of a normal-sized body should have been.

He turned the shovel upside down then and used the grip of the handle to punch through the coffin lid next to the original hole he'd stomped. A couple of plunges cracked off another foot of rotted wood and the whole upper part of the casket was soon visible in the harsh light of his lamps.

He stopped after a couple more stomps and stared into the hole.

"Huh," he said.

The coffin was clearly empty.

"Well, that's disappointing," Katie said.

"And weird," he said.

She nodded agreement. "That should make you feel better about digging up bodies down here, though."

"Yeah," he said. And then he put the spade into the earth and began digging around the outside of the coffin.

"What are you doing?"

"What are *we* doing," he corrected. "I'm not going to leave a big hollow spot under my basement floor. This thing's coming out of here. And since you're my new apprentice, you're going to help me move it."

★   ★   ★

Once Mike trenched around the old coffin, they lifted and walked the rotting thing to the far side of the basement and set it down against the wall. "I'll let Perry decide what he wants to do about it," he said.

Then he filled in the hole in the earth, scooping soil from all around the area to even out the surface.

"I signed on to this project as a carpenter, not a gravedigger," he complained.

Katie smiled from where she sat nearby. "You do what you gotta do," she said.

"Well, what I gotta do is get a shitload of work done," he said.

"I'm here to help," she offered.

"That's great," he said, as he tried to quickly do some math in his head. "But I can't really pay you much. This contract is a one-man job. And they got me cheap."

She shook her head. "I don't want money. I just want to watch what you do. And I might not be able to be here every day or anything. But I'll help when I can."

He nodded. "Fair enough. But I'm going to tire you out while you're here. It's a lot easier to carry wood with two people than one."

"Most things are easier with two people," she said.

Mike thought of his recent history with Mia and frowned. "I wouldn't know about that."

"Maybe I can show you then," she suggested.

"We'll see," he said and looked at his watch. Somehow the afternoon had moved on, and it was already past four-thirty. "Right now, I'd like to get some things ready for tomorrow. Because it's quitting time."

"What do we need to do?" she asked.

"While you're here, I'd like to move some boards inside so I can start right in tomorrow morning."

She agreed, and together they carried stacks of 2x4s and some 2x6s into both the basement and the first floor. At some point, Emery had shown up and helped with the carting. When they were finished, Mike's forehead was dripping with sweat and Emery's normally pale face looked flushed, but Katie looked none the worse for wear. She smiled as he put his hands on his thighs after moving the last load and took a deep breath.

"You look like you could use a drink," she said.

He nodded, too hot and tired to speak.

"Did you bring a cooler today?"

He nodded again. "Yeah, in the bed of the truck," he said.

"Meet you on the deck?" she said, and disappeared out of the room.

★   ★   ★

"They say that the woman who lived in this house was a witch," Katie said.

Mike tilted back a Pabst Blue Ribbon and shook his head. "Yeah, I've heard that," he said. "Not surprised. I don't know who else would choose to live out here in the woods."

"Oh, come on," she said. "Back then, this whole area was woods. But the woman who lived here, they say she killed her husband in a ritual to gain power over life and death."

"She sounds lovely," he said.

Katie shrugged. "He was an asshole anyway."

"Why, did you know him?" Mike asked with a smile.

Katie's face looked odd for a moment. Then she laughed. "No, of course not. That was like, fifty years ago or something. But they say she had his baby and he treated her bad and then killed her baby in a fit of rage. So...she took his energy for her own."

Mike emptied the last drops of the can before crumpling it in his hand. He tossed it to the side, and after a moment of consideration, pulled another from the cooler and popped the tab. He offered it to her, but she put out a hand and raised her can in the air. "Still working on it," she said.

He leaned back against the gray wooden siding of the old house. Katie shifted her position and a moment later, rested her head on his shoulder. Mike tensed a little, but then went with it. He slid his back down a hair against the house and slowly moved his arm until his hand gripped her shoulder, pulling her closer. She sighed and took a sip of her beer.

"It's so peaceful here, isn't it?" she asked after a minute.

The sun had disappeared behind the house and the upper leaves of the forest before them glowed with the rays of the setting sun. Bird noise colored the breeze that shivered through the trees, making the leaves shimmer with light and shadow.

"Yeah," he said. "You almost can't hear the turnpike back here."

"It's like a secret place," she said. "Hidden from the world."

Mike nodded. "It won't be hidden for long. This fall there will be lines of people from the turnpike to this house."

She pulled closer to him. "Well, for now, we can enjoy it like it's our own secret place."

Mike felt the buzz of his second beer beginning and looked down into the girl's face in the crook of his arm. She didn't look away.

Part of him wondered exactly what was happening here. The other part was an opportunist. Mike bent down and kissed her.

Katie's lips were cool and moist and he felt his entire body relax as her tongue slipped into his mouth.

What the hell? a voice in his head asked.

Another voice countered. *Shut up and kiss her.*

Soon he was lost in her mouth and her touch. His beer can rolled across the deck, nearly empty, and he used the freed arm to slip around her, drawing her closer. Never mind that he was sweaty and probably smelled like shit. She didn't seem to mind and he wasn't going to miss the opportunity for the first real taste of a woman since his wife had left him months ago.

Maybe she was too young. Maybe it was wrong. He didn't care about anything but the soft touch of her lips against his, and the feel of her skin as his hand slipped inside her shirt and rose up toward her....

"No!" she said suddenly, and broke the kiss, moving away from him across the deck.

"Not here," she said. "Not now. I'm sorry."

She got up and ran down the steps to disappear into the trees.

Mike picked up her beer, with beads of sweat running down the can, and downed a slug. It was still mostly full, and cold.

The forest was silent, except for the evening hum of crickets. Once again, he was alone. Just when it had felt good to be near someone again, he'd fucked it up.

He guzzled the rest of the can and closed his eyes before the tears came.

CHAPTER SEVEN

"You are my favorite Asian zombie ever!" Jeanie said as Bong walked into the living room of her small apartment. She threw her arms around him and kissed him as if she hadn't seen him in weeks. Never mind that they'd gone out to Teehan's just last night for drinks.

"Wha—" he said, between her frantic kisses.

"I got it!" she said. "I got the haunted house job!"

Bong smiled. "Ah. And here I thought you were just happy to see me."

She slapped him on the shoulder. "Well, I *am*, silly. It was the makeup I did on you that got me the job. Plus – and here's the coolest thing – they said that they wanted you to work as one of the actors who scare people at the house. Can you believe it? We can be together all of October and you can get paid too!"

She took in his look of dismay and put a finger to his scowling lips before he could say a word. "Say that you'll do it? Please?"

"Why would I want to be a spook in a haunted house?" Bong asked. "I already have a job, I don't need another one."

"Because we'll get to do it together!" she said. "They want me to do makeup, but they also want me to be a spook too. So, we can haunt the house together. How awesome will that be?"

He looked up at the ceiling, and then back at her. He couldn't complain too much. He enjoyed being with Jeanie. And to be with her while she was in her element, having fun….

Bong nodded in a hesitant yes.

"Oh, I love you!" Jeanie said, bouncing up and down on her toes and planting kisses on his lips with every move.

"I'll cross off every free minute in October," he said. "But as for today…."

"Oh, that's what I wanted to tell you," Jeanie said. "There's a meeting today for everyone who's going to work in the house. I thought since you were coming over anyway, maybe we could go."

"But we had a date…."

"It'll still be a date, silly," she said. "Only we'll be with a bunch of other people who love haunted houses as much as we do."

She looked at his face and quickly corrected herself. "Okay, as much as *I* do. But we'll be together?"

"Okay," he said.

"Good," she said, and walked across the room to pick up her makeup kit. "Can you drive? Because the meeting is in fifteen minutes."

★   ★   ★

They pulled up in front of a tan duplex house in Oak Forest as dusk was setting in, and clearly, they were not the first to arrive. The street was filled with cars on both sides of the street.

"How many people are coming to this?" Bong asked.

Jeanie shrugged. "I dunno. But I know that anyone who works on haunted houses on the south side wants to be part of this, since it's at Bachelor's Grove. So, I'm not surprised if it's crowded. This is so cool. It's a total honor to be part of this."

Bong couldn't hide the fact that he didn't put the experience on quite the same level she did. But she grabbed his hand and dragged him forward down the sidewalk to the doorway of the host house. There was a picture of Jack Skellington from the movie *The Nightmare Before Christmas* on the window.

"This is it," she enthused. She lifted her hand to knock on the door, and a face appeared in the window. A black man with almost no hair, and a t-shirt that featured the steel claws of Freddy from *A Nightmare on Elm Street,* opened the door.

"Do you know the password?" he asked. "I have just one clue for you: Haunted."

Jeanie grinned. "House?"

"You're in," he said, and pushed the screen door open wider.

"Hi, I'm Lenny," he said, extending a long thin hand once they were inside.

Jeanie took his hand and introduced herself and Bong. "Is this your house?" she asked.

Lenny laughed. "Oh no," he said. "I don't play that way. I live in an apartment down on Harlem Avenue. This is my pal June's place. She's got the big corporate job and mortgage and all, but I don't rib her about it too much. Because, well, she likes haunted houses and shit still."

"That and the fact that I let you sleep here most of the time," a woman's voice said from behind him.

A thin girl with pale features and long auburn hair walked up behind him and smacked him in the back of the head before smiling and ducking left down a hall.

Jeanie and Bong followed Lenny into a crowded kitchen that connected to an equally crowded living room. There were at least thirty people in the house, and half of them seemed to be wearing shirts from horror movies.

Jeanie squeezed Bong on the arm and gestured at the group with a grin. "I feel like I just came home," she said. "And I don't know any of these people."

Bong smiled. "So…what are we supposed to do here exactly?" he asked.

Jeanie shrugged. "I don't know. But I guess we'll find out."

At that moment, a guy in a shirt dominated by a decayed face with gnarled teeth and maggots crawling from a rotted eyeball (the text beneath the photo said *Zombi*) stood up in front of a widescreen TV that was playing *Halloween III: Season of the Witch* with the sound turned off. Jeanie could hear the 'Silver Shamrock' theme from the movie instantly play in her head. The thing was so obnoxiously addictive.

"Hey everyone!" he said, calling out to still the room. "Some of you know me and some don't, but we're going to be working together a lot over the next few weeks. My name is Lon, and I'm the production manager for Bremen House, the Bachelor's Grove Haunted House attraction. I've done a lot of work on stage design, and worked for a couple seasons on the Stateville Prison haunted house. Plus I've always put together a haunted house in my garage for the kids, so I'm really psyched to be working with you on this. It's going to be awesome."

He looked around the room for a minute and then grinned. "There you are. June, come on up here."

The auburn-haired girl slipped between a couple guys in Metallica and Anthrax t-shirts, and joined him at the front of the room. She hung her head a little, clearly uncomfortable with being the center of attention.

"This is June," Lon said. "For any of you who haven't met her, she's the best monster makeup artist you're ever going to meet, and she'll be leading all of you who are here to work on makeup and costume design. She's really amazing, and if she didn't hang out so much with Lenny, I'd ask her to marry me and turn me into a zombie."

June looked up at Lon, clearly mortified.

"I'm kidding," he said. "But she is really good. And in a couple minutes, I'm going to ask all of you who are here for makeup to follow her for direction. But some housekeeping first. I'm your official 'stage manager' for the next few weeks, so if you have any problems or questions on anything, I want you to let me know. We'll figure out how to fix it. Or kill it. Whatever it takes."

He motioned for a thin guy in a *Suspiria* t-shirt to step forward. "This guy calls himself Argento. You'll always be able to find him – just look for the *Suspiria* or *Opera* or *Four Flies on Gray Velvet* or *Deep Red* or *Phenomena* t-shirt. I don't think he owns a shirt that isn't a Dario Argento movie. Don't ask me what his real name is; I don't know and I don't care."

He pointed at another wiry guy with brown hair standing nearby. "And where you find Argento, you'll also find Lucio. I'm guessing that's not his real name either. All I know is they make amazing sets – if you went to the Rob Zombie Great American Nightmare house in Villa Park last year, you know what I mean. Argento's going to be in charge of designing all of the rooms in the house. Anyone who's doing painting and set stuff, you'll be working with him. And please feed him some ideas – because we can't have every room in this place end up looking like a set from *Suspiria*."

"I don't see why not," the guy who called himself Argento said, but Lon just shook his head. "No. But I don't want to see a *Sharknado*-themed room either."

"This is a twister…*with teeth*," someone yelled.

Lon held up his hands and smiled. "So, here's the way it's going to go down. For the next month or so, there's a guy out at the house fixing it up. Don't go out there; you can't get in. He's putting down new floors and shit and fixing it up so the place is useable for us. While he's doing that, we're going to be planning out the room themes. We want every room to reference a really cool horror movie. I know the people who walk through in October probably won't always get half the references, but if the rooms are good – really good – then they'll have an awesome time anyway. And for those who are really big horror movie fans…they're going to be in heaven. So once we have the themes all mapped out, the set folks are going to work with Argento to figure out how to make the rooms look real. And the makeup peeps are going to plan out their spooks based on the room themes. We'll have a couple big group meetings between now and September, but mostly we'll be working in smaller groups and we'll communicate what's going on with everything in a private Facebook group. Before you leave here tonight, make sure you write down your Facebook ID on the signup sheet in the kitchen so we can add you."

"Are those knives on your fingers?" Jeanie whispered. Lenny had ended up next to them. He raised his hands and flexed his fingers with a smile. His fingers were the color of milk chocolate, but the blue blades of the tattoos looked dangerous. He nodded.

"Are you a *Nightmare* fan?" he asked.

Jeanie grinned. "Freddy forever."

"Then you have to see this." He nodded his head toward the back of the room, and then turned and walked.

Jeanie and Bong followed.

Lenny led them up a short flight of stairs to a bedroom. He grinned as he pushed a door open and gestured for them to enter.

"What do you think?" he asked as they stepped inside.

"Holy shit, what happened in here?" Bong gasped.

The pale lavender walls were splattered with spots of what looked like blood. It dripped down the walls in dark, dried trails but the real disturbing part was on the ceiling. A life-size female manikin hung from the center of it, just above the bed. Her nightgown hung in tatters and her mouth was open in a silent scream.

"June let me decorate the bedroom," he explained. "So, I chose the film that started it all."

"*A Nightmare on Elm Street*," Jeanie said.

"Reel One!" he grinned.

Jeanie smiled in appreciation, and noted that one wall appeared to have a phrase on it finger-painted in what looked like more blood. It read, 'To Sleep, Perchance To Dream…'

"It's really cool, but I don't know how you sleep in here," Jeanie said.

"Nah," he said. "It's comforting. A refuge. The world of *Nightmare* is way more safe than the world out there." He pointed out the bedroom window. "Human beings, those are the monsters that you've gotta fear."

Jeanie nodded. "Can't argue with you there."

He walked to a closet and opened the door. A moment later he turned around, a latex mask of Freddy Krueger covering his face.

"Do you think you can make me look like this with makeup instead of a mask?"

She frowned. "I dunno," she said, hesitating. "Your skin is already pretty dark."

"See, that's what I'm always talking about," he said. "Black guys never get the good parts in horror movies. We're always just bums or zombies or shit like that. And just look at this cast for the haunted house. I'm the only black guy in the group."

"I'd guess that's just because no other guys came out for this," Jeanie suggested. "Or…if this is like a horror movie, maybe it means you're the only one of us who is going to survive the entire month of haunting the house."

Lenny shook his head. "More likely, it means I'll end up dying in some ridiculous way on Halloween night when this thing is open to the public… and everyone will just think I'm a prop."

At that moment, June walked into the room, shaking her head.

"Are we back to the poor black man bit again?" she said. "Just get over it. There are plenty of black guys in horror and they have great roles, not just victims. What about Tony Todd in *Candyman*? What about Duane Jones in *Night of the Living Dead*? If horror discriminates against anyone, it's women. Always whiny screaming victims who can't run more than five feet without falling down."

"Not true," Lenny said, quickly warming up to what was obviously a continuing argument. "How about one of the strongest characters in a horror movie ever – Sigourney Weaver in *Alien*. Or even Heather Langenkamp as Nancy in *Nightmare*? She's a kid but she goes up against Freddy. She doesn't just run away and whine."

"Exceptions," June said. Then she turned to Jeanie and asked, "What do you think? Who gets the short stick more in horror films, girls or black guys?"

"I think you can make a generalization about pretty much anything to support whatever argument you want to support," Jeanie said. "If you're a black guy, you're the victim of racial prejudice. If you're a woman, there's the glass ceiling of The Man keeping you down. If you're a white guy…all of the minorities – and women – are out to get you. Everybody can point to some one or some group that is 'keeping them down'. So…I just don't go there."

June grinned and clapped Jeanie on the shoulder. "Well said! I think I'm going to like you…um…."

"Jeanie," she answered.

June grinned. "June and Jeanie. Let's make some monsters," she said, leading them back into the hall. Jeanie saw Bong waiting for her at the foot of the stairs and waved.

"Black or white or Korean," June continued, noticing Bong. "They're all going to be scary as hell."

CHAPTER EIGHT

The field grass around the cemetery was wet with dew as Mike pulled the truck down the slim gravel road bordering the old stones. It was going to be a hot one; while the air was heavy with the fresh smells of summer and a gentle morning breeze, he could taste the coming heat of the day in the air. The moisture beading on the tips of the grass right now would be burned off in an hour.

He parked and pulled his cooler and toolbox from the back bed of the truck. He had a feeling he was going to need the former more than the latter in a couple more hours.

Despite the outdoor weather, the basement of the house was cool and dank as he went down the steps and turned on his utility lights. As long as he had to work down here, the day might not be too bad.

All the lights on the far end of the basement were off, and then Mike remembered that he had unplugged part of the strand yesterday when he'd been digging, because the hanging lamps kept hitting him in the head. He'd ended up laying the problem lights on the ground out of the way, and using a camping lantern he had in the truck to light the area of the dig.

As he walked a few steps from the door, the basement turned pitch black almost immediately. Mike reached down and grabbed the extension cord that fed power across the room and used it as a guide to trace his way across the floor until its end, walking slowly step by step into the darkness. When he found the end, he felt around on the damp earth until he located the disconnected cord that fed the lights in the back half of the basement. He plugged it in, and the dark disappeared in a wash of yellowish light, though some was beaming directly into the earth, where he'd laid the lights down yesterday.

When he stood up with the cord in hand, something *thunked* against the back of his head. He jumped, and then turned around.

A dark object swayed from the joist above.

"What the hell is that?" he whispered, and grabbed for the nearest light lying nearby on the ground. It was encased in a metal hood with a protective lattice across the open portion so you could drop it without breaking the bulb. The casing had a hook and typically hung from a nail in one of the joists; the open end of the case where the light came out was currently beaming into the ground. He lifted it up by the hook and turned it around to point the light at exactly what he'd bumped into. Mike felt his jaw drop as he took in what the bulbs illuminated. He slowly aimed the light from left to right, noting one carcass after the other hanging from the beam.

They all looked like bloody lumps of fur. Three raccoons. A couple of squirrels; small striped things that he guessed were chipmunks; a rabbit. One pale gray thing with a long snout that boasted a row of sharp yellowed teeth. An opossum.

The animals were strung from the beams in a circle all around the old coffin area that Mike had dug up and then immediately re-buried yesterday. Beneath each body, the ground was dark with drained animal blood. And in the center, above where the coffin was buried, a symbol was drawn in the earth. It was faint, but Mike could see it still. He guessed that someone had made it using the animal blood, and while it might be dry, the earth would hold that darker color for a long time to come. The symbol looked like something he'd seen in a horror movie dealing with witches and the devil. A circle, with a star inside it.

"Okay, that's really it," he whispered and backed away from the scene, step by step. He could feel his heart beating, harder and harder with every second that passed.

What the hell was going on in this place?

★   ★   ★

Once he got outside and could take a couple of deep breaths in the dappled sunlight that came through the trees, he dialed Perry's number with shaking fingers.

"Hello, Bremen Enterprises," his friend's voice answered.

"Your devil worshippers are still here," Mike growled. "The work site is full of dead bodies."

"Bodies, what? Is this Mike? What are you talking about?"

Mike quickly explained what he'd seen, as he walked around the outside of the house and back up the porch steps to return to the main level. He could feel his emotions growing with every word that described the scene with the blooded animals.

"That's it, I'm done," he said. "This place is rotting, stinking and creepy. It should be left alone to rot into the earth and disappear. That's what it was in the middle of doing when we started trying to save it. There are animals in the walls and fucking devil worshippers apparently hanging out here at night. I don't want any more part in it."

"Whoa, calm down, man," Perry said. "We'll work this out. I need you to finish this now, I really do. We've got the set builders and decorators ready to come out in two or three weeks to start working on the rooms. I can't lose even a day now."

"I'm not working in a place where people are killing things," Mike said. "For all I know, they're just waiting around in the trees and I'm going to be their next human sacrifice."

Perry laughed on the other end of the line. "It's just kids screwing around. You're overreacting. But I get it, I do. You're kind of remote out there. How about this? We'll put a night watchman on the place from now on, so nobody can get in there when you're not around."

"I don't want to work in this craphole," Mike complained.

"Nobody does," Perry said. "Trust me, I asked around."

"I thought I was your first choice?"

"You're my friend," Perry said. "But originally I tried to get a couple of bigger contractors in to do this job faster."

"Well, I suggest you give them a call again," Mike said.

"Time and a half," Perry said. His voice sounded panicked. "We'll give you a watchman and time and a half for the rest of the month." His voice calmed then, and he said softer, "I need you to finish this, Mike. Please."

At that moment, Katie walked into the room, and leaned against the doorway. Her eyebrows lifted in askance, as if to say, 'what are we gonna do today?'

His fear of devil worshippers suddenly dissipated, and Mike thought of the opportunity to work with Katie at his side all day.

"Okay," Mike said into the phone. "But only because it's you."

*And only because Katie is here…*his mind added.

Perry said something that he only half heard. And then Mike was mumbling goodbye and thumbing the end call button. He dropped the phone into his pocket and took a step toward the doorway.

"Hi," he said. "I thought I'd scared you off for good."

Katie smiled and shook her head. "Can't scare me," she said. "What's the project for today?"

It was Mike's turn to smile. "Well, after I bury a bunch of dead animals, we're going to put down a wood plank floor and make sure that nobody can stumble on any other hidden coffins or blood puddles from sacrificed animals. Basically, we're going to make the scary basement not scary so that they can come in with a bunch of paint and props and make it scary again."

"Seems like a waste of time," Katie said.

"Yep," he agreed. "But you know, it pays the rent."

★   ★   ★

Katie held a plastic sheet as one by one, Mike clipped the strings that held the animals suspended from the beams. When all of the bloody balls of fur were lying on the sheet, he grabbed the opposite side of the plastic and walked it to her. When his hands brushed hers, he felt a spark shoot down his spine. His skin grew strangely warm. He was sure he saw a glint in her eyes as he took the plastic from her hand and pulled the ends together so that he could drag the plastic out of the cellar without losing any bodies. Or blood.

"Thanks," he said.

"Whatever you need," she answered. Her voice was soft. Like rose petals.

He dug a hole on the edge of the cemetery, away from the house, and dropped the animals in. Katie moved boards into the basement as he piled dirt back in the hole and retrieved his saw from the truck.

"How's this?" she asked, as he came down the steps to find a neatly stacked pile of 5/4x6 boards on one side of the door, and 2x4s on the other. Emery stood nearby, leaning against one shadowed basement wall. He nodded at her but she didn't move.

"Um, perfect," he said to Katie. "We'll frame it out with the 2x4s today and depending how far we get, slap down the wide boards tomorrow."

With Katie's help, the rest of the day passed quickly. And at the end, she brought him his cooler as they sat on the edge of the deck near the entry door. He popped the top on a PBR and almost couldn't wait for the telltale sound of the hiss of carbonation to down the first gulp. He hadn't eaten or drunk anything in hours, he realized. But he'd been more productive than he'd been on a job in months. Maybe years.

"Thanks for your help today," he said to Katie. "I couldn't have done it without you."

"Whatever you need," she said again with a slight smile. "I just want to help you get it done. My friends and I are looking forward to a haunted house this Halloween."

"Well, they will have you to thank for it," he said.

Katie smiled, but said nothing.

★   ★   ★

Over the next three days, Katie turned up shortly after Mike arrived, usually with Emery in tow, and they helped him carry, cut and measure wood as he framed out and ultimately hid the dirt floor of the basement. Mike had covered the earth beneath the wood with a heavy plastic sheet to help keep the dampness and mildew odors contained.

"Why do you always use that?" she asked at one point, as he slapped a square on the board he was measuring. "My dad used to just mark wood really fast using another board."

"Maybe I'm not as good as your dad," he said. "This helps me make sure my cuts are always ninety degrees."

"Does it even really matter down here?" she said. "I mean, it's a basement floor that is just to give people something dry to walk on. It doesn't have to be perfect."

"Maybe not," he said. "But I don't work sloppy. Every cut you make says something about the carpenter. Whether I'm building a treehouse or a mansion, I make my cuts true. It's just how I roll."

She shrugged. "Just was curious. That's good, I guess."

Once they finished the floor, Katie helped him place plywood sheets over the frames he'd put from floor to ceiling on two sides of the basement. Perry had asked him to divide the basement into three rooms since they were taking the time to floor it. The division gave them two additional rooms to 'haunt' come fall.

He didn't bother to put full doorways on the carve-outs, since people would just be filing in and out anyway. The decorators would probably hang plastic or beads or something to screen them off.

"Just hold it right there," he said, as Katie held the last piece of plywood square to the ceiling. Her arms were outstretched, crucifixion style, to press the board in place, and he came up behind her with the nail gun to reach over her head, press the trigger and shoot the top nails in. His chest pressed the back of her head as he bent forward to hold the gun in place. When he'd set the last nail, he dropped a hand to her shoulders. He knew he shouldn't touch her that way, but he couldn't resist. Every hour she was near he found himself more and more drawn to her. He said things to her as they worked just to hear her talk. When he got in his truck at night to go home, he found the silence without her voice almost deafening.

He craved her company, almost as much as he craved a cold one.

You're fucked, a voice in his head noted.

"All right," he said, looking at the plywood that sat snug to the beam. "We are officially done down here. They can paint these walls or put spiderwebs on them or whatever…but the walls and floor are in. Now it's time to move upstairs."

"What room is next?" she asked, not moving from beneath the press of his hand.

"I thought we'd start in the attic and work our way down," he said.

"Sounds like a plan," she agreed.

She moved away from him, but not without a knowing look in his direction, and the faint hint of a 'I kinda liked you touching me' smile.

He led the way back up out of the basement, which now smelled like clean fresh-cut lumber instead of mold and blood and rot. Maybe not the best prerequisite for 'haunting'. But that wasn't his problem.

They passed into the house through the kitchen and walked up the creaking steps to the attic.

"If we find any dead deer or raccoons hanging from nooses from the rafters, I'm leaving," Mike said.

"I'll be right behind you," Katie said. "That's gross."

There were no dead animals in the attic. But there was a lot of dust. And a dry smell of age. The heat was palpable; the air felt thick enough to cut with a knife.

"We need to get these windows open," Mike said. He walked to the right side of the long room and pulled with all his might on the handle of a window. It didn't move.

"Shit," he said. Crowbar time again.

"I got this one," Katie said at the other end of the attic.

The window squeaked, but seemed to rise easily under her hands.

"How did you do that?" he said, walking across the attic to join her. "The other window is dry-rotted shut."

"Magic," she said with an eyeroll.

He ran his hand over the edge of the window sill and shook his head. "Magic is what we're going to need to keep this place from falling down once hundreds of people start walking through it."

"I thought you fixed all that," she said. "I mean, all of the stuff you did in the basement made it more sturdy, right?"

He shrugged. "Well, I don't think the first floor is going to fall into the basement," he said. "But that doesn't mean this place is sturdy. Look at this wood. It turns to sawdust under your fingers."

As he said it, a chunk of the window frame snapped under his fingers, and an inch-long piece fell to the attic floor.

"See what I mean?"

She grinned. "Well, I guess that just means you can show me the best way to fix a rotted-out window."

"I'll tell you how," he said. "In this place? Just board it up."

He ran a hand around the window frame, and then pounded a fist against the wall. He repeated the motion a foot or so out from the window, and then stepped down the wall and did it again, cocking his head to listen at each spot.

"What are you doing?" she asked.

"Just trying to get a feel for what shape the walls are in up here."

He stomped a foot on the floor, close to the wall. His face filled with worry lines as he did it. He stepped a couple feet away from the wall and tried again, looking as if he expected to punch one boot through the floor. After several stomps, his face lost its look of trepidation.

"I'm shocked, but happy," he said. "Amazingly, it sounds pretty solid up here."

Then he put his foot down again and frowned. "That will teach me to open my mouth."

"What is it?" she asked.

"*That* sounded hollow."

He stomped again, a few inches away, and then dropped to the floor. With one finger, he followed a line in the wood. A gap.

"I think there's a trapdoor here," he said. "You almost can't see it, because the handle is fashioned to drop down into the wood and basically disappear."

Mike slipped his fingernails between two indentations a few inches apart and lifted. A slim wooden handle rose from the floor.

"Now that's craftsmanship," he said. "Nicely done."

He began to raise the door, but Katie put a hand on his shoulder. "That's probably just an old laundry chute," she said. "I don't think we want to go down there."

He raised it a foot, and could only see blackness below. A cloud of stale, foul air filled the corner of the room as he peered below. "It looks wide for laundry."

She shook her head. "All these old places had them. And there would be a small ladder, in case something got stuck on the way down and you had to go chase it."

Mike sneezed then, the cloud of dust and mold from below hitting his sinuses like a sledgehammer. He dropped the door and fumbled in his pocket to look for a tissue.

"Maybe you should build, like, a wall or platform or something here to block this corner off, so you don't have a bunch of people stepping on the door?" she suggested.

Mike stood up and sneezed again and again. When the fit passed, he nodded. "Probably not a bad idea. First thing is to make sure the rest of the floor is solid I suppose. I think I'll need to come back with a dust mask and a flashlight to check the chute out."

He blinked his eyes to clear the tears, and went back to stomping on the floorboards, slowly moving away from the trapdoor. His thumps got harder and faster as he felt more and more confident that the floor was still solid.

Just before he reached the other end, a bell chimed from his pocket. Mike pulled his phone out and shook his head. "Damn, it's four-thirty already," he said. "I don't think we're going to start up here tonight. I should start packing things up."

Katie shrugged and looked at him with wide eyes designed to ensure a positive response. "Do you have time for a beer before you go?"

"If you have time to drink one with me," he said.

"Only one?"

"Bad girl," Mike said. But he couldn't help grinning as he said it. "I am pretty sure there are a few still in the cooler."

CHAPTER NINE

"We have to go back there tonight," Jillie said. She punctuated that statement by pointing at him with a long, fresh-cut French fry. They were having lunch at Nicky's Carryout, arguably the best greasy spoon in the south suburbs. It had been there on the corner of 143rd Street, just a couple miles down the road from Bachelor's Grove, for decades. There was history in that grease stuck to the old tile walls.

Ted shook his head. "What's that going to accomplish? You've already lodged a complaint with the county, and you know what that got us. Exactly what you expected. This state has just about the biggest debt in the nation; there's no way they're going to turn down some easy money on a broken-down old house because somebody thinks there might be angry ghosts."

"I just need to know," Jillie said. "I want to feel what the state of the place is. Are the spirits dangerously angry? Are they quiet?"

"And if they're pissed off and grinding skull teeth, what are you going to do about it?" Ted said. "Do you think the county board is going to act differently if you go in to their board meeting in August and say, 'You can't open that haunted house, the dead are really teed off about it'?"

Jillie shot him a just-shut-the-hell-up glance, but said nothing.

"This isn't your fight," Ted said. "Don't go to war on something you can't win."

"Is that what you would have told Washington and Jefferson and the rest?" she asked. "Don't bother, you can't win?"

Now it was Ted's turn to roll his eyes. "What, you're the daughter of the Revolution now? Look, all I'm trying to say is—"

"I get it," she interrupted. "But that doesn't change things. I understand Bachelor's Grove. I know what could happen there if things really get tilted. I have to at least try my best to not let that happen. It's my responsibility."

"So, we go there tonight and...what?" Ted asked.

"You bring the EMF meter and full spectrum camera, and I'll just listen. I want to see what kind of activity there is now that this guy is in the house all the time."

"You think we're going to pick up a lot of stuff?"

"I would make sure your battery is charged and you have plenty of memory," she said. "Yes."

"Okay," he said. "Pick you up at eleven-thirty?"

"Perfect," she said. Then she looked at his plate. "Are you going to eat your pickle?"

★   ★   ★

The Midlothian Turnpike was dark and empty when they edged over to the side and parked Ted's car on a gravel shoulder close to the small bridge near Bachelor's Grove. Fleetwood Mac was singing 'Go Your Own Way' on the radio and the reflection of the radio LED tinted Jillie's face a strange electric blue.

"This is it," Ted said.

She nodded. "Kill the lights before anyone else sees us."

He did, and then got out and pulled the sensing and recording equipment from the trunk. Most of it was stuffed in a backpack, which he shrugged with a grunt over his shoulders. A minute later, they were trudging down the weedy gravel path that led past the old fence beneath the heavy tree cover and into the cemetery grounds.

"Did you bring the flashlight?" Jillie asked as they moved down the darkening path away from the turnpike.

A second later, a light flicked on, and Ted pointed it ahead of them at the path.

"I can always count on you," she said.

"Remember, I have a digital recorder," he said.

"Anything recorded can be erased," she countered.

He snorted. "Not if it's saved to the cloud."

"Trust me," she said. "Everything on the cloud is going to get wiped out one of these days by a thunderstorm."

"Always so negative about progress," he said.

"I didn't tell you to carry cassette tapes, did I?" she asked.

"Touché. Shhh," he said, pointing ahead. "There's a car here."

"Interesting," Jillie whispered. They approached the dark shape carefully, but once they arrived at it and peered into the windows, she pronounced it safe.

"Maybe someone drove it off the road and abandoned it here," she suggested.

"Or someone's in the house," he said.

"I guess we'll see," she said. "But I don't think so. Nobody that we can see with our own eyes, anyway."

They walked silently across the grass to the old house at the end of the clearing. Jillie stepped up the two stairs of the porch and walked quickly across the deck to the door.

"Do you think it's actually unlocked?" Ted whispered.

She put her hand on the doorknob. "Only one way to find out."

The knob turned.

"Check this out," she hissed, and pushed the wooden door inward.

It opened with a slow creak.

Jillie didn't hesitate, but stepped inside.

Ted followed her through the foyer, flashing the light ahead of them. She walked into the front room, and pointed to a spot not far from a dark hole in the floor.

"Set up right here," she said. "We should get started at the front of the house."

He nodded and pulled out a small tripod and camera from the backpack, along with another oblong shape. It glowed with thin blue LEDs when he pressed a button on the side.

"Any focal point?" he asked.

"Your guess is as good as mine," she said. "Maybe the hole in the floor? Maybe there's activity transgressing the basement? I don't know."

"Done," he said, slapping a lock on the tripod base to hold it steady. "Now what?"

Jillie plopped down on the floor with a wall behind her, and crossed her legs Indian style. "Now we wait."

"No. Now you go," a gruff voice said from behind them.

Jillie jumped to her feet. Ted, who had been in the process of easing himself to the floor, fell backward on his ass before scrambling clumsily to his feet. A short but solid-looking man in a blue button-up shirt and dark pants stood in the doorway.

"What do you think you're doing here?" he asked.

Jillie recovered herself quickly.

"We're looking for EMF activity. Who are you?"

"I'm the guy who's supposed to keep people like you out," the man said. He pointed at the guard badge he had pinned to his shirt. "You're trespassing."

"We're not doing any harm," Jillie said. "We're just trying to see if there is paranormal activity in this place since it's been put under construction. That could cause a surge in—"

"Get out now or I call the police," he interrupted.

"As you like," she said. "But you'll be sorry when people start dying in here."

"Actually, I'm here to make sure that doesn't happen," he said.

She snorted. "Good luck with that." Then she motioned to Ted, who was already fumbling with the latches and trying to collapse and pick up all of their equipment.

"Come on," she said. "We'll have to do this another time."

CHAPTER TEN

Mist still hung in the air just above the long grass as Mike drove down the gravel path and into Bachelor's Grove. It was an eerie blanket across the earth that looked like a special effect for a movie…but it was just the natural state of a cool August morning in the forest. When he pulled to a stop at the clearing in front of the house, Mike saw someone sitting in a canvas chair on the small deck. It looked as if he was sitting in front of a house in a cloud. The guy was sipping from a thermos and wearing a black pullover Blackhawks hat – an odd thing to see in August, but it had been dipping into the cooler temperatures overnight this past week.

Seeing someone at the house momentarily startled him, but when Mike got out of the truck he nodded at the man on the deck. Because the man wasn't a stranger. He was the night watchman, Gonz, who'd been there the past few mornings when he'd arrived. It was still disconcerting to see someone at the house, but it also made Mike feel better. He knew if Gonz was here, then nobody had turned up overnight to perform animal sacrifices in the basement…or God knew what else.

"Quiet night?" Mike asked as he walked up the two stairs to the deck.

Gonz shook his head. He was a short, thickset man with the darker complexion of a Mexican farmhand. Mike had worked with several guys like him on construction crews and maybe because of that, he'd quickly warmed to Gonz when the man had shown up on the site. He trusted him instantly.

When the watchman shook his head, Mike's chest clenched. Damned if this place didn't have him on edge.

"What happened?" he asked.

Gonz rolled his eyes and pushed himself up and out of the canvas chair.

"I took care of it," he said. His brown eyes met Mike's, and the carpenter could see how tired the watchman was. But there was a hint of amusement in that tired gaze as well.

"Couple of ghost hunters showed up and set up their cameras in the front room. Like they owned the place. I told them to take a hike."

The watchman shrugged and took another swig of his thermos. Coffee? Mike wondered. But the guy had been out here all night. Part of him wondered if it was a beer. That same part of him got excited when he thought of that possibility.

"Did they give you any problem?" he asked.

"Not once I threatened to call the police."

Mike nodded. "That can scare people off."

"That and a switchblade," Gonz said.

Mike raised an eyebrow. "Did you really pull a knife on them?"

Gonz laughed and shook his head. "No, no…just sayin'."

Mike let out a sigh of relief. "Good, I wouldn't want you to have to… though, you know, the closer we get to Halloween…."

Gonz nodded. "I know. They told me all about this place. And how the crazies would be coming out in droves."

"Do they let you carry a gun?" Mike asked.

The watchman nodded. "Yeah, but I don't like to have to bring it out. People see that and everything just goes south, you know?"

Mike nodded. "Sure. But good to know you're protected."

Gonz grinned, showing a mouth full of yellowed teeth. "Don't you worry about me," he said. "I can take very good care of myself. And your house."

He turned around and folded up his chair with one quick snap. "And now I hand it over to you," he said. "Go get some work done."

Gonz grinned and slapped Mike's shoulder as he walked past and down the steps. "Maybe I'll see you tonight," he said. "If you survive the daylight."

"No worry about that," Mike said. "You keep surviving the night and we'll both be all right."

But the watchman was already loading his chair into the back of his old rust-ridden red Toyota pickup truck and didn't give any indication that he heard.

Mike got to work and in a few minutes the clearing was filled with the whir of a circular saw. His first mission was to stack up a large reserve of boards… and once he was done with that, spend hours pounding them into position.

The day went quickly, and for once, without any instances of stumbling upon coffins or dead and bled animals. Katie was absent too, and Mike found himself missing her. When he packed up his tools at the end of the afternoon, he took his time, hoping she would turn up. But when five-thirty had come and gone, he had to admit to himself that she wasn't coming. He tried to find the silver lining; at least he'd get home for once before dark.

CHAPTER ELEVEN

Another day had disappeared like a summer breeze. Once again, Gonz Torrenz was back on the job as dusk fell. Considering he slept through the daylight hours, his life sometimes felt like one long string of silent nights. He pulled down the gravel path and parked the car just a few yards from the front door of the old house. The carpenter seemed to have already left for the day; the clearing was empty.

Gonz had worked a lot of oddball locations as a night watchman. But guarding a broken-down haunted house behind a cemetery in the middle of a forest preserve had to be the strangest. Who would *want* to get into this crap heap? Who even knew it was here? From the road, you couldn't see the old cemetery stones, let alone the old house.

He shrugged and took a chug from his thermos. Didn't matter in the end. It paid the bills. He just had to try to stay awake. It may have looked like a cush job, but he'd learned the hard way not to take those for granted. Every now and then the agency would send someone around to check on their watchmen, and you did not want to be sucking Zs when that guy came walking up to your vehicle.

Gonz knew. He'd been written up once for just that thing. On one easy night watch job, he'd leaned back in the truck after downing some cookies and a couple cups of coffee, and suddenly the low buzz of Zeppelin on the local classic rock station had been lulling rather than energizing. The next thing he knew, there was something tapping at his window. And then…he'd been written up. If it happened again, he might have to look for real work. And Gonz didn't have the education or resume to nab himself a desk job somewhere. He'd have to go back to using his hands and his back to clear a check. He'd worked for a bricklayer once; he didn't ever intend to go back.

No, he liked watchman work a lot more than busting his back. He needed to stay awake tonight. He had his phone set to go off every half hour, to make sure he got out of the truck and walked around – and walked around inside the house. It was an annoying ritual for the first couple hours…but he'd found on watch gigs at remote locations like this, it became necessary by two a.m.

So, Gonz was completely alert at twelve-thirty when his watch announced that it was time to head into the house. He'd changed it up so that he sat for an hour or so in the house, and then listened to the radio for an hour or so in the truck. Or sat on the back of the truck bed. The change of venue helped keep him alert (along with the coffee and phone alarms).

He stepped outside the cab and stretched. It was a warm night, with just the faintest of breezes to tickle the nose. The moon was low in the sky still, but it gave the clearing in front of the house an almost magical glow.

Gonz walked past the tombstones of the cemetery and stepped onto the new front porch of the house. He took a deep breath of the night air, before unlocking the door. The air inside was not nearly as fresh or pure. He wrinkled his nose and turned on a flashlight to illuminate the dark foyer. The light of the moon did not reach far through the dirty windows, and Gonz didn't want to trip over anything. He walked down the hall to the kitchen. Now and then, a floorboard creaked as he passed.

"Who's there?" he called, as he saw a white shadow pass in the hall.

The watchman stood still and just listened. You couldn't move in this house without making some noise. If he really had seen someone, there would be audible evidence that they were here. There were no rugs or draperies to deaden the sound. No matter where someone was in the house, you'd hear them.

Gonz held his breath and listened.

Something in the depths of the house creaked.

"God damn it," he mumbled under his breath. Someone had managed to get into the place while he was sitting right outside watching it. So now it was up to him to shoo them away.

He walked down the hallway and shone the spot into two of the bedrooms on the first floor. They were empty, stripped of any furnishings. There was no place for an intruder to hide. He moved on.

"I know you're here," he called. "Nobody's allowed in this place. Come out now and I won't get the police involved."

He stood still and listened then, hoping for some telltale movement indicating the person was going to leave quietly. Instead, there was a creak over his head. And another. Slow and repetitive and steady.

Like footsteps.

Gonz walked over to the attic stairs. He'd been up there once, on the day he'd started, just to get the full layout of the place in his head. He didn't have any desire to go back. It was creepy up there, full of dusty boxes and spiderwebs.

He put his foot on the first step and shone the light upward. It caught the rough beam of the attic ceiling. He called again. There still was no answer, but something above creaked.

Gonz shook his head and stepped slowly up the stairs. He debated going back to the car to get the gun he kept in his glovebox, but then shook his head. There was no reason for any intruder in this place to be armed. It had to be a kid, checking out the 'haunted house' after midnight. They were probably scared shitless right now that someone was on to them.

When he reached the top of the steps, he was careful as he put his head above the floor and into the attic itself. He quickly shone the light 360 degrees, and then did it again, moving slower. The flash didn't pick up anything but dusty boxes and bare walls.

Gonz frowned and stepped the rest of the way up until he stood in the room. He shone the flashlight to the right, letting it linger on an old rope coiled atop a wooden crate.

Something creaked again behind him, and then came a wooden snap, almost like a door closing. He turned quickly and moved toward the source of the sound. Or at least where it sounded like the noise had come from.

The carpenter had framed out a wall in the corner near the window. It looked as if he planned to barricade off a small finger of the room, but hadn't put up the plywood to wall it in yet. Gonz stepped through the frame and looked around, shining the flash into every corner. There was a screwdriver lying on the ground; the watchman bent down to retrieve it. As he did, he noticed the gap line in the floor. He followed it with his eyes until it turned in a 90-degree angle and cut across the floorboards. He saw the inset handle, and fingered at it until the handle lifted upward. Then he pulled. The floor door opened with the same kind of creak he'd just heard a moment before, and he grinned.

So. *You can run, but you can't hide from the watchman,* he thought.

He lifted the door all the way back, and aimed the light downward. He could see the plank ladder, and dusty floor below. There were footstep tracks all over at the base. Someone had been down here a lot.

He stepped down, and after just three steps, jumped easily to the bottom, anxious to catch whoever was down here by surprise…or if not by surprise, at least catch them before they expected him to make it down.

He saw her as soon as his head ducked below the surface of the attic floor.

She didn't look surprised by his entrance.

The woman stood just three feet away, in front of a small bed covered in a tan and green afghan. Was she a squatter? They had told him this place was empty, but that sometimes kids came and trashed it. But this bed was about the only piece of furniture he'd seen in the house. And it was in something of a hidden room. Maybe she'd managed to escape detection until now. She stood in front of him barefoot, in a stained blue t-shirt and ragged jeans. Her face appeared starkly pale in the light of the flash, her hair long and wispy and pale brown. It reminded him of the mane of a horse his mom used to ride, back when their family could afford to go to the stable and ride horses. She didn't move or speak. Her eyes didn't blink.

She simply stared at him. It was a little creepy.

"This is private property, ma'am," he said. "You'll have to leave."

She didn't answer.

"What's your name?" he asked. "What are you doing here?"

The dark of her eyes remained unblinking. She almost seemed a statue. But she was clearly human. He could see the slow rise of her chest.

"Look, you don't want to talk, that's fine. But you can't stay here." He gestured at the ladder with the flashlight, pointing up.

"If you would…?"

Then she moved.

Slowly.

He tensed involuntarily, but she walked past him and in almost slow motion mounted the steps of the ladder. She never said a word. Her dirt-smeared feet were at the level of his face when he let out a breath. She was leaving without any trouble. Thank God.

But then the door above snapped shut. Only, she was still on the ladder. She had simply pulled the trapdoor closed.

Step by step, her feet descended, moving a little faster now.

When she turned from the ladder to stare at him again, her eyes looked black as the void.

"You have to leave," he said.

She shook her head, no.

Then she jabbed out and slapped the flashlight from his hand. Caught by surprise, he dropped it, and the light rolled across the floor to rest, with the light trained on one wall.

A weight hit him then, as the girl's full body piled into his.

Gonz fell backward, landing with his ass on the floor. She was upon him in a heartbeat, pinning him to the floor with her weight.

That's when he saw the other one stepping out of the dark shadows. She was pale and comely and grinning. But that grin did not hold any humor.

Gonz opened his mouth to scream.

But only the gravestones heard his cry for help.

CHAPTER TWELVE

When Mike arrived the next day, he found Gonz's old red pickup –
with the bed door still hanging down – but no night watchman. Which
was unusual. Although he had missed seeing him last night because he'd
actually headed home on time, for the most part they had 'handed off'
the house over the past few days, Gonz arriving to work just as Mike was
getting ready to leave, and vice versa. Mike was 'day shift' and Gonz was
'night shift'. That way the place was always under someone's eye. And,
not surprisingly, there had been no further evidence of ritual sacrifices
discovered, which had helped Mike's work go faster.

Mike unloaded his own truck and trudged his box of tools up to the
attic. He needed to finish roughing in the corner where the laundry chute
was so nobody ended up falling down a hole during their walk through
the haunted house. Then he was going to finish another wall that he'd
framed to divide the space – it would serve as both structural support and
allow the decorators another room to haunt.

He'd left the circular saw upstairs and so, after taking his tools up, he
stayed there and measured and trimmed a couple pieces of wood right
away, nailing them quickly into place. Since there was already a pile of
lumber there, he measured and marked a couple more and did the same.
Quickly the upstairs spaces filled in.

By lunchtime, his face and back were completely drenched in sweat,
but he had finished the attic area – he'd shored up the side walls and added
new walls to barricade off sections of what had previously been one long
room. He wiped his face with his sleeve for the fiftieth time, and surveyed
the work.

Mike nodded. It was good.

So. Now he'd taken care of the attic and the basement. It was already
August, and finally time to power through the main floor. The haunted
house people would need to get in here soon to start decorating the place.
Perry had hired a deep-cleaning crew to go through the place so at least

Mike wouldn't be running into piles of dirt and dust on every surface. But he would be replacing the floor in the kitchen and patching several walls where animals and leakage had taken their toll.

He picked up the saw and some wood and moved them downstairs. It took a couple more trips before he'd carted all of his equipment to the front room of the old house. He realized that he hadn't seen Katie yet today and frowned. She'd been turning up every day by late morning, and here it was afternoon, with no sign of her. He hoped she wasn't mad at him; last night, he'd put his arm around her and kissed her, and she hadn't resisted…but when he'd slipped a hand up the back of her shirt and started moving his fingers to trace the line of her bra, she'd suddenly pushed him away and said no. He'd gotten frustrated and walked away to take a piss, and when he returned…no Katie.

Mixed signals. Always the story of his life, it seemed.

Mike shrugged, feeling defeated as always by women in general, and attacked the old yellow linoleum with a crowbar, peeling the stuff off the wood beneath a chunk at a time. By the time he had a sizeable pile stacked up, and was nearly done with the removal project, he heard a familiar voice.

"Looks like fun," Katie said from behind him.

Mike straightened up with a groan. "Not so much," he answered. "Where ya been?"

"Aw, did you miss me?" she asked.

"Could have used a hand, yeah," he said.

She pouted. "So, I'm just an extra hand to you?"

Mike tilted his head and rolled his eyes. Then he reached out and slipped a hand around her thin waist. With a tug, he pulled her close to him.

"Not just an extra hand," he said.

"Hmm," she answered, and took his free hand and pressed it to her breast. "Just an extra chest?"

"Not just that either," he said, but there was a catch in his voice. He could feel his jeans growing tighter.

"Tell me you missed me," she said, and pressed her lips to his for just a second. Then she pulled away. "Tell me."

"I missed you," Mike said. "A lot." In his head, he was thinking that she didn't have any problems bailing out on him last night, but he held his tongue.

Katie smiled. "Good. I work for love."

"Sounds like a Ministry song," he said.

Katie only looked confused. Probably too young to catch the reference.

She shrugged. "I hope you don't mind Emery helping out today. We were hanging out so I brought her along."

"Sure," he said, while inside he groaned. So…today she brought reinforcements. Why? To fend him off?

"Does she like tearing things apart?" He hefted the crowbar with one arm before holding it out.

Katie shrugged. "She'll do okay."

At that, a floorboard creaked in the hall outside. A moment later, Emery's dour face peered around the corner. Mike thought she looked as if someone had kicked her dog. She did not look like she wanted to be here. *Well,* he thought, *the feeling is mutual. I don't want you here, either.*

"Here she is," Katie announced. "C'mon, Em. Mike wants you to help dig up the floor. You're good at digging things up, right?"

The other girl said nothing, but moved forward to take the crowbar from her friend. Then she stood still, waiting for instructions.

"Do you have another one for me?" Katie asked.

Mike picked up a hammer and pointed to the teeth at the back. "You can use this. We're just trying to peel up all the old flooring, so that I can get at the boards beneath. Most of this material needs to be replaced if we're going to have hundreds of people walking back and forth through this room."

He demonstrated swinging the hammer to catch at the old linoleum and pulling it up by the back of the hammer. After cracking off a couple squares, he handed Katie the tool. "I'll be right back," he said. "I should have something else we can use in the trunk."

When he returned a couple minutes later, the two girls were both leaning over the hole in the floor, looking down into the basement.

"Not exactly where we need a window," he said.

"What about a door?" Katie asked.

He shook his head. "Not that either."

Mike got down on his knees and pulled up the old flooring with a second hammer. Emery stared at him blankly for a minute, and then gouged at the floor on the other side of the hole from him.

Katie's lips pursed in a faint smile, and then she began working between them.

With three of them working on it in tandem, the ten or twelve feet of old flooring quickly turned into piles of scrap.

"All right," he announced finally, wiping the sweat off his face with the bottom of his shirt. "That was the easy part. Now we need to pull out the old wood. You might want to let me take care of this part."

He swung the hammer at a blackened part of the plywood near the rotted-out hole, but instead of going through, the tool only bounced back, as if it had hit a springboard.

Emery stepped closer and held the crowbar out in front of her. But before he could take it, Mike realized she wasn't holding it out for him. She was getting ready to swing.

And then the heavy iron hit the board and something cracked. A moment later, she pulled back on the tool, and a two-foot chunk of old flooring popped up and out. It landed next to his feet, and Emery looked up at him. She didn't smile.

He did. "Well, I guess I was wrong," he said. "Looks like you can take care of this part just as well as I can."

Katie raised an eyebrow and he quickly amended. "Okay, maybe better than I can."

He picked another spot, and began working on removing the old wood a few feet away from Emery, who worked like a piledriver, jamming the crowbar down and then bringing it back up only to slam it back again.

The room was filled with the sounds of crashing tools and splintering wood for over an hour, until Mike called a time out.

"All right," he said, standing straight up with a groan. "I think that's enough for one day. It's after five."

Katie rose from where she'd been kneeling on the far end of the room from him. Emery simply stopped moving. She watched Katie expectantly.

"Do you have any beer?" Katie asked.

"I thought you worked for love?" he answered. With the back of his hand, he wiped a river of sweat from his forehead.

"And beer," she said. "Plus, I was really thinking of you. Because you look really hot."

"Thanks," he said. "Nobody's told me that in ages."

"Never let them see you sweat," she said.

"Come on," he said. "The cooler should still be full."

★　　★　　★

"You know they killed people here," Katie said.

Mike crumpled an empty PBR in his hand and tossed it to the side of the porch. "What are you talking about?"

"I'm talking about human sacrifice," she said matter-of-factly. "They hung them upside down from the rafters and bled them like cattle. And as the victims died, the coven lay on the floor naked beneath them. The blood of the innocent rained on their chests and privates, and they moaned in ecstasy as the hanging ones screamed."

"You're making this shit up," Mike said.

Katie shook her head. "I'm not. Haven't you heard people talk about Bachelor's Grove?"

Mike nodded. "Of course. I've heard all the stories. People have picked up hitchhikers along the turnpike for years. But before they ever get the hitchhikers home, they disappear into thin air. Ghosts."

"Ghosts of the hanging ones," she said. "Ghosts trying to find their way home when their homes have disappeared with their lives, and time."

"Why would anyone have done such a thing?" he asked.

"Anger," she said. "Revenge."

She held a can to her lips, but then didn't drink. She set it back down on the fresh wood of the deck. "You've never heard people talk about the sacrifices here then?"

He shook his head and popped the tab on a new can.

"They talk about ghosts, and strange lights bobbing between the cemetery stones. And they talk about the ghost of a woman, who's often seen crying as she cradles the ghost of a baby. That's probably the thing people talk about the most when it comes to Bachelor's Grove. The woman with the lost child."

Katie nodded. "Well, they have that part right then, at least. Everything that happened here happened because of her. The jealousy, the murder, the rituals and revenge."

"What did she do to cause all of that?" he asked, still not understanding.

Katie handed her can to Emery and stood up.

"She did what every woman does, only she refused to do it the way most women do."

Katie met Mike's eyes with a sad, long gaze before she said simply, "She loved."

Then she walked to the door of the house and went inside.

Mike felt a chill suddenly, as the sounds of the forest birds and bugs hummed unbroken all around him. He looked up, and found Emery staring at him. She said nothing, but raised the PBR to her lips and took a long swig. He sat there with her in silence for several minutes waiting for Katie to come back, feeling increasingly uncomfortable.

Finally, he shook his head and stood up. "I really need to get going," he announced.

When she didn't answer, he picked up his empty cans and the cooler and walked it to the truck.

When he came back, Emery was gone. He picked up another empty beer can, and then emptied another that still was mostly full over the banister. Then he called into the house.

"Hey girls, I've gotta get going."

When he received no reply, he walked inside and checked the kitchen and back bedroom and upstairs.

There was nobody there. They had vanished again. He didn't know where they'd gone; apparently they'd disappeared into the woods surrounding the old house, because they hadn't walked out the main gravel path that led to the turnpike. They'd have passed him.

"So long and thanks for all the beer," he murmured. He locked the front door and went back to the truck. He noticed Gonz's vehicle still remained where it had been this morning. He'd have to call Perry if the guy wasn't back tomorrow.

"People," he said, pulling with a crunch of gravel onto the turnpike and gunning the engine.

"Can't live with 'em, can't gut them with a knife and leave them to bleed out over a coven of devil worshippers."

He looked back at the entry road to the cemetery in the rearview mirror.

"Usually."

CHAPTER THIRTEEN

Sweat trickled down Mike's back in multiple mini-rivers. It was supposed to hit ninety degrees outside today, but the house felt like a hundred and ten, especially in the back bedroom, where he couldn't budge the window. He was going to have to fix that, or the fire marshal wouldn't approve the place for opening. But he'd skipped working on it this morning when he'd started on the outer wall. Animals or an old leak, maybe both, had led to a large rotten section that he had to repair. When he'd first come into the house, he'd found that one corner of this room had a pile of drywall chunks and wood and mud. You could see a small glimmer of outdoor light if you looked into the blackened hole in the wall. Luckily, this was the only full breach he'd found between the house and the outside, and it was small. But it needed to be sealed and patched.

He stood up from gouging out the soft drywall and groaned. His back got stiff way too easily these days. Thanks to his efforts, the hole in the wall had grown from something a mouse or chipmunk could have fit through to a three-foot-wide explosion in the wall. But he'd finally found solid drywall. The outer structure was solid except for a small area where the original breach had begun, so he'd shore that up and then bring in some new drywall to cover the hole. But first he had to get something to open this window. He couldn't work in this heat anymore.

Mike walked through the hallway, wiping the sweat from his forehead and neck. He hadn't realized just how hot he'd gotten until he stepped out of the bedroom, which had to be one of the most stifling spots in the house, since he'd gotten all the other windows to open and shut.

He stepped out onto the front porch and the temperature dropped at least ten degrees.

"Whew," he said out loud. And then he realized that he wasn't alone.

A thin man with dark unruly hair leaned against the banister. He appeared to be sizing Mike up. But he didn't say a word.

"Um, can I help you?" Mike asked, wiping his wet hand on the thigh of his jeans.

The man nodded slowly. He looked to be in his thirties, and was slight of build – maybe five and a half feet tall. He had a narrow nose and dark, shadowed eyes, and when he looked down – which he seemed to do often – his hair covered his face.

"Sure," he said. "Can you show me the house?"

Mike was taken aback.

"I don't think so," Mike said. "It's not open for visitors."

The guy nodded his head. "Yeah, I know. But I'm not visiting."

"Who are you?" Mike asked.

"Sorry," the guy said, sticking out his palm. "They call me Argento. I'm in charge of decorating all the rooms in this place for the haunted house."

Mike grinned then and shook Argento's hand, which felt thin as a girl's. "That's different," he said. "I'm Mike, I've been fixing the place up for you."

The guy nodded, but said nothing.

"When are you planning to start working?" Mike asked.

"Tonight," Argento said.

"Oh," Mike said. "I didn't realize you guys were going to be coming in yet."

"So, can I see it?" Argento asked, ignoring Mike's comment.

"Yeah, sure," Mike said, and opened the door. "No air conditioning, so it's not exactly pleasant right now."

"No worries," Argento said. "I like to work at night. Should be just fine." He walked inside, and Mike followed with a frown. Something about this guy was off.

Argento stopped in the kitchen and pointed at the faucet. "Does that work?"

Mike shook his head. "No. I'm assuming it used to be connected to a well, but nothing comes out."

"Good, we can make a fountain of blood there."

"Yeah, sure," Mike said, and shook his head. *Of course*, they'd make a fountain of blood in the rusty sink. Why hadn't he thought of that? Ha.

They moved slowly through the house, Argento walking up to corners and touching doorways. Now and then he mumbled something to himself, but Mike didn't answer. The words weren't for him. And he honestly had no idea what they meant. It sounded like a barrage of random syllables.

"*Phenomena*," Argento murmured at one point, while touching a window. And then, "*Tenebrae, Suspiria…. Zombie. Duckling.*"

Zombie duckling? Mike thought. *What the hell?*

Every time Argento's finger touched a surface, it seemed to evoke a new disconnected word. "*Beyond. Demons. Fascination.*" At one point, he laughed when they were in the large master bedroom with a connected bath. He swung his hand out in a wide gesture and announced to a nonexistent audience, "*Bay of Blood.*" Then he shut up for a while, as he opened the closet and returned to the hallway to look in the other rooms.

After they'd walked the rest of the first floor in silence (aside from a couple more of Argento's nonsensical whispers), the thin man suddenly looked at Mike and said, "Stairways?"

Mike took him to the attic staircase, and they quickly ascended.

As soon as Argento reached the top, a smile broke out on his face. "Yes!" he said. "Oh, yes!"

Mike had no idea what he was agreeing to. The man continued to hold a conversation with himself.

"*Grudge. Suspiria.* Even *House on Sorority Row* maybe…" Argento said, peering into the side room that Mike had walled off.

"Are there any drains up here?" Argento asked after a moment.

"You mean, like bathroom faucets or toilets?"

The man nodded quickly.

"No," Mike said. "Only on the first floor."

"Pity," Argento said, and went back to touching the walls. He pulled out a phone and snapped some pictures, and Mike kept moving to stay out of the way. Then the decorator abruptly turned and walked back down the stairs without another word.

"Freak," Mike whispered to himself, before following.

When he got downstairs, he led Argento to the den and showed him the new flight of steps leading down to the basement. When he moved the bookcase, the man's eyes lit up. "*House by the Cemetery*," he whispered, and immediately disappeared through the opening.

Mike followed, and after watching the man skulk around in the basement for a few minutes, he walked to the exterior stairwell and called to the man. "You could have them either enter or exit the house here," he said, pointing at the stairwell that led back up to the outside.

"Yes, yes," Argento said, but didn't follow him out.

Mike shrugged and walked up the stairs. He waited for a few minutes on the porch, before noticing Argento's face peering out of the attic window. The guy was re-walking the whole place again, apparently.

"Whatever," Mike murmured, and pulled out his cell phone. He'd been meaning to call Perry all day to let him know that the watchman had apparently abandoned his vehicle and his job.

His friend answered on the second ring. "Hey Mike, what's going on? I've been meaning to call you this week."

"Well, it looks like we need a new night watchman," Mike said. "That Gonz guy hasn't been back in a couple days. But his truck is still parked here."

"Damn, when was the last night he worked? I'm not paying the service if he hasn't been showing up."

Mike frowned. "Tuesday, I think he was here? Not since."

He walked down the steps of the porch to move out of the sun and into the shade of the trees. He found himself in the graveyard, and sat down on the top of one of the taller stones.

"I'd call them, and have them send out someone else," Mike suggested.

"No need," Perry said. "I'll call them and tell them to have that truck towed if their guy isn't going to show up. And then I'll fire them. We won't need them anymore. The set people are going to start working nights on decorating the rooms you're done with. That's why I was going to call you today, to let you know."

Mike laughed. "Well, thanks for the warning but…you're too late. One of them is already here. Some nutjob called Argento."

Perry laughed. "Go easy," he warned. "He's a talented nutjob. You stay out of his way, and he'll stay out of yours."

Mike nodded. "I can see that. I'm not sure he's even aware that other people exist."

"How much more time do you need to finish your part?" Perry asked.

Mike outlined the few projects remaining, and said he should be done by the week after Labor Day.

"Good!" Perry said. "Though if Argento or the rest need any help building stuff, I'd like you to stay on, and help them out. We need to open in a month. It's going to be a race."

"Sure," Mike said. After a few more words, they hung up, and he turned to look at the house.

"Who was that?" Katie asked.

Her voice made him jump; she was literally a foot from his shoulder.

"Don't do that!" he complained.

She grinned and slipped a cool hand across his neck. "Do what?" she asked innocently as her fingers ruffled his hair and then trailed down the line of his spine. "This?"

"No." He grinned. "That you can do."

"So, who were you talking to?"

"That was Perry," he said. "The guy who's running this whole renovation. He was just telling me about the decorating crew that's going to start painting the place and I told him about our missing night watchman."

"What do you mean?" she asked.

"Guy who was keeping an eye on the place at night," he said. "Hasn't been here in a couple days, but you can see his truck still sitting right over there."

He pointed at the glint of silver through the trees.

"Huh," she said. "That's weird that he'd leave his truck. You're sure he's not around?"

Mike shook his head. "I looked. Plus, we've been sitting on the deck the past couple nights when he should have been here. Anyway, these other people are going to start being around, so it doesn't really matter, I guess. There will be someone in the house pretty much all the time from now on to get it ready."

Katie frowned. "Does that mean you're not going to have a beer with me at the end of the day?"

"I think we can still squeeze that in," he said with a grin. "Oh, right there. Don't stop," he begged, as her fingernails found the perfect place.

"Where, here?" she said. Suddenly she moved her hand from his lower back to cup the crotch of his jeans. Her fingers and palm moved up and down slightly as she put on enough pressure to feel his balls shift inside the heavy fabric.

"Um, yeah," he groaned with surprise. "That's really good."

"Okay," she said, removing her hand as fast as she'd surprised him with it. "Good to know."

She planted a kiss on his mouth, and then traced the outline of the chain and locket he still wore through his shirt before she backed away. "I've got something to do this afternoon, but I'll be back later and we can see if that is still really good."

Katie winked and turned around to walk through the gravestones toward the turnpike. She didn't follow the gravel path, but instead circled the lower half of the small pond before disappearing into the undergrowth.

Mike had to take several deep breaths before he finally got off the stone and walked back to the house. Going back to work was going to be a bitch after that tease.

He desperately hoped it wasn't an *idle* tease. She'd been leaving him blueballed for the past couple weeks, and he wasn't sure how much more he could take. On a couple nights, he'd literally been in pain as he'd driven home after the sudden cessation of her kisses, his testicles filled and anxious, with no release allowed.

As he stepped up on the porch, the front door opened and the wiry man stepped out.

"I'll be back," Argento announced.

"When do you think?" Mike asked.

"Maybe late tonight. Maybe tomorrow night. I need to get some supplies together, but I have to work until ten tonight."

"Do you need me to leave the front door unlocked?" Mike asked. "I'm not sure how that's going to fly, but I won't be here that late."

Argento shook his head and held up a bronze key.

"I'm good."

And with that, he marched down the steps to the gravel lane.

Mike shook his head and went to the truck to get the crowbar to force open the bedroom window.

After being outside for a while, once he was back in the bedroom, the air really felt stifling. Mike worked at shifting the window with his hands for a minute and had exactly the same success as he'd had this morning. None.

So, he finally sprayed some WD-40 on the dry-rotted window tracks, and then pressed the crowbar into the small gap.

The window ledge cracked as he pressed down.

But he moved the crowbar from side to side, pressing it down just a little, and then shifting it to the other end, trying to edge the window up centimeter by centimeter without having the frame skew further and get completely locked.

After a few moves from one side to the other, he had raised the window up enough to wedge his fingers in beneath the old wooden frame. He set the crowbar down and with both hands shoved beneath the window, gave a solid heave-ho…and the thing slid up another inch.

Air came rushing into the room in a welcome gust. It wasn't cool, but it was *cooler*. He kept working at it and could hear things shifting inside the wall as he jimmied the window another inch and then two more. Once he'd gotten it halfway up, he sprayed the track beneath it with WD-40 and pulled it down most of the way. He sprayed the top half again, and then pushed the window back up. It moved easier now. He repeated that twice more, until the window moved up and down without too much effort. The sides gleamed with oil, but he didn't care. The key was to be able to open the window without a crowbar. Hopefully, he'd worked out the seal that time had put in place.

Mike fingered the edges of the hole he'd made in the drywall, confirming it was solid. Then he lifted the biggest pieces of debris from the gap between the inner and outer wall and stacked them up with the pile he had accumulated in the room already. He'd bag and toss the whole mess once he finished mudding in a new piece of drywall.

As he reached in to pull one last piece from the area near the window, he saw a glimmer of something white on the ground. Something white but not drywall.

He reached over inside the wall and brushed off the dirt that partially obscured it. He could see a somewhat rounded knob; it didn't look like anything that belonged to the architecture.

Mike grabbed the end and pulled it toward him, and a long piece emerged from the dirt. He pulled it out of the hole in the wall and held it up, not quite believing his eyes.

It was a bone.

And not the skeletal remains of some mouse or rat or squirrel that had skulked in the passage and died.

This was a human bone.

Arm or leg, from the size of it.

As that registered, Mike opened his fingers and let the thing fall. It rolled across the floor to lie next to the pile of drywall.

He was reminded suddenly of Katie's story about people being hung and bled to death in secret, gruesome rituals in this house, and shook his head. He looked again inside the hole, and saw other bits of yellowed bone sticking up from the dirt and debris that littered the narrow passage.

Someone had walled in a body…or parts of one…behind this wall at some point long ago.

"Fuckin' A," Mike whispered to himself. He stepped away from the hole, shaking his head. "This is not a good house."

He took a deep breath and imagined he smelled the stench of dead bodies. He could guess at the horrible stench that must have once permeated this place, if Katie's stories were true. And with a human bone buried here in the wall, he thought that they very much could be.

"I need a drink," he whispered, and walked out of the room to head to the cooler in his truck.

The first PBR went down really fast.

He slowed down a bit with the second. He needed to. Because he wanted to close up that hole before the daylight waned. He pulled a fresh piece of drywall from the back of the truck bed and marched back into the house.

Some things should remain buried.

CHAPTER FOURTEEN

"Here's what I'm thinking," Argento said. Lucio, Lon, Jeanie and June all huddled around the kitchen table at June's house. Three pieces of paper lay in the center, with boxes and notes sketched all over them.

"We've got three floors to play with," he continued. "But the place isn't huge. So, I think we set up the ticket taker outside on the deck."

He pulled one of the sheets of paper closer and pointed out a path with his pencil as he talked. "We have them enter through the foyer, walk through the front room and the dining room, then cross the hall into the kitchen. There's a back doorway to the kitchen, so we can have them go right through there and cross the hall into the back bedroom. If we have the carpenter cut through the back closet of that room, it would enter right into the den. And if we can cut through the back wall of the den, you'd be in the second bedroom. Exit through that main door, walk around a corner and you've got the stairs up to the attic."

"Do you really think he can just knock out the walls like that?" June asked.

Argento shrugged. "It looked like it to me. We'll have to ask him. If it doesn't work…then people are just going to have to go out through the same door they came in."

Lucio shook his head. "I don't like that. We want a straightforward funnel, no backtracking."

Argento nodded. "That's the goal."

At that moment, a loud yawn erupted from the hallway outside the kitchen. A moment later, Lenny walked in, stretching his arms toward the ceiling with his mouth wide open.

Lon turned and shook his head at June. "Does this guy ever go home?"

She shrugged. "When he needs to pick up his mail."

"Morning, haunters," Lenny said. "What are we all plotting today?"

"Well, for starters, it's afternoon," Lon said. "Didn't you go to work today?"

Lenny shook his head and walked to the fridge. "Didn't feel like it," he said, rummaging around inside. He came out with a can of Coke and popped the tab. "I called in sick. I'm *sure* I'll be fine by Monday." He grinned and took a deep slug of the pop.

"And that's what's wrong with America today," Lon declared. "No work ethic. You better not call in sick to the house."

"Don't worry," Lenny promised. "Showbiz is different. The show must go on and all that."

June sighed and rolled her eyes. Then she returned the conversation to the topic at hand. "Do you have ideas for the room themes yet?" she asked Argento.

"I have a few," he said. The way he smiled, it was clear he had more than just a few.

"I thought we could make the dining room a big *Texas Chainsaw Massacre* theme. And the den could be our giallo room. I'm thinking a combo of *Opera, Inferno, Suspiria, Phenomena.*"

"I'd argue that those aren't really all giallos," Lon said, but Argento ignored him.

June leaned over to Jeanie and explained. "Those are all Dario Argento films," she said.

Jeanie nodded. "Got it."

"I thought the first bedroom could be the *Nightmare on Elm Street* room," Argento continued.

June and Lenny both lit up. "Now you're talking," Lenny said. He grabbed June's shoulders and squeezed.

"I thought we could borrow the stuff from your bedroom," Argento said, looking at Lenny. He shrugged. "Sure, why not?"

"We have to have a Fulci room," Lucio said. "It'd be cool to do something from a Jean Rollin film too – a *Living Dead Girl* or *Fascination* theme? I'm thinking we could stage the scene of the ghoul girl at the piano or maybe something like Brigitte Lahaie in that long cape threatening people with the big scythe. Or maybe have a vampire walking out of a grandfather clock? Or how about a Jess Franco thing…we could have the girl from *Countess Perverse* running around in a loincloth with a bow and arrow."

Argento laughed and shook his head.

"I don't think we're going to get away with having a nude girl sitting at a piano, or a bunch of women in see-through silk waltzing around," Lon said. "Or really anything from a Franco movie. This is a family show."

"But the girls could have long, fake-looking fangs," Lucio offered.

Lon shook his head. No.

Lenny laughed. "Yeah, gore is great, but no tits, God forbid."

"How about an homage to the films on the 1980s Video Nasties list?" Lucio suggested.

"I think 'banned in Britain' might be a little obscure for our audience," Lon said. "I don't think most people in the suburbs are too familiar with *Cannibal Holocaust* or *Antropophagus* or *Unhinged* or *Flesh for Frankenstein*."

"Maybe not," Lucio said. "But they know *The Evil Dead* and *I Spit on Your Grave*. And some will recognize *The Beyond*."

"I have white contacts, so we can have someone dressed up like that girl from *The Beyond*," June offered.

"That would be awesome!" Lucio said.

Argento nodded. "I think you get the second bedroom for Fulci stuff."

"So…it sounds like you have the first floor pretty mapped out," Jeanie said. "Where do they go next?"

Argento pointed at the thin hall that ran along the left side of the diagram. "They walk down this hall and reach the stairways. We want to have someone stationed there probably, to make sure people go upstairs first or else they'll miss the attic."

"Brigitte Lahaie lookalike with the scythe," Lucio suggested.

"Maybe," Argento said with a grin. "It would be better if the stairwells were in different parts of the house, but we're stuck with this setup. You go up or down right here."

"And what happens in the attic?" June asked.

"We've got rafters, so we've got to do a noose," Argento said. "I'm thinking we should play off the whole attic thing though, and have some old trunks up there that people can pop out of, maybe an old woman in a wheelchair, like Norma Bates, and then a row of old costumes that people have to walk past, like that room in *Curtains*. We could even have someone in the hag mask from there stalking the aisles."

"Nice," Lucio said. "I get to be the old crone with the sickle!"

Argento grinned. "Sold. But I thought you'd want to be a zombie?"

Lucio shrugged. "I can switch off."

Argento shook his head. Then he pointed at the large space at the far end of the attic. "Here we've got a nice back room which I was thinking we could turn into a creepy kid's playroom, like in *House on Sorority Row*. They'll have to criss-cross here to get back downstairs, because there's only one way up and down to the attic, so people will cross through the playroom and out the back door, which points them right back to the stairwell they came up on. We can divide the stairway, maybe?"

June pointed at the other piece of paper on the table and looked at Argento. "So what happens when they go in the basement?"

He grinned. "They enter…'The chamber of horrors'!" he declared.

Lon laughed. "So, you're decorating the basement to look like your bedroom?"

Argento snorted. "Downstairs, we've got two walled-in rooms, and a small area along the northern wall that's enclosed to hide the utilities. I thought we could set up an aisle of exhibits with iconic monsters there."

"An Aisle of Atrocities!" Lucio said.

"As people walked down the aisle they would see some of the most famous horror themes and film scenes. Countess Báthory, *The Exorcist, Hellraiser,* Romero's zombies…."

"How about Fulci's zombies?" Lucio asked. "They had better makeup. And maggots."

Argento shrugged. "Rotting zombies, clean zombies, whatever. We can have a dungeon, and I thought one room could be a Vlad the Impaler room – I've got a friend who works at Ellis Manufacturing. I've already talked to him and we could get a bunch of tall metal spikes from him and hang some latex bodies on them. Easy setup, great spot for gory makeup skills," he said, nodding at June and Jeanie.

"What about a *Re-Animator* set?" Lenny asked. "Or *Dead Alive*? That scene mowing down the zombies with a lawnmower is classic."

"Maybe," Argento said. He clearly had other thoughts and pointed at the corner of his diagram. "On one end of the aisle, there's another enclosed area that we could turn into a wax museum."

"And where the heck are you going to get wax figures?" Jeanie asked.

"They don't need to really be wax," Argento said. "I've got a couple manikins that look like wax…and I know Lon has a dead whore that we could use."

"What?!" Jeanie yelped. "What do you mean he has a dead whore?"

Lon laughed. "It's a conversation piece I got last year for my Halloween party. It's a latex body, but damned if it doesn't look completely real. You should see the detail in her toes. She's got bruises all over her and she's kind of scrunched up. When you walk into a room and see her lying in bed, she looks completely real. My parents walked in and saw her at the party last year and, I kid you not, they stood there waiting, watching for her to finally take a breath or jump up at them. They really thought I'd hired someone to lie there in the bed and spook people."

"That's fucked up," Lenny said.

"And having a bloody girl hanging from the ceiling over your bed isn't?" Lon asked. "Give me a break."

"That's a *Nightmare on Elm Street* homage," Lenny argued. "It's not the same as having a fake dead whore *in* your bed. And showing your parents!"

Lon grinned but said nothing.

"So where are you going to get all of these manikins and sets and everything?" Jeanie asked.

"Well, Lon and Lucio and June and I all have a bunch of stuff we can use," Argento said. "I've also got a lot of my own lighting equipment that I've bought for other houses I've worked on."

"And we do have a budget for buying stuff," Lon offered. "But it's not huge, so we really have to try to build or borrow as much as we can before we spend it."

June looked at Argento and Lucio. "Are you guys going to be able to build all of those sets? If we have an aisle of different exhibits downstairs, that sounds like a lot of false walls and stuff. We only have a few weeks."

Argento grinned. "That's why we have a carpenter on the payroll. We just need to tell him what to build."

"Within reason," Lon cautioned.

"So, when do we start decorating?" Jeanie asked.

"Tonight," Argento said. "I'm going there after work. Anyone who's free after eleven is welcome to join me."

CHAPTER FIFTEEN

"Did you miss me?"

Katie's voice echoed in the empty room. It sounded as if she was right behind him.

"Yeah, actually," he said. "Can you reach over my shoulder and hold this in place while I screw it in?"

He had just finished cutting the drywall to size and was holding it up to the wall joists.

"Sure," she said. Suddenly he felt the soft weight of her breast on his shoulder, as she draped her body over him and pressed her fingers next to his hands.

"I could hold it like this for you," she said.

"You *could*," he said. "The problem is, I need to move. The drill and screws are over there."

He pointed to one side, but made no attempt to leave the shelter of her chest. You took what you could get. And he was definitely taking this for all he could milk it for. So to speak.

"Emery can get it for you," she said.

As if on cue, a pair of hands held out his drill and box of drywall screws. When he took them from her, Emery leaned in front of them both and pressed her hands to the wallboard.

"Thanks," he said.

She didn't answer.

A moment later, the whir of the drill cut the air. Emery kept holding the board, but Katie let her hands drift back to Mike's neck and side. She ghosted his movements from behind, her arms draped over his, her chest pressed softly against his back; he found himself growing uncomfortably aroused as he punched screws through the drywall. He was pretty sure that he had never gotten a hard-on while working on drywall. Then again, nobody had ever touched him like that while he was working. He feared he was going to be incapable of work in a few more seconds. Which only made him work faster.

When he punched in the last screw, Mike leaned back into Katie's embrace.

"That's it." He looked at Emery and said, "You can let go now. We just have to mud it in and we're all set."x

"Did I help?" Katie whispered in his ear.

"Couldn't have done it without you," he answered.

"Good," she said. "I wanted to help. Because I have something I need your help with later."

"What is it?" he asked, turning in her arms to look at her.

She kissed his lips and then sat back, releasing her hold on him. "Later," she said. "After you're done here."

"Just gotta slap on some mud, and it's Miller Time," he said.

"You don't drink Miller," she said.

"It's a figure of speech."

She smiled. "Should I go get a shovel from your truck?" she asked.

"Why?" He looked confused.

"For the mud," she said.

Mike laughed. "No, no," he said. "It's not that kind of mud. Come on, I'll show you."

He got up and led her out to the truck. Once he let down the bed, he picked up the can of drywall joint compound and a spreader. When they got back in the room, he popped open the lid and showed her the white paste within.

"If you like, you can spread it by hand," he said. "You just want to fill in all the cracks and cover and smooth it enough so that when you sand, you'll have a nice smooth surface. But you don't want to put so much on that you have to sand a lot, because then it's a pain."

He cupped his hand and dug out a big hunk of mud, and demonstrated working it into the cracks around the piece of drywall.

"Do you want to try?" he asked.

Katie shook her head. "I think I'll pass this time."

Mike grinned and slapped on a couple more handfuls before pulling out his joint knife and working the mud to an even covering across the edges of the piece. Katie sat and watched, keeping her hands to herself.

"I don't think I ever saw my dad do that," she offered at one point.

"Not something most people should have to do," he said. "Unless someone punches holes in their walls."

After another couple swipes of the metal blade, he finally sat back and nodded.

"I think that is about as even as we're going to get. Now they can paint it black or red or whatever the hell they want."

"Are you ready for a beer?" Katie asked.

Mike laughed. "I've been ready for hours."

He stood up and picked up the mud bucket, spreading knife and drill. "I just need a bag to put all of that crap in," he said, nodding at the pile of debris in the corner. "I don't like to leave a mess where I've been working."

He took all of the materials back to the truck and grabbed a black plastic bag to put the chunks of drywall and dirt and wood into. Katie followed him but Emery only sat in the corner of the bedroom, waiting for them to come back. When they did, she rose and took the garbage bag and he offered an end to Katie. He slipped the blade of a shovel under the pile and began moving the debris into the bag.

"I actually found a bone in that wall," he announced, when he recognized the long, ragged piece of wallboard that slid onto the top of his tool.

"Not surprising," Katie said. "They killed all sorts of people here. The walls are probably completely lined with bones. It keeps the wrong spirits out and leads the right ones in."

"And exactly which are the right ones?" he asked.

"That depends on who's laying the bones," she said.

"Touché," he said.

He picked up the bag, bucket and spreading knife and led the girls out to the truck to put them away. He set the joint compound bucket on the bed of the truck and used a paper towel and a splash from a water bottle to wipe off the spreading knife. Then he pushed the end of the bed up and slapped his hands together to knock off the dust and paste.

"That's it," he said. "Another day done."

"Well, not completely done," Katie said suggestively.

He grinned. "Nope, now it's time for a little relaxation."

He walked around to the cab of the truck and pulled the cooler from the passenger's side. "Who's up for a PBR?" he asked.

"I'd like one," Emery said. Her voice was low and strangely intense.

Mike was surprised to hear it, but glad at the same time. The girl's persistent silence creeped him out a little. "We can accommodate," he said.

They walked back to the deck and he opened the cooler, handing out cans to both girls before popping one himself.

"Oh yeah," he said, after downing the first three gulps of the can. "That hits the spot."

Katie grinned. "You looked like you could use a drink," she said, holding the can to her lips. "It was hot today."

"Hotter than hell," he said. "I thought I was going to melt."

"You don't know what hot is then," she answered, looking at him with eyes wide over the rim of her beer can. She didn't blink.

Mike suddenly felt aroused again.

"I think I'd like to know," he answered.

"I'd like to show you," Katie answered. Her eyes still didn't break contact with his.

"I don't think Emery wants to hear about that," he suggested.

Katie shook her head. "Em's cool. She knows me better than anyone."

At that moment, Emery held out another can of PBR to him. He emptied the last sip of his current can and cracked open the next.

"Whatever you say," he said, between gulps. The night suddenly felt both cooler and hotter than the sweltering humid soup of the day. And he was okay with that. On either extreme.

"So…what was the favor that you wanted to ask me for?" he said.

"It's kind of weird," she answered. "It's a family thing."

"Families are weird," he agreed.

"That's easy to say," she said. "Because it's really true. But…my family was *really* weird. Did you ever have an uncle who collected bugs?"

Mike shook his head.

"Well, I did. He used to say if you listened to them, you'd understand everything there was to know about the world. Personally, I thought he was crazy."

Mike laughed. "He sounds a little off."

She shook her head. "He was the least of them. My sister used to sleep with my cousin whenever our relatives came to visit. It started out that our parents put them in the same bed because they were little. But then when we were in our teens, they still did it. And they didn't sleep in pajamas, once our parents were in bed. Do you know what I mean?"

"That…doesn't sound right," Mike acknowledged, taking another sip of his beer.

"What's your family like?" she asked.

He shrugged. "Not much to speak of. My dad died when I was a kid – heart attack. My mom is still around, but she's losing it at this point. Sometimes when I visit her she asks if I'll go tell my dad it's time for dinner. He's been gone thirty years. So…she's not all there."

"Do you have a brother or sister?"

"Brother," Mike said. "But he's out in Kansas City. I almost never get the chance to see him. And neither one of us is very good with the telephone."

"That's it?" she said. "No wife, kids, pets?"

"No pets, no kids…just one ex-wife," he said. "She left me last year for a guy who wears a tie and takes the train into work in Chicago every day. A guy who saws wood and hammers nails wasn't enough for her, I guess."

"Girls don't usually care what you do for a living," she said. "As long as what you do after the lights go out is good. Did you…."

"Please her?" he finished. "I did when we first got together. I'm not a pencil dick or something. But she wanted prestige and a fountain of cash. And after a while it was pretty clear that I was never going to give her either one of those."

Mike shook his head and pounded the rest of his PBR.

Emery popped the top on a new can and handed it to him. Mike didn't think twice; he upended it and sucked half of it down before slamming it to the wood. Thinking about Mia made him drink more. And faster.

"I was a good husband and I made a decent living for us," he said. His voice cracked a little and Mike looked out at the deep blue sky that shone just barely through the tops of the trees all around. Night had fallen fast.

Katie's arm slipped around his shoulder. Her lips tickled the edge of his ear. "I'm sure you were," she whispered. "Sometimes you just meet the wrong girl."

Mike nodded and took another pull from the can.

"And sometimes," Katie continued, "she rips your heart out like a fishing lure stuck inside the throat of a five-pound bass."

Mike snorted at that, and looked up from his contemplation of the deck wood. Katie's eyes were right there, and they didn't pull away when he met them.

"I wish I'd met you five years ago," he said.

"I wish I'd met you a long time ago too," she whispered. "But... you can't go backward. Only forward. And you know me now. And I know you."

"Yes," he agreed. Mike realized he suddenly didn't know what else to say.

He took a sip and said nothing, and then suddenly heard another beer tab pop nearby. The can in his hand was pulled away, and a new cold one took its place.

"Thanks," he said, but even as he did, Katie's lips were on his, and her tongue tangled itself around his own. He set the beer down on the deck and slipped both arms around her. She not only accepted his advances tonight, but she made one of her own. Katie flipped one leg over his and smiled, her lips just inches from his own. She straddled him and pressed his head back to the post of the deck. Mike felt his head swimming amid the chiming hum of the crickets and locusts, and the call and response of the night birds throughout the forest, there on his deck beneath the light of the stars. He could feel her crotch shifting and grinding slowly against his as she nuzzled his lips and face with her mouth. Part of him knew that Emery sat quietly close by, and part of him didn't care.

"I want to stay with you tonight," she said at last, pulling back for a moment from kissing him. "I want to show you what it can be like to be with a woman who loves you."

Mike felt his heart thump hard. An explosion of pressure and need and blood. "You love me?" he whispered.

"Shhhh," she said, and buried him in her hair. When she pulled back from that kiss, she grinned slyly and whispered, "Don't tell Emery. She'll be mad."

She moved against him then, in a way that was more than just suggestive. It brought him to full erection in just seconds. He slipped his arms around her and ran his hands down to her ass, cupping the full, soft roundness of her, and pulling her even closer than she'd come on her own.

Her tongue slipped across his lips, tracing his smile, and she pressed him back until he lay down on the porch of the soon-to-be haunted house.

"Yes," he moaned.

"I need you tonight," she whispered, her lips just a breath away from his.

"You have me," he answered.

"There's just one thing we need to do first," she said.

"What's that?" he asked, moving his hands beneath her shirt to feel the soft curve of her waist.

"Not yet," she said, and slid her leg off him.

Mike blinked his way back into focus, and sat part of the way up. The sky was rich and dark blue above them, and the sounds of night filled his ears in a humming symphony. Thousands of locusts and insects and birds hummed and chirped in the distance. The sound was lulling; with Katie lying on top of him, he could have let himself go entirely. But she had moved.

"We need to do one thing first," she said. "Emery tried to do it on her own, but it's too much."

"What?" he asked again.

"I need you to help me move something," she said. "But we have to dig it out some more first."

"What is it?" he asked.

Emery held out a hand and pulled him to his feet as Katie rolled away.

"Do you have a shovel?" Katie asked. "We do need one for *this* kind of mud."

"Sure, in the truck," he said.

Together they walked to the bed of his truck and Mike pulled a spade out from the back.

"Do you have a light?" Katie asked. "It's dark over there."

Mike smiled. "I've got it all." He reached into the back of the cab, where he kept a large battery-powered lantern. You never knew when the power was going to go out on a new job.

"Follow me," Katie said, and led him down the gravel path a few steps, before veering into the woods. Mike followed, though the darkness and beer left everything around him in a haze.

At one point he stopped, and Emery slammed into him from behind.

When he turned around to apologize, she shook her head and put a hand on his back to push him forward.

They emerged from the short path through the brush at the middle of the small cemetery surrounding the pond. Katie turned around just as he realized where they were. She pointed at a small pile of dirt near her feet. A weathered gray headstone marked the top of a plot just a couple feet away. The inscription was lost in the shadows.

"Emery couldn't do this herself," Katie said. "I really need your help."

"Help to do what, exactly?" Mike asked.

Katie's eyes wouldn't meet his right away. She looked at the ground for a long moment, before they finally rose up, big and desperate looking.

"I need you to dig up my mother's grave," Katie said.

Mike's eyes grew wide.

"It sounds weird, I know," she said. "But it's really not. I told you my family was kind of messed up. Well, my mother took most of our family's money to the grave with her. She was buried with a family jewel, and I need it back."

"Oh no, no, no," Mike said. He dropped the shovel on the grass. "I've dealt with just about enough dead bodies this month. I am not about to dig one up on purpose. It's not right."

Katie shook her head. "I wouldn't ask you to help with this if it wasn't really important," she said.

"I'm sorry, Katie, but…I can't. I just can't."

Katie stepped closer, and leaned into him as she gave him a hug. She rested her head on his shoulder and whispered, "I promise you that if you do this for me, I'll do whatever you want tonight. Anything at all."

She raised her head up and met his eyes. "And I know what you've been wanting the past few nights. I'll do that for you, everything you've been thinking of. I'll be glad to do that with you. Just do this one thing for me before all those people start working on this house. You said this place is going to get crowded pretty soon, and it'll be impossible then."

The lights of a car passed by just a few dozen yards away on the turnpike.

"We're awfully close to the road to be digging up a grave," Mike said.

"That's why Emery couldn't do it alone," Katie said. "We need to do this fast and stay out of sight."

"I can't believe you'd want to dig up your own mother," Mike said. He still sounded unsure, though Katie's promises had nearly leveled any sane reservations he'd had. Beer and the promise of what he knew would be heaven had worn down nearly all of his will.

"She was buried with a family jewel that must be worth tens of thousands of dollars by now," Katie said. "And at the moment, I'm about to lose my house. If I can get the jewel back, I won't lose the house. You don't want me to lose the house I grew up in, do you?"

She looked at him with wide, dark eyes. For the first time since he'd met her, he saw the glint of panic, or at least, desperation, in her gaze. "I don't want to end up wandering the turnpike at night without a home like those lost ghosts you told me about."

Mike shook his head.

"Please," she begged, holding his shoulders. "Just get it out of the ground for me, and Emery and I can take care of the rest."

The night seemed to move like liquid around Mike's head, and he shook away the sense of disorientation as he reached down to retrieve the shovel he'd dropped. And then words came out of his mouth that he didn't think he'd say. But he heard his voice say them.

"Only for you," he said to Katie.

She smiled and leaned up to kiss him. "Thank you," she said. "I owe you. And I *will* pay you back."

Mike pushed the spade into the earth already loosened by Emery, and threw a load onto the small pile next to the grave. Emery herself held a shovel and did the same on the other side of the hole. Between the two of them, the piles on either side of the grave grew to be three feet high in almost no time.

A couple times they dropped their spades and ducked when cars passed on the turnpike, but it was later now, long after dark, and traffic was rare.

Mike dug until the sweat dripped off his forehead and onto his arm. At one point, the tip of his spade hit the iron of Emery's tool with a clang, and he looked up at the girl to apologize. Her face was flushed; her shirt covered in dirt and perspiration.

"Sorry," he said.

As usual, she said nothing. Emery only pulled her spade away and dug in to a new area of the grave.

Mike's spade hit the hollow sound of wood first, but Emery's was only a few seconds behind. And then her thrusts rang with the empty sound of hollow wood below. Together, they began to scoop instead of slice down, and in a few minutes, they had completely uncovered the surface of the casket.

"That's perfect," Katie said, standing watch nearby. "Can you lift it out?"

Mike looked at Emery, who had dropped her shovel and stood silent, arms at her sides.

"Want to give it a shot?" he asked.

The girl moved to the foot of the grave and reached down to find the handles they had exposed on the sides of the casket. She began to pull before he'd even bent over, and he hurried to get his hands placed on the other side of the wooden box from her.

The thing did not want to move.

Mike yanked and groaned and swore but it did no good. Finally, he pushed back from the edge and told Emery to stop. "We have to clear more from the sides."

He slid his legs back into the hole and stood on the top of the casket, and with the spade edged out the sides all the way around the wood farther than they had before, careful not to go too far so that the wall of earth above collapsed down. When they tried lifting it again, the casket moved. A little.

After shifting and moaning a few minutes more, the heavy box of wood finally jerked and shifted upward. Mike and Emery dragged it to the side, away from the hole and onto the grass. As soon as they stopped, Mike fell back to the ground, panting. When he opened his eyes again, Katie and Emery stood there looking down at him. Their eyes were simply watching him. It was a little unnerving. Mike sat up.

"There you go," he said. "You can open it and get whatever you're looking for but…I'm not going in there. I dug it up, but that's where it ends."

"Can you at least help us move it to the basement of the house?" Katie asked.

"And just leave a big hole out here?" Mike asked. "No way! Someone would see that."

"Take it to the basement for me, so I can open it when nobody's around," she said. "I don't want to be doing it here, when someone could stop on the side of the road at any minute. The two of you can come back and fill in the hole quickly for tonight and nobody'll notice."

Emery stood on one end of the casket, grabbed the handles and lifted. Her end of the box rose a foot and she stood like that, casket partly raised, waiting. Mike shook his head, but didn't protest. It was all a little surreal and foggy right now, and he just wanted this inexcusable exercise over with. He took the handles on the other side and lifted. Seconds later, Emery was walking backward as they moved through the cemetery and across the grassy clearing toward the house. She watched him, instead of where they were going, as they walked. He recognized that she was completely dependent on his navigation, and extra carefully guided them around the corner of the house toward the back.

"Down the cellar steps," Katie directed.

Mike shifted the box to the left and said, "Let me go first." Then he backed down the stairwell, grunting with each step. When Emery and he were both on level ground, he asked, "Okay, where should we set her?"

"Let's go to the old cellar," Katie said. "That way if any of the decorating people come down here...."

He nodded and hefted the casket higher. "You got it," he said, and began walking backward once more. At last they stepped down a few inches to the original earth floor and walked through a door to go behind the barricade wall he'd set up. It was effectively a secret, hidden room in the cellar.

"Here?" he asked.

"Perfect," Katie said.

Mike dropped his end and sat down on top of the coffin. His underarms were soaked, his forehead dripped sweat into his eyes.

"I'm not opening it," he reiterated.

"No need," Katie said. "Emery will help me. But...I really do need your help with one more thing."

Mike let out a faint moan and Katie grinned. She stepped up to him and bit the bottom of his earlobe before whispering, "I promise I'll make it worth your while."

Her lips felt like an electric shock, and he straightened. He was stung but it felt like the prod of heaven.

"What else?" he asked.

"Fill in the hole?"

He sighed and nodded, and then walked back through the 'public' basement and up the steps.

The night felt good. The air had cooled since the hot August afternoon, and once alone, Mike was lulled by the steady oscillating hum of the locusts in the trees. Their call was warm and placating, as he scooped the loose dirt shovel by shovel back into the hole. He only ducked down twice when lights from the road announced themselves through the forest trees.

After he patted the earth down and tried to loosely rearrange the hunks of sod on top, Mike took the shovel and dropped it back in the bed of his truck. He grabbed his cooler then, and walked toward the house. Half of him expected to find the girls gone; how many times over the past month had Katie ditched him?

But the memory of her electric touch kept him walking quickly to the house. And as he stepped up on the porch, he found Katie waiting there, in the shadow of the doorway.

"All done?" she asked.

He nodded.

"Then I think you've earned a reward."

Mike felt a stirring below the belt and couldn't help but smile. "Do you want to go back to my place for a while?"

She shook her head. "Actually, I had someplace else in mind."

A pair of headlights broke through the tree line, and Mike heard the crunch of gravel as a car pulled down the entry road from the turnpike. The first of the decorator crew was probably here.

Katie opened the door to the house and disappeared inside. Mike followed, and a moment later they were walking up the stairs to the attic.

"They're going to be working up here tonight," Mike said as he followed her across the floor.

"Not where we're going," she said. Katie led him behind the barricade he'd constructed to hide the laundry chute secreted in the flooring.

"Well, it's tucked away," he said. "But I think they'll still see us back here."

She shook her head and pointed to the floor. "We're going down there."

Just as she said it, the trapdoor opened, and Emery's head emerged. She climbed up the ladder stairs and stood beside the entryway, holding the door open.

Katie stepped into the hole and began to descend. When her head disappeared, she called up from below.

"I don't have all night."

Mike put his foot on the ladder and stepped down into the darkness.

"Or maybe I do," Katie's voice whispered, as his right foot suddenly left the ladder to touch hard floor at the bottom.

"This isn't really a laundry chute," he observed. He had been so focused working on other areas of the house over the past few weeks that after Katie had given him the glimpse of the trapdoor in the floor of the attic, he'd never bothered to pull it open again to look more closely inside. It simply wasn't part of his plan.

She didn't answer, but her hands slipped over his shoulders, and her lips brushed against his neck. He closed his eyes, and let the feeling wash down his skin. And then he jumped as the trapdoor above them slammed shut.

He heard Emery's feet creaking on the ladder near them in the dark, but couldn't see her. With the upper door closed, the room was absolutely pitch black, a silent tomb of a space. No exits, no windows. He should have felt a touch of fear, or at least claustrophobia. But all he could focus on was the tantalizing whisper of Katie's fingers on his skin. He felt as if he were floating in an endless dark, as tiny orgasms of touch moved across his body.

A light flickered on then in the corner of the room; just a single candle flame. Emery stepped away from it and suddenly Mike could make out the basics of the hidden space. It was very small with a low ceiling; he almost needed to duck. The walls were dark wood varnished planks, which seemed to mimic the floor, if they weren't made from the exact same material. The result was that even with light, it was a very dark room. Stifling. You could touch the ceiling just inches above your head and probably lie down on the floor and be able to reach the far wall. There was a small dresser in the corner, which was where the candle was perched. A scattering of matchbooks and pools of wax surrounded it. Given the small size of the room, one thing took up almost the entire space.

The bed.

Or, maybe more correctly stated, the torture device.

There was no mattress on this bed, though there was a headboard, and the wrinkled rumple of a blanket bunched up at the end. But it was the uncovered portion of the bed that made Mike blanch.

The sleeping area of the bed was not a solid surface, but instead, it was made up of row upon row of thin metal spikes. They were close together, but there was no question about what the owner of the bed slept on.

It was a bed of nails.

"This is Emery's bed," Katie said. "She says all of the points remind her to feel. We can use it tonight, though I don't think you'll need the reminder."

Mike considered the potential feeling of a hundred sharp-spiked nails all digging into his back as he lay down and shook his head.

"I don't think so."

Katie laughed. "Are you afraid of a little poke and bite?" she said. "I'll give you more than that. You'll forget all about the nails."

She pointed at the blanket and another bundle of fabric lying on the far side of the bed on the floor. "Emery, why don't you make your bed for us so it's not so scary?"

Katie moved in front of him and raised herself on tiptoes to press her lips to his. "It looks like it would be painful, but it's really not," she said. "It's just firm. Very firm." She pressed her hand to his belt and ran her fingers down. "Like you."

Mike took a deep breath and the whole room seemed to spin. He didn't think he'd had that much beer, and all the digging should have sobered him up regardless, but....

"You should lie down," Katie suggested. "Trust me, you'll be okay."

Mike put the cooler down next to the bed, and sat on the old blanket that Emery had pulled over the top of the nails. She was right, he didn't feel the nails digging in at all. The nails were close enough together that with a little fabric over them, they absorbed the weight with an evenness that avoided the presumably unavoidable spiky pain.

He heard the cooler click open and then a cold can was pressed into his hand. He saw Emery's dark eyes for just a moment before she stepped back and out of sight. Almost without thought, he popped the tab and took a drink.

"Relax now," Katie said. She sat down on the bed next to him. "Thank you so much for helping me tonight. I couldn't do it myself."

Mike shrugged. "You know I'll help you however I can."

She slipped an arm around his shoulders and kissed his cheek.

"I know you've been really patient waiting for me," she said. "And I really appreciate it."

She slipped a hand under his shirt, and he felt the tee riding up. Hands pulled at the ends and he lifted his arms without thinking, holding his beer can in the air. Then the can suddenly disappeared from his fingers and his shirt soon followed before the cold aluminum of the can returned.

"You don't have to be patient anymore though," Katie said. "Lie down."

He took a gulp of his PBR and set the can on the ground before lying back on the *very* firm surface of the bed. Hands worked at his belt, and then his jeans were falling to the floor. It was hot in the enclosed room, and finally being out of his clothes was a welcome relief. He closed his eyes and took a breath as his briefs slid down his thighs and away. His penis felt thick and instantly alert as it tasted the open air, and felt the faint brush of a woman's hand.

"I've wanted to bring you here since the first day I met you," Katie whispered.

The floorboards creaked above them, and Mike began to sit up.

Katie pressed him back, rolling over on top of him. She bent down and kissed him and then made the faintest "shhhh".

"What if they hear us?" he whispered.

"Don't scream and we'll be fine," she said. "You're not going to scream, are you?"

He shook his head, and she smiled before melting her lips over his.

Mike slipped his hands beneath her shirt and pulled her tight. Katie shifted against him, her lips now urgently hard on his. As he breathed, he breathed her. His thighs ached at the silk of her skin. His hands moved across her back; he wanted to feel every pore of her.

"Oh my God," he whispered, when she broke their kiss. "I've wanted this for so long."

Katie smiled, and with one hand fondled the evidence of his need between them. "I know," she said.

He moaned at the attention, and then lifted his hands to push her shirt up. He couldn't wait anymore. He wanted to have all of her, naked, pressed against him. He couldn't get close enough to her body.

Katie pulled out of his embrace and lifted her arms to let him strip her.

"There's just one thing," she said, as the shirt came off. The first thing he saw in the dim candlelight was that she wasn't wearing a bra underneath.

The second was that her chest and belly were crisscrossed in ragged scars. They still showed twists of black thread from the stitches that had obviously pulled her back together from whatever hideous accident had ripped her open.

"What happened?" he whispered. His fingers traced a line from her sternum to her groin, and he felt the hard points of the stitches shift like stubble beneath his hand.

"I will tell you all about that day," she said. "But…not tonight, okay?"

She pushed his hand down to the silver buckle of her belt, and Mike didn't argue. He was not going to screw this up, after waiting so long, by asking questions. There would be time enough for answers later. He unzipped her shorts and began to slip them down her thighs. She moved down to the bed so he could pull them past her knees and off. When he dropped them off the bed on the floor, he saw the shadow of Emery still standing at the back of the room. His stomach constricted for a moment; he'd been so lost in Katie, he'd forgotten there was anyone else in the room. But the other woman didn't move or say anything and again, his crotch told him not to fuck this up. If Katie didn't care, why should he? He slid his fingers up Katie's inner thighs, and slipped his thumbs beneath the elastic band of her panties when he reached them. She arched her back and he slid the silk down, gasping with desire as he exposed her.

"Hurry," Katie whispered. She spread her legs apart and held her arms open for his embrace. He accommodated, pressing himself between her thighs and diving into her kiss. She took his breath away; her every touch sent jolts of fire down his back, up his thighs, into his crotch.

It had been months since Mike had had sex, and foreplay with Katie had gone on for weeks. He wasn't slow or tentative about pressing inside her. He literally couldn't wait. She accepted his entry with a quiet moan, and then Mike felt the threads of her scars – or wounds – scratching against his belly as he moved with her. The sensation was strange, but weirdly exciting. He had all of her, even if it was a ragged her, against him. He poured himself inside Katie, rolling her back and forth on the bed in the dark. Her hands pressed against his thighs and ass, massaging him and stroking his body as he moved the most sensitive part of himself inside her. At one point, he felt lips and breath on his neck even though Katie was beneath him. But he didn't question it; his climax was too close to think.

Katie groaned and gasped in small tight sounds, and he struggled to hold his own sounds in, still aware that the decorators were working just a few feet above their head. When he finally let go inside her, a warm weight pressed down on his back. The soft flesh of breasts and the hot lips of a mouth that was not Katie's kissed his back and neck, as he moaned into Katie's shoulder.

Emery was lying on top of him, naked and hot. He was pinned between them, and his eyes rolled back. This was the strangest heaven. And then Emery's hands were urging him to roll over, off Katie to lie on his back. He did, and before his thighs had fully touched the bed she was on top of him, her wetness pressing down on his erection, still bone-hard from the excitement of plumbing the depths of Katie.

"Oh my God," he whispered, as the heat of her engulfed him. Compared to Katie, she was like a furnace, dripping with desire and panting with need. She pressed his wrists to the bed and rode him hard, with each motion bleating a tiny catch of a sound from her throat.

Mike couldn't believe he was still hard enough for her to use; he couldn't possibly come again, but Katie leaned over his face and kissed him as Emery used her hips and worked him inside her. He could feel the nails in his back now, as she pumped herself to orgasm, slamming his ass again and again toward the thousand nails beneath the sheet.

And then it was over. Emery let out something that sounded like a wounded animal caught in a trap. She froze above him, her breasts hanging down to just barely brush his chest. Then she lifted her hips and pushed off the bed, leaving him alone again with Katie.

"Thank you," Katie said. "She deserved that. It's been a long time for her."

"Nice of you to share," he said, laughing just a little. Nervously.

"If you take me, you get Emery," she said. "We're like a set."

"Whatever you want," he said.

Katie's eyes squinted with humor. "I didn't think you'd mind," she said. "You're a man, after all."

"What are you saying?"

"I think you know," she said. "None of you can say no to the kitty."

He snorted and slipped his hand between her legs. She was still wet with the evidence of their orgasms. "You weren't exactly resisting, yourself," he said.

She ran her hand up his arm to touch his chin. "No," she admitted. "But women can choose to resist. Men are slaves to their penises."

Mike ran his fingers over the rough stitches that marred her middle. The flesh felt angry, puckered and hard. The black stitches scraped his fingers like wires.

"What happened to you?" he asked. "How did you get all cut up?"

"Are you sure you really want to know?" she said.

He nodded.

"They did an autopsy on me," she said.

Mike made a face and shook his head. "They can't do an autopsy on you while you're alive," he said.

Katie nodded.

"I know," she said. "They did it after I died."

PART TWO
THE HAUNTING

CHAPTER SIXTEEN

"They're lined up all the way to the turnpike!" Jeanie exclaimed. She pushed the black drapes back over the window and walked across the room to her impromptu makeup station. This was the *Nightmare on Elm Street* room, so it was decorated like a girl's bedroom. Which meant she had a full vanity where she could work on makeup. Once the house opened for business each day, she could easily stow her stuff in a drawer as the house haunters made their way to their stations in all of the themed rooms. At the moment, everyone was gathered there for a last makeup check and a pep talk from Perry Clark, the guy who had masterminded this whole thing. Lon, the house production manager, stood at his side. Lenny and June stood in the front row waiting for Perry to talk. Both of them were visibly beaming with excitement. This was the night they'd been working toward for the past two months.

"Quiet down for a second," Lon called. "It's almost show time."

Jeanie slipped past Lenny to stand next to Bong. She'd played off his ethnicity and turned him into a pale Asian ghost with a long wig and black contacts. Against the pancake white of his face, his eyes were like dark pools of hell.

"Thank you all," Perry said. "You have done an amazing job here. Lon just gave me the tour, and I have to say, this place gave me the creeps – and you all weren't even in your places to jump out at me. Thank God!"

Perry grinned and nodded at the grizzled carpenter in the corner. The thin, quiet girl who was always with him, Katie, stood at his side.

"The first time I saw this place, I didn't think it would be safe for people to walk through without tearing it down," Perry said. "But Mike, here, managed to bring this place back from the dead."

He pointed at Argento and Lucio. "And you two…well, you made it *look* like the dead! I don't even want to know how you got the blood splatter to look so real. It's disturbing, I have to tell you."

Perry waved his hand around the room at the collection of ghouls and zombies and gutted 'haunters' and grinned. "And all of you look… disgusting. Huge thanks to June and Jeanie for turning you into…well… whatever you are. You're all amazing. And that's really all I have to say. I just wanted to let you know that I'm so proud of what you've all done. This is the first time in decades that Bachelor's Grove has had something positive happening within its gates. So, I just want you to go out there tonight, and the rest of the month and…have fun scaring the hell out of people."

Lon grinned and held up his hands. "Thanks to Perry for making this all happen. Haunting Bachelor's Grove was a stroke of genius. Once they walk through, I know people are going to be talking about this house for the rest of the year. Just remember, we're here to have fun. If you see someone having a real problem – like they get so freaked out they're crying or won't leave a room or something, fade back and text me. I'll be just outside or downstairs in Ops every night to deal with anything that comes up. I want the rest of you to stay in character for our guests."

He looked at his watch and nodded. "Front door opens in fifteen minutes. So…places, everyone. Let's haunt this house!"

The cast began to file out of the room, and Jeanie walked over to her makeup station to hide the rest of her things for the night. As she passed Perry, the businessman shook his head.

"That's disgusting," he said.

"What, this?" she asked, turning her belly to face him. She had worked with latex to create a grisly twine of guts. It was held fast to her back with flesh-colored straps, allowing the fake intestines to literally hang and sway out of her belly. They glistened with something that looked like blood mixed with a yellow slime.

"Go ahead and feel it," she offered.

Perry grimaced, but put a finger out to touch one curled rope of guts. He instantly pulled his hand back.

"It's good, isn't it?" she asked.

"Maybe too good," he said, and shook his head, grimacing. Then Lon came up and grabbed him away to talk about some issue with ticket processing out front.

She saw that Katie and Mike still remained in the back of the room, talking quietly. Katie's face was pale, and she wore a crop top halter and Daisy Dukes to show off her midriff to maximum effect. Her midsection was crisscrossed with scars and stitches. The effect was striking, yet also subdued. Jeanie wondered if everyone moving through the house would catch the grotesquerie of it, especially with the low lighting and moving quickly through the rooms. Jeanie stepped over to the two, interrupting their conversation with a smile.

"Do you want me to add some blood to that?" she asked, pointing at Katie's belly.

The other woman shook her head. "Nobody does my makeup but me," she said curtly, and went back to saying something to the carpenter. Mike had gotten her the job as a 'floater' at the last minute. She was not assigned to a particular room, but would simply be wandering the house looking spooky. But she had refused all of Jeanie and June's offers to help with her makeup. Jeanie didn't like her; she seemed just a bit too full of herself.

"Suit yourself," she said, and went back to her vanity to put the last tubes of blood and spirit gum to attach all of the latex appliances to the haunters back in the drawers.

"Ten minutes," Lon called from somewhere out in the hall.

Jeanie felt a lump in her throat and shut the last drawer. Bong stood next to her, and she leaned up on tiptoes to give him a small peck on the lips. She barely brushed them but apologized. "Don't want to ruin your lipstick," she said.

"I can't believe you made me wear lipstick," he complained.

"I can't believe it's opening night," she said. "Are you excited?"

He shrugged. "I can think of better ways to spend a Thursday night."

Jeanie frowned. "But think of all the nights we'll be together this month," she said. "We'll see each other more than ever."

"I like seeing you better without your guts showing," he said.

"I don't know," she said. "I might like you better with lipstick." Jeanie grinned and took his hand. "Come on, it's almost time to begin."

Mike bent down to kiss Katie, now that they were the last people remaining, and she shooed him from the room. He would be hiding out with Lon in Ops each night, helping with any problems. His official job had really ended three weeks ago, but Lon and Perry kept finding new reasons to keep him on the payroll. He didn't mind, since it gave him a good excuse to hang around Katie. "See you later," he told her, and exited the room.

★　　★　　★

Emery emerged from the closet then, wearing a black cowl and holding a long, curved butcher knife.

From somewhere in the house, someone yelled, "It's showtime. Let's get bloody!"

Katie nodded, and whispered, "Oh, we will."

CHAPTER SEVENTEEN

There were far more people tonight in Bachelor's Grove than had ever been there before for a funeral. And the people in line were buzzing with excitement. Many of them had heard of the haunted cemetery, but never actually been there before.

"...I can't believe they actually are doing this here..."

"...what if it really is haunted, like they always said..."

"...best gimmick for a haunted house ever. As soon as I heard about it, I was in..."

"...I'm going to scream, I just know it..."

Jillie Melton heard it all, and shook her head. She stood near the front of the line with Ted. She hadn't been able to enter the house or get it shut down since the carpenter had sent her away, so she'd bought a ticket to get in on opening night. They couldn't keep her out with a valid ticket. The county forest preserve commissioner had listened patiently before dismissing her as a kook with the explanation, "This is the best way to put all of that haunting nonsense to rest. Instead of having people sneak past the police and possibly get hurt in there at night in October, we're turning it into an attraction. For the first time in years, Bachelor's Grove will actually be a safe place to go at Halloween. The only ghosts that will be there will be the ones we *put* there."

Jillie didn't believe that for a heartbeat, but she knew when to give up on a full-frontal assault. She was going in tonight to feel just how dangerous this attraction was likely going to be.

"I'm really worried about this," she said.

Ted shook his head. "I think you're working yourself up over nothing," he said. "All this construction, all these people? I think they've probably driven away a lot of the energy here."

"You know better than that," Jillie said. "Spirits don't just get up and move. Most of them can't leave the place they're tied to without intervention. That's why you see the repetition over and over. The ghostly hitchhiker getting in cars on the turnpike happens again and again and again. The mother and her baby. The apparition of the house, with blood painted all over its front door. That energy is tied to the graves and the house, and all this activity is going to feed it, not send it away. And the spirits here have never been happy ones."

"Most of the negativity that's been here was because of the devil worshippers that desecrated this place in the Sixties and Seventies," Ted said. "The dark stuff that happened here was all caused by living, breathing humans, not ghosts."

She shook her head. "There were sacrifices here," she said. "That blood remains in the ground. The darkness may have been started by the living, but the spirits they tied here remain. There's been death here, violent death. And I just have this horrible feeling that there's going to be more."

The line suddenly shifted, as the first ticket holders were ushered past the gate on the front of the porch. As they stepped up on the first wooden stair, Jillie felt a chill down her back. An invisible pressure, like two cold hands, pushed against the front of her shoulders, trying to repel her backward. Trying to send her away.

"I can feel them now," she whispered. "Stage Three and we're not even inside the house."

Ted looked at her with concern.

"I don't know what we're going to find once we actually get inside. But I don't think these kids have any idea what they're going to be dealing with."

She nodded at the group of high schoolers ahead of them. There were a half-dozen of them, and two were wearing black and gold Oak Forest High School jackets.

A man wearing a hideous mask that looked like the skin of someone else's face held up a chainsaw as he stood guard at the door. He only let in one group at a time to the house. He opened the battered screen door and motioned with the chainsaw for the high schoolers to move forward.

"Step inside," he said. "Don't slip on the blood."

CHAPTER EIGHTEEN

Larry led a group up the steps to the house at Bachelor's Grove. They had all met for drinks at The Edge and planned to head to Naperville for a Halloween movie night with friends afterwards.

"We're going to get as much horror in as possible tonight," Diane had told the bartender just a half hour earlier, before her husband Troy had pulled her back to their table with Larry, Lisa, Amy and Pam.

"Everybody in the world doesn't need to know," Troy said.

"But everybody in the world should be going to haunted houses and watching scary movies this week," she'd insisted.

Now that they were finally about to enter the haunted house, Diane could barely contain herself.

"Who's ready to scream?" she asked.

Amy smiled and shook her head. But Lisa grinned. "Let's see what they got!"

They crossed the porch after getting their tickets. The door was opened by a man dressed as Leatherface.

"Good thing I wore my red shoes," Larry said, as the *Texas Chainsaw Massacre* doorman ushered them inside. "You won't be able to see the blood on them."

Lisa laughed and bit his ear. "After what you drank, you won't be able to see anything soon," she whispered.

"I can see just fine," Larry said. "Like right there. Isn't that a human thigh on the dinner platter? I'm gonna pass on that, but the liver and onions might be good if it's not overcooked."

The dining room table was made of weathered wooden planks and set with three table settings. A series of serving plates covered the middle. It looked like the preparation for a feast…if you were a cannibal. A pale, gray, disembodied head perched at the top of the table, and a silver platter was piled high with amputated hands and feet. The bloodied fingers and toes were piled next to a long hunk of human thigh. Behind the table, a blond girl in a thin blue shirt was tied to a chair that appeared to be made of human arms. Her hands shook and pulled hard at the bindings, trying to get away from the dead fingers that made up the ends of the chair arms beneath her.

"Help," she pleaded at them. "Get me out of here."

At that moment, a chainsaw growled to life in the background, and a hulking man wearing a pig's head stepped out of the shadows behind her.

"Holy shit," Amy said from right behind them as the smell of gasoline and blue smoke filled the room. She shoved at Larry to keep walking, and he and Lisa laughed and stepped through the doorway back out into the hall, and then into the kitchen. Diane and Troy followed with Pam lagging just behind.

"That was pretty awesome," Troy said.

"Gross," Pam complained. She had not wanted to come, but Lisa had insisted. "You are not pussying out on this one," Lisa had said. "A Bachelor's Grove Haunted House? And Lon managing the props and shit? It's gonna be epic."

The kitchen was lit with one bare bulb, which hung from the ceiling on a wire that swayed back and forth, throwing weird shadows on the room. The place looked as if it had recently been used as a slaughterhouse. Blood was splattered on the peeling old country wallpaper, and an axe was embedded in the far wall. A woman's body lay on the floor, blood pooled all around her head. A butcher knife handle stuck out of the back of her head; the silver tip of the blade protruded from her forehead. The tip of it gouged the floor.

"Damn, that looks real," Troy said.

Lisa laughed. "You know it's all just for show. I don't know how anyone could be scared of this shit."

She looked pointedly at Pam, who looked away. She stepped closer to the sink. One side had what looked like a human heart sitting in the middle of the basin. Around it, a thousand squirming maggots jittered and shifted.

In the basin next to it, a human head sat with its neck over the drain. Its hair was matted with blood, and gore streaked its cheeks.

"Oh my God," Pam said and stepped away.

"You are such a baby," Lisa said, and bent closer to the sink. "They sure did good work here though."

The eyes of the face were bloodshot and glossy; she could have sworn she saw the damn thing blink.

"Hi there," the bloody lips suddenly said.

Lisa shrieked and jumped back two feet.

"Gotcha," the human head laughed.

Behind her, Troy and Diane were bending over the woman with the knife in her head. Just as Lisa jumped, the dead woman began to rise up from the floor.

"That's it," Diane said, and bolted for the next room.

The rest of them followed, and a moment later, they found themselves in a bedroom with floral wallpaper. The sheets of the bed were rumpled, and a pool of red marred the center. The reason hung from the ceiling above. A girl in a white nightgown drenched in crimson hung from the ceiling. She looked as if she were crouching there; both of her legs were stretched out like a sprinter at the starting gate while one hand clutched the ceiling, surrounded by bloody handprints. Her other arm reached out toward the bedroom door, as if she were begging for help.

"She better not move," Diane said.

"No way they could hang someone up there every night," Troy said. "I don't think we have to worry."

The closet door creaked open at that moment, and they suddenly heard the singsong chant of a group of children. "One, two, Freddy's coming for you…."

A hand emerged from the closet, wearing a glove tipped with long knife blades. The blades trailed down the wall with a faint scraping sound, before Freddy Krueger emerged in his familiar red and green sweater from the closet, his face a burned mass of scars. "Welcome to my nightmare," he said and started toward them.

"Time to go," Pam said, and bolted back out of the room. Lisa laughed and followed her down the hall to a room that offered two exits. The walls shimmered with red and blue light, and hidden speakers played a taut, synthesizer-dominated soundtrack that gave Pam the creeps almost as much as the setpieces of the house. A sign seemingly written in blood said 'Don't Go In The Basement'. A human skeleton seated in what looked like an electric chair pointed with one bony finger toward the stairs that led upward.

The darkened stairs that led down had another placard nailed to the wall next to them. 'No Exit', the sign said. Screams erupted from the dark below, and they didn't sound like a recording.

"I guess 'up' it is," Pam said.

She started up the steps. The walls were covered in a strange array of taxidermy. There were animal pelts stretched out with pins, and the full heads of a raccoon, a squirrel, a goat and other creatures emerged from the wall at odd intervals.

There were also the stretched-out skins of three human faces.

As she passed one, it let out a scream, and Pam jumped. "Jesus," she complained. Her heart was pounding a mile a minute now. "I really just want to get out of this place," she murmured.

"Gotta love a skinhead," Larry laughed behind her.

The attic was creepy. The music here was louder, and the first thing they saw was a girl's head lolling through the broken glass of a window. The shards had clearly punctured her throat, and her mouth hung open in a silent scream.

"Ouch, I bet that had to hurt," Larry said.

To their left an old woman sat in a wheelchair. A rope was fastened around her neck and stretched up to a hook in the ceiling. To their right were racks and racks of what looked like costumes. It could have been the props department for a horror movie. There were lots of velvet vests and gowns on hangers, but there were also rubber masks of all sorts of monsters, from the overt Frankenstein's monster to more freakish things with three eyes and hag hair.

The floor had an arrow painted on it in red pointing the way into the aisle in the center of the costume collection. Words were painted on the floor next to the arrow.

'Shed Your Skin and Choose Another,' they said.

"I'm not going first," Pam announced.

"Chicken," Lisa taunted. "Let me show you how it's done."

She held out her hands and began to walk through the aisle of outfits, making them all shift and move as she passed through.

Larry grinned and patted Pam on the head as he passed her, pulling Lisa by the hand behind him. Amy followed closely behind them.

"Come on, Pam," Diane urged, as she and Troy walked into the aisle. "The sooner you get through it, the sooner you'll get through it."

Troy laughed at that, and the two passed into the aisle of clothes. Pam was about to follow, when she heard Lisa scream ahead.

"Oh shit," she whispered. Her knees were shaking and she couldn't seem to walk forward.

Just then, someone in the mask of an ancient woman with frizzy hair and a horrible wrinkled face poked out of the aisle. She held a sickle in her hand and made a pass of it through the air in front of Pam.

The girl shrieked and leapt backward, shocked out of her paralysis. The figure disappeared back into the aisle and a moment later, Diane screamed.

Pam staggered backward, past the old woman in the wheelchair. That monster, at least, she knew wasn't real.

She rounded a corner and bent over, trying to catch her breath. "I just want to go home," she whispered. "I just want to go home."

From the far end of the attic, she heard Larry laughing, and then another shriek. It sounded like Lisa. Then Diane was demanding, "Go, go, go."

The upstairs grew silent, except for the eerie music overhead. Pam took a deep breath, steeling herself to follow them alone through the costume maze.

Something creaked in the floor in front of her, and Pam looked up to see two hands reaching out of a door in the floor toward her. Before she could move, the hands grabbed her ankles and yanked. Pam fell backward, as her legs slid forward.

She hit the ground hard, her head bouncing on the wooden floor. Pam opened her mouth to scream, but hardly any sound came out.

And then the hands pulled her down into darkness, and the door above her head slammed shut.

She hadn't had the chance to voice even the faintest scream.

CHAPTER NINETEEN

"Perfect," Jillie said. They had just entered the *Nightmare on Elm Street* room. "There's a bed in here," she whispered. "Unless someone's already under it, that's where I'm staying."

The sound of children singing the Freddy Krueger song suddenly began, and Jillie pushed Ted in front of her. "Don't let anyone see me," she said, dropping to the floor.

The closet door opened and a moment later Ted was face-to-face with the infamous boiler room killer.

"Welcome to my nightmare," Freddy said, clicking his finger blades together.

"I was just leaving," Ted said. He turned and hurried back out of the room.

Jillie lay perfectly still beneath the bed. There was nobody else there, and she held her breath until she heard the closet door close again. She intended to stay here until the place closed for the night. And then, once she was alone, she'd be able to walk around and really take the pulse of the house. She would text Ted to come back then, and let him in so they could set up their EMF meter and take some readings. Not that she couldn't feel some of the energy here herself. But she wanted recordings and scientific readings. Maybe with some evidence, she could get the county to reconsider what it was doing. Show them the danger they were exposing all sorts of people to, especially all the kids who would be walking through here in the next three or four weeks.

Jillie edged her way to the center of the space beneath the bed, put her hands on her chest and closed her eyes. For a few hours, she needed to be very quiet.

Outside in the room, the closet door opened again and Freddy said, "Welcome to my nightmare."

He was greeted with the shriek of a teenage girl.

CHAPTER TWENTY

"That's a wrap," Lon called. "All of the living have left."

Argento stepped out of the closet on the first floor. He pulled the black hood from his head, and began to peel off his black leather gloves as he joined the others in the gathering room.

"How was your body count tonight?" Lon asked with a grin.

"I think I made a woman pee," Argento said.

"Nice!"

Lucio came walking down the stairs first, still wearing the old hag mask and carrying the sickle. Bong was just behind him, and June followed. Her throat appeared cut from ear to ear and one of her eyes appeared gluey white.

"Oh my God, that was so much fun," Jeanie said, emerging from the basement stairs. She was followed by three zombies. They made for a strange sight, as all of them were laughing.

Chelsea, the girl with the knife through her head, came staggering out of the kitchen. "Lying on the floor all night is going to get old really fast," she complained.

"Did you freak anyone out, though?" Jeanie asked.

"I made one guy scream like a little girl." She grinned. "He really thought I was just a dummy, and was about two inches from my face when I jumped up."

Lenny came out of the back bedroom still wearing his Freddy mask. He clicked and clacked his blade fingers together while the family room filled with the cast of the house.

"All right," Lon said. "Great job, everyone. That was an excellent night's work and we sent a lot of people home happy. With wet underwear, maybe, but happy. But now it's late and we do it all again tomorrow. So, get out of your costumes, leave them on hangers upstairs, and let's get the heck out of here. Thanks for making it creepy!"

"Did you have fun?" Jeanie asked Bong. She gave him a much longer kiss than she had at the start of the night.

He shrugged. "People don't seem to like Asian ghosts who crawl down the hallway at them. So I really didn't meet any new friends, although I talked to June a bit. Plus, now my arms are tired."

"I'll rub you down when we get home," she promised.

"I'm counting on it," he said.

"Somebody help Allen out of the sink in the kitchen," Lon called.

Jeanie grinned and patted Bong's shoulder. "I'll be right back," she said.

She walked to the kitchen and found June already there, with the front cabinet open. "I'll lift while you push," Jeanie offered. The counter creaked upward on hinges, and Allen rose up slowly, rubbing his neck.

"Damn, that's a long night," he said. "How long are we doing this?"

"All month," June said. "We'll get you some Bengay."

Allen snorted and staggered off toward the bathroom.

"How are you doing?" Jeanie asked.

"What do you mean?" June answered.

"Well, it's none of my business, I guess, but...I thought you and Lenny...."

June snorted. "Lenny spends too much time at my place, that's all."

"But," Jeanie began. "With the *Nightmare on Elm Street* room and all, I thought...."

June grinned, but she didn't look happy. "Yeah, a lot of people think. But, if you're interested, he's available."

Jeanie's eyelids shot open. She put her hand up. "No, I didn't mean...."

June shook her head. "Look, I don't care," she said. "He crashes at my place a lot, that's all."

"I have Bong," Jeanie said. "I'm not after Lenny."

June shrugged. "Suit yourself," she said, and began to walk away. But then she looked over her shoulder and said something that made Jeanie's stomach go cold.

"Lenny's a good lay if you're feeling dry. Just sayin'."

Jeanie took her time putting the kitchen countertop back in place and closing the cabinet doors before she returned to the bedroom where Bong waited. She didn't know why June had said that, but she couldn't stop hearing it in her head.

She shook her head until it went away, and then she raised her chin and kissed Bong on the lips.

"Hey," she said. "Wanna take me home?"

★   ★   ★

The voices had been silent for a while now. Jillie slid out from her hiding place beneath the bed and stretched. Her back was stiff. She walked over to the window and peered out the black curtains. The forest outside looked completely dark. No headlights in sight. She pulled out her phone and texted Ted.

> *Jillie: Where are you now?*
> *Ted: Went home. Are you ready for action?*
> *Jillie: Think so. All is quiet.*
> *Ted: Be there in ten.*
> *Jillie: Cool.*

She walked to the hallway and peered up and down it for several seconds, listening for any sound in the house. Hearing none, she finally stepped into the hall, and walked down to the dining room and kitchen. There were no lights on. She hit the flashlight app on her iPhone and shone it around the rooms. Nothing there but props. Grotesque, red-splashed walls and chains and furniture.

Jillie walked to the other end of the house and found the room with the stairs to the attic and basement. She shone the light on the darkness going down, and carefully stepped on the first stair. She hadn't gotten this far on her tour earlier.

One by one she crept down, pausing to listen at each step. When she reached the bottom, she flashed her phone in a 360-degree arc, absorbing the layout. The place looked like a junk shop, with mirrors and bureaus and boxes all stacked in rows. She peered at herself in one mirror and almost jumped. A ghostly white face appeared just behind her own. Then she realized the 'ghost' was fastened to the beam just above her head – so anyone who looked in the mirror (which was tilted upward) would get a shock.

She moved down the row of junk, strategically placed to allow 'zombies' or other 'monsters' to hide and jump out, no doubt, while corralling the patrons down a specific path. And that path now resembled a museum of horror. Every twenty feet or so, there appeared to be a small set constructed to represent some kind of horror theme. To her left, she saw the half-nude manikin in a tub of red, meant to depict the Countess Báthory. But that gory tableau wasn't what made her pause.

There was something wrong here.

Jillie had followed her career as a ghost hunter because she had always been sensitive to things. She knew most people thought she was a nut, but that didn't change the fact that she *sensed* things. Her spine seemed like an antenna for ghosts; it chilled and sparked whenever she was in areas reputed to be haunted...and often in places that were not. She could always seem to find cold spots in old buildings where there was no breeze. There had been many times walking through a cemetery that she had felt fingers brush across her face when she bent over a gravestone to read the inscription. As if the dead were reaching up from the earth to greet her softly. She had felt things that other people didn't ever since she was a kid. It had all started when her family moved to an old house in Virginia for a couple years when she was four. Every time she'd gone into the basement, her mother had found her standing in the corner, talking to someone. She barely remembered those early years, but her mom had told her later how unnerving it was to see her conversing with the wall. But kids often had imaginary friends, so her parents had chalked it up to that.

When they moved across country to the Chicago area, she no longer talked to walls...but there was one place in the house that bothered her. It felt wrong. Every time she'd walked into the room she'd felt cold, sometimes to the point of shivering. It was her dad's den, and over time she began to avoid going there, which her father never questioned, because he didn't want to be disturbed when he was working there anyway. Every time her mother sent her there to call her father or take him something, she'd complained that it was too cold in there.

"It's the same temperature as the rest of the house, baby," her mom insisted. And Jillie had argued over and over again that it was not.

"It's like walking into a freezer," she remembered saying.

Later, as an adult, she'd researched the house and found the probable cause. In the Forties, there had been a horrible crime committed in that room. Domestic violence that had turned into a murder-suicide.

That had always given Jillie proof and validation that her 'feelings' were not imaginary. She had lived with ghosts and felt their frozen rage. The dead were not gone, she knew. The dead were everywhere. So now, when she reached the end of the basement and felt something twist in her stomach, and a chill begin to creep up her back, she trusted her instinct. There was something here.

She walked through a tableau inspired by *The Exorcist*, pushed an old dresser out of the way and stepped behind the construct to the other side of the aisle, toward the back wall of the basement. It was a newly constructed wall. A quickly thrown together barricade of plywood and 2x4s.

What was it here to hide?

She moved the light along its length until she found a hinge. Three hinges actually. She moved the phone around until she discovered the foot-long piece of board that served as the knob and lock. It was positioned horizontally to hold the door in place, but when she twisted it vertically, the plywood swung inward. There was another small room here in the basement, hidden away from the 'attraction' area.

Jillie stepped down a few inches from the wooden floor to an earthen one. The air here was immediately more dank and chill than in the rest of the hastily 'finished' portion of the basement.

There was a coffin against the wall to her right, but she barely noticed it because in the middle of the small room, lying with her face to the ground, was a teenage girl. She looked like one of the kids in the group that had entered the haunted house before her earlier tonight – the girl wore a thin Oak Forest High School jacket, and a swirl of long brown hair covered her eyes and cheek before cascading to the dirt.

"Hey, are you okay?" Jillie called softly. When the girl didn't answer, she repeated the question, a little louder. And then she stepped closer.

There was blood on the girl's neck. Jillie bent down and brushed some of the hair from the girl's face; her skin felt cool and Jillie could now see the long gash that cut across her neck. The ground beneath her chin glistened with the girl's blood. She hesitantly reached out her hand to touch the darkened earth, and her finger came back wet with blood.

"Oh no," Jillie whispered, just before her spine suddenly turned cold as ice water.

A woman's voice spoke from behind her. It sounded deathly serious.

"Get out!" it said.

Jillie looked behind her but saw nothing. However, her legs suddenly felt like wet spaghetti. The ice spread from her spine to her chest, and Jillie held a hand to her breastbone as she found herself struggling to breathe.

"Get out now!" the voice demanded again. She couldn't see where it was coming from, though it sounded like it was right next to her. She backed away from the girl.

Jillie staggered to the door and dove through the furniture to return to the haunted house path. It felt as if two fists were beating her back, and she stumbled and half-ran back along the aisle until she came to a door. It was locked, but she fumbled with the doorknob until the metal latch turned. Then she ran up the steps, not closing the door behind her.

When she reached the grass, she fell to her knees. When she got back up, she realized the pressure inside her was gone, and the hands no longer pushed her. But she wasn't going back. Jillie moved quickly toward the front of the house. Behind her, she heard a door slam shut.

"There you are," Ted's voice said from across the clearing. "I was looking for you. Are you ready for us to set up?"

Jillie shook her head vigorously. "No," she gasped, bending over and putting her hands on her knees as she caught her breath. "Call the police. There's a dead girl in the basement."

Ted shook his head. "They did a really good job decorating the place," he said. "But I can't believe they freaked you out."

"I'm not joking and the body wasn't a prop," Jillie said. "I touched her face. There was blood all over the ground. Somebody was murdered in there tonight. And that's not the worst of it."

"What could be worse?" Ted asked.

"I *felt* her," Jillie said. "*Physically*. She wanted me out of there so I wouldn't interfere. She actually pushed me. But I know it was her, and I think I know what she wants."

"She who?" Ted said.

"The witch of Bremen Coven," Jillie said.

"She died fifty years ago," Ted said.

"Exactly," Jillie said. "And she's been trying to come back ever since. I think that girl in the basement was a sacrifice, and if I'm right, she won't be the last one."

She looked at him with wide eyes. "Now call the police!"

CHAPTER TWENTY-ONE

Two cop cars arrived a few minutes later, with red and blue lights flashing, but no sirens. They pulled past the gravel onto the grassy clearing just in front of the porch, where Jillie and Ted waited.

Four officers emerged. A tall, thin one with a day's growth of stubble and tired eyes walked quickly toward them. He introduced himself as Officer Mulkin and pointed at Ted. "Did you call in a homicide?"

Ted tilted his head at Jillie. "I did, but she's the one who saw the body. It's in the basement."

The cop nodded and looked directly at her. "You're sure you saw a body and not a prop?" he asked. "This is a haunted house, after all. I'm sure they have some very realistic-looking stuff in there."

Jillie shook her head vehemently. "It was real," she said. "It was a girl from Oak Forest High. Her throat was cut."

The cop looked skeptical. "What were you doing in the building after hours?" he asked. "Are you working in the house?"

"No," Jillie said. She looked at Ted and made a face before continuing. "I'm a paranormal investigator, and I was here trying to see what kind of impact turning this place into a circus has had on the ghosts inside."

"Uh-huh," Mulkin said. "So you were trespassing."

"I think the fact that there's a dead girl in there is more important right now," she said. "I bought a ticket to go inside tonight, and then I waited until the house was closed to look around." Briefly she explained how she had hidden beneath the bed and then used her cell phone to explore the house in the dark.

Mulkin pursed his lips and nodded. "Show me."

Jillie stepped down the deck and began to walk around the perimeter of the house. Ted and the four officers followed right behind her, but then they stopped as two headlights cut through the forest and moved straight up the gravel path toward the house.

A silver Mitsubishi stopped right next to the police cars, and a stocky man in Dockers and a blue polo shirt got out.

"What's this all about?" the man called, as he walked toward the group.

"Are you in charge of this place?" Mulkin asked, as the man reached them.

"Yeah," he said. "I'm Perry Clark. Someone from the police station called and told me there was a problem out here."

"This woman has reported a dead body inside," Mulkin said.

"There are all sorts of 'dead bodies' in there," Perry said angrily. "It's a haunted house, for Christ's sake. And it's closed. Nobody should be here at all right now. I don't want anyone messing with our sets for tomorrow."

"This is county property, so we were going to take a look," Mulkin said. "You can join us and make sure we don't damage anything if you like."

Perry glared at Jillie. "I should have known," he said.

"Do you know this woman?" Mulkin asked.

Perry snorted bitterly. "Yeah, she's the ghost hunter nut who tried to get the house shut down last month before we opened," he said. "I'm guessing this is another one of her stunts."

"You're welcome to press trespassing charges if you like," Mulkin said. "But first let's see exactly what she saw."

He pointed at Jillie. "Let's go," he said.

Jillie walked around to the side of the house and led the way down the steps to the door. She paused at the bottom and took a breath. She did not want to go back in there. When she put her hand on the knob and turned, it didn't budge.

"It's locked," she said. "But I didn't lock it. In fact, I left the door open when I left."

Mulkin showed no expression. "Do you have a key?" he said to Perry.

The businessman nodded. "Yeah, but it's to the front door, not this. C'mon."

They walked back up the steps and around the house to the front. Perry let them in and flipped the switch for the lights. Then he led them down the hall to the basement stairs. When they reached the bottom, Jillie pointed to the far end. "It's over there," she said.

When they threaded through *The Exorcist* exhibit and reached the false back of the basement, she lifted the wooden latch and pushed the door.

Mulkin stepped inside, followed by the other three officers. Jillie did not go in. Instead, she looked around the area, now that the lights were on. She didn't feel the sensations she had down here just fifteen minutes before.

"Ma'am," Mulkin called. "Can you come in here please?"

She stepped down onto the dirt and walked over to where the officers huddled over a figure on the floor.

"Is this what you saw?" he asked, looking up from the body to meet Jillie's eyes. She could see the legs and pale bare feet, but the rest of the girl was blocked.

"Yes," she said. But then she saw the face through the gap as Mulkin straightened up and her forehead creased in confusion. "I mean, no! That's not the girl who was here before."

The body on the floor was clearly a manikin. It wore jeans and an Oak Forest High School jacket. But the face was clearly plastic. A wig lay slightly askew, covering part of the face, and a line of red – maybe lipstick – cut across the neck.

"Somebody took her. This isn't what I saw."

"The basement lights were not on when you were here, were they?" Mulkin asked.

She shook her head. "No, I used my iPhone as a flashlight."

One of the cops was grinning and Jillie closed her eyes for a moment to still her frustration. "You have to believe me," she said finally. "This is not the body that was here earlier. I touched the skin, I had blood on my finger. Somebody moved this here after I left – probably the same person who shut and locked the cellar door. There must have been someone else in the house with me."

"If it's okay with you, we'll take a quick look around," Mulkin said to Perry. "Make sure nobody else is in the house."

Perry nodded.

"You can go outside, but don't leave the premises," Mulkin told Jillie. "We'll want to talk further with you."

He motioned to one of the officers who started walking the perimeter of the basement, as the other three headed upstairs.

"Let's wait outside," Jillie said to Ted.

Perry glared at the two of them, but held his hand out to point the way to the stairs. "After you," he said with mocking politeness.

Ten minutes later, the officers all returned to the porch.

"Well?" Perry said.

Mulkin shook his head. "There's nobody else in there. You have some very sick artists, however."

Perry grinned. "They're the best."

Mulkin turned his attention to Jillie. "Breaking and entering is a crime. Filing a false police report is a crime. It could be a felony."

"I didn't file a false report," Jillie said. "And I didn't break and enter...I just didn't leave on time."

Mulkin ignored her and looked at Perry. "Would you like to press charges?"

The other man frowned and opened his mouth to say something, then thought better of it. After thinking another moment, Perry shook his head.

"No," he said. "I don't want to waste any more time on this and I don't want to encourage any other stunts through media coverage of this."

He turned his gaze on Jillie. "However, I don't ever want to see you near this house again."

She opened her mouth to protest and he put a hand up. "Seriously. You had your say to the county and they ruled against you. I do not appreciate getting calls from the police at one in the morning. If you cause any more trouble here this month, I will make sure they throw you in jail."

Perry turned and thanked the officers and then walked back to his car.

"I think you'd be best served by listening to him," Mulkin said.

"Do we have to go to the station with you?" Ted asked.

Mulkin shook his head. "Not this time. However, I would advise you to not come back here again."

Ted nodded and took Jillie's arm in his hand. "C'mon," he said, and guided her across the grass to his car.

"There was a body there," Jillie said. "I'm not lying."

"I believe you," Ted said, though he didn't sound one hundred percent convinced.

Neither of them saw the curtains in the attic of the house move as they pulled out onto the path around the cemetery.

But Jillie felt a tremor in her heart. The witch who had led Bremen Coven had been associated with other murders at the house in the past. Jillie knew all the stories, and more than one said the witch had been working with an incarnation spell that needed blood. Lots of blood.

"Something bad happened in there tonight," she whispered. "And I think it is going to be just the beginning."

CHAPTER TWENTY-TWO

Mike lay beside Katie on the bed of nails. With one hand, he traced the puckered lines of her ravaged body. She shifted next to him, and then tilted her head to gaze into his eyes.

"I don't think I've ever been this happy," Mike whispered.

In answer her hand reached down to his thigh and with one fingernail drew a line from his knee to his balls. Then she cupped his manhood in her hand and squeezed just a little.

"I'm glad," she said. "It's hard to find a good guy when you're dead."

"I still don't buy the dead thing," Mike said. "You seem perfectly alive to me. And you're not some brain-eating zombie or anything."

Katie slipped her fingers around the knuckles of his right hand, and drew it up to her breasts. She held it between them, and whispered, "What do you feel?"

"A beautiful woman," he answered.

"No," she said. "What do you feel? Do you feel warmth? Is there a heartbeat?"

Mike paused. He let his fingers spread out, for once not with erotic intent, but simply to feel more of her. And then he finally had to admit the answer to both questions.

"No."

"There you go," she said.

Both of them were silent for a minute. Mike ran his hand over her breast, lingering for a second on the hard nub of a nipple before slipping his fingers across her bellybutton and down into the soft hair of her pubes. He was so confused. She felt so good; she wasn't some rotting corpse. How could he be making love to a dead woman? How could a dead woman talk to him? For a moment, he thought about all of the beer he'd been drinking. Could he be hallucinating? For two months? That thought was more disturbing than lying with a dead woman who talked to him.

"Okay, then how did you die?" he asked finally. Maybe knowing more about how she had gotten this way would help?

"Does it matter?" she asked. "The end result is the same no matter what."

He shrugged. "I'd like to know."

"My husband stabbed me with a butcher knife because he thought my baby wasn't his."

Mike's eyebrows rose. "Why did he think that?"

Katie's lips gave a faint smile. "Because it probably wasn't."

Mike's eyes bugged a little. "Oh."

"I loved a lot of men," she said. "I didn't want to only give myself to one and he said he could handle it. But in the end, he got jealous and crazy."

"Did it happen…here?" Mike asked.

She nodded. "Downstairs, in the master bedroom. I'd just come home from being with some friends and he had been drinking. He was passed out on the couch when I came in, so I just went to the bedroom. I had just taken off my clothes to put on my nightgown when he came in. His eyes looked all wild. 'Slutting around again?' he asked me, and I just ignored him. But that just made it worse. 'Who was it this time?' he asked. 'Randall? Ted? That black guy? Tell me you haven't been sleeping with him at least. I will not be the laughingstock of this town walking around with you holding a little mulatto. Because that bump in your belly isn't even mine, is it? Tell me the truth.'

"I told him, 'It could be from any of you, but it won't *belong* to any of you. The baby will be its own person, just like me.'"

She shook her head. "Things got ugly then. He slapped me around and I kicked him. Then he raised his fist to punch me and stopped. He got a look in his eyes that was just pure crazy, and he walked out of the room. I should have run then, but I didn't. And he came back a minute later holding the butcher knife. 'I should never have married you,' he said. I can remember every word. 'You're the devil herself,' he said. 'You probably conceived that kid on the altar during one of your pagan rituals that you never want me to be part of. But I have eyes and ears. I've seen things when you didn't know. But I'm not going to be the cuckold for someone else's brat. I won't do it. We'll just cut that thing out of you right now and be done with it.'

"I screamed and threw stuff at him but he was bigger than I was, and eventually he caught me and pinned me to the bed. He smelled like a whiskey bottle and I pleaded with him to see reason, but he was seeing something else entirely. He had the knife at my throat and then all of a sudden, he raised it and jabbed it just below my chest. 'We'll see if you've got that dirty black guy's kid right now,' he said. 'Or maybe that Mexican you were hanging around last fall.'

"The pain was horrible, and I screamed and screamed, but he just laughed and twisted the knife around until he could reach his bare hands inside me. I could feel something horrible moving and pulling inside and then his hands were in my face all covered in blood and he was saying something about the baby but…I didn't hear anything else. That's when I died."

"Jesus," Mike breathed, and took her into his arms. "I am so sorry."

After a few minutes, he loosened his embrace and asked the most obvious next question. "But, how did you come back?"

Katie smiled. "Emery did it," she said. "She's my anchor. If it wasn't for her, I'd be in that cemetery out there right now."

"Emery?" Mike asked. His voice sounded more than a little incredulous because, well, from what he'd seen, the other girl didn't seem to have a lot going on. "How did she manage it?"

"She was one of my secret sisters," Katie said. "There were five of us. We weren't related by blood but we were closer than family; you'd say we were a coven. That's part of the reason I moved out here to the forest. So we could practice our rituals without being seen. We came from different mothers and backgrounds, but together we formed a circle of unified power."

"You were witches?" Mike asked. This just kept getting weirder.

"That's the way most people label it," she said. "We were connected to something bigger, that's all I know. And Emery used her connections to stop me from leaving this world behind, even though Patrick had gutted me and killed my baby. She used her power to keep me from disappearing into the void, and I used mine to keep her alive all these years, just as she was then."

She rolled over on the bed to lie across his chest and stared down. Her face looked worried. "Are you okay?" she asked. "Do you still want to be with me?"

Mike wrapped his arms around her slight bare shoulders and crushed her against him. "Yes," he said. "I don't care what happened in the past. All that matters is that you're here now. And you might be the only woman I've ever really loved."

Katie smiled and planted a soft kiss on his lips.

"You don't know how glad I am to hear that," she said.

CHAPTER TWENTY-THREE

Bong got down on his hands and knees in the attic room and steeled himself for another long night. June walked up the stairs and into the room a moment later and took her place on the chair. People would focus on her and assume she was the 'jump scare' of the room, when actually, it was Bong's job to jump out and scare people. She was the distraction.

"Looks like you nicked yourself shaving again," he joked as she lolled her head back, exposing the red gash.

She held up the large straight razor from the table next to her. "Yeah, seems like it happens every day. This job is a killer."

"I'm not sure my knees are going to take this abuse for an entire month," Bong said. "I may end up becoming the scary Asian ghost in a wheelchair!"

"I'm not sure that's going to have quite the same impact," she said with a laugh.

Her voice made him grin. She was one of those people who always made people feel up.

"Are you wearing kneepads?" she asked.

He shook his head. "Nah, hadn't really thought of that. I don't think it's part of the costume."

"I think we can find some pads that nobody will notice," she said. "I think that's a much better plan than the wheelchair."

He shrugged. "Probably a lot cheaper too."

"I work at Oak Forest Hospital," she said. "I think I can find something that won't cost you a dime."

"That suits my budget perfectly," he said.

Just then, Lon's voice interrupted from the base of the stairway.

"The living are coming!" he said. "Let's make some screams tonight!"

That was the cue to shut up because the doors were opening. Bong flashed June a row of blackened teeth and moved back into the closet out of sight.

Someone downstairs shrieked, and Bong grinned. It wasn't really the kind of job he was interested in doing, but there was very clear affirmation if you were doing the job right. And so far, based at least on the number of screams, jumps, squeezed hands and quick exits, they all seemed to be haunting the house well.

Bong wondered how Jeanie was doing. She was one of the floaters on the first floor, and sometimes played the ravenous zombie, while other times she simply held out her guts, trying to get people to touch them. She said the guys sometimes would, but usually the girls yelped and said 'no way'.

This was supposed to be a job that brought them closer together, but honestly, Bong felt like it was going to have the opposite effect. He'd been so tired the past few nights that he'd passed out as soon as he took her home. The only time they'd had to talk was on the car rides to and from the house.

Three boys walked into the room. They looked college age and one of them was prodding the other one forward.

"Touch it," he said. "You know that's a dummy."

They stepped closer, and the provocateur pushed his friend to bend over.

"Ten bucks if you give her a kiss."

The other one stepped forward then, so all three of them were hovering over June, who managed to stay amazingly still. "Hell, I'll do it for ten bucks," he said.

Bong couldn't watch anymore. He pressed the button to start the strobe and began to crawl quickly toward them just as the guy bent down over June's face.

"Oh shit," the ringleader said when he saw Bong coming out of the dark, eyes and teeth blackened, his movements made more jerky and strange by the lights.

They were all so focused on June, that Bong's entry really freaked them out. The 'brave' one probably leapt the most. Bong kept relentlessly moving toward them, and while one of them started laughing at their surprise, the threesome quickly exited the room. Bong crept back to the closet.

"What did you do that for?" June asked before the next group arrived. "You didn't wait for my cue. I think I could've made one of them piss his pants!"

"Sorry," he said. "I knew I was early, but they were just making me nervous with all the kissing talk. They were getting a little too close, I thought."

"Thanks," June said. "That's sweet, and I appreciate it, but I can handle the frat boys, don't worry."

Bong nodded and ducked back out of sight as the next group entered the room. *Stupid, stupid, stupid*, he told himself, and steeled himself to make sure to wait this time for June to move. Then he laughed inside at his own private joke. Seemed he was always waiting for a girl to make a move.

June jumped, and Bong started out of the closet toward a handful of high school girls.

When they saw him, they screamed. "It's like *The Ring*," one of them said.

He had to grin at that. Sometimes the wait was worth it.

CHAPTER TWENTY-FOUR

Mike walked the attic, making sure all of the props were where they should be. He rehung a costume that had fallen to the floor and pushed a trunk back in place with his foot. Then he shut out the lights and went down the stairs to do the same on the first floor. He and Lon were taking turns handling lock-up each night, so one person didn't always have to be at the house insanely late.

It was hard to even recognize this as the same smelly, rotten and forgotten house he'd walked into less than three months before. Between his renovations, coats of paint, props and gelled spotlights, it was like a whole new, ancient museum of movie sets.

He walked down the stairs and shook his head at the dining room, decked out in the most suggestive cannibal décor possible. The leg bone – red with fake meat – still gave him the creeps and Argento and Lucio had finished what they called the 'Tobe Hooper Room' over a month earlier. It was their first project, because they wanted people who walked into the house to be immediately reminded of Hooper's most famous, most harrowing film.

Mike flipped off the hidden red spotlights and then walked down the fingernail-etched hallway toward the den. That remained one of his favorite spots in the house. He still couldn't believe that someone had built a hidden bookcase/stairway there, or that it still actually functioned, decades later. But he'd oiled and cleaned it, and now the room served as a great scare for the house. When a group entered the room, they found a suspiciously cozy spot with a glowing fireplace (electric) and a smoking pipe in an ashtray next to an easy chair. But then they noticed the pool of blood on the floor beneath the chair, and then maybe they noticed the giant framed portraits hung all around the room depicting serial killers, each grinning and holding his or her weapon of choice.

That's when the door slammed shut, and something groaned behind them. Some patrons screamed, some turned and ran for the door. But either way, they were forced back into the center of the room, faced with a man in a terribly deformed rubber mask who was holding a large axe. When they became sufficiently freaked out, the bookcase would click and swing open with an extended creak. The flickering red and orange lights that escaped from the dark stairwell behind it did not provide any confidence for the haunted house visitors, but the room's axe-wielding mutant didn't give them much of a choice. They headed toward the stairwell down to the basement every time. For those who did get past the axeman (or when they needed to jam groups through the house faster), there was a back door that led back out to the hallway where both the stairwells up and down were. But Lon wanted them to use the bookcase basement entry as much as possible. It was a great gimmick and they hadn't even had to build it.

At the moment, however, nobody was in the house but Mike. He walked over toward the coffin that leaned sideways against the far wall and reached behind it to shut off the glow of the fireplace and a couple other quietly shifting LED lights tucked around the room. The cords were hidden behind the coffin, so patrons couldn't see the source of the 'atmosphere', which Argento said ruined the effect.

As Mike reached behind the coffin for the switch, someone screamed in the basement.

His heart froze.

Nobody was supposed to be left in the house.

"What the fuck?" he asked. Luckily, nobody answered.

Mike walked toward the bookcase and fingered the hidden latch that remained where it had been set up dozens of years before. The wall of books and skulls and other arcane decorations swung inward at his touch.

The scream did not repeat, but now Mike's ears were tuned. He listened to the air move as he stood at the top of the steps, waiting for some sign that someone was alive and moving downstairs.

None came.

Mike took a deep breath and forced his foot down on the first rung of the staircase he'd rebuilt. He had heard something down here, he was sure of that. And he couldn't leave the house without checking it out.

Carefully he eased his foot down another step, and then the next. He didn't want to make the steps creak. He still had visions of some coven of devil worshippers stabbing wild animals in the heart and then hanging them to bleed out over the original earth floor of the basement, as he'd discovered in his first couple weeks on the job. Whoever had been responsible had never been caught, and he didn't fully believe that they were gone. It occurred to him suddenly that Emery may have actually been the culprit, which was something he would have to ask Katie about. But if she hadn't been…well… the haunted house activity may have chased them away for now, but….

When he reached the bottom, Mike blinked as a red spotlight moved across his face. The room had been set up to have slowly shifting colors and hues, and noise or not, he would have needed to come down here regardless to shut everything down. He stepped to the side wall and lifted a fake wood shingle to expose the lighting switches. He flicked the colored bank off, and then flipped a switch to light the downstairs in a series of cool white lights. The non-haunting bank.

The bulbs lit the long expanse of the basement without revealing any people. Just long empty aisles in between setpieces of horror.

Mike stood and simply listened for a moment, waiting to hear if any sound repeated the anguish he'd heard before. He could hear his heart beating louder than any sound in the room. But the sound, whatever it had been, didn't reoccur.

He turned to flip the downstairs lights out completely, when something thumped at the end of the aisle. It seemed to come from somewhere behind the Báthory and *Exorcist* tableaux.

Mike frowned.

There was nothing down there, except the long false room where the water heater and furnace were. The small room where he'd put Katie's coffin was also down that way. Nobody should even know that room existed, let alone be in there. Even the haunted house cast didn't know about Katie's room. They knew about the other section though, because Lon ran Ops out of the utilities room. Mike started walking down the aisle.

As he drew closer, he heard another noise. Something like a gasp.

Mike's chest constricted. Nobody should be down here. Especially not in the hidden basement room. He'd seen all of the regulars leave the house.

"Why me?" he asked silently, and then reached for the inset latch of the door. It opened quietly, and for a moment he was able to see what was going on within without alerting the people inside.

The glimpse made his heart ice over.

Inside the small hidden room, Emery held a long knife to the bare side of a man who'd been stripped naked. The man appeared to lean heavily against his captor. Mike couldn't see his face, but Katie was walking around the two of them in a circle, whispering things. Emery spoke along with her in unison. As Mike watched, trying to figure out exactly what Katie and Emery were up to, he saw Emery lift the silver blade higher in the air. Before he could react, she brought it down and drew it across the man's side. Then she reached across his middle and ran her hands over the wound, cupping and gathering the blood that welled.

Katie walked around and around the two of them, but Emery never looked at her. Instead, she moved to where the coffin that they had dug up sat. Only, the cover had been removed since Mike was here last. Emery held her hands out over the open coffin and let the blood drip off her fingers. She shook her hands then, sprinkling it on the bones that Mike dug up from the cemetery.

The victim himself didn't move, he just stood there in a trance, bleeding and blinking until Emery turned back and rubbed her hand over the crimson wound again.

Mike couldn't hold back then, and stepped down onto the dirt floor.

"What the hell are you two doing?" he asked. His voice was quiet, but his tone told how freaked out he was. Katie moved away from the still, naked man who, strangely, remained standing, and put her hands on Mike's shoulders. "It's okay," she said. "We just need to siphon a little life from him for me to hang around." She kissed him, wrapping her arms around his neck to pull his eyes away from the naked, bleeding man.

"What are you talking about?" he asked, moving to push her back. But she didn't let him get away. When the touch of her lips had calmed him somewhat, she pointed to the wooden box at the far side of the room. "That coffin that you dug up for me?" she said.

He nodded.

"Those bones are mine," she said.

"What are you talking about?" Mike asked. "You're right here. You're not a ghost."

"Aren't I?" she answered. "Take the chain off from around your neck."

"The one I found in the house?"

She nodded. "Give it to Emery."

He frowned, but raised the necklace past his chin and over his head. Emery took the chain and locket from him and slipped it into her jeans pocket.

The naked man now stood abandoned in the middle of the room; he remained still as a statue, though he could have easily walked out of the room.

"So now what?" Mike said, when Emery had hidden his locket.

"Now try to touch me," Katie said.

Mike shrugged. He had held Katie before they'd gone to the stupid expensive Red Robin for half-assed burgers a few hours ago, and he'd held her again later tonight when she'd dressed up in her witch-ly 'haunt' costume and prepped to walk the halls and scare people. Not to mention touching her as she kissed him seconds ago. He didn't see why taking off a necklace would change anything there.

He held out his arms to pull her close but instead she sidestepped them, and whispered in his ear. "I need you to finally understand," she said.

"Understand what?" he asked.

"Understand that I'm dead," Katie whispered.

When he shook his head and turned to look at her, she kissed his lips and pulled away. He felt the faint spark of electricity that he did every time her mouth met his.

"You're not going to like hearing this, but it's true," she said. "I died a long time ago, and while I've told you that, what I haven't told you is the body you've been holding isn't real. But I want it to be. I want to come back. And if you help me…you can be with me forever. I've kept Emery with me all these years… I can do the same for you."

Mike shook his head. "You're real," he said. "I can feel you. I've kissed you."

Katie smiled, but it was a sad smile. "You think you have. Now give me a hug," Katie urged.

Mike put his arms around her and started to pull her close.

Only.

His hands went right through her.

"What the hell?" he whispered.

"I'm dead," Katie said. "I've been telling you."

"That's insane," Mike said. "I've been with you for weeks. We've made love; we've eaten and drunk beer together. You've been working in the haunted house – other people have seen and touched you."

"You *thought* you felt me in bed," she said. "And you've dumped out a lot of nearly-full cans of beer after our nights together, haven't you?"

He shrugged at that. He had simply figured that Katie was really a lightweight.

"I can make people see me pretty easily," she said. "But without the locket, nobody can feel me. I've been careful not to get too near to anyone in the haunted house, so nobody has touched me."

Mike kept shaking his head, as if in pantomiming *no* he could make the past few minutes disappear.

"I have been dead for a long, long time," Katie said. "But I don't want to be any longer."

"So…" he said.

"So, I need the blood," she said. "Living blood to touch my bones. Every night. And with every drop, I'll come closer to being real again, instead of a ghost."

"But I've touched you," he said. "You're not a ghost. I've felt you."

"You *think* you have," she said. "That locket is the key. It lets you feel me when I'm not really here."

"What about Emery?" he asked. "I've touched her. She's shoveled dirt and lifted boards with me."

"Emery's not the one who's dead," Katie answered. "I've kept her just as she was on the night she saved me. She sleeps on that bed of nails to constantly remind herself that she's still alive. She grows distant, but she's not dead like me."

She waved a hand at the still silent man standing alone by the coffin. "If we can dress my bones with the blood of thirty victims – one every night in October – on Halloween night, my body will be reborn and my spirit will finally be able to walk again in the flesh. You'll be able to hold me again."

Mike shook his head as the enormity of what she suggested dawned on him. Katie was talking about stabbing people down here every night for the rest of the month. "No, no, no," he said. "You can't do that. If people start disappearing every night from here, they'll shut this place down. And they'll find you."

Katie laughed. "They won't find *me*," she said. "They might find my bones. But I don't think they'll know what to do with those. They're not taking a skeleton to prison."

Mike couldn't help but smile at that idea.

"But it doesn't matter," she said. "People aren't disappearing. We're not killing anyone. In fact, right now you can help Emery bandage this one up and take him back to his natural habitat."

Mike frowned at her. "This guy is going to go straight to the police and tell them about the two women who cut him. And now he'll probably mention me too."

"He won't remember anything," she said. "He'll wake up and wonder how he got hurt and who bandaged him… but that's as far as it'll go. He'll count the money in his wallet, count his blessings that he's alive, and do his best to forget about it all. Does he look ready to tell tales?"

Mike looked at the man, who remained staring straight ahead, slack jawed. Blood dripped down his waist from the slice in his side.

"Fix him up," Katie said to Emery. "It's getting late and we don't want him to be missed."

Mike watched as Emery retrieved paper towels, tape and gauze from behind the coffin. She wiped off the blood, then held a piece of gauze over the wound. She looked up at him then, as if waiting for him to do something. When he didn't move, she spoke softly. "Hold this," she said.

Mike held the gauze in place and she covered it with medical tape. Moments later, she was guiding the man's legs back into a pair of jeans, and Mike helped her pull a t-shirt over the man's head. They might as well have been dressing a warm dummy; the man hadn't moved on his own or said a word.

"When will he wake up?" Mike asked, as Emery worked on getting his shoes back on.

Katie shrugged. "Once he gets away from this house, the spell will wear off. Emery will take him to his car and drive him down the turnpike a ways. When he comes to in his car, he'll wonder how he got hurt, but won't remember anything. He might not even remember coming here. But a little piece of me will be reborn from the wash of his blood."

"This is crazy," Mike said, shaking his head in disbelief.

Katie leaned toward him and planted a kiss on his lips. He felt the spark, but as his arms instinctively went around her, they passed right through her shoulder blades.

"If you want to feel me again, you need to help Emery," Katie said. "This is a matter of life and death. Mine."

Mike took a breath and nodded. "C'mon," he said to Emery and took the man's elbow. Together they started walking the zombie-like man toward the door. When Mike looked over his shoulder to catch Katie's eye, the room was empty.

All he saw behind him was the coffin.

CHAPTER TWENTY-FIVE

"I knew it," Jillie said. She pointed at a small article in the Oak Forest *Daily Southtown* and then reached over the table and grabbed a handful of Ted's fries. "There was a Missing Persons Report filed a couple days ago with the police. A girl from Oak Forest High School didn't come home, and her friends said they didn't know where she disappeared to. They said they lost her inside the haunted house."

Ted's eyes rose. He took another bite of his greasy cheeseburger.

"They said we were nuts. Well, I'm sure this is the same girl that I saw in the basement of that house. I'm going to the police station to show them this missing person notice. Maybe now they'll want to talk more about what I saw."

She reached across the table and Ted slapped her fingers away from his plastic container.

"I'm going to file a Missing Persons Report on my fries if you keep that up."

"They're not good for you anyway," she said, and avoided his hand to snatch one.

"And they're good for you?"

She shrugged. "I have more nervous energy than you. I'll work it off."

She crumpled up her sandwich wrapper from inside her red plastic container and stood up suddenly. "C'mon, let's go over to the station."

Ted shook his head. "I don't think that's a very good idea. They already let you go once. You want to tempt fate?"

"No, I want to prove that they should have listened to me," she said. "And then I want to get that house closed down before the witch gets anyone else."

She snatched up Ted's basket of fries as he shoved the last bite of his burger into his mouth.

"C'mon," she said, and walked the basket to the trash. She took a handful of fresh cut fries and stuffed them in her mouth before emptying the rest in the trash.

"Damn, those are good," she said, as Ted launched himself from the table to try to stop her.

His hands passed through air as she emptied the basket and set it on the top of the garbage can.

"Drive me to the police station?" she said. It was framed as a question, but there was no query about it. Ted sighed and looked longingly at the garbage can for a moment, before walking to the exit.

★   ★   ★

Jillie was three steps ahead of him as they walked into the station. She marched up to the intake window, where a woman in a blue uniform shirt sat behind a (presumably) bulletproof pane of glass. Her voice came through a round silver vent in the glass.

"How can I help you?" the woman asked. She sounded bored.

Jillie waved the paper in the air and then set it down and pointed at the Missing Persons Report. "I need to talk to an inspector," she said. "I saw this girl murdered at the Bachelor's Grove Haunted House two nights ago."

The woman behind the desk looked skeptical. Then she fingered a button on the phone next to her. "Hey Bill, can you come up here a moment?" Then she pointed at an uncomfortable-looking plastic couch with orange vinyl cushions on the side of the room. "If you would wait over there..."

Jillie walked triumphantly over to the couch and flopped down on the edge. She could not wait to let the cops know they'd screwed up when they refused to listen to her. She felt bad about the high school girl, but she felt good about the chance to shut down the house before more people were killed.

Ted sat next to her, but he slouched into the chair. He did not look anxious to face the police for the second time this week.

A minute later a white steel door opened to the right of the reception booth and a big man in full officer uniform stepped into the lobby.

"Can I help you?" he asked the two of them. A silver rectangle pinned to his blue shirt said 'Richton'. Above it, a thin badge boasted, 'Detective'.

Jillie leapt back to her feet, and crossed the room in a heartbeat, holding out the newspaper.

"This missing girl from Oak Forest," she said. "I saw her dead the other night at the Bachelor's Grove Haunted House. She was downstairs in the basement after the house closed."

Detective Richton nodded slowly and took the newspaper from her. "You're the one they found trespassing there, aren't you?" he said.

"Yes," she said. "That doesn't matter though. The point is, I saw the girl. She was lying in a pool of blood and the cops that night didn't believe me because someone came back and put a manikin in her place before they got there. Now you need to listen to me, because she's missing. I was right. And someone or something at that house did her in. You need to shut the place down and actually investigate it."

The officer looked at the newspaper article and shook his head. "I don't think so," he said.

"Why not?" she said. "I'm telling you, the house is connected with this girl's disappearance. And you're not going to find her alive. She may be at the bottom of that pond by the cemetery."

Detective Richton shook his head again.

"No, she's not," he said. "And we are not looking for her either."

"What do you mean?"

"That article was out of date before the newspaper was even printed," he said. "That girl is safe and sound back home with her family. She bumped her head, got lost and scratched up wandering around in Bremen Woods, but found her way out the next day. She's fine."

Jillie frowned. "You're sure?"

He nodded. "She'd been in the haunted house the night before and got separated from her friends. But she's fine."

"Maybe the girl I saw was someone else then," Jillie said. "Are you investigating any other missing persons?"

Detective Richton handed her back the newspaper. "No," he said. "We are not."

He turned to return to the interior of the station, but then paused.

"Remember what they told you," he said. "Stay away from that house. Stop making trouble where there isn't any."

Jillie's eyes caught fire and she started to spit back a retort, but Ted grabbed her arm.

Detective Richton disappeared through the door without another word.

"C'mon," Ted said. "Let this one die."

"I swear that girl already did," Jillie said.

CHAPTER TWENTY-SIX

The night was alive with screams. Recorded, and real.

Mike stood behind the barricade on the left side of the attic in the dark, and watched groups of patrons thread their way through the costume aisle at the right. Periodically one of the haunters would jump out at them from a hidden location and someone would always let out a yell. Then they'd disappear into the room at the end of the path and be sent down the back stairway before the next group came into the attic.

One thing that Lon and the rest of the group had been good about was separating the groups. Some haunted houses just jammed people through in an endless line, so the rooms were never vacant enough for the scare factor to really work. Sure, there were jump scares, but it was all too fast and crowded. Lon had insisted on limiting the flow of people into the house, so they could really 'work' each room.

That was playing well for Mike now, as he waited in the dark.

A hand gripped his shoulder from behind. Mike jumped a little. The pale face of Emery emerged from the shadows. She said nothing, but pointed at the stairwell coming up from downstairs. Mike nodded. Then he walked out into the main room and stood next to the stairs on the other side.

When a single girl stepped up and into the room, Mike said nothing. As she saw him, he stretched out his right arm and pointed toward the small entry to the alcove that led to Emery's secret bedroom.

The girl had neon-blue hair and wore a black t-shirt with a pattern that glowed in the black light beaming across the stairwell to illuminate a pile of bones in the corner. She was chewing gum and grinned as she saw him. Without questioning him, she moved into the small side room where Emery waited. She assumed he was a haunted house guide. Mike followed her.

When she walked two steps in and reached the center of the small space, she stopped and looked confused. Her face turned one way, and then the next, searching for where to go next, and then she turned to walk back toward Mike. There was only one way out, and that was the way she had walked in.

He said nothing, but shook his head. No exit.

Then he pointed at the floor.

The girl gave him a look. "Okay," she said. Then she bent down and looked at the floor where Emery's door was concealed. Mike noted that she wore a black skirt and ripped fishnets above black boots. A goth chick. Probably here on a dare that she wasn't afraid to do the house on her own. Nothing could scare her.

We'll see about that, Mike thought.

The door in the floor suddenly opened and Emery's face emerged from the darkness. The goth girl jumped backward, but Mike caught her in his arms easily. Then he lifted her in the air and dangled her feet into the opening in the floor. Emery grabbed the girl by the waist as Mike took over holding the door.

"What the fuck?" the girl yelled.

But before she could get out another word, she'd disappeared down the stairs pounding at Emery's shoulders. Mike lowered the door gently back to the floor, and the sound of her struggles disappeared. In moments, the girl would be silent, captured in whatever spell Emery and Katie wove.

He looked out at the empty attic, making sure none of the haunters had seen the girl's abduction. At that moment, a gang of rowdy teens ascended the stairs and a few seconds later the room was echoing with laughter and screams again.

Mike watched them disappear down the hall and nodded to himself. Then he opened the door in the floor and slipped down into the secret heart of the house.

★   ★   ★

Jeanie walked down the hallway with slow, exaggerated steps. She was roaming tonight, moving from one area of the house to the next, making sure there were no stragglers. With one hand, she cradled her fake guts to her middle, as if preventing her intestines from completely falling out of her body. With the other, she touched the wall. It was a convincing gimmick that usually sent patrons moving quickly to get out of her way.

A middle-aged guy in glasses and a blue polo shirt walked out of Argento's favorite room, with two teenage boys behind him. The group stopped when they saw Jeanie, and she reached out a hand to them and let out a horrible moan. The older guy smiled and nodded, clearly impressed with her makeup. But the younger-looking teen led the trio quickly ahead, sidestepping past her in the hall.

They ducked into the next room, and instantly she heard a scream from one of them. One of the haunters, Darren, was in there, with a huge machete. Jeanie grinned and slipped into Argento's room for a moment to check it out.

The room was awash in red and blue spotlights, and a tapestry shivered on the wall to the left. A woman's head was impaled on the blades of glass remaining in a broken window on the far end of the room. Overhead, the ceiling was a moving mass of maggots. When someone stepped on the spot in the center of the room, a handful of the tiny rubber things fell from the ceiling. That typically elicited some solid shrieks from any women who walked through and suddenly saw white maggots stuck in their hair.

Jeanie didn't walk to the center of the room, but before she'd gone inside two steps, a black-gloved hand grabbed her from behind, and held her mouth shut. The cool touch of a metal blade touched her neck. "Take another step and I'll cut your guts out for real," a voice growled in her ear.

Jeanie laughed. "And I'll shove fake bugs in your mouth."

She turned around and grinned at Argento. The set designer loved playing the part of a giallo killer.

He dropped the knife (which had a completely filed down rounded edge) to his side, and smiled through the black latex hood that covered his head.

"Getting hot in there?" she asked. "Need me to give you a break?"

He shook his head. One of Jeanie's roles as a floater was to give the other haunters a chance to go to the bathroom, or take a breather from sweaty costumes for a few minutes each night.

"I've got to rack up more kills tonight," he said. "Can't afford to stop."

He and 'Lucio' had a bet going. Every time one of them used their favorite director's 'weapon of choice' on a guest, and that guest screamed, it counted as a kill. Whoever elicited the most total kills in a week bought the other's bar tab on their night off.

So far, Lucio was winning this week. They turned in their totals to Lon each night at close, and he was keeping the running totals on the notes app in his phone.

"What's the score so far?" she asked.

"It's 113 to 97," he said. "People hate zombies."

Lucio's makeup this week was that of one of Fulci's zombie creations, and featured an eyeball hanging down his face. He'd flipped from wearing the murderous crone mask when one of the other haunters had developed a rash from the zombie makeup. The hanging eyeball was a particularly gruesome bit of makeup that Jeanie wished she had done. But June had designed it.

Outside the door, they heard steps moving quickly in the hall. "You better walk," he said.

She nodded, and exited the room, just as a new group rounded the corner of the hall. She held her arms out to them, and a girl with blond hair laughed and shook her head upon seeing Jeanie's guts. "That's so gross," she said. But her friends dragged her into the room Jeanie had just left, and within a few seconds she heard a scream.

Jeanie smiled.

"Ninety-eight," she murmured, and walked toward the stairs to the attic. She wanted to check out how Bong and June were doing.

The eerie keyboard-driven music of a band – that Argento had once impatiently explained to her was called Goblin – jittered and added to the creepy atmosphere as she walked up the stairs. She abandoned her shambling gait to reach the top floor before a new group caught up to her from behind.

She slowed for a moment though, as she saw a lone girl with blue hair walking up the stairs ahead of her. Jeanie stopped on the stair and waited. Someone upstairs yelled, "What the fuck," and Jeanie grinned. Probably the blue-haired girl meeting up with the old crone mask…and the sickle. A guy named Ben was playing that part tonight, and he loved to wave his weapon.

Jeanie counted to thirty, and then walked up the rest of the stairs. The blue-haired girl should be through the costume aisle and past the old hag slasher and in Bong and June's room by now. Another few seconds and she'd be on her way back down the stairs to head toward the basement.

When she stepped onto the floor of the attic, the room appeared empty; she headed toward the costume racks. She waved off Ben and walked down the clothes aisle and into the room that Bong was haunting. But when she stepped inside, neither of them were to be seen.

"Bong?" she called.

There was a creak on the other side of the room.

A second later, the black hair and white face of Bong emerged from the space behind a large old projection television set. Someone had donated it from their basement since it didn't work well anyway, and it was a great prop for an 'Asian ghost' to hide behind, since it brought back thoughts of *The Ring*. They ran a loop of TV static on it to help set the mood.

"Hey," Bong said. He pursed his lips like she'd taught him to spread his black lipstick better. "I was just talking to June. It's been a while since anyone came through…is someone behind you?"

Jeanie frowned. "Didn't a girl with blue hair just go through here?"

Bong shook his head. "I don't think that was the last one."

June walked out from behind the TV then, and pulled down the hem of her white, bloodstained dress. Her milky eye was creepy even to Jeanie, who knew it was just a contact.

"Do either of you need a break?" Jeanie asked.

June shook her head and looked at Bong. "I think we're both okay right now."

He nodded quickly. "Yeah. You'd better head down before the next group gets here."

"No worries," Jeanie said. "I won't blow your scare!" She stepped up to Bong and pecked his lips lightly. He instantly rubbed his finger over his lips to smooth out the black. Jeanie frowned before walking to the back stairwell beyond them. "I'll be back in an hour."

"Cool," Bong said. "We'll be here."

As Jeanie walked down the back stairwell, she had a cold feeling in her stomach that had nothing to do with scares and haunting. She couldn't help but feel as if she'd just been pushed out of the attic room.

CHAPTER TWENTY-SEVEN

Emery stood next to the blue-haired girl in the basement. She held the docile girl's arm out over the coffin on the back wall, and massaged the biceps until ribbons of red dripped out of the cut she'd made and onto the bones below.

The house had been closed for a half an hour now, and Mike had turned off all of the upstairs lights before descending into the basement. When he arrived, he found Katie and Emery whispering strange words together as Katie walked round and round the punk girl, who stared off into some space that nobody else could see.

It was eerie to see, but also something he was used to by now. He'd helped Emery for the past two weeks to pick off lone victims toward the end of each haunted house night. The women somehow quieted and calmed their 'bleeders' and kept them hidden away in the secret room until the house was closed. Then they bled them in the basement over the casket, before bandaging them up and sending them back out in a confused and disoriented state to the world. Mike had helped drive a couple of them down the road to the parking lot of a strip mall, when the victims lacked any car keys. If the lot was empty when they took the bleeder out of the house, they knew that they'd picked on someone who'd been dropped off or had come with others, even if he or she had been walking the house solo.

He stood back and waited until whatever magic the two were spinning was spun; he'd learned quickly to stay out of their way when they bled their victims.

Emery slid her knife across the girl's arm in another spot, an inch or so away from the first cut, and fresh blood surfaced on the white skin of her lower biceps instantly. They cut every victim in a slightly different place. Katie smiled and nodded, and the two began a chant once again.

Mike pulled his cell phone out of his pocket, and skimmed his email. It was hard to believe, but after watching this strange ritual night after night, he no longer was fascinated or repelled by it. This was just what Katie and Emery did...and he would be there at the end, ready to help take their 'bleeders' outside to safety, so that they weren't missed. His biggest fear was that sooner or later one of them would remember how and where he or she was cut...and the whole thing would be blown before Katie's resurrection was complete. But Katie assured him that none of the victims remembered a thing. He had to believe her, since so far not a single one had come back to the house with the police in tow the next day.

He looked up from his email, which was empty other than spam from banks that he didn't hold accounts at, and coupons from White Castle and TGI Fridays.

What if this was all just bullshit? he wondered. What if, after a month of cutting people, Katie remained a ghost, a phantasm who slipped through his fingers when he went to hug her?

The thought made his stomach churn. Since the night that he'd discovered Katie and Emery's ritual, Katie had remained noncorporeal to him. Emery had kept the locket from him, and Katie used it as a bit of sexual blackmail. "I need you to help Emery make me whole," she'd said, when he asked for the necklace back. "I want you to remember that I can't really touch you until we're done with all of this. So, for now, Emery is going to keep the necklace."

He'd not been happy. Every night, he asked the same question: "Can we be together tonight, please?"

Katie only looked at him with wide, sad brown eyes and whispered, "Soon."

Having sex with her again was bait – so he would keep bringing her people to bleed. Mike thought about it a lot at home, in his bed at night. But every time he questioned himself, he came to the same conclusion. She was worth it.

But now, as Emery moved the girl away from the coffin, and beckoned him over to help her bandage the wound, Mike found himself doubting again.

"Is all of this really doing anything?" he said, as he held the gauze in place and Emery taped it down.

Katie's eyebrows creased, and her ethereal fingers stroked his forehead. He couldn't really feel her, but there was still some connection, some spark that his skin felt as she brushed her spirit over him.

"You still don't believe me?" Katie whispered. Her voice sounded girlish. And hurt.

Mike licked his lips and clenched his fists before he answered. He didn't want to say the wrong thing. He didn't want the necklace to be withheld forever. "I believe you," he said. "But I just worry if something doesn't go right...."

Katie smiled. "Everything is going fine," she said. "Come here and see for yourself."

She motioned him closer to the coffin, as Emery led the punk girl away.

"Look at me," Katie said.

"I am," he said.

She shook her head and pointed into the open coffin. "No, look at *me*," she insisted. He leaned over to peer inside the wooden box.

"Do those look like the bones you brought here?" she asked.

As Mike peered into the cavity, he gasped.

He'd expected to see white bones stained in blood, because they'd been drenching the coffin in it every night.

He hadn't expected to see bones with sheathes of...meat covering them. In fact, there was so much pink in the coffin now, he could barely see the shards of white where Katie's skeleton had once lain dry and white. The bones of her feet and hands still were clearly naked in the box, but even those had a spiderweb haze of *something* starting to grow on them.

"It's actually working," he whispered.

"You doubted me?" Katie asked.

Mike shrugged. "I didn't know what to think. It all seems so unlikely."

Katie smiled, sort of, but her lips stretched thin. "You have to learn to trust me," she said. "Relationships are built on trust, right?"

He nodded, and the words hit him. He had a *relationship*. Sure, it was with a ghost but...he hadn't had a relationship with a woman since his wife had left him. And arguably, he hadn't really had one with her for months, or maybe years, before that life-decimating event.

Mike found himself smiling for the next fifteen minutes as he walked the blue-haired girl to the lone remaining car in the parking lot, fished out her keys from her purse, and then drove her a few blocks down the turnpike before putting the car in park, and moving her over to the driver's seat. He knew from past experience that by the time he locked up the last rooms of the house and drove past here himself, the girl would have woken up, and the car would be gone.

When he walked back into the haunted house, it was silent. Emery and Katie had disappeared. But it was late and Mike knew that he'd see them again tomorrow. And that was one day closer to the day when he could hold Katie in his arms again and actually feel her. He felt better about that day coming than he had before. Because...they had a relationship, right?

CHAPTER TWENTY-EIGHT

Jeanie wondered if she really had a relationship. Over the past couple weeks, Bong had grown increasingly quiet. Admittedly he was always quiet; it was just his nature. But the past couple nights, he hadn't even come inside with her when he'd dropped her off after the house had closed.

"I'm really tired and tomorrow is going to be a long day," he'd said last night. He'd planted a kiss on her cheek and sat back, waiting for her to get out of the car. As she did, she'd seen his phone light up with a notification. "Who's texting you?" she wanted to ask. But she didn't dare. It probably wasn't even a text, just a Facebook notice or something.

The problem was, she'd wanted to ask.

She had never felt like that before with Bong. And that sucked. She wasn't really sure what had changed. She knew he'd never wanted to do the haunted house, and had agreed to do it for her. So, he had been a little grumpy for the past month or more. But she figured that would pass and he'd have fun with it, the same as she did.

But instead, he'd just grown quieter.

And then last night, when she'd seen him talking animatedly to June, when he'd not said more than a few sentences to her all day, well… that's when her heart suddenly screamed a warning klaxon. Was he just unhappy with her, or was he getting happy with June?

Fuck.

June was her 'boss', and she seemed really cool. She knew more about monster makeup than Jeanie had ever dreamed of knowing. Jeanie had already learned a ton from her.

So she didn't want to think that June was making time with Bong. She wouldn't do that, right?

Jeanie walked back into her kitchen and pulled a Milky Way bar from the cabinet. She always craved chocolate when she got upset. She ripped the paper wrapper off and bit down hard.

When Bong rang the doorbell a few minutes later, the candy bar was gone and Jeanie sat on the couch in a worse funk than before.

"Ready to go?" he asked through the screen door.

She didn't answer, just stood and grabbed her purse.

"How was your day?" she asked once they were on the road.

Bong shrugged. "Same as ever. Wish it was Friday night."

"Me too," she said. "Maybe you can stay over this weekend."

"Maybe," he said, staring straight ahead.

Her belly felt a pang of ice, and she said nothing else for the rest of the ride.

★　★　★

"Okay, it may be hump day, but I don't want to see any humping going on in these halls tonight," Lon said. He was giving their nightly pep talk in the *Nightmare on Elm Street* room. "I want to see people too creeped out to kiss," he said. "So, let's get our game on and keep the blood flowing fast. Less than two more weeks to Halloween, you know that?"

Lon pulled his phone out of his front jeans pocket and thumbed it on. He hit the touch screen a couple times and then held the phone in the air for everyone to see. Not that anyone really could.

"Last week, you know that Lucio took home the scream prize. So far Lucio is poking out Argento's eye this week. He's already ahead 77 to 49 on the scream-o-meter. Maybe people just aren't a-scared of black-gloved, leather-masked killers these days. But they still do love their zombies. At least, that's what these two are reporting. Maybe neither one of them is getting the scream on, I don't know."

"Hey, hey, hey!" a voice called out of the crowd. It was Lucio, wearing his trademark *Zombi 2* shirt, with maggots crawling out of a decaying face's eyeball.

"I have earned every one of those screams. And you can audit me if you want. Maybe you'll scream too while you're at it."

"Somehow, I doubt that," Lon said with a grin. "All right, the point is, let's give 'em our best tonight and make 'em wanna come back and do it again. And good luck catching up tonight, Argento. Creeps dismissed!"

"See you later," Bong said, and reached down to fondle her fake intestines. "Maybe suck it in?"

"Ha ha," she said, and grinned in spite of herself. That was more like Bong.

But then she watched him walk through the crowd to catch up with June. And she saw June's face light up with a smile before the two of them exited the makeup room to head upstairs to their spots.

All of a sudden, her stomach felt like her guts were all twisted up again. The weird thing about it was…if she looked down at her waist, they were.

Jeanie realized suddenly that this wasn't fun anymore.

And that sucked.

★   ★   ★

"How are your knees?" June asked.

Bong shrugged. "Dreaming of the day after Halloween," he said.

She snorted. "Not enjoying your nights as a Korean ghost?"

"I think I'm supposed to be Japanese," he said. "But what difference does it make? I mean, jet black hair, slanty eyes, we're all the same, right?"

"You don't think Jeanie knows the difference?" June asked. "C'mon, I don't think she's that clueless. She really likes you."

"All she thinks about is this place," Bong said. "That's what she cares about."

June shook her head. It was a little disconcerting to see the bloody gash in her neck twist in the flickering red light. "She's living a dream right now," June said. "But in a couple weeks, she'll be all yours again."

Lon's voice echoed up the stairs. "Get your spook on!"

June gripped Bong's arm and leaned in close to him. Close enough that he could smell the faint flower scent of her deodorant. "Of course, in a couple weeks, you may be in a wheelchair," she laughed.

"You're evil," he said with a grin. "Now go…slit yourself."

★   ★   ★

Argento adjusted the black leather hood over his head. Damn thing was hotter than hell, and the sweat dripped around his ears and down his cheeks. But no matter how uncomfortable the getup was, he was bound and determined to get ahead on the count tonight. Truth be told, he wasn't aggressive enough on the floor. He knew it. He loved decorating the rooms and setting the lights and coming up with the 'look'. Because every 'look' was really a homage to his favorite movies and director. But when it came to playing a part...he was, by nature, too shy. And shy monsters didn't scare people.

Lucio wasn't that much more outgoing than he was, but he had more disgusting makeup. That trumped a 'quiet killer' every time.

"Not tonight," Argento whispered. He walked to the back of the room and reached behind the set tapestry to turn up the Goblin soundtrack to *Suspiria* two more notches. Music helped set the mood.

So he'd let the masters talk for him. He just needed to act the part more.

He just needed to be more menacing with the (fake) knife.

The first footsteps sounded in the hallway outside, and he held out the knife and assumed the position.

Tonight, he was going to freak people out.

Or he'd sever his own neck on a broken window.

★   ★   ★

Tonight's bleeder, according to Emery, was a forty-something guy with a long ponytail and a Dio t-shirt with ripped sleeves.

Mike wasn't real happy when he saw the guy stomping up the stairs. Emery had done her usual quiet appearance behind him and pointed at the stairs. Meaning, corral the next person who came up here. But railroading a big dude was way different than scaring a thin girl into the hole in the floor where Emery waited. Hell, how did Emery even think she was going to carry this guy down her secret ladder?

"Fuck," Mike whispered under his breath. But he'd learned not to question Katie. And if Emery said it, it was Katie who spoke. He'd realized that much a while ago. There was only one girl calling the shots here.

Mike pointed toward the alcove behind the bureau, and the guy looked at him hard for a second, and then started walking toward the entry point without a question.

Thank God for small favors.

Mike followed him into the half-hidden area and pointed dramatically down at the floor. They guy looked confused for a moment, and then as if on cue, the floor door opened and Emery came out.

She stood next to the open door and pointed, just as dramatically as Mike had, for the man to walk down the ladder.

The guy hesitated for just a moment, and then turned and began to descend the stairs.

Emery looked at Mike and for the first time in the entire time he'd known her, he swore the girl smiled.

When the big guy had stepped down four or five stairs and the door was closing behind him, Emery took it in her own hands, and waited for him to disappear below her before she followed.

When the door closed, Mike heaved a sigh of relief. Whatever shit happened down there, it was on her, not him.

After the next group passed by on the stairs and began screaming down the aisle as haunters with hag masks and knives jumped out at them, Mike quickly slipped down the stairs before the next group could ascend.

He was going to check in with Lon and see what else was up for tonight. Because his job for Katie was done. At least for the next 24 hours.

CHAPTER TWENTY-NINE

Thirty-seven out-loud screams tonight. Argento was happy. He hadn't heard Lucio's score yet, but his own was better than he'd charted on any other night for the past two weeks.

Sometimes pressure was what drove you to succeed.

And sometimes you were just lucky.

He didn't know which of those scenarios he owed his numbers to, but he was proud of the rank he'd racked up. It ought to put him back in contention with his friend.

Lon had just called the 'spooks out' call, which meant that all guests were out of the house, and they were closed for the night. He walked out of his room with a faint grin and headed to the makeup room to get rid of his gear. There was a line at June's mirror, but he didn't need to worry about that shit. He pulled the gloves and mask over his head and went upstairs to hang it on the rack with the others.

"So, what did you hit?" he asked Lucio when he got back down.

"Twenty-nine," Lucio said.

Argento grinned. "Creeping up on you, man. Thirty-seven."

"Bastard," Lucio said. "I even made a girl piss her pants, I swear I did."

"Sometimes the knife is better than the maggot," Argento said.

"Yeah, sometimes." Lucio grinned. "But rarely. You want to grab a drink? A few people are going."

Argento shook his head. "Wiped. Maybe tomorrow. I just want to head home."

Lucio shrugged. "I hear ya. See you tomorrow."

Argento smiled as his friend headed out the front door. There was one thing he wanted to do before he left. Lon had mentioned earlier that a couple of the lights in the basement were out. So he grabbed replacements from a pack he kept in the *Nightmare on Elm Street* bureau and headed to the hall. Lon was talking to Lenny at the end of the hallway, but looked up as Argento came out.

"You're gonna be the last one out," Lon said.

Argento shrugged. "Nah, you guys are still here. I just wanted to fix those lights before I go."

Lon nodded. "Fair enough. Mike's closing up tonight, so we were just leaving. You want to meet us up at The Edge in a few? We're going to have a beer."

He shook his head. "Lucio already asked me. I gotta get some sleep."

Lon grinned. "Save up your energy for another big scream night tomorrow? Got it. See you then."

Lenny waved and the two of them walked toward the front foyer.

Argento had second thoughts for a moment about following, and then shook his head. He needed some sleep; his throat had been scratchy earlier, and he couldn't afford to be sick for Halloween.

He descended the 'Don't Go In The Basement' stairs and saw the problems. There was a floor spot out on the far right, which was easily fixed. But there was also a top spot out near the middle of the maze, and he needed a different bulb for that. He replaced the first one, and smiled as a red glow instantly lit the wall. It was a small change, but every light made a difference.

Argento went back upstairs, but left the lights on. He thought he had a replacement for the other spot in his trunk; he hadn't used many of those and they were LEDs so they should have lasted the whole show. He replaced the other extra bulb and went outside.

The night air was cool, but a little humid. It smelled of the forest, and he took a deep breath. There was nothing better than the night. He preferred to sleep all day and work at night, when he had a job that allowed it. For a long time, he'd been a stock boy at a Jewel supermarket, and it was perfect. He had a night shift, but could drive home long before the sun came up.

He stood still for a few minutes, just breathing the air and listening to the chime of the night bugs. They buzzed and droned and chirped like an orchestra, a steady, constant background of natural music.

Argento smiled and finally walked to the car to retrieve the bulb. He opened the trunk and found he did, indeed, have a pack of them tucked in the back. He grabbed the box and decided he might as well keep some extras in the house with the other bulbs.

When he went back inside, he paused for a moment, listening for any sound to tell him where Mike was. He hadn't seen the carpenter in hours, though Lon said he was here. He should let him know that he was still here so he didn't lock Argento inside.

"Mike?" he called. "You around?"

When there was no answer, he shrugged and dropped the spare bulbs in the *Nightmare* room and grabbed a screwdriver before heading down the stairs. The mount for these spots was a little more difficult to get to – he had to take off a plastic guard – but he should be out of here in a minute anyway. Maybe the guy was taking a dump somewhere.

Argento walked over to the dead lamp and reached up to unscrew the housing. The whole mount moved, instead of the screw, and he frowned. With one hand, he held it fast to the beam and tried unscrewing it with the other hand. The screwdriver promptly jumped out of the hole and gouged a hole in the joist.

"Damnit," he whispered, and tried it again. He tapped the back of the screwdriver to jiggle the screw mount, and then twisted…this time it unlocked. He grinned and got the rest of the housing off and then swapped out the bulb. A blue halo appeared, bringing out a splatter pattern on the wall nearby that he was particularly proud of. It was all a part of a whole. No light, no swatch of paint was unnecessary.

Some artists worked on canvas, but Argento liked to think that he worked in three dimensions. Five, really, because he also used music and sometimes scent to fill out the atmosphere of a room.

Something thumped at the end of the basement.

Argento froze. The aisle he was in appeared completely empty, just shadows of red and blue and green light melting and merging across the empty plank floor.

Another noise then. A scraping. As if something was being dragged across a floor. For a second he thought maybe it was Mike putting something back in place, but the noise sounded closer than that. And he saw nobody else in the basement. Could an animal of some kind have gotten in? Raccoon?

"Shit," Argento whispered. Slowly, he began to walk toward the back of the basement, where the source of the sound seemed to be. It was dark back there, by design. Every few seconds a strobe went off and illuminated a gutted man that June had created. It looked pretty good, but Argento didn't think it was quite good enough to have a solid light trained on it.

The impression the strobe made was better than letting people stare at it too closely.

He stared at the area behind the gutted man for a moment, watching as the strobe illuminated the dark space near the back wall three or four times. Nothing.

He walked over to the wall at the right. It was the back of the house, the side that faced the cemetery. But there was nothing there. He stepped around the false prop wall to look behind the room that the public saw, and the space was dark.

Then he heard a voice through the wall. Someone was talking in low tones close by. It sounded like a man. Mike?

Argento frowned and stepped closer to the back wall. He cocked his head to see if the sound was coming from upstairs, but no. His ear said it was directly in front of him. Behind a wooden wall which he thought butted up to the cement foundation. But maybe not.

He ran his hands over the wood, pressing on it to see if it gave somewhere. That's when he found the cavity in the wood. And when his hand slipped into it, he found the door knob. There was a room down here? How had he decorated this space and not known this?

Argento turned the knob and the door swung inward. The hinges were on the inside – so that's why you couldn't see the door from inside the basement.

He stepped inside and saw Mike standing on the right side of the room. Katie, his girlfriend, was next to him, and another girl, a stocky woman with a head of knotted brown hair, stood next to them. Only, she was propping up a body that appeared to be slumped against her. If the guy really was relying on her for support, he couldn't figure out how she managed it. The guy looked like a construction worker; his shoulders were broad and he must have stood well over six feet.

Argento opened his mouth to call out to Mike, who still hadn't noticed him enter the room. But then he shut it. The slumping guy was naked from the waist up, and the chunky girl was holding his arm over what looked like a casket at the end of the room.

He frowned. What the hell was going on here? Then he saw the girl lift a silver blade, and swipe it across the guy's arm. A spout of blood erupted from the man's bare arm to spray across the casket, and a light went off in Argento's head. That's not makeup, he realized.

"What the hell are you doing?" he yelled and bolted forward.

Mike turned and moved to intercept him but before he could, Argento had grabbed for the knife arm of the girl. She didn't flinch. Instead, she released her hold on the big man and lunged.

Something cold touched Argento's neck. He opened his mouth to cough, and then the whole world lit on fire. He grabbed for his neck but it was too late. Emery pulled back the blade and the knife left his throat, which instantly filled with blood. Argento choked and blinked and struggled to scream. This couldn't be happening.

He heard Mike yell something but he couldn't understand the words. Everything seemed like it was closing in and he felt hands grabbing at him, but Argento found that he could only see the thick lips of the big girl as she bent over him and stared at him with dull brown eyes.

Argento kicked and twisted on the floor as he clutched his neck and tried to stem the tide of hot blood flowing out. And then all of a sudden he was lifted into the air by the girl.

"We need to get an ambulance," Mike said.

CHAPTER THIRTY

Mike's stomach sank as he turned and saw Argento standing in the hidden basement room. They'd managed to keep the room secret this whole month, but now, as they approached the final days, the set guy had stumbled not only on the room, but on the bloodletting.

"Shit," he said under his breath and turned to head the guy off. Emery was busy washing Katie's bones with blood, but maybe he could steer Argento off before he really got what was going on.

"What the hell are you doing?" Argento yelled and bolted toward Emery. Mike moved to intercept him, but missed. And the next thirty seconds played out like a slow-motion film in his eyes as Emery's knife swung around and stabbed, catching Argento right in the side of the neck, piercing, sliding in like it was a sheath and then pulling back. And then the wiry little set and lighting guy was clutching at his neck, as red blood splashed through his fingers and he fell to the floor.

Emery scooped the man up and Mike grabbed for her arm. "We need to get an ambulance," he yelled. "Put pressure on his neck."

"It's too late for that," Katie said behind him. "He's going to be gone in seconds. Just look at his eyes."

Emery struggled to hold Argento over the coffin so the blood dripped inside.

"Help her," Katie urged. "Don't waste his life. He's going to be dead in seconds no matter what."

Mike's head swam with conflicting emotions but he had followed Katie this far, and somehow that made him go once more with what she said. He grabbed Argento's black-booted feet and hefted the man up and over the coffin, trying to hold him steady as the man's feet kicked and his middle tremored. Emery gripped him by his shoulders and tilted his upper half so that the blood dripped in a steady river across the raw sheaths of muscle and meat that had taken shape in the coffin. After a couple minutes, the body grew still, and one arm hung limply across the meat of the growing body below.

"Lift his feet higher," Katie urged, and Mike did, closing his eyes when he saw the blood flow increase.

This wasn't happening. None of it. Mike held his eyes closed and wished himself back to that meeting with Perry. He imagined himself turning down the job, and muddling by these past few weeks with normal jobs. Maybe he would have fallen into a full steady gig without Perry's help. Or maybe he would have lost his house. But either way, he wouldn't have been standing here holding a man's legs in the air so that he could bleed the body's last blood onto a ghost's reborn corpse.

"That's enough," Katie finally said softly.

Mike opened his eyes as the body began to move – because Emery was pulling it. He followed her lead to lay Argento on the ground. The man's eyes were wide open, staring at the wooden ceiling as if in shock at what he saw. Mike swallowed hard and reached over to finger the man's eyelids closed.

He couldn't look at him that way.

"What the hell are we going to do now?" he whispered. "You promised that we weren't going to kill anyone. They'd all go home and wake up with a bandage and a weird scratch on them that they couldn't recall getting and that was it."

"Curiosity killed the cat," Katie said. "He shouldn't have come here."

"That doesn't help," Mike said. "The police are going to come. They'll arrest me and Emery and this whole thing will have been in vain."

Katie shook her head. "No, they won't," she said, and then pointed at the big guy who lay unmoving on the floor next to Argento. "First, you're going to take our friend here for a walk so that he can get home and not wake up here. Then you're going to come back and help Emery bury this other one."

Mike felt a tear running down his cheek. "I can't," he whispered.

"You have to," Katie said. "You want to hold me in your bed every night, don't you?"

He nodded.

"In just a few more days, I'll be yours to hold forever. Right now, we have to finish the plan. This is a setback, but we need to work with it. You need to make it right."

"We can't make it right," Mike said. "Argento's dead."

"And his death will help in bringing me back to life. It's a trade. Don't waste his life by stopping on me now."

Emery was starting to bandage the arm of the big man who remained alive, and after a minute, Mike bent to help her. When the gauze was taped in place she began to pull a t-shirt over the guy's mostly bald head.

Then the two of them put the man's arms over their shoulders and lifted him to his feet. His body seemed to unconsciously respond, and together they walked him like a zombie out of the basement.

There was a pickup parked just down the gravel path, and Mike patted the man down and found the keys in his right pocket. Emery helped load the man into the passenger's side and then Mike drove the truck down the road toward Cicero Avenue. He pulled off on the side of the road and pushed and pulled until he'd shifted the guy into the driver's seat, all the while looking over his shoulder to make sure no cars were coming. An unlikely, but occasional, risk at one a.m.

Once the man was in the seat, Mike rolled down the window and closed the driver's side door.

"You should go home," he said in the man's ear. He repeated himself twice more, and then stepped backward, away from the truck. He was only a few yards down the road when he heard the crunch of gravel. He turned and saw the pickup moving slowly down the shoulder of the road. After a moment, it eased hesitantly onto the asphalt. The brake lights went on and off a couple times, but then the truck suddenly accelerated.

One problem out of the way.

★　　★　　★

"What are we supposed to do with him?" Mike asked when he got back to the basement. Emery had closed the casket and put away the bandages. But Argento still lay, very dead, in the middle of the floor.

"Put him in my grave," Katie said. "The earth should still be loose there."

"And his car?"

"Find his keys and drive it away from here. I'm sure you can lose it somewhere."

Mike wanted to protest, but what was the point? If he ditched the body somewhere so that someone could find it, the police would be all over the haunted house. And if he tried to come clean about what had happened…he'd be in jail. To be honest, he was more worried about getting rid of the car than the body.

With the latter, the only option was to bury Argento and hope that the body was never found. And who was going to look in an existing old grave for a new body? So that was a good solution.

After he searched Argento's pockets and found a set of keys, he looked at Emery.

"Let's go," he said, and the two of them picked up the body by its arms and legs and walked it across the basement and up the stairs outside. They laid it on the ground near the grave, and then Mike retrieved two shovels. In a half hour, the two of them were dripping with sweat, but the pile of earth on the side of the grave was high. When they'd gone down about as far as they'd dug originally, Mike stopped and put up his hand. "That's enough."

They lifted Argento's body once again, and held it over the center of the hole. "One, two, three," Mike counted aloud. They both let go, and the body dropped with a thud to the clay base below. Part of him wanted to straighten the arms and legs, which twisted at odd angles. But instead, Mike just took a deep breath, and started shoveling earth back into the hole. He moved fast, anxious to stop seeing the empty face of the haunted house decorator.

When they were finished, Mike patted the earth down firm, and got down on his hands and knees to push the piles of brown and red leaves around, hiding the evidence that the ground here had been disturbed.

They walked back to the house in silence, and Emery didn't slow when they stepped inside. She walked down the hallway and a moment later he heard her feet on the stairs going up to the attic. Apparently, she was going to bed.

Mike went downstairs and walked down to the hidden room behind the sets. It was empty. Katie was gone. Part of him had thought maybe she'd be waiting here for him. He was disappointed, but also relieved. Part of him didn't want to see her now. All he wanted was beer. Many beers.

There were splatters of dark on the floor, but other than that, you couldn't tell that a man had been murdered here just an hour before. Mike shook his head and backed out of the room, closing the door behind him.

He quickly made the rounds of the rest of the house, turning out lights. He fumbled with the keys to lock the front door, and swore. When he finally got the lock to click shut, he looked over through the forest to the faint silhouettes of the tombstones nearby.

Then he pulled the keys from his pocket and got into Argento's car. There was a road a quarter mile down the turnpike that led back into the heart of the forest preserve. He could drive the car back there and off the road into the trees. It should stay undiscovered for a while if he went back far enough.

Mike started it up and eased the car across the gravel road and onto the asphalt. A few minutes later he was maneuvering through brush and trees until he was well off the small access road that led into the forest preserve. At this time of year, nobody came back here.

When he was satisfied that it was well secreted behind a thick wall of scrub and branches, he turned it off, but left the keys in the ignition. It would be a favor if someone found it and stole it. Mike looked at the car for a minute under the light of the stars and shrugged. Then he began the long walk back to the turnpike and the haunted house.

When he finally got back to Bachelor's Grove, he was sweating. And exhausted. He looked at the dark, silent house across the clearing and considered going back inside to look for Katie. Then he shook his head in denial and walked quickly to his truck. He needed to be away from here. When the truck started and he pulled on to Midlothian Turnpike, Mike reached up to scratch his cheek. His fingers came back wet, and angrily he wiped the back of his hand across his face.

When he walked in to The Edge, he went straight to the restroom and washed his face and hands clear of tears and dirt. And any blood that he might have touched. Then he took a seat at the bar and ordered a PBR.

"Last call in a few minutes," the bartender said.

Mike nodded and shotgunned the beer. The bartender looked at him with concern.

"Been a long day," Mike said. "Hit me again."

CHAPTER THIRTY-ONE

"You good?" Jeanie asked.

Lenny shrugged. "This hood is sweaty, but I'm all right. I don't know how Argento's been wearing this every damn night though. He better show up tomorrow, because I'm not doing this all weekend."

Jeanie grinned. "I thought being the masked killer was a step up from being just another zombie."

Lenny shook his head. "Black guys don't wear masks and gloves. We don't need to hide – we put it out there."

"So, you're breaking typecast now," she said. "You're always saying black guys get all the shit roles…now you've got a lead shot."

Lenny shook his head. "The masked killer always gets killed in the end. He's not the hero."

"Maybe," Jeanie said. "But I think some people think Jason is the hero. And he never seems to die."

"Oh, he died," Lenny said. "He just keeps coming back from the dead."

She grinned. "Whatever. I'll be back later. People on the floor."

She quickly exited the room before the footsteps of the next group reached them. She turned to face them before they entered Lenny's room and let out a horrible moan as she massaged her bloody guts. One of the girls in the group turned her head away and complained, "Oh my God, that's so gross."

Then they disappeared inside, and Jeanie headed upstairs to check on Bong and June.

★　　★　　★

"This is driving me insane," June said.

"What's the matter?" Bong asked. He crept out of his hiding spot. A group had just exited the room and they should have a minute or two before the next.

"I got like five mosquito bites on my back last night. There must have been a swarm of them in my bedroom."

June twisted and turned, pushing on her elbow with her hand to try to guide her arm to an untouchable spot on her back.

"Fuck," she complained. "I can't reach it." She backed against the wall and started to rub her back against it.

Bong laughed and stood up.

"Here, let me," he said.

He reached around her back and began to scratch. "Tell me where," he said, watching her eyes. He knew that he'd be able to see it when he found the spot.

"A little to the left," she said. "And up."

He moved his fingernails up and over, and then he smiled as her face suddenly took on the look of an orgasm.

"Holy shit," she moaned and arched her back against his hand, expanding the radius of his scratching.

"God yes," she said. "That's it, right there. Dig in. Rip my fucking back open, I can't stand it anymore."

"I don't want real blood on my hands," Bong said. He kept scratching for a few more seconds, and then began to slow. "We probably need to stop. I think I heard someone on the stairs."

June nodded, but her eyes looked up at him in pure adulation. "Thank you so much. I can't tell you how good that felt. It's been driving me crazy for hours."

She tilted her face up and went to kiss him on the cheek. But Bong moved. He couldn't have told if he did it on purpose, or instinct, but his lips connected with hers and instead of jumping back, he only pressed forward.

He loved Jeanie, but there was something about June that drew him so much. Talking with her every night for the past month…he felt close to her. Closer to her than Jeanie lately. He welcomed the intimate touch of her lips on his.

"We shouldn't," June whispered, but didn't pull her lips away.

"No," he agreed, and kissed her harder, wrapping his arm around her back and digging his nails in where the mosquito bites were.

"We should get in position," he said, his lips still touching hers. He could taste her breath in his mouth.

"Yeah," she said, not moving. "We should."

Bong's eyes met hers, and saw the desire and anxiousness there. This was wrong, and they both knew it. Might never act on it again. But it had happened.

He pressed his mouth to hers one last quick time and then pulled away.

"Showtime," he reminded her, and moved away from her to hide again.

★   ★   ★

Jeanie walked down the long attic floor to the back room that June and Bong 'haunted'. As she reached the threshold and opened her mouth to ask how they were doing, she suddenly bit her tongue.

Bong's hands were all over June, and then their mouths were touching. They kissed again and again, and Jeanie felt an icy stab in her heart.

She wanted to run into the room and punch them. She wanted to kick Bong in the nuts and pound June in the face with her fist.

But instead, she stood there rooted to the floor as her boyfriend kissed her monster makeup mentor.

The dream of this haunted house was now a nightmare.

Jeanie wanted to scream, but instead she backed quietly away. She couldn't face them now. Maybe not ever.

On the far side of the room, a group of people were just stepping into the attic from the stairs, and Jeanie ran toward them. The group split, one of the women screaming at her aggressive approach, as one of the other couples moved quickly to one side.

Jeanie didn't slow until she was down the stairs. Then she ran out the front door, surprising the group in line outside. She ran around the house and into the trees, stopping only when she came to Bachelor's Grove Cemetery. There, she sank down on the toppled stone of a grave and finally let out one long, plaintive howl.

The tears came hard and ruined her makeup.

And for the first time, Jeanie didn't care.

PART THREE
CLOSING NIGHT

CHAPTER THIRTY-TWO

"Looks like you were celebrating a little early," Lon said.

Mike moaned, and then held a hand to his forehead. It hurt to moan. "Yeah, I might have crushed one too many cans last night."

"You know *tonight's* closing night, right? Post-party at The Edge?"

Mike nodded, and moaned again at the ache. He had to stop doing that. "Oh yeah, right."

Lon tilted his head slightly and stared at him. "You gonna even make it through tonight?"

"Yeah, I'll be fine in a couple hours," Mike said.

"Good, because I think things are going to get a little crazy later."

"What do you mean?"

"It's Halloween, man," Lon said. "The big night. People are going to be lined up down the turnpike to get in here. And the gang is psyched. I know they're going to be working overtime on the scream factor tonight. Wait until you see Lucio. I think he's been working on his makeup since three o'clock."

"How gory can a zombie get?"

"You'll see."

"I guess I will," Mike agreed. "I'm going to go set up downstairs."

"Don't go to sleep down there," Lon warned. "We open in a half hour."

"The basement is the last place I want to fall asleep," Mike said. Lon could have no idea why the basement was any different for Mike than the main floor or the attic, but in his head, he had visions of the bloody meat-covered bones that lay pulsating in the coffin behind the door of the hidden room. Lon just looked at him and shrugged.

"I dunno. It's cool and dark down there. If I was you, that's where I'd head for a nap. But…don't do it!"

"All right, all right!" Mike said shaking his head. And then he put his hand to his forehead and mumbled, "Ow," as he walked away.

Lon grinned and turned his attention back to the room of bloody, creepy, excited people and held up a hand to get their attention.

★   ★   ★

In the back of the room, Lenny pulled on the black leather giallo killer hood.

"I did not want to still be doing this," Lenny said. "Where the hell did Argento disappear to this week? I can't believe he's missing closing night."

The man with the hanging eyeball and gory cheeks next to him shook his head. "I wish I knew. I'm pretty worried."

Lenny nodded. "Yeah, I know man. I'm sorry. I'm sure he's okay, just got called away on a family emergency or something."

"Argento doesn't have any family," Lucio said.

Lenny didn't have an answer for that.

"Hey," Lucio said. "I know you hate the outfit but…make 'em feel like you're really gonna kill them tonight, okay? For him?"

Lenny suddenly felt his throat closing up. He opened his mouth to speak but instead, just nodded.

★   ★   ★

"All right!" Lon yelled from the front of the room. "This is it. I can't believe I'm saying this, but…it's fucking Halloween!"

The room erupted in cheers.

"I can't believe it's all come down to this. Hell night. Hallowmas. All Hallow's Eve. Night of the demons. We have been scaring people almost every night for a month, and tonight's the final night. This is our last hurrah. Last time to make one of those girls from Tinley Park High pee her panties. Last time to make one of those jocks from South Suburban College run like a baby out of your room. So, let's make it happen. Let's scare the hell out of them!"

As the motley, blood-soaked crew exploded in whistles and claps, Lucio walked up to stand next to Lon. The house manager nodded and took a step back, ceding the floor.

Lucio didn't talk much, and so the room quieted when he stepped up to speak. His voice was quiet and a little shaky as he began.

"You all know that this place looks like it does because of Argento. He designed most of these sets and this lighting. I don't want to bring anyone down, but I know that he'd be here tonight if he could. This should have been his crowning night, and I know he would have been challenging me for the scream title big time tonight. I don't know what's happened to him this week. I know...." His voice broke and Lucio hung his zombie head for a moment before continuing. "I know he'd want us all to scare the shit out of people tonight, so...." Lucio raised one blood-streaked hand. "Do it for him."

Lenny raised a black-gloved fist in the air and yelled, "Hell yeah!"

Jeanie raised a hand next to his and grabbed on to his hand as she yelled out, "For Argento."

Everyone around the room joined suit, and raised their fists as they yelled in unison, "For Argento."

★   ★   ★

Lon retook the floor and closed the 'rally' down after a couple chants. "I know that there's one thing for sure that Argento would say if he was here: Quit jerking around and get the fuck out there and scare people."

People laughed and clapped and Lon pointed toward the door. "Go out there and get it done. Let's have a good time tonight!"

★   ★   ★

Lucio walked out of the makeup room and down the hall to his station. Part of him wished that the night was over now. And part of him wished it would never end. He was here because of Argento. And his friend hadn't answered a call, email or text in a week. From what he could tell, he hadn't been home either. His car was missing, so the police suggested that maybe he'd left town.

Lucio didn't believe that.

He believed something horrible had happened, though he hoped it wasn't the case. Still, his friend had always been a strange one. Anything was possible. In his heart though, he knew better. If Argento was alive, he would not have missed the chance to wear the leather mask and gloves on the final night of the haunted house.

And while part of him wanted to just walk away, the part of him that had been friends with Argento heard the same words in his head that Lon had suggested just a couple minutes before. "Go out there and get it done."

CHAPTER THIRTY-THREE

"You don't look so good," Katie said.

Mike looked up from the spotlight he was adjusting and smiled. Thinly. "I don't feel so good," he admitted.

"Why don't you come upstairs?" she said. "I might be able to help."

"I don't see how," Mike said. "I can't even feel you anymore."

Katie nodded. "I know," she said. "But that's all going to change soon."

"You keep saying that," Mike said. "But we're kind of out of time. After tonight, this place is closed."

"Tonight is the last night I need," Katie said. "And I want you to be ready when it's all over."

"I'll be fine," he said. "I've had a hangover before."

Katie raised her eyebrows. "Yeah, I'm sure. Come upstairs, okay?"

He nodded, and once again cursed himself. Then he finished resetting the light and turned to follow her.

"Shouldn't you be staying here to haunt the basement?" he asked.

Katie nodded. "Yeah, I'll be back. But let's get you set first. They haven't opened the front door yet."

She led him up the back stairs, and a moment later they were in the attic. After ensuring that nobody was in the vicinity to see, Mike opened the door in the floor and let Katie step through. He followed and pulled the door down behind him.

In the hidden room, Emery stood in the corner.

But Mike was used to that by now. He ignored her and only looked at Katie.

"Why are we down here?" he said. "I can't even touch you anymore. Coming here is pointless."

Katie shook her head and held a finger to his lips. He couldn't feel it.

She looked at Emery and motioned with her other hand. The surly girl moved from her spot across the room. Katie leaned toward her and whispered something in her ear. Then she leaned back, and Emery reached into the pocket of her jeans.

When her hand came out, she held the locket that Mike had once found lying on the floor of the old house, before ever meeting Katie.

The locket that had allowed him to touch Katie.

He snatched it out of her hand, and pulled it over his head. When the cold kiss of metal met his chest, he turned from Emery and looked at Katie.

"I hope you mean this," he said.

Katie grinned. "Of course I do," she said. "You've been so good to me the past couple weeks, I wanted to give you something special so that you'd know I was serious."

"Serious about driving me crazy," he asked.

She took his hand, and a spark shot up his arm as he realized he could feel her grip. With her hand, she pressed his fingers to her chest. Mike's heart jumped as he felt the swell of her breast beneath his fingers. "Only in a good way," she said.

Katie stepped backward, toward the bed, and Mike couldn't help but follow.

"Come here with me," Katie whispered, drawing him down to the bed of nails with her. Mike melted into her arms. The touch of her on his skin felt like heaven. For days, he had only been able to *see* her. Every brush of her skin, every kiss, had been like touching the wind. He'd felt a spark now and then, but no substance.

Now she hugged him and he actually felt her body there. Mike didn't resist; he wrapped his arms around her slight shoulders and pulled her close.

"God I've missed you," he whispered.

"I don't know why," Katie said. "I've been right here all the time."

"I've missed feeling you," he said.

"Oh, that," she said. Katie laughed, and he couldn't help but smile at the wide grin that she gave. Her teeth were long and white and she looked mischievous and happy. "I wanted you to remember what it was you were fighting for," she said.

Mike had no answer for that, so he bent down and kissed her. Her tongue answered his with electric energy. In seconds, she had wrapped her legs around him as well, and rolled him over and back on the hard, pointed bed. Somehow their clothes disappeared, one piece at a time, and Mike realized that most of his headache was gone as he moved between the silken skin of her naked thighs and pressed himself into her.

"Oh, I have missed that," she gasped, as he rolled her beneath him, tilting her head back against the bare nails.

Mike groaned and pulled her tighter. "Then you should have left me with the necklace," he whispered, as her lips brushed his.

"Shhhh," she said, and pressed her mouth hard on his lips. When she pulled back, she said, "Soon you won't need it."

"Jesus, I hope so," he gasped and thrust his hips hard against hers.

"Jesus has nothing to do with it," she answered, and pressed his hips back to the bed.

Then they were quiet, at least with words, and focused on moving together across the bed of nails.

When their motions finally slowed, Katie pushed Mike over and onto his back. "How's your head now?" she asked, licking a pink tongue across his lips.

Mike smiled. "Better," he said. "But even sex can't cure a hangover."

Katie nodded. "I figured," she said. "But Emery's got something that does."

She motioned behind her, and Mike's heart skipped a beat as he saw the chunky girl move out of the shadows toward the bed. Once again, he'd forgotten she was there. He shouldn't care if Katie didn't, but there was something creepy in having sex in front of a big wallflower girl who just stood…still…against the wall. (*Kind of the definition of a wallflower, moron*, he said to himself).

Emery dropped three white tablets on the small table next to the bed, and set a bottle of water next to them.

Mike didn't question it. He knocked back the tablets and slugged down the bottle of water. When he'd swallowed them, Katie wrapped her arms around him and straddled him. She kissed him again and again until he felt almost smothered; the room began to fill with amber shadows.

"I am so exhausted," he said, stifling a yawn.

Katie smiled. "Then you should sleep for a while. I have work to do downstairs anyway. I'll be back."

She got up from the bed, and then, as Mike felt the waves of dark and sleep wash over him, Emery took her place, and reached down to take the necklace back from around his neck. He wanted to protest, but realized that he really couldn't move. His limbs felt like lead.

"Wait," he whispered, suddenly feeling helpless and wondering what had become of his arms.

"Shhhh," Katie said, returning for a moment to push a finger across his lips. Without the necklace, he only felt the hint of a spark.

"You won't need that again," she said. "I told you, tonight's the night. Now…get some sleep so you can really enjoy it."

He wanted to argue, but dimly he saw Katie walk away, and then Emery, too, disappeared from the range of his vision. He wanted to sit up and see where they were going, but instead, his eyelids slipped closed, and Mike let the heavy cloak of sleep spill over him. He didn't fight it.

★ ★ ★

Lucio went to his room but he couldn't settle in. Jeanie had helped him put on what was probably the best, most elaborate makeup he'd had all month, but he just didn't feel like scaring people tonight. It was a weird feeling, but all he wanted was to know what had happened to Argento. The guy had been his best friend for three years now, ever since they'd met at a Terror in the Aisles film night in Chicago where they were showing *Suspiria* and *The Beyond*. They'd talked, at first haltingly, about their favorite directors, and quickly realized that they not only loved the same era and style in films, but that they lived close to each other, too.

It was a match made in heaven. Or hell, as Argento would have insisted. They quickly began getting together on the weekends and staging film fests. It was Argento who had introduced Lucio to Lon, who didn't fixate like they did on Eurosleaze, but still had an amazing library and palate for obscure horror. Lon had actually convinced the two of them to watch some comic horror movies from Australia, which they were skeptical of, but ultimately loved. Lucio would never forget the time they all got together for beer at some log cabin bar near Lon's place, and the guy had suggested they watch a horror movie about a tire.

"C'mon," Lon had said. "It's a killer tire. The audience breaks the barrier of the fourth wall. It's called *Rubber* and I know you're going to love it. Plus, I've got bourbon."

Argento had shaken his head in feigned sadness, but Lucio had grinned.

"I'll watch any movie if bourbon is involved."

"Be careful what you promise," Lon said. "I've got an Australian movie about killer sheep too."

"Oh my good lord," Argento had moaned.

And in the end, they'd all loved *Rubber*. And had watched dozens of crazy horror films together ever since.

Only…maybe they wouldn't be doing that anymore now.

Lucio pressed his eyes closed. He needed to take a walk before the house opened. He stepped into the hallway and then remembered that Argento had always checked the lights in the basement before the house opened. He had a bunch of sets going down there, and some of the incandescents seemed to burn out quick. As far as he knew, nobody had really looked at them since Argento had disappeared early this week.

Lucio shrugged and took a walk down the hallway toward the stairs. It was something to do. Something that Argento would have wanted done.

Even with his costume on, Lucio felt the chill as he stepped down the stairs into the basement. The house had been hot most of the time when they'd first come here to decorate and set it up, but now, at the end of October…it was drafty and cold. There was no furnace, so some nights over the past couple weeks, he'd been able to see his breath as he closed up at the end of the night. It wasn't that bad so far tonight, but the temperature had definitely dropped since the sun went down.

Lucio stepped onto the floor of the basement and stood still, taking stock of the room. His glance went from one spotlight to the next, and the spaces in between, where perhaps there was supposed to be a light, but wasn't. The front end of the basement looked good. He walked down what Argento had dubbed the 'Aisle of Atrocities', where they had constructed several sets that played off famous horror tales and grinned at the setpiece that took its premise from the story of Countess Báthory. A half-nude woman hung from the ceiling, tied with her wrists and feet behind her back to a hook in the ceiling so that only her belly hung down. Her gut was…gutted. Intestines hung out like a rope, and a steady stream of red dripped into the white porcelain tub below, where another woman luxuriated in the deep red bath.

Argento had outdone himself there – he'd rigged a hidden fish pond pump that took the red water out of the tub back up in the air and into the 'corpse' so that it could be a continuous blood fountain.

Something rustled in the blue shadows down the aisle and Lucio walked toward it. The 'haunters' of the basement ought to be down here any minute, but he hadn't seen anyone yet.

Someone flipped on the music soundtrack then and the room was filled with the eerie synthesizer tones of Goblin. Argento had nicked the soundtrack from *Suspiria* for this area. It worked great in a heavily shadowed basement. Lucio turned toward the back of the room, but didn't see who had turned on the music.

"Andy?" he called out. "Karen? Is that you?"

Nobody answered. Lucio shrugged and continued his survey of the lights. Something moved amid the hanging chains of the *Hellraiser* display. He walked across the aisle and saw the shadow of someone standing still there, in front of the tortured body strung up with hooks and chains. They were in front of the lights, so he couldn't make out the face. But whoever it was wore a dark cape and cowl, and held a long blade in front of their chest. It looked like a classic devil worshipper pose.

"Very funny," Lucio said. "But you're in the wrong Atrocity for that outfit."

The figure didn't answer, but instead raised the knife with both hands in the air. As it did, the cowl fell back and Lucio saw that it was a woman. She was a big woman, with ratty brown hair. He didn't recognize her at all.

"Hey, who are you and what are you doing down here?" he demanded.

She didn't answer, but instead suddenly lunged forward and brought the knife down.

Lucio was caught by surprise and started to jump backward to avoid the attack, but he was too late. The knife plunged right through the false eyeball stem that hung from the rubbery mask he wore.

Lucio felt a white-hot explosion in his eye, and grabbed for his face. But the woman pulled the knife right back out of his skull, and brought it back down in his other eye.

The world became a sea of hideous, bloody black pain.

But only for a moment.

Then Lucio didn't feel anything anymore.

CHAPTER THIRTY-FOUR

Bachelor's Grove had never had so many people trying to get in. Word of the haunted house had spread throughout the south suburbs of Chicago over the past few weeks and everyone wanted a look before it closed for the season. The line of people stretched from the ticket taker on the porch all the way down the gravel road past the cemetery and pond, and out onto Midlothian Turnpike. Both of the forest preserve parking lots that served the attraction just down the road were full, and police were directing and stopping traffic on the turnpike to allow people to cross the busy street safely in the dark.

"This is crazy!" Jeanie said to Lon. She had ducked into the hidden main level Ops room – the converted master bathroom. The cast needed to pee over the course of the night, so they'd cordoned this room off from the rest of the rooms as a refuge. And when this was in use, Lon used the hidden room downstairs for Ops. "We're never going to get all of these people through the house in one night!"

"Yeah, I know," Lon said. "Can you let everyone know that they have to speed up their throughput tonight? I don't want to ruin the impact, but we have to move this line faster."

"I would, but Lucio has been missing for the past hour, so I've been working his room. That's why I'm here. Have you seen him?"

Lon shook his head and frowned. "Fine time to get lost. Parker is a zombie – he's downstairs in the basement near the Romero Atrocity. Can you grab him and send him up to the room? We have plenty of people down there tonight and I need you roving to help people out. I need to go back outside and help with crowd management."

"Sure," Jeanie said. "But I wish I knew where Lucio was. I spent a ton of time on his makeup tonight. I wanted him to be seen."

"Yeah," Lon agreed. "I'm just glad we got some extra haunters for this week. Because we sure need the help tonight."

He got up and closed the laptop screen where it sat on the sink. "Just four more hours until the witching hour!" he announced.

Jeanie held her guts out for several groups as she tried to move down the hallway to the basement. She had to stay in character, which meant that every few steps she had to stop and mug for a group of visitors. The house was alive with screams and laughter – though mostly screams. Eerie music streamed from every room and groups of people were going room to room just yards apart from each other. They'd never allowed people to stack up this thick before. The ticket takers were already moving people through the house at twice the speed and volume as they had earlier in the week.

She reached the basement finally, and quickly moved to the left side of the room before another group confronted her. She saw Parker lurking to the right of a prop zombie. He stood still as a statue, but she knew the makeup. She stopped and waited, as there was a crowd of people moving toward the exhibit ahead of her.

Parker's gimmick was to let the group be lulled by the 'fake' bodies in the display space and then, just before they moved on to the next display, he came to life. His gray hands touched the shoulders of one of the women, and she shrieked as if she'd been stabbed. Her boyfriend or husband laughed, and she slapped him. "Ass!" she said, but he pulled her down the aisle away from Parker, who was now lurching toward another girl in the group. The girl had her own zombie makeup on and Jeanie grinned as she saw it. Peeling flesh, glistening red blood around her mouth...the girl had done a good job.

Parker held out both hands toward her, as if to hug her. "Friendddd," he growled.

The girl laughed and swatted his arm away. "Freshhhh!" she said, and quickly ran to rejoin her friends.

Jeanie hurried forward then, before another group turned up behind her.

"Nice one," she said. "I thought you had a new recruit there for a minute."

"She just doesn't appreciate my sensitive side," Parker moaned.

"You mean the side that has watched *Return of the Living Dead* thirty times?"

"It's a deeply moving examination of the youth culture in our society and their need for connection."

"That and Linnea Quigley lies naked on a gravestone."

"You just don't appreciate the deep and life-changing symbolism of that moment," he said.

"Uh-huh," Jeanie said. "Hey, Lon asked me to come down and get you. Lucio disappeared somewhere and we need a zombie in his room. He wanted to move you up there."

Parker shrugged. "I can stagger and beg for brains wherever he wants me."

"Cool," she said. Then she nodded toward the exhibit, which had both the standing zombie at the side and another one half crouched in the back. In between was a row of gravestones. Next to one of them, a hand emerged from the fake earth. And nearby, a body lay bloody and disheveled. One hand was draped over a gravestone, as if it were trying to crawl away when the end came.

"Did Lucio add that this week?" she asked, pointing at the bloody body. "I don't remember that prop there before."

Parker nodded. "Yeah – he must have brought it down this afternoon, because it wasn't there yesterday. Pretty freakin' awesome though, isn't it? You almost feel like the blood is fresh and wet."

Footsteps tramped down the stairs behind them, and Jeanie grinned. "You better take care of this group and then head up," she said. "I'll go check on Maggie while I'm down here."

"She's by the Wax Museum," he said.

"Thanks," Jeanie said and began walking as quickly as she could without attracting attention toward the middle of the basement. Behind her, she heard the chatter of a group, and then the sudden growl and scream as Parker leapt out at them. Jeanie smiled. Damn, she was going to miss this. She was already thinking ahead to next year.

CHAPTER THIRTY-FIVE

"He's asleep now?" Katie said.

Emery put her hand on his forehead and drew her fingers lightly across his forehead.

Mike didn't stir.

She nodded.

Katie pointed at the small dresser. "Take the knife and the glass, and get some of my blood in it."

"But I can't cut you, you're not…" Emery said slowly.

"From my real body," Katie said. "Go downstairs. I need my blood to be inside him tonight."

Emery nodded, picked up the implements and climbed up the steps to leave the room.

Katie stood over Mike's body and smiled. "Soon," she promised. "You and I will truly be bound together as one, just as you've wished for. I hope you'll still feel the same when it happens."

★　　★　　★

When Emery's feet returned a few minutes later, and stepped slowly down the ladder, she set a glass down on the tiny nightstand next to the bed. It was about a quarter full of a dark liquid. She set down the blade next to it. The blade was stained.

"Now what?" she asked.

"He needs to drink this from me," Katie said. "Once he does, I can join with him for a short time, while my blood is mingled with his and running through his veins. Lift his head and feed him my communion."

Emery put one hand behind Mike's snoring head and propped him forward. He was heavy, and she didn't get his head far up from the pillow. But it was enough. With her free hand, she held the glass to his lips. His head remained angled backward, his mouth parallel to the ceiling. Emery pressed the glass down on his lower lip until she could see the dark space between his teeth.

And then she poured.

Mike's throat gulped automatically and he choked. Flecks of blood escaped the sides of his lips, but the majority of the blood from Katie's 'unborn' body remained in his throat.

"Perfect," Katie said, and Emery let his head rest back on the bed. A trickle of blood slid from the corner of his lips to disappear down his neck. The ghost of the witch climbed onto the bed and lay down on top of the carpenter's body.

She kissed his sleeping mouth briefly, and then said something. Her voice was silent, but her lips moved and she stared into Mike's sleeping face.

A moment later, her body began to sink, as if he were quicksand and she was trapped in his pull.

Just seconds later, she had fully disappeared into his form.

Mike's head shook, as if fighting off a bad dream. His arms moved too, grabbing at the steel points that served as the mattress of the bed.

Then he opened his eyes, and sat up to slide his legs over the side of the bed. He raised one arm and looked at it. Then he flexed the other hand in front of his face.

Mike's lips split into a wide smile.

He stood up, walked past Emery, and climbed up the stairs.

CHAPTER THIRTY-SIX

"You've got the switchblade, right?" J.T. asked.

Nikki nodded. "How many times are you going to ask that?"

"I'm just anxious," J.T. said. "Did you put the blood packs in or do we need to find a bathroom?"

Nikki shook her head. "If I slap you in the head a few times, do you think it would break some of your brain free?"

J.T. grinned. "This is going to be so awesome. We'll just see about who is scaring who here tonight."

J.T. and Nikki had gone through the house the weekend before, and when they'd reached the Argento room, a man in a black mask and gloves had leapt out at Nikki so fast and threatened her with the knife so close that she'd literally peed her pants. J.T. had jumped, himself, but when they left the room, he was not amused. When Nikki whispered to him that she needed to change her pants, he shook his head in anger.

"That's too much," he'd said. "They're going too far. I'm going to get our money back when we get out of here."

But the ticket taker had refused a refund, suggesting that if they got the piss scared out of them, the house had done exactly what it promised.

That had not set well with J.T., and he'd stewed on it for a couple days before coming up with his solution.

Scare the crap right back out of the people in the haunted house. How? By surprising them with something they wouldn't expect.

"We'll start with that bastard in the black mask," J.T. said.

"If we ever get inside," Nikki said.

"Almost there," he said. Then he pointed. "Look, they're taking that whole group in at once."

A dozen people in front of them all marched up the steps and disappeared inside, and then one of the wranglers walked down the line asking for the number of people in each party. A group of three and another group of five were ahead of them. J.T. held up his first two fingers and the wrangler nodded and checked on two more parties before returning to the front of the line. They only waited a couple more minutes and then they were being ushered up the steps and into the house.

"What if he doesn't buy it?" Nikki asked.

"He'll buy it if you do what we practiced," J.T. promised.

They passed through the *Texas Chainsaw Massacre* dining room and ducked around the hulking Leatherface that darted toward them with a chainsaw held high.

They didn't slow down in the kitchen to let the bloody girl on the floor try to lure them in for a jump scare. Instead, they moved quickly down the hall to the first bedroom, where the masked killer had been last week. As they stepped into the room, they heard the tense music cycling in the background, and the lights flared.

It was a gimmick; the room was wired with motion sensors to trigger things whenever someone walked into the room. J.T. knew that the killer lay in wait just behind the old couch. Instead of moving further into the room to trigger the cue for the killer, he stayed near the door, and took the chain that he'd attached to a leather collar around Nikki's neck.

He noticed that another haunter stood still in the shadows in the back of the room. Nice. He'd get to freak out two of them.

"I'm not coming in any farther until I see you," J.T. called out. "I know you're waiting behind the couch. Stand up."

A black-gloved hand slipped fingers over the top of the couch back and then the black shine of a leather hood appeared. The figure stood, holding a long silver blade in its free hand. It began a silent walk toward them.

"Hold it right there," J.T. commanded.

The figure hesitated. J.T. laughed inside; he was sure the guy was not used to anyone ordering him around while in costume. Probably didn't know quite what to think right now. Which was exactly what he wanted at this moment. This scare was *his* to give.

J.T. suddenly yanked Nikki's chain and pulled her in close to him. He put one arm across her throat and pulled the switchblade out. Then he tripped the release and the blade shot out. He held it in front of her face.

"I want to see your face beneath that mask," J.T. said. "Take it off."

The figure did not comply. Instead, it began to move toward J.T. and Nikki.

"I'm serious," J.T. warned. "I want your mask. I've always wanted your mask. Give it to me. And your gloves too."

The figure hesitated, but then held its own knife out and took another step toward J.T.

"This is not a joke," J.T. warned. He held the blade of his knife above Nikki's left breast. "I'll kill her right here in front of you if you don't take off your hood and give it to me right now. This is not a joke."

The guy froze. He clearly didn't know which way to turn. He was pretending to be a psycho and scaring people, but here was a real possible psycho in the room with him. J.T. guessed the guy probably was shitting a brick right now wondering exactly what was going on here.

"That's it," J.T. said. "I gave you the chance, and you decided your mask was more important than this poor girl's life. Her blood is on your hands."

He lifted his knife away from Nikki's chest and the guy began to move toward him quickly.

"No, wait!" the guy yelled.

But J.T. just smiled and brought the switchblade down hard. He felt the haft smash into the thin plastic bag of blood just beneath Nikki's shirt, as the trick blade retracted.

Her shirt suddenly blossomed blood, as the hooded man reached out toward them.

Nikki screamed on cue.

"Back up, man," J.T. yelled.

He pulled the knife back, thumbing the mechanism to release the blade again so that to an onlooker it appeared as if he pulled a deadly blade back out of Nikki's chest. He held it up again as if he were going to stab her once more. Nikki screamed and thrashed in his grasp, just as they'd practiced.

"No, no," the black-masked man cried. "Don't! I'll give you the mask."

The man dropped his blade on the floor and reached around to the back of his head and unzipped the leather so that he could slip it over his head. "Don't hurt her anymore."

The guy yanked the hood over his head to reveal a near-bald, black scalp and threw the mask on the floor in front of J.T.

"Let her go," the man said, as he began peeling off his gloves.

J.T. found it funny somehow that it was a black guy underneath the black leather mask. The whites of the man's eyes seemed to glow in the weird lighting of the room, and J.T. shook his head.

"Too late," he said, and slammed his knife down again, smashing another bag of fake blood which instantly soaked through Nikki's shirt.

She screamed and threw her head back as J.T. pulled his knife-hand back up and showed the unhooded man his knife.

"I wanted to do that with your hood," J.T. said. He let go of Nikki and she crumbled, falling to the floor. The chain clanked to the wood next to her. "But maybe I'll just have to wear it while I kill you!"

The man backed away from him, and put both hands in the air in front of his chest.

"No man, c'mon, I just work here. My name's Lenny. I'm not a real killer or anything. I'm just here to make it a good time for everyone, you know what I mean? This isn't even the normal room I work. I'm usually in the *Nightmare on Elm Street* room. Do you like Freddy Krueger?"

J.T. bent down and picked up the hood. He grinned as he felt the leather between his fingers. This was playing out exactly the way he'd hoped. The guy was eating it up.

"Get down on your knees," J.T. demanded.

The guy dropped to his knees instantly, and J.T. stifled a snort. This was too easy.

"Now put both of your hands on your chest."

The guy complied, and J.T. smiled. "I'm going to see how it feels to be you," he said, and pulled the other man's 'killer' hood quickly over his head. He adjusted it with one hand as he held the knife out toward the kneeling man to keep him still.

Nikki lay still on the floor, presumably dead.

"I wanted you to have a taste of your own medicine," J.T. said as he stepped closer to the man with his knife raised high in the air. The feeling of the hood over his face was energizing. He felt as if he really could knife the guy and walk away untouched.

"Please just let me go," Lenny cried. He took his hands off his chest and J.T. shook his head. "Oh, no," he taunted. "I don't think so."

J.T. raised his knife high in the air, and Lenny cowered, shaking his head and leaning backward.

And then suddenly Lenny's mouth gaped open.

His eyes bugged wide.

J.T. didn't know what he was doing at first, and then the man's frightened eyes looked down. J.T. followed the man's gaze.

A triangular barb of metal protruded from between Lenny's fingers. A splash of gore painted his knuckles.

"Oh, that just fucking figures," Lenny wheezed. "I told June the black guy always gets it."

J.T. looked up, confused at what had happened. The figure from the far end of the room moved toward them. She had some kind of arrow launcher in her arms.

He realized then that he'd been made.

What he had been doing to the 'hooded killer', she was doing to him. Only…she was using real weapons. Blood streamed across the kneeling man's knuckles and there was no way that it was fake. Lenny gasped one last time before toppling over to hit the ground.

J.T. looked up and met the eyes of the woman who held the weapon. Her face was blank, as if she didn't have a thought in her head other than to put a spear through his heart. "Get up, Nikki," he said through gritted teeth. Then he turned to leave the room.

Something clattered to the floor behind him and J.T. couldn't help but look back. It was a fatal distraction. The woman in the cowl had dropped her arrow launcher and now held a long silver knife in the air, not dissimilar to the fake one that J.T. had used to 'stab' Nikki. And she was almost on top of him.

"Wait," he begged, but the glint of metal was already in the air and moving. When it hit him in the chest, for a moment he barely felt a thing. It was as if the woman had tapped him.

And then the pain began. The heat spread down his ribs and his shirt suddenly felt heavy and wet.

"Why?" he asked. This wasn't fake. He'd hoped the guy with an arrow through his chest was somehow false, despite everything, but this… this was his own death.

J.T. sank to his knees, holding the wound in his heart. He knew that he wasn't getting out of this alive. Behind him, he heard Nikki finally moving. Finally realizing that something had gone wrong.

"J.T.," she finally said. "What's the matter?"

He opened his mouth to tell her, but when he did, he choked instead, and something hot and thick suddenly slipped over his lips.

"Go," he whispered, and fell backward then, landing on the floor next to her feet.

Nikki screamed.

J.T. felt something weird spreading across his chest. Not a cold feeling, but not hot either. It was the same and different, everything and nothing, and he knew that it meant only one thing.

The end.

"Run," he croaked with his last gasp of energy.

She bent over him for a second, her face a mask of horror and concern and fear.

"Please," he begged.

She got up then, finally realizing that she was in danger. But it was too late.

J.T. saw the pale fat girl move toward Nikki, with the knife that was still red with his blood held over her head. She didn't say a word, but simply brought it down fast and hard.

Nikki's eyes went wide and she squealed for a second. It wasn't a yell or a shriek…just a thin sound of tortured surprise.

And then she fell to the ground next to J.T.

He tried to say her name, but nothing happened. No words would come out. And his arms wouldn't move.

J.T.'s last vision was of the killer wiping Nikki's blood off her blade with her fingers and walking away.

CHAPTER THIRTY-SEVEN

"How are things with Jeanie?" June asked.

Bong had crept out of his hiding spot for a few seconds between customers. Though he knew they didn't have much time. The groups were moving through the house fast tonight.

"She's still pissed off," he said. "I can't blame her, but I can't really prove to her that nothing was really happening either. At least she drove in with me tonight."

"That's something," she agreed. "I'm sorry if I got you in trouble."

Bong shook his head. "I got me in trouble, and I'm not completely sorry."

June raised her eyebrow.

"The best thing about doing this whole haunted house thing was meeting you. I'm not sorry about that."

June smiled. "I'm not sorry about that either. But I really like Jeanie. I didn't want to do anything to hurt her. She hasn't talked to me at all the last three nights."

Bong nodded. "She's stubborn. But she'll come around."

"Are you guys going to come to the after party tonight?" she asked.

"Are you going to throw your arms around me and kiss me there?" he asked.

June snorted. "Would you be happy if I did?"

"Not the right question," Bong said.

"Okay," she said. "Do you want me to?"

Bong shifted, suddenly looking uncomfortable. "Also, not the right question."

Something creaked on the wood planks outside, and Bong stepped back. "I think we have company."

A guy with a short blond goatee and a black shirt that had a ski mask design on it stepped into the room. He pulled a woman wearing a *Nightmare Before Christmas* sweatshirt into the room after him. Bong ducked back out of sight before they saw him. He hoped.

June played it perfectly. She faded back at first, and then, when the guy saw her, she lunged forward again, staggering and clutching at the gash in her neck. The *Nightmare* girl pulled back but her boyfriend laughed.

"Come on," he said. "She's just dead, she's not scary."

That was, more or less, Bong's cue.

He started out of the hidden passage on the floor, moving with an awkward crab crawl toward them. When the guy registered that something was coming at him on the floor, he looked down and then leapt a yard away from her.

"Shit," he complained.

His girlfriend jumped with him. But she didn't scream. She pointed at Bong and said, "It's just like that movie *The Ring*."

"Yeah, or *Tomie*," he agreed. "Nice one," he said, pointing at Bong. "You got me there."

Then he pulled his girlfriend around June and back out of the room to take the stairwell down. He didn't acknowledge June at all.

When they disappeared, Bong stood up and grinned. "Well, I guess I got them."

June pouted a little. "Yeah. Well…they didn't think I looked creepy at all."

Bong smiled. "Sure they did. They were just too afraid to say anything. I thought you were great."

June stepped closer to him and shook her head. "The gash isn't what's making them freak in this room," she said. "You're doing the work."

"Without your gash, I couldn't scare them," Bong said.

"That's so romantic of you," she said.

"You think that's romantic?"

"I take what I can get."

Bong suddenly felt nervous. He hadn't wanted to start something with June. And he'd been telling Jeanie that there wasn't anything, that the kiss a couple nights ago had been an accident. Just a crazy moment.

But now….

"What exactly do you want to take?" he asked.

"What exactly will you give?" she answered, moving closer. "I'd take a kiss again."

Bong felt his heart pounding suddenly. June had been totally cool the past couple nights, no flirtation. And he'd been both disappointed and thankful. Now…he was nervous. He didn't want to lose Jeanie. And he didn't want to say no to June. Classic love triangle disaster in the making.

"I guess a kiss couldn't hurt," he said. As he did, he looked at the doorway. Would not be good if Jeanie walked in again right at that moment.

Before he turned his head back, June's lips were touching his. He closed his eyes and savored the touch. Forbidden and wrong. But he couldn't pretend she didn't feel good. He'd run their first kiss over and over again in his head like a film loop this week and he ultimately had to admit that he wasn't sorry for it. June was really amazing.

The problem was, he loved Jeanie.

The other problem was…he was really feeling like he liked June a lot too.

He returned the kiss.

When he looked up, there was a woman in the doorway.

His stomach leapt, as his first thought was that it was Jeanie.

But it wasn't.

It was a woman, but he hadn't seen her before. She filled the doorframe. And she held a knife in her hand.

"We have company," he whispered, pulling back from June's touch.

"Shit," June whispered and backed away. Starting a 'scare' with a kiss was not exactly optimum haunt behavior.

Bong backed away from her, but he knew he couldn't 'disappear'. Instead, he tried to get in a position where he could at least be…less seen.

The woman walked into the room, and as she did, Bong quickly realized she wasn't a normal 'guest'. She didn't have the same hesitant step as a normal haunted house patron. She walked with a purpose. And she was walking directly toward them.

Bong raised his arms, and opened his mouth as if he were a vampiric ghost.

The woman raised her arms, and that's when he saw she held a knife.

A long, silver, very real-looking knife.

CHAPTER THIRTY-EIGHT

Jeanie was shambling through the front of the house when she saw Lon standing in the foyer. He ushered a group of five teenagers into the *Texas Chainsaw Massacre* room and then motioned her over.

"What's up?" she asked.

"I've gotten a half dozen different complaints tonight from people who've gotten their clothes ruined. Big red stains on them from somewhere. I don't know what you guys did different tonight with makeup, but we're going to end up with a bunch of dry cleaning bills."

"I didn't do anything different," Jeanie said. "Maybe someone spilled something. Did any of them say what room they got it in?"

Lon shook his head. "Nope. They haven't noticed it until they're outside and walking to their cars. And then they double back to complain to me or Andreas at the ticket stand."

Jeanie shrugged. "Well, I don't know what to tell you. I can keep a look out but I haven't seen anything messy so far tonight."

The house manager nodded. "Keep your eyes open. If you see anything…clean it up. I don't want to end the month on a big drag. They're rubbing up against something messy somewhere."

"I'll look," Jeanie said. "But if people are getting messed up, they must be banging into someone. It's not like we poured fake blood on the walls or props. That stuff's all dry."

Lon made a face. "Well somebody dumped some shit somewhere."

Jeanie shook her head. There was only one answer that was going to be acceptable, so she gave it. "On it."

"Good," Lon said, and ducked back out the front door. She stole a glimpse after him and saw the line still stretched down the gravel path and out of sight. She hoped Lon was cutting it off soon; it was already after ten p.m.

She decided to take a walk through the whole place from the start to see if she could spot any fake blood spills to make Lon happy. She couldn't imagine why there would be any though. Jeanie walked down the hall to the *Nightmare on Elm Street* room. When she looked inside, she saw someone disappear into the closet. She assumed it was whoever was wearing the Freddy suit tonight. Angie was hanging from the harness in the ceiling, the front of her nightshirt shredded and stained in red.

"How's it hanging?" she called into the room, but Angie didn't say a word. She just hung there, staring at Jeanie.

"Nice," she said. "Fine, stay in character."

She backed out of the door before a group trapped her in the room. Seconds later a couple slipped by her and entered the room. She heard the guy exclaim in awe, "Wicked!"

Jeanie moved down the hallway and decided to go upstairs to check on Bong and June.

The attic was strangely quiet. The last group must have just moved through and headed down the back stairs because nothing was moving here. Above her, hanging from the ceiling, was a new prop. She looked and grinned. It was super realistic. A woman with blue hair, a tight black t-shirt and bare feet hung from the rafters on a rope noose. That noose had been hanging dramatically empty for the month, but she appreciated that someone had finally filled it. A bit too little, too late, though. What was the point on the last night?

Jeanie walked beneath the figure and felt something wet splash on her face. When she touched a finger to her cheek, it came away shiny and red.

"What the fuck?" she said, and looked up at the figure again. She could see now that the woman had cut marks all down her arms and chest. And those marks appeared to be dripping with blood.

"So that's where the mess is coming from," she said. Jeanie looked at the floor beneath the figure and realized it was slick with red. "Stupid," she said. "No wonder people are getting their clothes fucked up."

She'd have to see if Mike could come up and cut it down quickly before anyone else got dripped on. What the hell did they hang it up there wet for? She shook her head and walked through the costume maze. Somehow, it seemed creepier tonight, probably because Bill and Tanya weren't jumping out at her. Speaking of which…where were they?

She frowned and walked over to the nursery. It was weird to have a nursery and no kids in the house, but Bong had been pretty effective in jumping out at people from his hidden vantage point. The room was scoring well with attendees, at least the ones they'd quizzed on the way out. Lon had been trying to gather some data from visitors on what they liked and what they didn't like over the past week as they left the place. He was already thinking about next year.

She ducked her head under the ragged overhang. The entry to the room was supposed to be reminiscent of the room in the climax of *House on Sorority Row*, though Jeanie doubted that anyone would ever place it. Especially since, though you walked into a room that was filled with a child's nursery items, instead of a kid or mutant childlike adult, you got a throat-slashed woman and a J-horror creeping adult. A little mix-and-match with the monsters.

Whatever. It had proven a solid room throughout the month, despite the mixed theme.

"Hey," she said, as she poked her head inside.

June was lying on the floor. Which wasn't usual. Ghosts didn't usually act like corpses. The weird thing was that she was covered in blood. Her whole gimmick had been a kind of zombie thing, with a throat slash. But tonight, she looked like someone had slashed her arms and legs and chest and…well…everything. She had cuts and blood splatter all over her.

Jeanie had to admit the effect was solid. But…she hadn't seen June do it. The last time she'd seen her, she just had the neck slash, as she had worn all month.

"Going all out tonight, huh?" she said. There was grudging admiration in her statement. At the same time, she looked at June and stifled a voice inside that said, *Too bad those aren't real, bitch.*

"Coast is clear for a second," she said with false buoyance, and looked away from June. "Bong?"

There was no answer.

Jeanie walked over to the faux hallway where she knew he hid, ready to crabwalk out when new 'victims' entered the room.

Bong was there, on the floor, where he usually was.

Jeanie screamed.

Because Bong wasn't going to be crabwalking out of the corridor again tonight.

His fingers were reaching out to the floor behind him, while his toes hung down on the blood-smeared floor near his vacant face.

Someone had chopped off his arms and legs and left them lying on top of his torso…only in the reverse order of where they should be. The raw gristle of his thigh was propped on the meaty opening where his arm should emanate. And vice versa.

"Oh my God, oh my God, *oh my fucking God!*" Jeanie screamed.

She looked back at June and realized the makeup artist had not added fake blood to her ensemble tonight. She had been slashed to death.

The blood was not makeup.

Jeanie dropped to her knees and reached out to Bong…but her fingers stopped short of touching him. Because…his feet were pointed at her, rather than his arms.

"Why?" she cried, and touched her fingers to his bare, bloody leg.

Somebody in the outside attic room screamed. It didn't sound like the scream of someone scared. It sounded like someone being killed.

"What's going on?" she whispered. Her stomach was suddenly a hard, clenched ball of fear. It hadn't all really sunk in yet, but she knew that Bong was dead, and she was in danger.

Self-preservation took priority over her emotions for the moment. Jeanie walked to the doorway, and carefully peered around the jamb.

Another scream echoed from the attic area outside.

Jeanie could only see the shifting blue and purple light reflecting off an old hag costume on the rack in front of her. A man's voice suddenly cried out from the direction of the stairwell.

"Please just let me go, I won't tell anyone, I promise."

A moment later, she heard something like a wet punch. There was something else, another soft noise she couldn't place. And a soft thud.

Then the eerie synthesizer music took over.

Jeanie stood there for what seemed like forever, breathing as quietly as she could. She hugged the wall and stared at the vacant eyes of the old hag mask, crazy gray hair streaming out in all directions around the face.

At any moment, she expected it to jump off the rack at her.

But the hag stayed still.

Jeanie started walking slowly down the aisle, straining to see past the 'maze' of weird costumes and masks that separated the 'secret attic nursery' room from the entrance to the attic. The bass on the soundtrack playing overhead was throbbing in a steady, tense rhythm. For the first time all month, Jeanie really wasn't happy to have the soundtrack to a horror movie playing overhead. She loved horror movies…but she didn't want to be in a real-life one.

She moved down the wall, step by step, until the main area of the attic finally came into view. She saw the feet of the corpse hanging from the ceiling and it suddenly dawned on her that it wasn't a prop. It was a dead body, hanging from the rope.

Bleeding.

Underneath the hanging body's feet, two other bodies lay spread out on the floor. A woman lay there on her back, black hair splashed across the wood like an explosion. Her pink t-shirt was soaked in the center with dark red color.

A man was just a couple feet away. He was curled into a half-ball on the floor, as if trying to shield himself from something. His back faced the woman's corpse and his hands were pressed outward, as if trying to drive something back. Someone had taken more time with him; his shirt had been cut to shreds (without concern for the flesh beneath it) and his shorts had been sliced down the thigh, opening them to the private spaces within.

Those…had been removed.

"Jesus," Jeanie whispered, as she saw the glob of red flesh that lay against the corner of the far wall.

Part of her knew what organ the glob was, and part of her refused to acknowledge it, despite seeing the man's pants cut open, and the splash of blood that stained the half-shorts that remained around his waist, and the wooden floor beneath him.

Somebody in the house had slashed the throat and chest of this guy's girlfriend, and then cut off his 'nads. Jeanie was about to run for the stairs down, when someone began walking up.

She saw the black hair of a thin, weathered woman with her hair tied in a ponytail, along with another fatter, pale-looking woman in a black t-shirt, plastic glasses and a plaid skirt, ascend the stairs and step onto the floor of the attic.

She saw them look at the hanging woman, and then down at the floor where the butchered bodies lay. She saw them grimace and then grudgingly approve, through the shifting lines of their faces.

And then she saw the figure moving behind the old bureau that stood on the side of the stairwell up. It was another woman, she noted, with bare pale arms, and a hand holding a long silver blade above her head.

The two women who had just walked up the stairs gave a typical, low intensity shriek and began to move quickly toward the costume maze.

Only, the knife woman followed.

And she wasn't there simply to scare.

The blade came down and stabbed hard and fast into the ponytail woman's shoulder.

The woman looked confused and surprised and hurt all at the same time. It made for a strangely impactful expression on her face as the killer lifted and brought the blade down again and again. The woman crumpled under the stabbing blows, before her friend even realized what was happening.

When she finally turned and saw, the plaid woman screamed. Then she ran toward the stairs. But the woman with the knife moved surprisingly swiftly. She brought the blade around in a horizontal arc and caught the fleeing woman in the cheek. Even in the garish light of the attic, Jeanie could see the line of the cut open, expand and burn red.

Plaid woman screamed and stumbled, slapping one hand to her wounded face. When she lifted it, her hand came back completely covered in blood. Her eyes bugged as she realized how badly she was hurt.

All of this happened in a moment, and in that moment, the killer did not stop moving. She stepped in front of the bleeding woman, lifted the blade and brought it down. Plaid woman made the mistake of looking up, which turned out to be the last mistake she would ever make.

The silver point flashed through the air. Then it connected with her right eye, and slid easily inside her skull.

It all happened in a flash, but the woman dropped like a brick. Her head slid back off the knife, and the killer simply stood back and watched as the plaid woman's body spread out and shivered briefly on the floor. Her hands tremored and grasped toward the stairway, but her legs kicked once and crossed over each other. The rippling flesh of her thighs was exposed all the way to the pale wrinkles of her ass, as the plaid skirt flipped up in the wrong direction. And then she went still.

It was anything but an elegant death.

Jeanie held her breath until the killer moved again. Satisfied, apparently, that she had fully dispatched the woman, the killer turned and walked slowly to the stairs. Jeanie watched as foot by foot her body vanished down the exit until her hair dipped below the floor and disappeared. Then

Jeanie crept out of her hiding place and took a deep breath. The air came in hitches, as she stifled her body from crying and yet still tried to catch her breath. She knelt down next to the body of the plaid woman and pulled her skirt down, giving her a modicum of decency in death. Something warm touched her hand, and she yanked her hand away instinctively. But it was just the growing river of Plaid's life leaking away. Blood was puddling around the woman's body fast.

Jeanie pushed back off the floor and forced herself toward the stairway. She wanted to go back to the farthest reach of the attic, crouch down and hide until daylight. But she knew in her head that she wouldn't be safe until she'd gotten out of the house. And neither would anybody else. Jeanie couldn't just curl up and hide as one by one the woman slashed and killed guest after guest. She had to find Lon and have all the houselights brought up. They had to evacuate the house. Her heart pounded so hard she could barely breathe as she leaned against the wall and crept down, stair by stair.

The house remained full of sound – creaks and moans and the tense tones of synthesizers that made each room feel like you were walking into a movie. And there were still the distant sounds of shrieks and laughter, the sounds of people enjoying a good scare.

But it all sounded smaller somehow, the guests far away. Jeanie knew how long the line was outside, and how fast they should have been cycling people through the house. But nobody had come upstairs in several minutes.

She could hear the chainsaw revving though, down in the dining room. It was a cycle. The motor would whine to life and then crescendo louder. It shook and screamed with deadly promise, usually corresponding to Brad holding it over his head and shaking it at the guests, who would screech and run into the next room.

But right now, while it sounded like Brad was scaring people with the tool, nobody was getting past the next couple of rooms and corridors to walk up the stairs.

Where were they going then?

CHAPTER THIRTY-NINE

The line stretched back to Midlothian Turnpike, and the buzz from the crowd was slowly growing louder as the night went on. Hidden flasks kept many people warm, and others had shown up already well-liquored. People laughed and yelled, and every little while a cop walked up and down the line, watching for…whatever warning signs cops watched for when they were on crowd control duty.

A woman with shock-red, kinked hair and a loose white suit full of multi-colored polka dots nudged a fat man wearing white-face and old bum clothes covered in blood.

"Hey, Ted," she said.

The bum-zombie next to her grunted.

"How much longer do you think?" she asked.

"What difference does it make?"

"Because I'm worried they'll cut off the line if it gets much later."

He shrugged. "Then I guess we'll get a good night's sleep at home."

She elbowed him. "Lotta help you are," she said.

"Sorry, but this just feels like déjà vu. Only this time, we have stupid costumes."

"Mine isn't stupid," she said.

"Like there aren't a thousand evil clowns out on the street tonight," he said.

"That's how I fit in without being noticed," she said.

"Hmmm."

"You have to admit, this should keep us from being stopped at the ticket stand because someone recognizes us."

"Nobody would have recognized us if we'd just come as ourselves," Ted said.

"That guy who called the cops on us last time would have," she answered quickly.

"Maybe. If he was here," Ted said. "But now, since you're in a clown suit, it's going to be really difficult to stay under the radar."

"O ye, of little faith," she said. "Just work with me here."

"The last time I did that, the cops came."

"This is different," she said. "It's the final night. And it's Halloween. If something happens here tonight, I don't think it's *us* that the police are going to be after."

The group ahead of them suddenly surged forward, and Jillie grabbed Ted's arm and squeezed. "There's something going on in there tonight," she said. "I can feel it."

"Indigestion," he said.

"I'm serious," she said. The crowd all around them filled the air with stories and voices, but Jillie still whispered. "I have this horrible, black feeling. Like I've never felt before. It's almost as if someone or something was sucking all of the life out of the sun."

"That's because it's eleven o'clock at night," Ted said. "And the sun went away a long time ago."

Jillie threw her head back to look up at the stars. The night sky was clear and cold. "You're impossible," she said. "Sometimes I don't understand why you do this at all."

"Mainly because of the beef sandwiches you buy me at Nicky's," he said.

"I'm not talking to you anymore."

They stood in silence for a couple minutes, and then surged forward again. There were only a handful of people between them and the ticket taker now. Behind them, there was a sudden wave of voices. They sounded angry. Someone yelled, "Fuck that shit," and another yelled, "Come on, we've been here…."

Ted looked back and then said, "Looks like they finally cut off the line."

Jillie nodded. "Figured that was coming soon. We're good though. We'll be in before midnight, which is all I really wanted."

"You know nothing is going to happen at the Witching Hour, right?" he asked. He looked up at her with black zombie eyes – God she hated those contacts – and raised an eyebrow.

"Maybe not then," she said. "But something *will* happen tonight. I feel like something is already going on in there."

"It's called having a good time," he said.

"Not the things I'm feeling. They don't feel good at all."

Ted had nothing to say to that.

The line moved forward again and suddenly they were standing at the two steps leading up to the porch of the house. "We'll take two," Ted said to the man sitting at the table with a cashbox. He pulled out his wallet to give the man thirty dollars.

"Buyer beware," the man said, and handed Ted their tickets.

"That's what I'm afraid of," Jillie whispered.

Ted didn't answer her, but led them forward toward the door. A man in a black suit with white-face makeup grinned at them through ruby-red lips. Inside Ted groaned at yet another clown outfit. But then the dark clown opened the door, and they stepped inside.

CHAPTER FORTY

Lon took his position in the den. He'd had to leave the ticket stand because for the third time tonight they were missing a haunter. First Lucio, then Brad and now Chris. He'd seen Mike was filling in for Brad when he walked past the dining room. It was too late now, but next year he had to put some strict things in place to stop this from happening. They couldn't run this place on the busiest night of the year with people abandoning posts. Maybe if you didn't show up, you got docked a week's pay?

He shrugged and took an appreciative look around the room. He had to admit, when it was empty, the den was pretty eerie. Between the music that was piped in, the red and blue and green spotlights that lent the room a surreal flavor and the stained glass (false) windows and dark shadows in every corner, the place was definitely prepped to scare.

Lon was prepped to scare too. He wore the grotesque rubber mask of a pustulating rotting corpse figure that looked surprisingly real, and he held a long dangerous-looking axe across his shoulder. Never mind that it was plastic, it *looked* good. If you were standing in front of him and it was pointed at you, you would not have blown it off. You would have backed away in fear.

He'd filled in at this position before, and virtually every time he jumped out from behind one of the alcoves of the room to hold the axe out at the patrons, somebody screamed.

Honestly, Lon hated the sweaty feel of the mask, but he loved the screams. It meant he was doing something right.

Tonight, he held his blade high. It was Halloween. If Argento wasn't here, he wanted to represent the guy well. This room, this costume, was Argento's creation. It's what the designer of this house had wanted.

Wherever Argento was, Lon wanted to make sure his vision was done right.

So he was ready when the door opened for his first 'victim.' He leapt out and stood at the ready with his axe.

The only problem was, the girl at the doorway did not appear in the least bit scared.

Instead, she stepped forward, with a long silver blade of her own cradled on one shoulder.

What is that about? he wondered.

All of his preparation suddenly fell to the floor. He was no longer the guy in place to scare…he was faced with a woman who was scaring *him*. Because…he was pretty sure her weapon was real. And he knew his was certainly not.

"Hey," he said. "Can I help you?"

It was the dumbest 'customer service' phrase he had ever spoken, but he had to say something. Why not ask it before he got cut into tiny scrubs. Why was she here? Who was she? And why was she threatening *him* in his own haunted house?

She didn't have the same kind of interest in communication.

The woman lifted her blade and ran toward him. Suddenly he realized that there wasn't any communication that was going to occur here. There was only victim and killer. And he was on the wrong side of the equation at the moment.

"Wait a minute," he demanded, dropping his fake weapon and frantically looking around for something to hide behind. Some way to avoid her blade. He ducked behind the couch, forcing her to choose which side she'd come after him on. When she hesitated, he ran to the bookcase and frantically toggled the lever to open the secret door.

It opened and he slipped through just as the crack of a blade fractured the shelf his fingers had just touched.

Lon stumbled into the secret room that led to the back stairs into the basement. The star within a circle symbol that had been etched into the center of the floor still remained from whatever Satan worshippers had put it there decades ago.

Argento and his team had played off that, and painted the walls with a series of symbols of witchcraft and the occult.

Lon ran for the stairwell, but the woman swung the long knife at him like a bat. The flat of the blade caught him in the hip hard, knocking him to the floor. He scuttled backward as the blade came down again, the business end this time, catching for a second in the floor before she pulled it up again and readied to strike.

He pulled himself up but there was nowhere to go. Lon stood face to face with the girl, and realized that he was really up shit creek here. This was not a prank. This girl was deadly serious. Her dark brown eyes never seemed to blink. Her jaw was clenched with fatal determination. She stepped relentlessly forward, one foot at a time, forcing him to the wall. A giant Ouija board was painted on the wall behind him and out of the corner of his eye he could see the arc of its letters. His face was next to the K.

"You don't want to hurt me, I work here," he said. "I'm helping to haunt this haunted house."

She shook her head, and pinned him against the back wall with her body. Then she held the blade to his neck.

"You can't haunt a house until you're dead," she said. "But I can help there."

She stepped back and with one fast motion brought the heavy blade up and then down, whispering one word as it connected with his face.

"Goodbye."

CHAPTER FORTY-ONE

Jeanie put her foot down on the plank floor that Mike had laid at the bottom of the stairs, and felt her heel slide forward. She lost her balance, but grabbed for the banister and saved herself from falling on her ass. When she righted herself, she looked down to see what she'd slipped on.

"Oh fuck," she whispered.

The floor was a river of red.

She looked to the left, and three bodies lay there in a row, their throats cut from ear to ear. When she looked to the right, the scene was worse. One by one she counted the bodies. Seventeen. Counting the ones on the right, there were twenty people dead in this hallway.

"Why?" she whispered as tears slid down her cheeks. She knew her makeup was running down to her chin, and for once in her life, it didn't matter.

Jeanie pursed her lips and forced herself to step forward, ignoring the fact that she was walking through pools of blood. She had to get to the front of the house, and find out if anybody was still alive. The chainsaw still whirred, so that said someone was still up front.

She resisted the urge to tiptoe, and instead walked flatfooted down the slippery hallway. The last thing she wanted to do was slip and find herself coated in the death of twenty people.

As she passed the Argento room, she looked inside and saw a man and a woman lying on the floor. And then she stifled a cry as she saw the dark face of Lenny lying equally still nearby. Her stomach clenched and she balled up a fist to wipe her eyes.

This really wasn't a dream.

She walked to the end of the hall to peer into the *Nightmare on Elm Street* room, and saw Angie hanging in her invisible harness from the ceiling, as she did every night. What was not the same as every night was the blood, which was literally raining down on the bed below. Jeanie restrained the urge to barf. This was not an effect. Angie was dead and bleeding as she hung upside down from the ceiling.

She refused to look again and turned back to the hall.

Jeanie stepped carefully past the dead bodies, worried that at any minute the killer would return around the corner. But the hallway remained empty of life. Step by step, she made her way to the end. When she reached the corner, she peered around to the right, and could see the black glass of a window at the front of the house looking out onto Bachelor's Grove.

The LED lights tucked into the corners of the hallway flared red and purple in the sidewell of her vision as she peered into the back entrance to the dining room.

The screams of the house seemed to have diminished now, and all she really heard were the tense notes of the Goblin soundtrack playing nearby and the buzz of an angry saw.

"Where is everyone?" she whispered, and hugged the wall closer.

She couldn't believe that nobody had tracked her down already.

Somebody screamed in the room ahead, and she didn't fade back. Instead, she stepped around the corner and into the room. She stood in the back quarter of the dining room that represented the *Texas Chainsaw Massacre* movie. The room was shaped like an L so she couldn't see the main attraction yet. Just around the corner she got a glimpse of Brad hefting the chainsaw. He was playing his part well; the blade of the tool rose into the air frequently and she could hear the patrons screaming in answer. But she couldn't see who he was threatening with it. Or what they did when he made the blades whine.

Jeanie crept forward, trying to see what was going on in the room ahead without anyone actually seeing her. She peered around the corner of the L finally and stifled a gasp.

There was a hole in the floor next to the 'cannibal' table. A big open rectangle cut through the floorboards that had not been there before. It was right in the path that people were supposed to take to walk through the *Texas Chainsaw Massacre* room. She crouched down, so that her head wouldn't be seen above the table, and slipped along the wall to position herself on the far side of the table. Even though the killer seemed to have left Brad alone, she instinctively didn't want to be seen. The killer could be lurking right around the corner.

But what the hell was with the hole in the floor?

As she reached the front corner of the room, its meaning became clear.

A group of four turned the corner. Two couples in their mid-twenties stepped into the room; they all looked as if they were well on their way to a hangover. One man with shaggy black hair took his arm off his thin, hawk-nosed girlfriend and threw it in the air in a fist. "Groovy!" he yelled.

"Wrong movie, asshat!" the other man said. "It's more like, 'You wanna have dinner with us? My brother makes great head cheese.' Get it?" he pointed at the head on the dining room table. "Head cheese?"

Brad/Leatherface had secreted himself against the back wall until the group was fully in the room, and then he revved the chainsaw and jumped forward behind them. The only way for them to go was forward...only, there was a big hole in the floor there.

"Nice," the 'Groovy' guy said. But almost immediately, his girlfriend screamed as the chainsaw clipped her on the arm. A gouge of red appeared instantly.

"Holy shit," the boyfriend said. "That thing's real!"

He turned to face down Leatherface.

"What the fuck man, you just hurt her for real! What do you think you're doing?"

Leatherface didn't say a thing. Instead, he simply revved the engine and jabbed forward with the chainsaw on full speed. It caught the complainer in the gut and suddenly the air of the room was filled with a red-hot mist. And the sounds of a hideous scream.

Leatherface pushed the chainsaw forward until the whirring blade came out the other side, next to the spine of the complainer. Then he pulled back the tool and let the body fall backward, into and through the hole in the floor. He held up the tool as the other three stood on the edge of the hole, screaming. Then he brought it down fast, catching the arm of the girl he'd already wounded.

But this time, it was more than a wound.

Shirt and skin and blood sprayed into the air and the girl's arm suddenly fell free. The knuckles of her lost hand hit the floor first, but then the arm toppled over, disappearing into the black space behind.

The girl grabbed for her shoulder, now spraying blood like a tiny hose, and seconds later, fell backward to join her lost arm.

That left the other couple, who teetered on the edge.

"Over the table," the guy screamed, and dove between the manikin figures toward the bloody props displayed on platters. But Leatherface didn't miss a beat. He brought the chainsaw down and severed the man's right hand. The fingers were still clutching for the tablecloth when the guy pulled back and screamed, blood spraying from the stump below his wrist. His girlfriend or wife echoed his scream and grabbed for his torso, but then turned her head away in disgust when she was suddenly sprayed in his blood.

Leatherface waved the chainsaw behind and in front of them. They twisted and turned, their feet just barely on the edge of the hole. And then the man lost his balance and toppled into the chasm. The woman grabbed for him, but all she managed to do was lose her own balance in the process of trying to save him. They disappeared into the hole, and a second later, the air filled with a sharp, horrible shriek. And then the only sound in the room was the background music soundtrack, and the idling groan of the chainsaw.

That wasn't Brad wearing the Leatherface mask.

Jeanie crept slowly along the floor out of sight behind the table. Maybe she could get on the other side of the madman and make a break for the front door before he turned from the hole.

But then she put her hand down on something soft.

Jeanie's whole body went stiff. Her hand had touched someone's arm. She looked down and saw Brad's stubbled jaw just a couple feet away.

But that was all she could see of Brad's head. Because the top half had been sawn off at the eyes.

Jeanie wanted to throw up. But she knew if she made a move of any kind, she'd be chopped up just like the foursome now at the bottom of the hole. She pressed herself tight against the corner of the room, trying to remain unseen in the shadow. Just a prop, not someone to be sawn up.

Leatherface returned to his own position standing back against the wall, awaiting the next group to appear.

No wonder nobody had been getting upstairs, Jeanie thought. They were all at the bottom of a hole, chainsawed into pieces. Everyone had to pass through this room before reaching the stairs.

Something tickled her nose. Maybe it was the smell of the blue smoke from the chainsaw. The room was thick with ghostly clouds that hung like demons in the air. She wrinkled her nostrils and breathed through her mouth, trying to hold the feeling down. Still, that tickle in the back of her nose grew and grew until her eyes began to water.

And then it couldn't be denied and came out, all in a loud, angry sneeze.

Leatherface turned and the eyes behind the mask glinted in the low red light.

She didn't move, but Jeanie knew he saw her. And then it suddenly dawned on her who the man behind the mask had to be. She knew his build, and his work shoes. He wore the same blue-checked flannel shirt she'd seen for weeks working around the house before showtime.

"Mike?" she whispered.

He revved the chainsaw and began walking toward her. Jeanie darted back the way she'd entered, but instead, Leatherface turned back and ran out of the room toward the front door. Jeanie hesitated, not sure why he was running away from her. But as she turned the corner of the L to leave the room out the back hallway, she understood.

Just as she reached the door, the chainsaw revved, and swung toward her.

Jeanie stumbled backward and he kept coming, waving the whirring silver teeth of the blade at her chest and head.

Jeanie turned the corner back into the dining room and started to run toward the front door. Only, she took the short way around the cannibal table, her habitual route for the past few weeks when walking through this room.

And a second later found herself standing on the edge of the big black hole.

She looked down and the garish lights of the basement played over a pile of body parts. There were heads, arms and torsos all glistening in a gory heap directly below. At the highest part of the mound of corpses, it was dark, but at the edges of the heap of bodies, she could see the tips of long, tall spikes.

She knew right where they were, in terms of the basement. The Vlad the Impaler exhibit was just below. Dozens of five-foot-high sharp metal spikes, all reaching for the ceiling.

Oh shit.

The chainsaw was in the air buzzing closer and closer behind her head. Jeanie had no options.

She jumped, aiming for the darkest part of the stack of bodies.

Her landing was soft, though something bit at her left calf. Above her, she heard the chainsaw connect with the floor where she had been standing a second before. Then the machine whine faded away, as Leatherface pulled it back and returned to his position at the front of the room to wait for new guests to enter the house.

Jeanie was safe for a moment.

Now she just had to get off the pile of bodies and back to the floor of the basement without impaling herself in the process.

She turned her head and found herself looking directly into the blood-splattered face of the 'Groovy' guy. His eyes were open in terror. Jeanie couldn't help it. She let out a short scream.

Then she tore her gaze away from that bit of horror and took in the rest of her situation. She felt wetness seeping into her clothes. And as she looked down the length of her body, she could easily see why. Her knee rested inside the crimson cavern the chainsaw had ripped into someone's gut. The gristle of the shoulder end of a woman's arm was shoved up against her chest. Something hard pressed against her groin, and as she shifted slightly, she saw what it was. The decapitated head of a man. He had a five-day growth of beard, but he was bald on top. His eyes were also open, staring sightlessly at Jeanie's crotch. She shivered and looked away, toward the hallway that led past this grisly exhibit. There were three rows of silver spikes between the edge of the pile of bodies and her escape.

Above her, the chainsaw let out an angry war cry as a woman screamed in true terror. Jeanie now realized that there was a difference between the screams that they'd elicited in patrons from an unexpected scare versus those in a true deadly situation. The cries of true horror sounded different. It wasn't something she could have explained, but you could hear it.

Something hit her in the back, and she gasped. It was heavy. She turned to see what it was and choked.

It was half of a woman.

Intestines slid over Jeanie's ribcage as they exited the shredded cavity of the victim. They looked like bloody snakes and she shrieked at the sight. But a second later, her scream was cut off when another weight hit her. The other half of the victim. The woman's pink gym shoe landed on top of the face of the dead woman beneath her. Before Jeanie could react, another body fell from above. She caught the blur of a heavyset man with glasses, and then heard the most horrible scream she had ever heard as he belly-flopped onto a handful of steel spikes next to the stack of corpses. His scream stopped abruptly as the spikes jutted through his back in three places. Another had caught him in the side of the head, and stuck fast in his skull. While his body slid down the spikes a couple feet, his head pinned him to the top of the spike.

"Jesus," Jeanie whispered. She resisted the urge to panic. While there was death all around her, she had escaped the chainsaw…now she just had to escape the spikes. The tops of the pointed spikes were all stained red, with bodies and body parts hanging on many of them halfway to the floor – like toothpicks with human olives. Argento had never imagined an impaling zone this cruel when he'd set it up with a handful of fake bodies streaming fake guts.

Jeanie grabbed at the dead woman's hand that hung over her, and pulled the woman forward. If she was going to get to the edge of the rows of spikes without being impaled herself, she needed to build a bridge. She rolled the ragged rib cage over to rest on the edge of a spike, but as soon as she pressed down on the woman's jacket, the spike slid through the bones, and the upper half of the woman began to slide down the spike. The next corpse was lodged at least three feet down.

No, she thought. *They can't slide. They need to wedge.*

She grabbed at the woman's long blond hair and held her from slipping down the spike. And then she had an idea, thanks to the fat man nearby.

Jeanie pulled the head by the hair and positioned the woman's mouth over the tip of an impaler. Grimacing but not giving in, she pressed the spike through the glossy lips of the dead woman. The head sunk, but caught.

That was the ticket.

If she could use a handful of heads to create the base, stopping the soft flesh of the bodies from slipping down the spikes, she could then layer the tops of those heads – anchors – with a couple other bodies. A gruesome human suspension bridge.

Another scream from above, and two more bodies fell through the opening. One landed on Jeanie's legs, the other impaled itself a couple feet away. Not where she needed it to be.

She took a breath, and smelled the strong scent of iron. And something far more pungent and foul. The bowels of dozens of people had opened beneath her.

Rather than throw up, she grabbed at the denim jacket of a man who now lolled across her legs, and dragged him forward and over the woman whose head she'd impaled. Jeanie could think of only one thing.

She was getting out of here.

A hot rinse of blood soaked into her shirt as she dragged his corpse, but she ignored it, focusing only on getting the man's mouth in the place she needed it to be. Fellating a silver spike.

As the bodies continued to fall in a grotesque rain of screams and blood spray, she grabbed and moved them, layering pelvises over skulls on the spikes. She layered their limp, heavy bodies across each other, crisscrossing the corpses in a Lincoln Log style. Her hands and arms were slick with blood, but she hardly noticed now. She shrugged off the fake guts that were strapped around her waist so that she could move easier, and slapped them across a spike. More building material.

A man's voice screamed from above her, and the chainsaw whirred again. An arm suddenly fell through the hole, and bounced off the corpse pile to fall to the floor a couple feet away. The rest of the man came through the hole a second later, screaming without stop. He missed the center of the bodies and a spike suddenly poked through his thighs. His chest, however, rested on the edge of the island of bodies and he reached out his hands to Jeanie.

"Oh God, fuck," he cried. "Please help me."

He struggled, but all that did was make his legs slip farther down the spikes. He was pinned like a butterfly. As his legs slid down, he let out a series of sharp guttural cries. Jeanie turned toward him and took his hand.

"Stop moving," she said. "You're making it worse."

And then another body fell from above. Another man. The guy landed on top of the pinned man's waist, and she saw his eyes suddenly bulge.

The force of the new body pushed his stomach down hard on a spike that had been buried in the chest of another pinned corpse. A rain of blood splattered on the floor and the man didn't scream or beg anymore. Jeanie let go of his hand, but took the hand of the body that had killed him. It had avoided getting wedged, so she dragged it behind her across the corpse bridge and laid it across the head of a woman.

That did it. She had wedged a bridge of ripped and bleeding bodies right up to the edge of the spikes.

She crawled across their still-warm flesh slowly, spreading her weight out as much as possible. Beneath her, she felt flesh shifting, sinking.

"Please, please, please," she whispered as slowly, carefully, she crawled across the dead. And then she had her hand on the back of the skull that rested on the final stake between her and the open ground below. She pulled herself forward, as the bodies beneath her shifted and moved. Something sharp poked at her thigh. Was it a spike or someone's broken bone?

She didn't want to find out. Jeanie pushed against the skull beneath her hand and felt it sink. The spike below was working its way through the skull of the corpse. But now Jeanie could look over the tower of spikes and see the open floor four feet below.

"Now or never," she whispered, and closed her eyes for a second, steeling her nerve. Then she rolled across the bodies, not stopping when she reached the edge. She flipped right over the edge as one of the bodies behind her gave way, sliding two feet down a stake that she'd been resting on. It didn't matter. For a second she was in the air, and then she landed hard on the ground.

Jeanie cried out as her thigh slammed the wood, but she kept rolling and staggered to her feet in a heartbeat.

She looked down at herself and grimaced. Her jeans and t-shirt were absolutely sodden with blood. Shreds of someone else's flesh stuck to her pants like lint. Jeanie looked up as another body came through the hole in the ceiling above to smack down on top of the pile.

She forgot about the gore and turned away toward the exit of the basement. She could be out of the house in seconds and then could finally find Lon and get him to turn the house lights on and stop sending people inside.

Her leg hurt from where she'd landed, but Jeanie limped toward the cellar stairway out.

She could see the Exit sign just ahead, with the white sign above it disputing the light. Argento had painted 'NO' in bright red letters above 'EXIT'.

Jeanie moved toward it, safe at last.

Someone moved out of the corridor ahead of her and took a position directly in front of the stairs leading out.

A figure with a long silver knife.

Jeanie began to cry.

The killer from the attic blocked her way out.

CHAPTER FORTY-TWO

Jillie tugged on Ted's arm as they stepped into the foyer. "See, I told you this would get us in okay."

"Yeah, but now you stand out like…a woman in a clown suit," he said.

The chainsaw whirred in the room to their right and Jillie pointed straight ahead. The arrows on the floor told them to turn right. 'This Way To Your Doom', the words next to them encouraged. The hallway ahead had police tape across it. Most of it had been knocked down already, but a couple strips still barred the way a foot above the floor.

"Let's go this way," she said.

"And get us thrown out for going the wrong way?" he said.

"I think this leads straight to the stairway to the attic," she said. "Come on."

She stepped over the tape and ducked into the hallway beyond. Ted followed, shaking his head. Screams erupted with the whir of the chainsaw behind them, and Jillie motioned Ted forward. When they reached the kitchen, Jillie stopped and crouched down.

"What is it?" Ted whispered.

She pointed at the puddle of blood surrounding the woman on the floor.

"That's real blood," she said.

"That's what they want you to think," he said. "Don't you remember, she's going to jump up any second and give you a heart attack."

Jillie shook her head. "Not this time," she said. She pushed the body over, and despite knowing that the woman was dead, she jumped back when she saw the ravaged torso. The woman's neck had been slashed ear to ear, and the blood was obviously real, when you saw it next to the makeup blood. Someone had slashed down the center of her shirt, severing both the cotton of her tee and the strap of her bra. It had also dug deep into the line of her sternum, ending in a foot-long hole in her belly. Wet red and yellow chunks of flesh hung out of the wound, and Jillie dropped the body back to the ground.

"It's happening," she said. "I knew it from the start."

She stood up and went to the sink. A blackened face with poached eyes glared back at her. The man was very, very dead. A spotlight lay in the water next to his face. It was still plugged in to the wall socket, but it no longer was giving out any light.

"So now that we know it's happening, how do we stop it?"

"Stop *her*," Jillie corrected. "This is all part of a ritual," she said. "We have to stop it before anyone else is sacrificed for it."

"Yes, but how?" he said.

"We have to find her heart," Jillie said. "And put a stake in it."

"But she's already dead," Ted said.

Jillie shook her head. "If this is part of a reincarnation spell, I don't think so. Not anymore. There have been too many sacrifices already."

Ted looked confused, but Jillie grabbed him by the arm and pulled. "Come on," she said. "She'll be in the basement. That's where all of the other events in this house have been. They found animal bones down there, and magic ritual symbols in the past. All in the same spot. All dead center of the structure. The house's heart. It's where she pushed me. It's where she's held on all these years, waiting."

Together they ran down the hallway past the strobing lights and howling music. When they turned the corner, they found the bodies.

"Oh my God," Ted said. "Is it too late?"

"I don't think so," she said. "It's not quite midnight yet. That's always the hour of change. The weakest moment in the fabric between today and tomorrow, natural and supernatural. Come on."

Carefully they threaded their way through the corpses blocking the hall until they reached the stairs down. Jillie didn't slow, but immediately launched down them.

"Wait," Ted called in a loud whisper. "Be careful," he warned. "Whoever did this is still here."

"I'm counting on it," Jillie said on the fourth step. Then she took the next three and in a second stood on the plank floor of the basement.

"What are we looking for?" Ted whispered.

She shrugged. "We'll know it when we see it. I don't know how all the sacrifices work, but her center is down here. That way," she said, pointing to the right.

Ted nodded, but didn't move. "Okay," he said. "Lead on."

Jillie shook her head. "Chivalry is dead."

Ted shrugged. "This is your party and I don't want to *be* dead."

Jillie rolled her eyes and began leading the way down the aisle. "We'll all be dead eventually," she said.

"Yeah, but we don't have to die tonight," he said from behind her.

"We're not going to die," she said. "We just have to avoid getting stabbed."

"Someone should have told that to him," Ted murmured, and pointed.

They were passing a display that was clearly an homage to *The Exorcist*; there was a bed and nightstand in the center, and a girl with a green-tinged face and glowing eyes sitting up in the center of the bed. Her hair was wild and the soundtrack overhead kept repeating two lines in the midst of a nerve-racking soundtrack: "The power of Christ compels you!" one voice cried and shortly thereafter, a demonic growl declared, "Your mother sucks cocks in hell!"

But the bed and the soundtrack and the flaring lights weren't what Ted was talking about. There was a man lying in front of the bed. He could have been part of the set, but a closer look made it clear he wasn't. The man wore jeans and a black shirt with a cartoon on it that boasted 'Fast zombies miss the brains'.

Jammed into his mouth was a long wooden pole; a crucifix was mounted on the opposite end. It had probably been a setpiece for *The Exorcist* room, but now it was a murder weapon. Blood pooled around the back of the man's head, where the end of the pole had plunged through his neck to gouge its way into the floor.

"I wonder who he pissed off," Ted said.

"I don't think he had to piss off anyone," Jillie said. "She wants the blood of everyone standing in that line outside spilled in here."

"But why?" Ted said.

"She needs their life to return," Jillie said. "She needs gallons of blood. This isn't just vengeance. There's a purpose."

"A method to the madness?"

She nodded. "Yeah, I just don't know what the method is. Or rather, what the last act is. I just hope we're not too late to stop it."

They walked past another display, this one an homage to *Hellraiser*. And like in the movie, a man had been mounted on a cross in the center of the space, with chains liberally covered in hooks attached to the body. The man's arms and legs and cheeks and abdomen were all gouged and pulled tight by hooks, his flesh stretched like yellowed taffy off his bones and pinched toward the walls.

But like the last display, the star of this torture scene was not a dummy. There was no makeup here.

The puddle on the floor beneath his legs was the result of a bladder voided, and the blood spatter rained on the floor was real blood, the trickle of life that had dripped from the holes of the hooks. The man had been bled dry as he hung helpless in the air.

Jillie walked into the set and reached up to put her fingers on the man's chest.

"What are you doing?" Ted whispered. His voice was sharp.

"Just trying to tap in," she said.

Jillie rested her head and stood there for a minute, not speaking. When she finally pulled back, Ted asked, "What did you feel?"

"Nothing," Jillie said. "I saw him die. And I felt nothing at all."

She looked perplexed, and Ted pulled her arm. "Come on," he said.

She nodded and stepped away from the body. Her face was troubled, but she walked back into the aisle and only paused briefly as they passed the next display. There was a woman's torso there, propped upright on a church altar, with her vacant eyes staring toward the aisle. Her waist and legs were missing, and a stream of blood leaked over the edge of the altar to drip down and spread on the floor.

Jillie only shook her head. "This is not good," she whispered.

"Ya think?" Ted said. "Should we be recording anything?"

"Sure," Jillie said absently. "If you want. But this is different. This isn't a haunting situation."

"What would you call it?"

"A ritual. A massacre."

Jillie walked further down the aisle, and the lighting changed. Ted reached into his backpack and pulled out an EMF reader. Maybe Jillie didn't care right now about documenting all of this, but later, she'd be asking what he'd been doing in here with her the whole night.

There were times she could be really unfair…and unforgiving.

The meters on the tracker were alive.

Ted held the tool out toward the aisle behind them and slowly moved it forward, watching the readings. The LED meters shivered and moved; nothing drastic, but they weren't still either.

"There's activity here," Ted announced, looking around the spotlit dark. "But nothing focused."

"That's all of the victims," Jillie said. "Not the main event."

He followed her around the corner and they began a new row of grotesque sets as they walked toward the exit. Having done this once before, Ted understood how it flowed, even if he didn't remember the 'kill' scenes exactly.

Ted reached out to grab Jillie's shirt. She slowed, and he pointed down the long aisle in front of her before whispering, "Who is that?"

There was a woman standing at the edge of the aisle. And she was clearly a woman, not some prop. Her face moved, and she looked both left and right as she studied the room. But when Ted trained the EMF reader on her, the dial did nothing.

"Jillie," he called. "Look."

He held the reader out in front of him, and she glanced at the dial.

"She's alive," Jillie said. "But there's no way that this is simply the work of one disturbed woman. Let's see what's really going on."

Jillie kept walking forward, toward the girl at the end of the aisle. She had unruly brown hair, kinked and curled in a wild way across her shoulders. She stared straight ahead though, her gaze focused on something down the other aisle, as she held a long silver blade into the air.

Ted followed behind, holding the EMF reader out in front of him. The needles looked nervous, but really didn't move. On either side of the walkway were sets depicting scenes from horror films, but Ted didn't look at most of them seriously enough to try to guess what they were. When he did look, he saw people bleeding from a wide variety of wounds. He didn't want to see those; instead he tried to focus on his EMF meter rather than the death that was clearly in evidence all around him.

"Who is behind all of this?" he asked.

"Someone with a plan," Jillie said. She strode forward then and held up her hand, gesturing for the woman to stop whatever she was doing. They were close, and she saw the opportunity to intervene.

The woman didn't see her right away, and instead lifted her knife higher to threaten somebody in the aisle ahead. Jillie and Ted couldn't see who, but they began to run forward.

"Stop!" Jillie screamed.

The woman paused, surprised by the interruption. She turned to face Jillie and changed the focus of the knife blade. At the same time, she kept her gaze divided, watching whoever she had been threatening. Without warning, she suddenly darted down the side aisle away from them.

Jillie ran to follow and Ted was right behind. When they reached the aisle, they finally saw who the woman was really after.

A girl stood just a few feet down the passageway from the killer. She was covered in blood, head to toe. She could have been representing Sissy Spacek from the pig blood scene in the movie *Carrie*. The woman with the knife suddenly ignored Jillie and Ted and moved toward the girl like a storm.

"Stop!" Jillie cried again.

But this time it was Ted who didn't hold back. He elbowed past Jillie and ran the five yards down the aisle to catch the woman.

"Leave her alone!" he yelled, as he drew closer to the woman.

The woman with the knife stopped midway down the aisle and turned toward him with the blade raised.

"Stop!" he screamed.

The woman's answer was to swing the blade like a scythe as she turned toward him.

Ted slowed his approach, but it was too late. The woman moved fast.

Ted gasped as the steel of the knife slipped easily through the cotton of his shirt and into his chest.

"*Noooo!*" Jillie screamed, but she could do nothing to save him.

Ted gasped and choked.

The knife moved fast through the soft flesh of Ted's belly. There was a pinch at his heart. It felt like it should have been more painful, really, but Ted didn't have the chance to say that to anyone. Instead he groaned and collapsed like a house of cards to the floor.

The killer only gazed at him for a moment, however, before turning her attention back toward the other woman waiting at the end of the passageway.

Jillie dropped to her knees, grabbing for Ted's hand. His shirt bloomed with blood and her fingers were almost instantly warm with his life.

"Hold on," she whispered to him. "I'll get an ambulance."

Ted grimaced and slowly shook his head. "I don't think so," he said. "Just don't let her get to you."

"You're going to be okay," Jillie promised. But she knew as she said it that he wasn't. His chest was like a well of blood, and his breath came in wet wheezes.

"You can have my fries," he gasped. His mouth twisted in a pained scowl, and then went still.

"Ted?" Jillie whispered. She repeated his name louder, but he didn't move.

His eyelids didn't blink.

Her eyes filled with tears, but then self-preservation forced her to look up from her friend. She knew the killer had to be just a few feet away, maybe already coming for her. But when she looked up, through her bleary gaze, she realized that the knife woman was gone. And so was her intended victim.

Jillie felt a small relief at that, since it allowed her to release her grief and hold Ted.

She put her arms around him, ignoring the wet blood that covered his chest.

"I'm so sorry I dragged you into this," she whispered, and laid her cheek on the stubble of his. "So, so sorry," she whispered, as her tears slipped down to pool on his bloody shirt.

CHAPTER FORTY-THREE

The nails hurt his back.

Mike screwed up his eyes and moaned as he rolled over on Emery's dangerous bed. How long had he been asleep there? he wondered.

He rolled his feet over the side and pushed himself up to a sitting position.

That's when he realized that he was covered in blood. He looked down his arm and saw his sleeve was dark with it. His other arm was the same.

He hadn't lain down in the bed that way. And he didn't feel injured. Had he gouged himself badly on a nail? He ran a hand up and down one arm and shook his head. The sleeve was damp with sticky blood. Only, nothing on his arm hurt. He didn't think he was hurt. He just felt a little...woozy.

So then...how had he gotten all bloodied?

Mike stood up, and tried to survey his body in the dim light of Emery's room. There was just a single candle, and Emery and Katie were nowhere to be seen. His sleeves were sodden with blood, and his chest and belly and crotch were all damp with it as well.

What the hell?

Mike started to walk toward the stairway when his foot connected with something on the floor.

He looked down and saw a chainsaw lying there.

A familiar Leatherface mask lay on the floor nearby.

"What did you do?" he whispered. Then he climbed up the stairs to reach the attic.

The eerie music played, but nobody was there. Mike descended the stairwell to the main floor and realized the house there also seemed empty. It was as if he had slept until after closing time. All the lights were on, but nobody was home.

Mike walked around the corner and abruptly stopped.

It might not be so much that nobody was home, but rather, that everyone who was home was dead.

The corridor was filled with bodies. And clearly these were not props, but real, bloodied, murdered bodies.

"What the fuck?" Mike whispered.

He stepped between the corpses until he reached the hallway that led to the kitchen and the front foyer. People were lying on the floor everywhere. His stomach contracted to a tiny ball of ice. The world had turned dangerous and strange in a way he had never imagined in his worst nightmares.

Mike walked toward the front of the house, intending to find Lon. But when he reached the foyer, he looked outside and saw that the deck was empty. The ticket-taker booth was untenanted, and the long line of people to get in to the haunted house…was gone.

How long had he slept?

And why was he covered in blood?

Mike stepped back from the door and looked instead toward the *Texas Chainsaw Massacre* room. The walls seemed painted in blood. He walked inside and looked around. The 'cannibal' table had blood spatter everywhere. The tablecloth was drenched. The 'props' that Argento had made were no longer creepy unto themselves – their fake blood was dripping with the real thing.

He looked at the plank floor and saw the oblong hole that had been carved into the basement. Why had anyone cut a hole in the floor?

Mike shook his head and stepped back to the main hall. He had to find Katie, and he knew where she probably was. He headed back through the hallway of bodies toward the stairway down. While the sounds of Goblin and John Carpenter still echoed through the air from the various rooms, otherwise, the house was quiet.

He stepped down the stairs into the basement and found it equally deserted. But then, as he walked down the aisle toward the secret room, he realized that it wasn't completely empty. While there didn't seem to be any living patrons roaming the halls in search of a good scare, there did seem to be plenty of dead patrons.

Each of the display rooms that made up the basement Aisle of Atrocities was now filled with dead people.

Some were chainsawed and some were stabbed…but all of the bodies he saw appeared very dead, no matter what 'set' they were in.

Mike felt frightened beyond anything he had ever been. Something terrible had happened here tonight, while he had been asleep. But what? And why?

He reached into the recessed opening and pulled open the door to the room where Katie's bones lay.

And almost instantly, he heard the first voice to break the silence since he'd awoken.

"There you are," Katie said. "We've been waiting for you!"

CHAPTER FORTY-FOUR

She had escaped the psycho who had cut off Bong's arms and legs, managed to slip past the maniac with the chainsaw, build a bridge of human bodies to avoid being impaled and land bloody but basically unharmed on the ground just yards from the exit to this slaughterhouse.

And after all that, she was going to die anyway. It wasn't fair.

Those were Jeanie's first thoughts as she confronted the girl from the attic with the bloody knife.

She stood in a faceoff with the girl, who barely seemed there at all. The killer's eyes seemed to stare right through Jeanie. But Jeanie didn't trust that blankness; she'd seen the damage this monster had done with her knife. The evidence lay bleeding on every floor of this house.

Jeanie feinted to the right, and the knife followed her. The woman's body did not. Her feet stayed planted in place, blocking the aisle. Jeanie could turn and run back the way she'd come, but then she'd have the knife at her back. She needed more distance between her and the killer before she could chance turning around.

Jeanie edged a step backward, and then another.

The girl with the knife stepped forward, maintaining the distance.

Fuck. What the hell was she going to do? She didn't have a weapon, and this girl was twice her size and held a knife that she clearly was not afraid to use.

She was going to have to turn and run and pray that she could put a couple steps between them before the killer reacted.

The knife suddenly raised in the air as the killer prepared to attack.

Jeanie steeled herself to go, when someone yelled from just around the corner.

"Stop!" a woman's voice cried.

The girl looked at the source of the voice, and as she did, Jeanie stepped backward a step. And then another. And another.

"Leave her alone," a man's voice cried.

And then the killer took off and Jeanie seized the opportunity. She turned and ran.

Behind her, she heard the steps of the killer, and the voices of the couple. She couldn't pause to look back, but when she turned the corner she realized quickly that there were no longer any footsteps at her back. She slowed her pace enough to glance behind, but didn't stop.

She was no longer being followed at the moment.

And then the basement echoed with a scream.

Jeanie swore beneath her breath. She knew the knife meant for her had just found at least one of the people who had given her the opportunity to escape. And if the killer had taken care of those two, that knife would be coming for her again any second.

Jeanie rounded the corner to the left, and then stopped before the pathway turned left again. The stairway out of this hellhole was at the end of this corridor. But was the way clear?

She hugged the false wall of one of the exhibits and peered around the corner. Spotlights showed blue and red and green against the walls and floor, and a strobe flickered in one of the exhibits near the end of the corridor. There were a couple bodies lying on the floor but otherwise, nothing moved.

Jeanie took a breath and stepped around the corner. But just as she did, something crashed in the hallway she'd just left.

She ducked into the exhibit to the left to get out of sight.

It was supposed to be some kind of dungeon; there were chains hanging from all of the walls, and a woman was locked in a wooden rack. The device had never been functional; Jeanie knew, because she'd helped Argento assemble part of it.

But it looked impressive, with its big wooden wagon wheels and plank backing boards. And iron manacles.

Somebody had made it look more real than it was. There had been a bloody manikin chained to the device, but now there was a real woman there. Her wrists and ankles were pulled tight to the opposite ends of the rack, which made what had happened to her midsection more dramatic.

She was broken open like a piñata, her groin and ribs yanked far apart to allow her intestines to cascade like bloody vines over the edge of the wood.

Jeanie grimaced and looked away. She slipped behind the Iron Maiden that Lucio had designed in his garage and crouched down on the floor. She should be able to stay safely out of sight here for a while.

She could just see the corridor from there. Jeanie let out a breath and then forced herself to take in another, trying to still the pounding in her chest. In the distance, she thought she could still hear the sounds of talking, or sobbing. But it could have been part of the soundtrack too; the whole basement had distinct zones of eerie sounds and synthesized throbbing all designed to make the walk through its exhibits more intense.

Something dripped on Jeanie's head.

And again.

She reached up to wipe it and her fingers came away dark.

Jeanie looked up and saw the source. A man in ripped jeans hung from chains attached to the rafters. His shirt had been removed. His throat was a red circle of slashed flesh that had dripped and drooled in a dozen different rivers down the hair of his chest and belly. His face hung down, and she could see the sightless whites of his eyes in the dark.

Without thinking, she started to rise, to get away from the blood, but just as she did, she saw feet in the corridor.

Jeanie froze in a half crouch. She didn't dare breathe.

Another drop of blood hit her forehead, and ran down to her nose. She screwed up her face in disgust but still managed to hold her breath. She would *not* let the killer know she was here.

Drip.

The white soles of tennis shoes moved a step farther down the corridor. And then slowly, another.

Drip.

Jeanie was dying to wipe her face, but she didn't dare move a muscle.

The feet turned then, and began to slowly walk back the way they'd come. The way she had come.

Jeanie slowly took a breath, and let it out. And breathed again. She raised one hand in slow motion and brushed it across her forehead, nose and cheek to clear the blood away. She wiped it off on her jeans, which were already heavy with other people's blood. She refused to think about that, and forced herself to stay focused on the corridor.

Nothing moved.

Slowly she relaxed a little, and settled down to wait. The seconds passed like hours, and she forced herself to count to one hundred.

From somewhere in the distance, she heard voices.

She rose, and forced her feet to step past the Iron Maiden and rack to the edge of the exhibit.

Jeanie looked to the left and right, and saw only spotlights and dry-ice fog.

Now or never.

She stepped into the corridor and walked toward the exit, her feet moving faster and faster the closer she got to the stairs that led up and out of the back of the house.

Something was dripping all over her face now; she didn't want to know what. Jeanie wiped it off her cheeks with the back of her hand. The red arrow on the floor directed her out of the basement and through the red-painted door. The cement stairs beyond looked like a life raft.

Jeanie vaulted up them and emerged outside behind the haunted house, beneath the dark of the midnight sky. She hurried around the side of the house and saw the pathway to the turnpike. It was completely clear. There was nobody standing in line to get into the house.

Because they were all dead, she thought.

There was nobody at the ticket-taker booth. It was weirdly empty and quiet. She could hear the light breeze riffle the leaves that still clung to the oaks that barricaded the house.

The moon shone icy bright through the tips of the trees on the edge of the clearing nearby, and Jeanie wiped at her face once again, looking down to see water glistening on the back of her bloodstained hand.

The drips on her face were tears.

When she realized that she was crying, the tears only intensified. She started sobbing and couldn't contain the noises that came from her chest and throat.

Jeanie shook her head and began to run down the gravel path toward the deserted turnpike.

She was all alone.

CHAPTER FORTY-FIVE

Katie stood near the coffin that held her bones, though they were no longer simply bones. When Mike looked inside it, he saw Katie. Or her doppelganger. Katie's double lay silent and naked in the coffin; her body now appeared fully formed, from the small creamy nubs of her toes to the dark thatch of hair at her crotch to the soft, round breasts that he longed to suckle again. Only her face remained slightly incomplete; her lips still didn't quite connect right…there was too much scarlet at the edges; he could see the white of her teeth with the front of her lips closed. Emery held a knife in her hand; she raised it in the air as she began to walk toward Mike. He backed away.

"Don't worry," Katie said. "Emery won't hurt you, I promise you that."

"Yeah, okay maybe," he said. "But who *will* she hurt? This place is a slaughterhouse. What the hell happened while I was asleep?"

"Just what had to be," Katie said. "You want me to be alive again, right? In the flesh, so you can actually touch and feel me?"

"Yes, of course," Mike said.

"Well, that's what we've been working on," she said. "We've been doing what we need to do to make that happen. Because, I want to be with you finally, too."

"But why so much blood?" he said. His voice rose with incredulity and anger. He waved a hand toward the coffin. "When this all started, you said we wouldn't have to kill anyone. You just needed a little blood each night. I was okay with that," he said. "But not this. This place was supposed to be a fun haunted house, not a death trap."

"There was only one way for me to return," Katie said. "I'm sorry it had to be this way but…you want me to be with you again, right?"

Mike nodded. "But why," he said. "Why did all those people have to die?"

"Power," she said. "On the night of the becoming, I needed all of their energy."

Emery stepped toward him.

"Emery, give Mike the knife," Katie said.

Katie's quiet but very bloody accomplice lifted the blade, and offered it easily into Mike's hands. He took the weapon, but frowned.

"What am I supposed to do with this?" he asked.

Katie stood just in front of her coffin and bowed her head as she answered.

"I need you to kill her," she said. "Her blood will complete my return to life."

Katie reached out a hand to touch Emery's shoulder. Without protest, the girl knelt, and offered her chest for Mike to address. He made a face and looked back at Katie.

"What are you saying?" he said. "She's been your best friend!"

Katie nodded. "I love her, I do. But...a witch can have only one familiar. And Emery has been mine for more than fifty years. She began the process of my return...and now she must give the final energy to complete it."

"But what about *her*?" Mike asked, pointing at the chunky girl who knelt and stared at his feet without looking up. "Doesn't *she* deserve something for her service to you? Something more than death?"

Katie shook her head. "Yes," she said. "She deserves to finally be set free. It is time for a new person to join me. Emery has helped me for many years but...she's been with me since I died in 1963. It's because of her that I'm here today. But now... I need someone who understands the world today. Someone who can help me not only survive, but thrive. Someone who can be my lover, as well as my familiar."

Katie looked at Mike with eyes that sucked out his soul. "I need *you*."

CHAPTER FORTY-SIX

Jillie wiped the tears from her eyes and rose from the floor. She couldn't bear to look at Ted's body anymore. She couldn't imagine life without him near, but what made it worse was the guilt of his blood that was on her hands. His death was her fault. She should never have dragged him into this. Her throat was thick with grief but everywhere she turned her head, it got worse.

There were mutilated people everywhere. Men held the red ropes of their guts between their fingers with the mask of surprise and sudden, unexpected death painted on their faces. Women hung from rusty meat hooks from the low ceiling. Bodies lay in gory piles on the floor and bled out from where they were pinned to the walls by nails and stakes. Nearby in a tableau that looked like an old barn with bales of hay and a rustic horse stall, a teenage boy wearing a Camp Crystal Lake shirt was staked to the wall with the tines of an old pitchfork. The decapitated head of a girl lay on the floor just beyond his feet. The girl's body rested nearby on a bale of hay, her open throat still dripping a slow trickle of blood on the floor below.

"This has to stop," Jillie whispered.

She walked over the bloody floor to an exhibit meant to look like an old crypt. Maybe it was supposed to reference *The Mummy*, she wasn't sure. The false walls were painted to look like roughhewn stone 'bricks'. In the center of the room, two stone sarcophagi sat with lids half removed. A hand gripped the edges of one, as if a figure were about to rise from the tomb.

On the floor between the stone coffins, a man lay with a long, silver blade jutting out of his middle. Jillie forced herself to walk over, grip the haft of the blade and…pull. She needed a weapon if she was going to track down the witch.

The blade slid out of the dead man easily, and she quickly turned away from the corpse.

The woman who had killed Ted had walked away from them toward the end of the basement, and that's the direction that Jillie headed. The haunted house theme music was still playing through speakers hidden in the ceiling, with groans and sighs and occasional screams adding tension to the already spooky rhythms. But above the soundtrack, she could hear voices.

Someone else was still alive down here.

Jillie moved toward the voices, passing body after broken body along the path. She stepped carefully, quietly. She couldn't tell where the voices were coming from; the Aisle of Atrocities hit a wall just a few yards away and nobody was alive in any of the macabre 'sets' on the right or left side of the walkway. But as she reached the end of the aisle, she saw an opening between the sets to a dark access corridor behind the fake walls of the horror 'exhibits'. And there was a crack of yellow light in the shape of a doorway just a few feet away.

So.

Jillie stepped over a dead girl and wound her way around a wooden post to emerge in the narrow corridor behind the sets.

"I never wanted anything like this," a man's voice was saying inside. He sounded upset.

"It's too late for that," another voice answered. A woman. The killer? Jillie wondered.

She took a deep breath and put her hand into the wooden inset that served as a handle for the door. The door opened inward as soon as she touched it. No turning back now.

Jillie stepped into a small room lit by a single bare bulb screwed into a fixture on the ceiling. On the right side of the room, an old coffin sat on the floor near the wall, its lid removed.

A beautiful young woman stood in front of it. She was slim with long dark hair that draped across her shoulders in easy curls. Her eyes were dark pools, her lips heavy and filled with a secret humor. Her hands were on her denim-hugged hips.

She was looking at another woman, a stocky girl with mouse-brown hair who knelt at the feet of a man. Jillie could only see the woman's back, but she could tell that her head was bowed down, as if awaiting execution.

Jillie wanted to rush forward instantly once she looked at the man. He was dressed in work boots, jeans, a t-shirt and a denim overshirt. All of his clothes, from bootlaces to collar, were spattered and dark with blood. There was a bloody handprint on his back.

The man held a knife. From his clothes, it was clear that he'd used the weapon, repeatedly. And from the stocky girl's position on her knees in front of him, he was about to use it again.

"You must," the pretty girl said. She was speaking to the man and didn't seem to have noticed Jillie's entry. "It's the only way. And the time is now."

"No!" Jillie ran forward, raising her own knife. She had to stop him. She aimed at the center of the man's back and brought her arm down as hard as she could. But the man moved at the last second, twisting away as she brought the knife down. Instead of his back, she caught the side of his arm. He yelled as the knife bit through his shirt sleeve and carved a channel in his flesh. A fresh bloom of red joined the sodden cloth all around it.

The man grabbed at his wound and staggered to the left. The kneeling girl came to life then and grabbed at Jillie's legs. But Jillie turned and twisted, throwing herself away from the girl and toward the coffin.

"Get rid of her," the pretty girl commanded, and the other woman rose from the floor. When she turned, Jillie realized in a flash that this was, in fact, the woman who had killed Ted.

Jillie retreated until her back hit the edge of the coffin. The touch of the wood startled her. Jillie glanced behind her and saw the body lying between the short wooden walls of the old coffin. The first thing she noticed about the body was that it looked fresh. Not rotten like the wood it lay within. That and its nakedness. And then she recognized the face. It had the same high cheekbones, narrow nose and black hair as the woman standing just a few feet away. A dead twin.

Jillie looked away from the body and held the knife out in front of her, threatening the thickset woman who was coming at her with both hands outstretched. The other woman didn't move, but seemed to be in charge. She directed the man.

"Help Emery get rid of her. Hurry, it's time."

"Can we use *her* blood on the body to finish it?" the man asked. He walked toward Emery holding his wounded arm.

The pretty girl shook her head. "Emery's blood began to raise me. Only Emery's blood can complete the spell and bring me back in my new skin. The hour is now. The power is thick in the house at this moment but it'll quickly drain away. Hurry. I want to be reborn for you."

The woman stepped closer to the coffin and put her hands on the feet of the body within, gently touching the ankles and calves of her twin as if marveling at their soft beauty.

It all hit Jillie in a flash. This woman was the witch of Bachelor's Grove. The girl who hundreds had reported walking half-dressed and chilled along the turnpike. The girl who consistently disappeared as soon as a driver picked her up and tried to take her home. The witch who had been trying to find a way back into the world for decades.

On a hunch, she took one hand off the knife. While she kept the blade trained on Emery to hold the woman at bay, with her other hand she grasped at the witch's arm.

Her fingers passed right through the woman's skin. As she'd expected.

"Your name is Katarina," Jillie said.

The girl looked up in surprise. And smiled. "Very good," she said. "Have we met?"

Jillie shook her head. "No," she said. "But I've felt your energy in this cemetery for years. And I've stood at your grave."

Katie nodded. "I see," she said. "Well, perhaps you can lie down in it. After tonight I won't be needing it anymore. Mike?"

The witch pointed at Jillie, and Mike began to walk forward with the knife in hand. Jillie did not understand exactly how Katie's body in the coffin had been reborn, but she understood that this night was all about reuniting the spirit of the witch with this flesh. The incarnation had not happened yet. But it was about to. And she knew how to stop that from happening.

Ghosts were fleeting, but flesh could be killed.

Jillie turned her back to Emery and raised the knife. She didn't know much, but she knew that whatever happened, she could not let the witch of a half century of legend return to the living. She brought the knife down.

Emery dove forward at the same moment.

Jillie's blade bit into something soft before lodging with a wrenching finality in bone. Blood sprayed, drops raining warm against her face. And then her arm yanked to the side, as the knife and the flesh it skewered moved.

The body she had stabbed was not the vacant vessel of the witch. The blade had stabbed deep into the chest of Emery. She had flung herself over Katie's unraised body at the last second.

The girl's eyes bugged out as she gasped and coughed while still trying to shield Katie's body from further attack.

The sudden cold bite of metal in her back took Jillie by surprise. It stabbed down from beneath her shoulder and in seconds she felt her chest fill with fire.

She cried out and struggled to turn as the man pulled a dripping knife out of her back. His face was twisted in anger and fear and horror and he screamed out a single word.

"Stop!"

Then he brought the blade down again. Jillie reached out with both hands, but the knife only sliced past them with an icy kiss that blossomed instantly into hideous fire. And then something hit her neck. Even as she felt her skin open, she heard the knife clatter to the floor and the man turned away to reach for Emery. He had abandoned his attack on her to lean over the coffin.

"How bad is it?" he asked.

"Bad enough," the witch answered.

Jillie felt the world ending. She opened her mouth to speak but only blood came out. Her legs suddenly gave out and she collapsed backward to slam her head on the floor.

The last thing she saw was the witch's ghost climbing into the coffin.

CHAPTER FORTY-SEVEN

"Hold her over my body," Katie instructed. With one hand, the witch gently stroked Emery's forehead as Mike cradled the dying girl's upper body in his arms, supporting her spasming form a couple feet above the vessel below. The back of Emery's thighs rested against the coffin.

"You have always been mine," Katie whispered, her lips just inches from Emery's choking mouth. Blood oozed steadily from the place where the knife had been buried near Emery's collarbone.

"There are no words that I can say," Katie said, bending low to kiss the girl's crimson lips. Emery's eyes stared wide and fearful, looking back and forth between Katie and Mike as the end crept closer.

"It's been a long road to tonight and you always walked it bravely," Katie said. "Go now into the night and finally be free. Free of earth. Free of me and my demands. I'll always treasure you."

Tears streamed from the corners of Mike's eyes as he held the body aloft. He let the blood drip across Katie's body's face and neck and chest. He painted the waiting flesh with Emery's blood as Katie's ghost looked on and said nothing.

When Emery's eyes glazed over and her lips stopped gasping, Mike lifted her body up and away from Katie's flesh. He laid her down gently on the floor next to the coffin. Then he knelt next to her and with his finger, closed her vacant eyes.

Katie stripped off her ephemeral clothes, letting each article drop to the floor. As they hit the earth, they disappeared. Figments of truth, no longer needed. When she stood completely nude, Katie pulled herself up and over the walls of the coffin. With a faint smile, she turned to sit on the coffin's edge, and then laid her back down on the chest of the blood-smeared body within.

"What should I do?" Mike asked. Katie didn't respond. Instead, she closed her eyes and then seemed to…sink …into the flesh beneath her.

For one strange second, there were two Katies visible. She looked like a double exposure, her two noses and chins at first an inch and then a centimeter apart.

And then there was only one.

A naked, bloody body that now displayed perfect butterfly lips.

As Mike watched, the tip of a moist pink tongue slid through those lips and licked the blood away.

Katie's eyes opened.

A smile crept across her lips and she turned her head to meet Mike's eyes.

"At last," she whispered.

She raised one arm and flexed her fingers above her face. Then she did the same with the other, her grin growing as she twisted her arms and fingers one by one. Then she put her arms back down and used them to push herself upright.

"Take off the locket," Katie said. Mike did, and set it into her outstretched hand. Katie dropped it into the coffin and then held that same hand out to Mike.

"Touch me," she said.

He took her hand, and she squeezed. "You can feel me, can't you?"

He nodded.

"And you're not wearing the locket," she said.

He nodded again.

"Because I'm real, not a ghost anymore," Katie said. "I'm alive again."

Mike shook his head.

"You don't know how long I've waited for this moment," she said. "All of the minutes and days and months and years stuck here in this house, doomed to wait and wait and wait until the time was right."

"All of the rumors were really true," Mike said. "You've been haunting this place all these years."

"I've been here," she said. "I've been waiting."

"And Emery?" Mike asked, pointing to the dead girl on the floor.

"She performed the ritual that started it all," Katie said. "After my husband killed me, she brought me back, using her own blood. At first, even she couldn't really see me. I screamed with all my might and she would squint, as if she maybe heard some faint sound in the distance. She didn't know that those sounds were me, trying to reach her. But she never gave up. She started performing other rituals. Blood rituals. And with every sacrifice, she gave me new energy. Made me stronger. Until she could actually see me and we could finally talk again."

"And your reward was to kill her," he said.

"That was always the price," Katie said. "She knew that on the very first night that she cut her wrist and dripped her blood on my corpse. She could shed the blood of others to give her spell more power – give me more power – but in the end, only the blood of she who woke me could fully raise me."

"Then why did it take so long for her to do it?"

"Because there was never enough blood," Katie said. She lifted one leg over the coffin and Mike reached out a hand instinctively, to help her step down to the floor.

"You know how many people had to bleed in order for my bones to grow their flesh back," she said. "Until you opened this house again, we saw one person in the cemetery every couple months. And almost none of them ever made their way into the house. There were never enough people to form a critical mass until you came. When I found out what you were doing, I knew that the time had finally come. I knew that you were here to save me."

Katie took Mike's face in her hands.

"Emery kept me from slipping away," Katie said. "But you made it possible for me to come back."

"Not just me," Mike whispered, pointing at the door that opened on the rest of the basement. "Dozens of people out there are dead."

"It takes an enormous amount of power to accomplish what we did tonight," Katie said. "But we can't look back now. The only way is forward."

Katie stared into Mike's eyes as she ran her fingers through the hair on the back of his head. "Will you move forward with me?"

Mike looked into her eyes and felt the power there. He tried to blot out the images of the blood in the hallways. He tried to forget the fact that two women lay dead on the floor on either side of them. He tried to remember sitting on the porch just a couple months ago in August with Katie, listening to her stories, living for the light lilt of her laughter.

"I want to," he said. "But I don't know."

"Come with me," she said, taking his hand.

Katie led him out of the basement and up the stairs to the main floor and then the attic. When he opened the trap door in the attic to finally descend into Emery's room, Katie reached up to the door in the ceiling and pulled a bolt shut. They were locked into the hidden room. There were still candles lit along the walls, just enough to allow Mike to see the nails of the bed and the naked woman who approached him now from the stairwell.

She moved like a ghost, gliding along the floor in her bare feet. But she was a ghost no longer. When her hands touched Mike's arms, she drew her hands up and under his sleeves, touching him and kneading his muscles with the tips of her fingers. Then she brought her hands down to his waist and drew them up under his shirt, ratcheting it up until he lifted his arms and allowed her to bring the blood-drenched, sticky cotton up and over his shoulders.

She threw the ruined shirt into the corner and then unbuckled his belt. As his jeans slipped down to the floor, Mike gasped.

"I don't know," he said. "I really don't know if I can do this now. After tonight…."

"I'm here," Katie whispered, her lips just centimeters from his. He could feel her breath. "I'll always be here for you," she said.

Then her mouth moved down his throat to his chest and belly and below.

Mike closed his eyes. And instantly he saw images of carnage. The reflections of the night had embedded themselves on the back of his eyes.

"I think…I think I'd like to go home for tonight," he said, despite the warmth that engulfed his erection.

Katie raised her head from his crotch and smiled sweetly. "This is your home now," she said.

Mike frowned. "No," he said. "I mean my real home. I could take you there. It has a real bed, with a real mattress."

Katie smiled thinly, but shook her head no.

"You can never go home again," she said. "Not after you killed all of these people. They'll be waiting for you."

"What are you talking about?" he said. "Emery killed those people, not me."

"You did your part," Katie said. "Emery used the knife, but you used the chainsaw."

Mike shook his head. "No," he said.

"Yes. While you were sleeping, your body let me in. And together, we cut through the hearts of dozens of people tonight. Your strength. My need. Together we swung the chainsaw back and forth and the people fell in pieces one after the other to the basement below."

"I don't believe it," Mike said, though, even as he said it, he could smell the ghost of engine oil in his nose and see the spray of blood as a whirring blade bit through tendons and muscle and bone. "And even if it was true, nobody would know it was me," he said. "Nobody is left alive!"

"There is one," Katie said. "She's probably reached the police by now. And even if she hasn't...your prints are all over that chainsaw. And you're the only other person running the house who isn't dead. But you're missing. Who do you think they'll blame?"

Mike felt his stomach and throat squeezing shut. "I have to go," he said. He pushed her aside and pulled up his jeans, fumbling to buckle them. He ignored the bloody shirt on the floor and headed straight toward the stairs back to the attic.

"If you leave me, they'll put you in jail for the rest of your life," she said. "Or give you the electric chair."

"Not if I get out of here now," he said. "I can wash my prints off the chainsaw, and go to the police myself."

"Too late," Katie said. She sat on the edge of the bed with her arms crossed. "Jeanie saw you doing it, and she's already gone for help. And who do you think they'll believe? A frightened girl who just escaped from a slaughterhouse...or the drunk that she says killed everyone?"

Mike hesitated. In the distance, a police siren began to whine.

"What do I do?" he whispered.

"You serve me," Katie said. "Just as Emery did."

She patted the bed beside her. "Come here. They won't find us here."

"I just want to go home," Mike whispered. Tears of frustration and fear rolled down his face.

Katie stood up and walked across the room. The red and white plastic cooler from Mike's truck was there. When she returned, she sat down again next to him and popped the tab on a Pabst Blue Ribbon and held it out to him. Cold drops slid down the can as a cocoon of foam arched out of the opening.

"Your home is with me now," she said. When he took the can and slugged back a long gulp, she brushed the hair away from his eyes. "Don't ever forget that."

When he finished the beer, she kissed the tears from his face, and pushed him down to the bed. Mike didn't protest too much. He really didn't know what to do at this point. He was overwhelmed. Lost.

And then her lips were on his, and his mouth filled with the heat and need of her tongue. For a few seconds, he forgot about the horror of the night and lost himself in the promise of her. The girl he had fallen in love with so many weeks ago. The girl who until tonight had seemed sweet and playful and innocent. The girl who had really been a ghost. The ghost of a witch who was anything but innocent.

He kissed her back with growing passion and then felt the wetness of her need upon him. And then he thought about nothing but filling her for what seemed like hours.

It wasn't hours.

But when he lay back, spent and gasping for breath, Katie rested herself half on, half off of him. She kissed him gently on the mouth and the cheek.

"Give me your hand," Katie said.

He didn't question her, but offered his left hand.

She took it and squeezed it in hers. "You are mine now," she said. "In heart and soul and body."

She lifted a knife in her free hand and he flinched.

But Katie only kissed him and lifted her hand from his clutch to the air above them. She pressed the blade into the center and drew it down. A red mouth opened in her palm.

She took his hand next, and touched the blade to it.

"My blood in yours, and your blood in mine," she said. "Forever and always."

She said other things then, words he didn't recognize. But he didn't pull his hand away as the cold steel threatened his skin. "You won't ever leave me?" he whispered.

Katie shook her head. And then she drew the knife down until droplets of red splattered Mike's chest. She tossed the knife away and gripped his wounded hand with her own. Their fingers entwined and locked.

"My life is yours," she whispered.

"And mine is yours," he answered. It seemed like the right thing to say. For better or worse, it was true.

She smiled and pressed her body against his, holding their bleeding hands up above their heads. She kissed him deeply, and he responded. He realized that he was already 'ready' to consummate their new bond. And she didn't hesitate to guide him inside.

He was lost in the smell and heat and feeling of her when he realized that there were sirens now just outside. And the tread of boots and steps overhead.

Katie's eyes drew him in, and she nodded. She heard them. She kissed him and pulled him close. Mike accepted her embrace and didn't pull out from her until they were both nearly asleep.

Voices and radio calls and yells and commands echoed from the attic above and the main level below.

Mike only barely heard them. He pulled Katie close and the whole world simply went away.

They fell asleep in each other's arms, hidden in the secret heart of the house, as just a few yards away, police officers and ambulance drivers began to lift body after body onto stretchers to move them to the many trucks with flashing red and blue lights that gathered outside.

EPILOGUE

A pickup truck rolled past the ribbons of broken yellow police tape that still fluttered loosely in the faint winter breeze. The truck bounced down the ruts of the old gravel road that led from the Midlothian Turnpike around the small pond that bordered Bachelor's Grove Cemetery. Its tires left darkened tracks in the hardened crust of snow that covered the ground in a blanket of white.

A pretty girl in an unseasonably short skirt and a half-buttoned yellow blouse stepped from the cab to the ground, her dark hair bouncing across her slim shoulders. Then the driver's door opened and a big man in a long black wool coat and blue jeans quickly got out to join her.

She took his hand in front of the truck and led him up the wood steps to the front door of the old gray house hidden deep in the shelter of the forest. A faint plume of smoke rose from the chimney on its roof above. When they stepped through the creaking door inside, the woman leaned up to kiss the man, and then drew him down the hall into the house toward the bedrooms.

When they reached the bathroom next to the master bedroom, she pulled him inside.

"I have a surprise for you," she promised.

But when the man stepped within the white-tiled room, the door behind him suddenly swung shut and an arm wrapped around his chest from behind. The steel of a cold blade slid firm against his neck.

The man struggled and kicked as the thick arm of the unseen man held him fast. But the knife only locked down harder, biting deep into his skin, and the man was forced to stop moving.

"You've been gone a while," the unseen man said from behind.

The girl shrugged. "Slow night. But I picked you up a twelve-pack of PBR. It's in the bed of the truck. Don't forget to get it out before you drive away the evidence."

"Small favors," he said, as the girl unbuttoned her shirt and then slid out of her skirt in front of them. Her bra quickly joined the clothes on the tile floor, and she scooped down her panties to step into a white porcelain tub.

"Brrrr!" she complained, as she sat down on its cold surface.

"This will make it better," said the man holding the knife. "Your weekly bath."

He pushed the man forward until they stood at the very edge of the tub, looking over the girl who lay within. The man gasped and renewed his efforts to punch and knee at his captor, but he couldn't seem to break free. Not with a knife at his neck anyway.

And then without ceremony, the knife wasn't simply *at* his neck…but *in* it. The blade dug across his throat and bit down hard. The captive man thrashed in desperation then, but couldn't escape the iron grasp of the other man. It was too late anyway even if he had; the knife sawed away at his soft flesh and in seconds his need to escape dissolved in a shower of blood. His life sprayed in a crimson mist across the tile, and the naked woman below closed her eyes and licked her lips as it rained down to cover her.

"Nothing takes away the chill of winter better than blood," she sighed.

The man holding the knife frowned but said nothing. Instead, he pulled the hair of the victim, yanking the head back to open the wound further. He aimed the open gash of the victim's throat carefully, working to ensure that every drop cascaded down the flawless white skin of the woman in the tub. Nothing wasted.

She reclined and arched her back, luxuriating in the warm spray of life that covered her. She may have returned from the dead, but she still needed the transfusion of life to keep her here.

★   ★   ★

Katie rubbed her hands across her belly and thighs and breasts, smearing herself in crimson.

A tear slid from the corner of Mike's eye as he drained the last weak spurts of blood from the man's dying heart, but he said nothing. He shook the tear away, and made sure that every last drop landed on Katie's thirsty flesh before he dragged the body back outside to add to the pile in the unmarked, hidden mass grave out back.

Bachelor's Grove Cemetery had grown a lot more crowded since Katie had come back to life.

When Katie had shown Mike what his new role was going to be, he had yearned desperately to leave. But every time he slipped out of the house and began to walk down the turnpike without her blessing, the hand that she had cut and shared her blood with burned as if it were being held to a fire. It grew until he was doubled over on the side of the road, and only abated when he returned to the house. Soon he stopped trying to leave. Every day now, he found it harder to contemplate walking beyond the boundaries of the cemetery. His past seemed like a half-remembered lost dream. The only thing that broke through the growing cloud in his brain was the smile of Katie each night when she drew him close in their hidden bed.

"I am yours, just like you wanted," she would say as she stroked and kissed him. "And you are mine. Forever."

★   ★   ★

As the echo of Mike's work shoes tromped across the deck out front, dragging the body away, Katie shifted and smiled with satisfaction against the cool porcelain of the tub.

"Home, sweet, home," Katie whispered.

FLAME TREE PRESS
FICTION WITHOUT FRONTIERS
Award-Winning Authors & Original Voices

Flame Tree Press is the trade fiction imprint of Flame Tree Publishing, focusing on excellent writing in horror and the supernatural, crime and mystery, science fiction and fantasy. Our aim is to explore beyond the boundaries of the everyday, with tales from both award-winning authors and original voices.

•

Other titles available include:

Thirteen Days by Sunset Beach by Ramsey Campbell
Think Yourself Lucky by Ramsey Campbell
The Toy Thief by D.W. Gillespie
The Siren and the Specter by Jonathan Janz
The Sorrows by Jonathan Janz
Kosmos by Adrian Laing
The Sky Woman by J.D. Moyer
Creature by Hunter Shea
The Bad Neighbor by David Tallerman
Ten Thousand Thunders by Brian Trent
Night Shift by Robin Triggs
The Mouth of the Dark by Tim Waggoner

•

Join our mailing list for free short stories, new release details, news about our authors and special promotions:

flametreepress.com